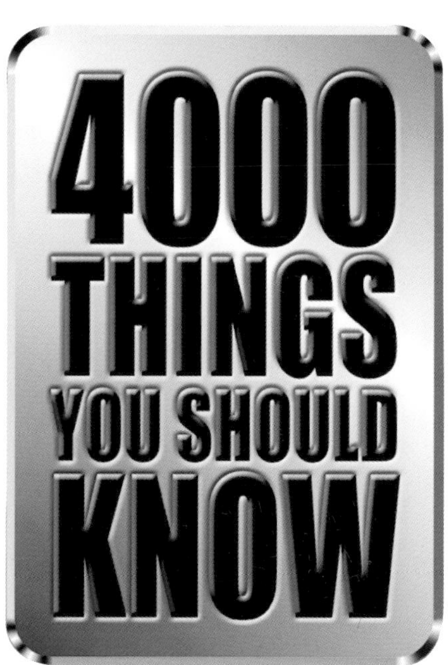
4000
THINGS
YOU SHOULD
KNOW

This edition first published in 2003
(originally published in larger format, 2000)
by Miles Kelly Publishing Ltd
Bardfield Centre, Great Bardfield, Essex, CM7 4SL

2 4 6 8 10 9 7 5 3 1

Project Manager: Ian Paulyn
Production: Estela Godoy
Written and designed by Barnsbury Books

British Library Cataloguing-in-Publication Data
A catalogue record for this book is available from the British library

ISBN 1-84236-318-2

Printed in China

www.mileskelly.net
info@mileskelly.net

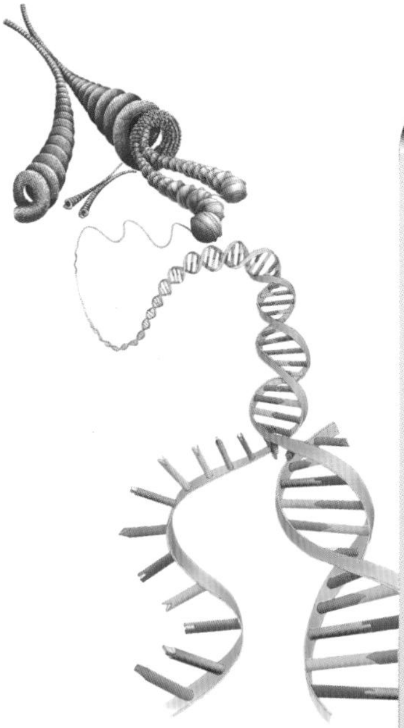

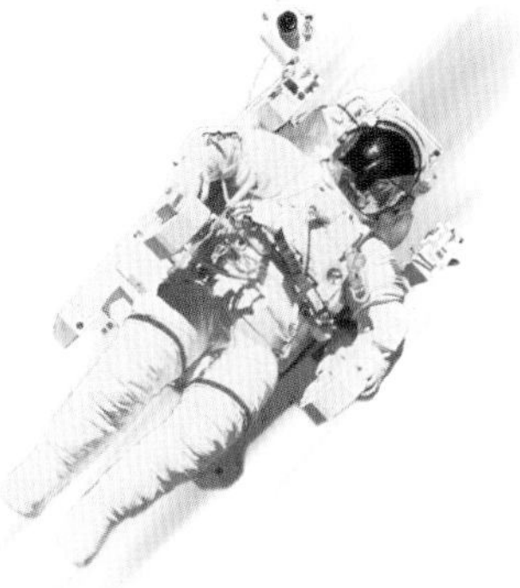

4000 THINGS YOU SHOULD KNOW

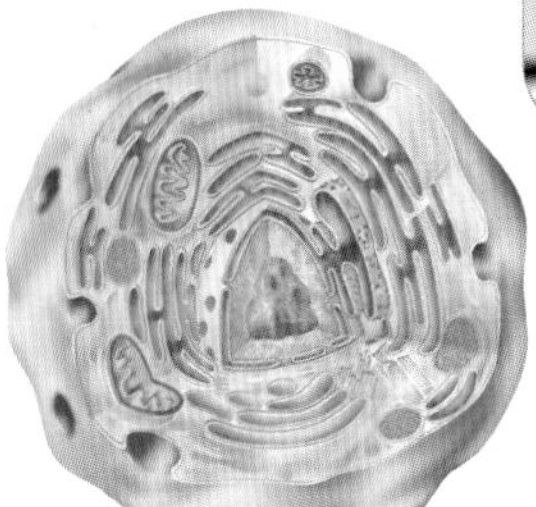

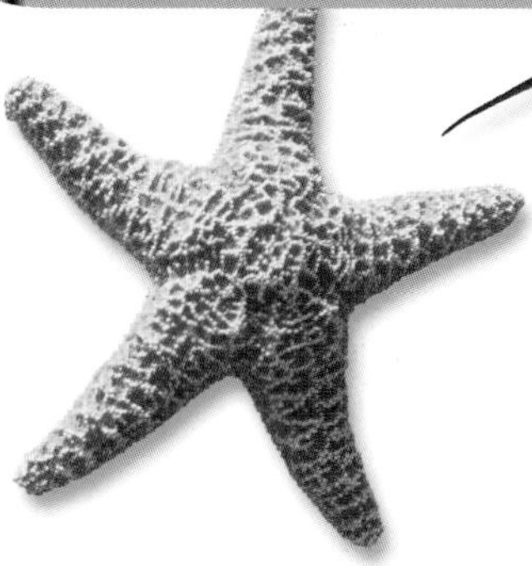

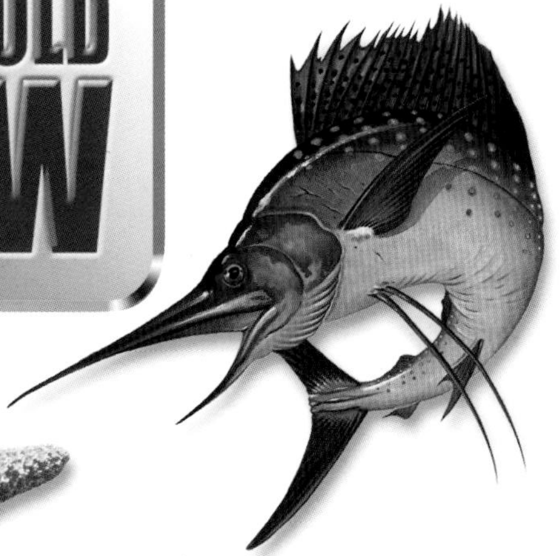

John Farndon

Contents

SPACE 12-69

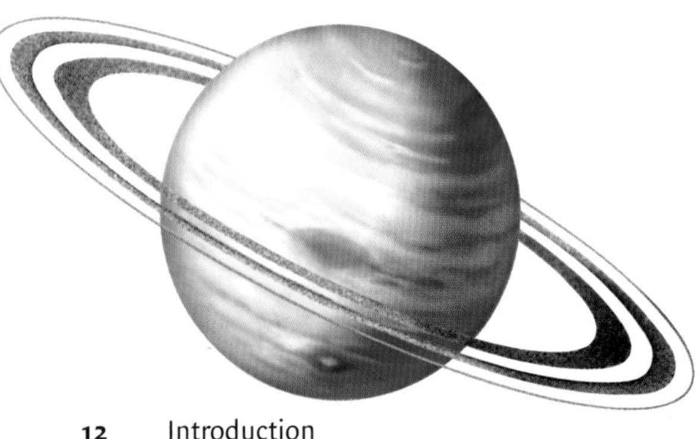

Contents

PLANET EARTH 70-127

Contents

ANIMALS 128-185

Contents

HUMAN BODY 186-243

INDEX 244-255

INTRODUCTION

This incredible reference resource provides knowledge, fascination and inspiration on every page. Its four hundred subject panels contain facts that will inform, amaze and entertain. You will find out quickly and effortlessly about space, the Earth, the world of animals and the human body. And you will learn through facts like these:

- *Mars's volcano* Olympus Mons *is the biggest in the solar system. It covers the same area as Ireland and is three times higher than Mount Everest.*
- *Factories in the Chinese city of Benxi make so much smoke the city is invisible to satellites.*
- *The Arctic beetle can survive in temperatures below -60°C.*
- *The reproductive system is the only system that can be surgically removed without killing you.*

Now discover the other 3996 brilliant facts in ***4000 Things You Should Know***

Using this book

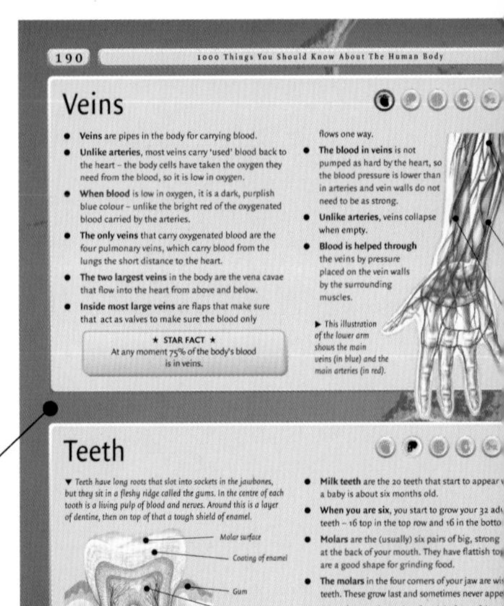

190 1000 Things You Should Know About The Human Body

Veins

- **Veins** are pipes in the body for carrying blood.
- **Unlike arteries,** most veins carry 'used' blood back to the heart – the body cells have taken the oxygen they need from the blood, so it is low in oxygen.
- **When blood** is low in oxygen, it is a dark, purplish blue colour – unlike the bright red of the oxygenated blood carried by the arteries.
- **The only veins** that carry oxygenated blood are the four pulmonary veins, which carry blood from the lungs the short distance to the heart.
- **The two largest veins** in the body are the vena cavae that flow into the heart from above and below.
- **Inside most large veins** are flaps that make sure that act as valves to make sure the blood only flows one way.
- **The blood in veins** is not pumped as hard by the heart, so the blood pressure is lower than in arteries and vein walls do not need to be as strong.
- **Unlike arteries,** veins collapse when empty.
- **Blood is helped through** the veins by pressure placed on the vein walls by the surrounding muscles.

★ STAR FACT ★
At any moment 75% of the body's blood is in veins.

▶ *This illustration of the lower arm shows the main veins (in blue) and the main arteries (in red).*

Teeth

▼ *Teeth have long roots that slot into sockets in the jawbones, but they sit in a fleshy ridge called the gums. In the centre of each tooth is a living pulp of blood and nerves. Around this is a layer of dentine, then on top of that a tough shield of enamel.*

Molar surface
Coating of enamel
Gum
Soft core or pulp
Dentine layer
Jawbone
Root canal

- **Milk teeth** are the 20 teeth that start to appear w a baby is about six months old.
- **When you are six,** you start to grow your 32 adu teeth – 16 top in the top row and 16 in the botto
- **Molars** are the (usually) six pairs of big, strong at the back of your mouth. They have flattish to are a good shape for grinding food.
- **The molars** in the four corners of your jaw are wis teeth. These grow last and sometimes never appe
- **Premolars** are four pairs of teeth in front of the m
- **Incisors** are the four pairs of teeth at the front o mouth. They have sharp edges for cutting food.
- **Canines** are the two pairs of big, pointed teeth b the incisors. Their shape is good for tearing foo
- **The enamel** on teeth is the body's hardest subs
- **Dentine** inside teeth is softer but still hard as b
- **Teeth** sit in sockets in the jawbones.

The organization of **4000 Things You Should Know** brings surprises and interest to every page.

The book is divided into four broad areas: Space, Planet Earth, Animals and Human Body.

On each double-page spread there are three or four subject panels. Each panel contains 10 key facts and is identified with a highlighted subject symbol. You can turn to subjects that interest you by looking for the subject symbols below.

The subjects covered on each spread are organized so that you will find interest and variety throughout the book. Use the subject symbols, the contents page and the index to navigate.

There are diagrams throughout the book.

SUBJECT SYMBOLS

SPACE

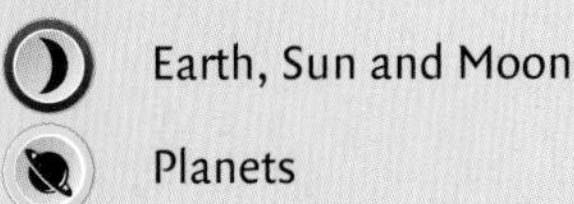

Earth, Sun and Moon

Planets

Stars

Universe

Astronomy

Space travel

ANIMALS

 Mammals

 Birds

 Reptiles and amphibians

 Sea creatures

 Insects, spiders and creepy crawlies

 How animals live

PLANET EARTH

 Planet Earth

 Volcanoes and earthquakes

 Shaping the land

 Weather and climate

 Continents

 Oceans

HUMAN BODY

 Breathing and blood

 Skeleton and muscle

 Body control

 Food and water

 Growing and changing

 Health and disease

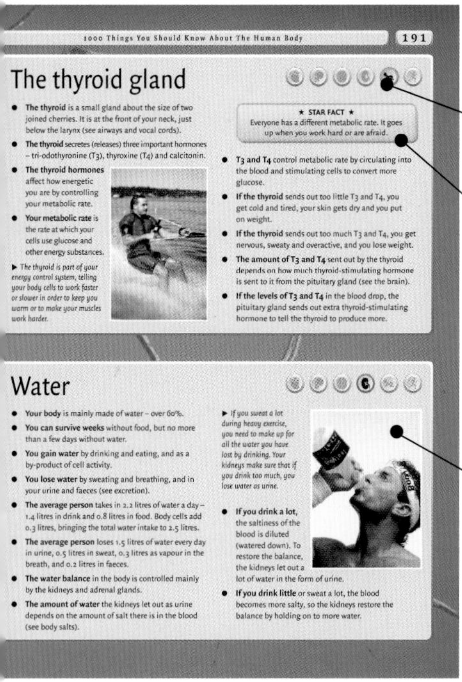

1000 Things You Should Know About The Human Body 191

The thyroid gland

- **The thyroid** is a small gland about the size of two joined cherries. It is at the front of your neck, just below the larynx (see airways and vocal cords).
- **The thyroid** secretes (releases) three important hormones – tri-odothyronine (T3), thyroxine (T4) and calcitonin.
- **The thyroid hormones** affect how energetic you are by controlling your metabolic rate.
- **Your metabolic rate** is the rate at which your cells use glucose and other energy substances.

▶ *The thyroid is part of your energy control system, telling your body cells to work faster or slower in order to keep you warm or to make your muscles work harder.*

★ STAR FACT ★
Everyone has a different metabolic rate. It goes up when you work hard or are afraid.

- **T3 and T4** control metabolic rate by circulating into the blood and stimulating cells to convert more glucose.
- **If the thyroid** sends out too little T3 and T4, you get cold and tired, your skin gets dry and you put on weight.
- **If the thyroid** sends out too much T3 and T4, you get nervous, sweaty and overactive, and you lose weight.
- **The amount of T3 and T4** sent out by the thyroid depends on how much thyroid-stimulating hormone is sent to it from the pituitary gland (see the brain).
- **If the levels of T3 and T4** in the blood drop, the pituitary gland sends out extra thyroid-stimulating hormone to tell the thyroid to produce more.

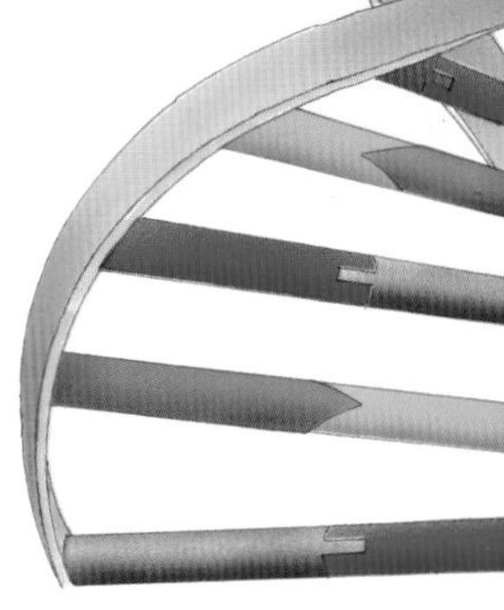

Subject symbols appear on every panel. Look for the ones that are highlighted.

'Newsflashes' give you up to the minute snippets of information. Star facts are strange-but-true.

Water

- **Your body** is mainly made of water – over 60%.
- **You can survive weeks** without food, but no more than a few days without water.
- **You gain water** by drinking and eating, and as a by-product of cell activity.
- **You lose water** by sweating and breathing, and in your urine and faeces (see excretion).
- **The average person** takes in 2.2 litres of water a day – 1.4 litres in drink and 0.8 litres in food. Body cells add 0.3 litres, bringing the total water intake to 2.5 litres.
- **The average person** loses 1.5 litres of water every day in urine, 0.5 litres in sweat, 0.3 litres as vapour in the breath, and 0.2 litres in faeces.
- **The water balance** in the body is controlled mainly by the kidneys and adrenal glands.
- **The amount of water** the kidneys let out as urine depends on the amount of salt there is in the blood (see body salts).

▶ *If you sweat a lot during heavy exercise, you need to make up for all the water you have lost by drinking. Your kidneys make sure that if you drink too much, you lose water as urine.*

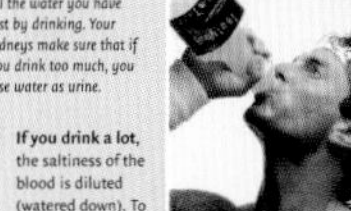

- **If you drink a lot,** the saltiness of the blood is diluted (watered down). To restore the balance, the kidneys let out a lot of water in the form of urine.
- **If you drink little** or sweat a lot, the blood becomes more salty, so the kidneys restore the balance by holding on to more water.

Over 300 photographs help illustrate the amazing facts.

Headings at the top of each double-page spread tell you which of the four areas of the book you are in – Space, Planet Earth, Animals or Human Body.

Ten key facts are provided in each subject panel. There are 400 panels making 4000 facts in all.

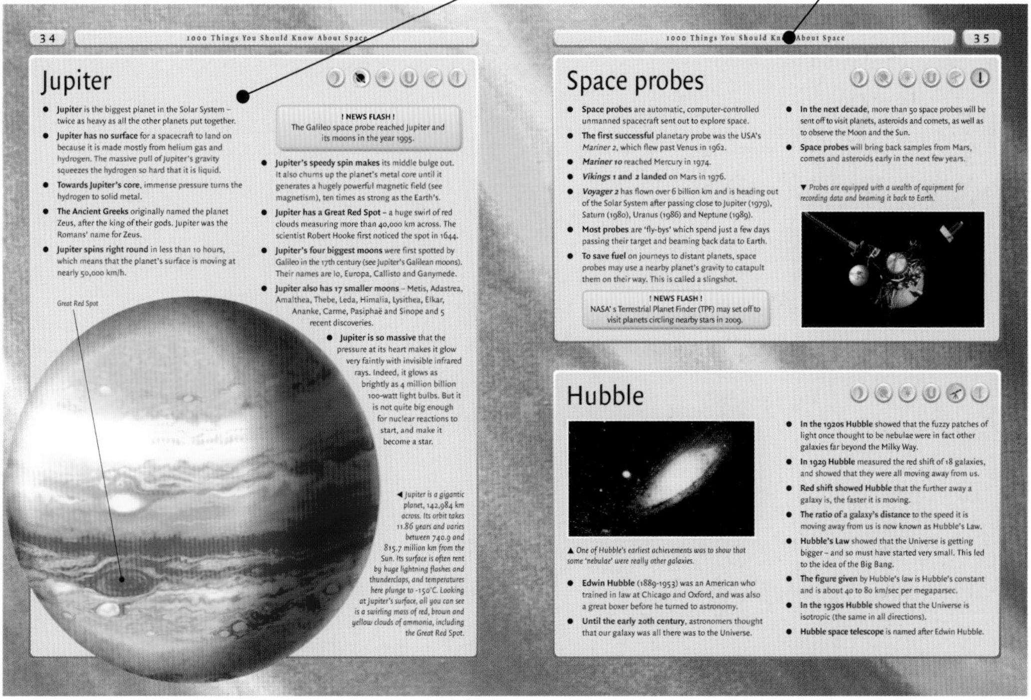

34 1000 Things You Should Know About Space

Jupiter

- **Jupiter** is the biggest planet in the Solar System – twice as heavy as all the other planets put together.
- **Jupiter has no surface** for a spacecraft to land on because it is made mostly from helium gas and hydrogen. The massive pull of Jupiter's gravity squeezes the hydrogen so hard that it is liquid.
- **Towards Jupiter's core,** immense pressure turns the hydrogen to solid metal.
- **The Ancient Greeks** originally named the planet Zeus, after the king of their gods. Jupiter was the Romans' name for Zeus.
- **Jupiter spins right round** in less than 10 hours, which means that the planet's surface is moving at nearly 50,000 km/h.

! NEWS FLASH !
The Galileo space probe reached Jupiter and its moons in the year 1995.

- **Jupiter's speedy spin makes** its middle bulge out. It also churns up the planet's metal core until it generates a hugely powerful magnetic field (see magnetism), ten times as strong as the Earth's.
- **Jupiter has a Great Red Spot** – a huge swirl of red clouds measuring more than 40,000 km across. The scientist Robert Hooke first noticed the spot in 1644.
- **Jupiter's four biggest moons** were first spotted by Galileo in the 17th century (see Jupiter's Galilean moons). Their names are Io, Europa, Callisto and Ganymede.
- **Jupiter also has 17 smaller moons** – Metis, Adastrea, Amalthea, Thebe, Leda, Himalia, Lysithea, Elkar, Ananke, Carme, Pasiphaë and Sinope and 5 recent discoveries.
- **Jupiter is so massive** that the pressure at its heart makes it glow very faintly with invisible infrared rays. Indeed, it glows as brightly as 4 million billion 100-watt light bulbs. But it is not quite big enough for nuclear reactions to start, and make it become a star.

Great Red Spot

◀ *Jupiter is a gigantic planet, 142,984 km across. Its orbit takes 11.86 years and varies between 740.9 and 815.7 million km from the Sun. Its surface is often rent by huge lightning flashes and thunderclaps, and temperatures here plunge to -150°C. Looking at Jupiter's surface, all you can see is a swirling mass of red, brown and yellow clouds of ammonia, including the Great Red Spot.*

1000 Things You Should Know About Space 35

Space probes

- **Space probes** are automatic, computer-controlled unmanned spacecraft sent out to explore space.
- **The first successful** planetary probe was the USA's *Mariner 2*, which flew past Venus in 1962.
- ***Mariner 10*** reached Mercury in 1974.
- ***Vikings 1* and *2* landed** on Mars in 1976.
- ***Voyager 2*** has flown over 6 billion km and is heading out of the Solar System after passing close to Jupiter (1979), Saturn (1980), Uranus (1986) and Neptune (1989).
- **Most probes** are 'fly-bys' which spend just a few days passing their target and beaming back data to Earth.
- **To save fuel** on journeys to distant planets, space probes may use a nearby planet's gravity to catapult them on their way. This is called a slingshot.

! NEWS FLASH !
NASA' s Terrestrial Planet Finder (TPF) may set off to visit planets circling nearby stars in 2009.

- **In the next decade,** more than 50 space probes will be sent off to visit planets, asteroids and comets, as well as to observe the Moon and the Sun.
- **Space probes** will bring back samples from Mars, comets and asteroids early in the next few years.

▼ *Probes are equipped with a wealth of equipment for recording data and beaming it back to Earth.*

Hubble

▲ *One of Hubble's earliest achievements was to show that some 'nebulae' were really other galaxies.*

- **Edwin Hubble** (1889-1953) was an American who trained in law at Chicago and Oxford, and was also a great boxer before he turned to astronomy.
- **Until the early 20th century,** astronomers thought that our galaxy was all there was to the Universe.
- **In the 1920s Hubble** showed that the fuzzy patches of light once thought to be nebulae were in fact other galaxies far beyond the Milky Way.
- **In 1929 Hubble** measured the red shift of 18 galaxies, and showed that they were all moving away from us.
- **Red shift showed Hubble** that the further away a galaxy is, the faster it is moving.
- **The ratio of a galaxy's distance** to the speed it is moving away from us is now known as Hubble's Law.
- **Hubble's Law** showed that the Universe is getting bigger – and so must have started very small. This led to the idea of the Big Bang.
- **The figure given** by Hubble's law is Hubble's constant and is about 40 to 80 km/sec per megaparsec.
- **In the 1930s Hubble** showed that the Universe is isotropic (the same in all directions).
- **Hubble space telescope** is named after Edwin Hubble.

SPACE

KEY

 Earth, Sun and Moon

 Planets

 Stars

 Universe

 Astronomy

 Space travel

Small stars

- **Small stars** of low brightness are called white, red or black dwarves depending on their colour.
- **Red dwarves** are bigger than the planet Jupiter but smaller than our medium-sized star, the Sun. They glow faintly, with 0.01% of the Sun's brightness.
- **No red dwarf** can be seen with the naked eye – not even the nearest star to the Sun, the red dwarf Proxima Centauri.
- **White dwarves** are the last stage in the life of a medium-sized star. Although they are even smaller than red dwarves – no bigger than the Earth – they contain the same amount of matter as the Sun.
- **Our night sky's brightest star**, Sirius, the Dog Star, has a white dwarf companion called the Pup Star.

◀ *Black dwarves are stars that were either not big enough to start shining, or which have burned up all their nuclear fuel and stopped glowing, like a coal cinder.*

- **The white dwarf Omicron-2 Eridani** (also called 40 Eridani) is one of the few dwarf stars that can be seen from the Earth with the naked eye.
- **Brown dwarves** are very cool space objects, little bigger than Jupiter.
- **Brown dwarves** formed in the same way as other stars, but were not big enough to start shining properly. They just glow very faintly with the heat left over from their formation.
- **Black dwarves** are very small, cold, dead stars.
- **The smallest kind of star** is called a neutron star.

Life

▲ *Saturn's moon Titan has plenty of evidence of organic (life) chemicals in its atmosphere.*

- **Life is only known** to exist on Earth, but in 1986 NASA found what they thought might be fossils of microscopic living things in a rock from Mars.
- **Life on Earth** probably began 3.8 billion years ago.
- **The first life forms** were probably bacteria which lived in very hot water around underwater volcanoes.

! NEWS FLASH !
Microscopic organisms have been found in rock deep underground. Could similar organisms be living under the surface of Mars or Titan?

- **Most scientists** say life's basic chemicals formed on Earth. The astronomer Fred Hoyle said they came from Space.
- **Basic organic (life) chemicals** such as amino acids have been detected in nebulae and meteorites (see meteors).
- **Huge lightning flashes** may have caused big organic molecules to form on the young Earth.
- **Earth is right for life** because of its gas atmosphere, surface water and moderately warm temperatures.
- **Mars is the only** other planet that once had water on its surface – which is why scientists are looking for signs of life there.
- **Jupiter's moon Europa** probably has water below its surface which could spawn life.

Space suits

- **Space suits protect astronauts** when they go outside their spacecraft. The suits are also called EMUs (Extra-vehicular Mobility Units).
- **The outer layers** of a space suit protect against harmful radiation from the Sun and bullet-fast particles of space dust called micrometeoroids.
- **The clear, plastic helmet** also protects against radiation and micrometeoroids.
- **Oxygen is circulated** around the helmet to stop the visor misting.
- **The middle layers** of a space suit are blown up like a balloon to press against the astronaut's body. Without this pressure, the astronaut's blood would boil.
- **The soft inner lining** of a space suit has tubes of water in it to cool the astronaut's body or warm it up.
- **The backpack** supplies pure oxygen for the astronaut to breathe, and gets rid of the carbon dioxide he or she gives out. The oxygen comes from tanks which hold enough for up to 7 hours.
- **The gloves** have silicone-rubber fingertips which allow the astronaut some sense of touch.
- **Various different gadgets** in the suit deal with liquids – including a tube for drinks and another for collecting urine.
- **The full cost** of a spacesuit is about $11 million although 70% of this is for the backpack and control module.

◀ *Space suits not only have to provide a complete life-support system (oxygen, water and so on), but must also protect against the dangers of space.*

Newton

- **Isaac Newton** (1642-1722) discovered the force of gravity and the three basic laws of motion.
- **Newton's ideas** were inspired by seeing an apple fall from a tree in the garden of his home in Lincolnshire.
- **Newton also discovered** that sunlight can be split into a spectrum made of all the colours of the rainbow.
- **Newton's discovery of gravity** showed why things fall to the ground and planets orbit the Sun.
- **Newton realized** that a planet's orbit depends on its mass and its distance from the Sun.
- **The further apart** and the lighter two objects are, the weaker is the pull of gravity between them.
- **Newton worked out** that you can calculate the pull of gravity between two objects by multiplying their mass by the square of the distance between them.
- **This calculation** allows astronomers to predict precisely the movement of every planet, star and galaxy in the Universe.
- **Using Newton's formula for gravity**, astronomers have detected previously unknown stars and planets, including Neptune and Pluto, from the effect of their gravity on other space objects.
- **Newton's three laws of motion** showed that every single movement in the Universe can be calculated mechanically.

▶ *Newton's theory of gravity showed for the first time why the Moon stays in its orbit around the Earth, and how the gravitational pull between the Earth and the Moon could be worked out mathematically.*

Nebulae

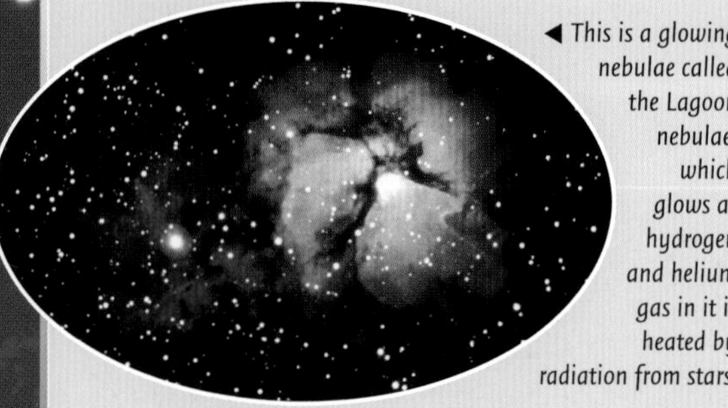

◀ *This is a glowing nebulae called the Lagoon nebulae, which glows as hydrogen and helium gas in it is heated by radiation from stars.*

- **Nebula** (plural nebulae) was the word once used for any fuzzy patch of light in the night sky. Nowadays, many nebulae are known to be galaxies instead.
- **Many nebulae** are gigantic clouds of gas and space dust.
- **Glowing nebulae** are named because they give off a dim, red light, as the hydrogen gas in them is heated by radiation from nearby stars.
- **The Great Nebula of Orion** is a glowing nebula just visible to the naked eye.
- **Reflection nebulae** have no light of their own. They can only be seen because starlight shines off the dust in them.
- **Dark nebulae** not only have no light of their own, they also soak up all light. They can only be seen as patches of darkness, blocking out light from the stars behind them.
- **The Horsehead nebula** in Orion is the best-known dark nebula. As its name suggests, it is shaped like a horse's head.
- **Planetary nebulae** are thin rings of gas cloud which are thrown out by dying stars. Despite their name, they have nothing to do with planets.
- **The Ring nebula** in Lyra is the best-known of the planetary nebulae.
- **The Crab nebula** is the remains of a supernova that exploded in AD 1054.

Extraterrestrials

- **Extraterrestrial (ET)** means 'outside the Earth'.
- **Some scientists** say that ET life could develop anywhere in the Universe where there is a flow of energy.
- **One extreme idea** is that space clouds could become sentient (thinking) beings.
- **Most scientists** believe that if there is ET life anywhere in the Universe, it must be based on the chemistry of carbon, as life on Earth is.
- **If civilizations like ours** exist elsewhere, they may be on planets circling other stars. This is why the discovery of other planetary systems is so exciting (see planets).
- **The Drake Equation** was proposed by astronomer Frank Drake to work out how many civilizations there could be in our galaxy – and the figure is millions!

★ **STAR FACT** ★
The life chemical formaldehyde can be detected in radio emissions from the galaxy NGC 253.

- **There is no scientific proof** that any ET life form has ever visited the Earth.
- **SETI** is the Search for Extraterrestrial Intelligence – the program that analyzes radio signals from space for signs of intelligent life.
- **The Arecibo radio telescope** beams out signals to distant stars.

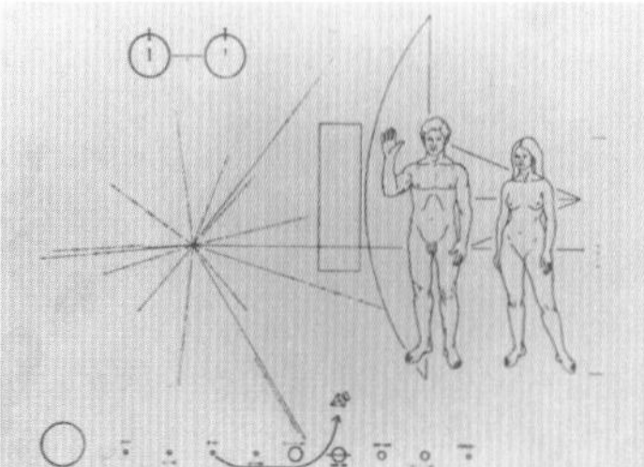

▲ *The space probes Pioneer 10 and 11 carry metal panels with picture messages about life on Earth into deep space.*

H-R diagram

- **The Hertzsprung-Russell (H-R) diagram** is a graph in which the temperature of stars is plotted against their brightness. The temperature of a star is indicated by its colour.
- **Cool stars** are red or reddish-yellow.
- **Hot stars** burn white or blue.
- **Medium-sized stars** form a diagonal band called the main sequence across the graph.
- **The whiter and hotter** a main sequence star is, the brighter it shines. White stars and blue-white stars are usually bigger and younger.
- **The redder and cooler** a star is, the dimmer it glows. Cool red stars tend to be smaller and older.
- **Giant stars and white dwarf stars** lie to either side of the main sequence stars.

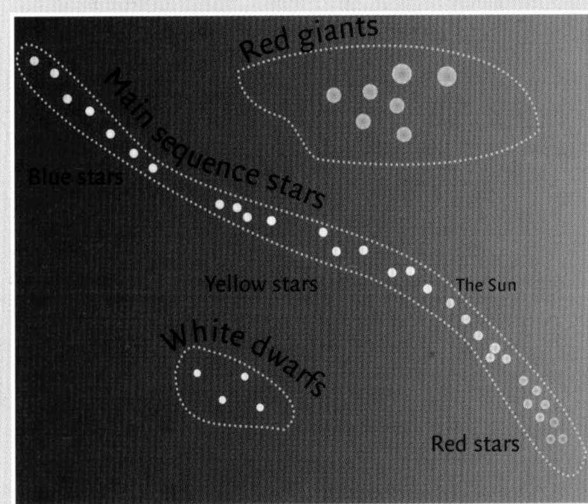

- **The H-R diagram** shows how bright each colour star should be. If the star actually looks dimmer, it must be further away.
- **By comparing a star's** brightness predicted by the H-R diagram with how bright it really looks, astronomers can work out how far away it is.
- **The diagram** was devised by Ejnar Hertzsprung and Henry Russell.

The Milky Way

- **The Milky Way** is the faint, hazy band of light that you can see stretching right across the night sky.
- **Looking through binoculars**, you would see that the Milky Way is made up of countless stars.
- **A galaxy** is a vast cluster of stars, and the Milky Way is our view of the galaxy we live in, called the Galaxy.
- **The Milky Way Galaxy** is one of billions in space.
- **The Galaxy** is 100,000 light-years across and 1,000 light-years thick. It is made up of 100 billion stars.
- **All the stars** are arranged in a spiral (like a giant Catherine wheel), with a bulge in the middle.
- **Our Sun** is just one of the billions of stars on one arm of the spiral.
- **The Galaxy** is whirling rapidly, spinning our Sun and all its other stars around at 100 million km/h.
- **The Sun** travels around the Galaxy once every 200 million years – a journey of 100,000 light-years.
- **The huge bulge** at the centre of the Galaxy is about 20,000 light-years across and 3,000 thick. It contains only very old stars and little dust or gas.
- **There may be a huge black hole** in the very middle of the Galaxy.

▼ *To the naked eye, the Milky Way looks like a hazy, white cloud, but binoculars show it to be a blur of countless stars.*

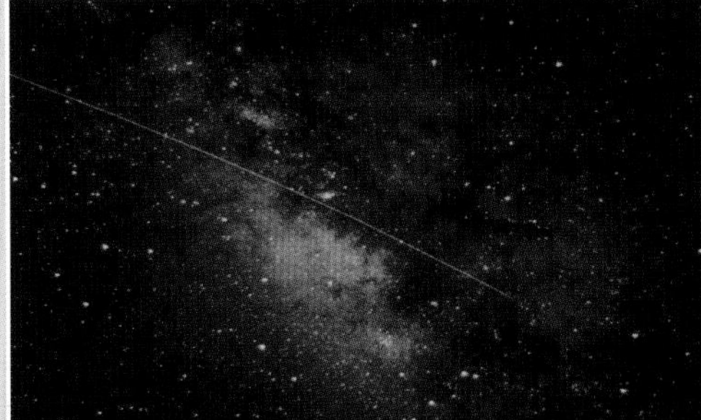

The Universe

◀ *The Universe is getting bigger and bigger all the time, as galaxies rush outwards in all directions.*

- **The Universe** is everything that we can ever know – all of space and all of time.
- **The Universe** is almost entirely empty, with small clusters of matter and energy.
- **The Universe** is probably about 15 billion years old, but estimates vary.
- **One problem** with working out the age of the Universe is that there are stars in our galaxy which are thought to be 14 to 18 billion years old – older than the estimated age of the Universe. So either the stars must be younger, or the Universe older.
- **The furthest galaxies** yet detected are about 13 billion light-years away (130 billion trillion km).
- **The Universe** is getting bigger by the second. We know this because all the galaxies are zooming away from us. The further away they are, the faster they are moving.
- **The very furthest galaxies** are spreading away from us at more than 90% of the speed of light.
- **The Universe** was once thought to be everything that could ever exist, but recent theories about inflation (see the Big Bang) suggest our Universe may be just one of countless bubbles of space-time.
- **The Universe** may have neither a centre nor an edge, because according to Einstein's theory of relativity (see Einstein), gravity bends all of space-time around into an endless curve.

★ **STAR FACT** ★
Recent theories suggest there may be many other universes which we can never know.

Black holes

▲ *This is an artist's impression of what a black hole might look like, with jets of electricity shooting out from either side.*

- **Black holes** are places where gravity is so strong that it sucks everything in, including light.
- **If you fell** into a black hole you'd stretch like spaghetti.
- **Black holes form** when a star or galaxy gets so dense that it collapses under the pull of its own gravity.
- **Black holes** may exist at the heart of every galaxy.
- **Gravity shrinks** a black hole to an unimaginably small point called a singularity.
- **Around a singularity**, gravity is so intense that space-time is bent into a funnel.
- **Matter spiralling** into a black hole is torn apart and glows so brightly that it creates the brightest objects in the Universe – quasars.
- **The swirling gases** around a black hole turn it into an electrical generator, making it spout jets of electricity billions of kilometres out into space.
- **The opposite of black holes** may be white holes which spray out matter and light like fountains.

★ **STAR FACT** ★
Black holes and white holes may join to form tunnels called wormholes – and these may be the secret to time travel.

Mercury

- **Mercury is the nearest planet** to the Sun – during its orbit it is between 45.9 and 69.7 million km away.
- **Mercury is the fastest orbiting** of all the planets, getting around the Sun in just 88 days.
- **Mercury takes 58.6 days** to rotate once, so a Mercury day lasts nearly 59 times as long as ours.
- **Temperatures** on Mercury veer from -180°C at night to over 430°C during the day (enough to melt lead).
- **The crust and mantle** are made largely of rock, but the core (75% of its diameter) is solid iron.
- **Mercury's dusty surface** is pocketed by craters made by space debris crashing into it.
- **With barely 20% of Earth's mass,** Mercury is so small that its gravity can only hold on to a very thin atmosphere of sodium vapour.
- **Mercury is so small** that its core has cooled and become solid (unlike Earth's). As this happened, Mercury shrank and its surface wrinkled like the skin of an old apple.
- **Craters on Mercury** discovered by the USA's *Mariner* space probe have names like Bach, Beethoven, Wagner, Shakespeare and Tolstoy.

★ STAR FACT ★

Twice during its orbit, Mercury gets very close to the Sun and speeds up so much that the Sun seems to go backwards in the sky.

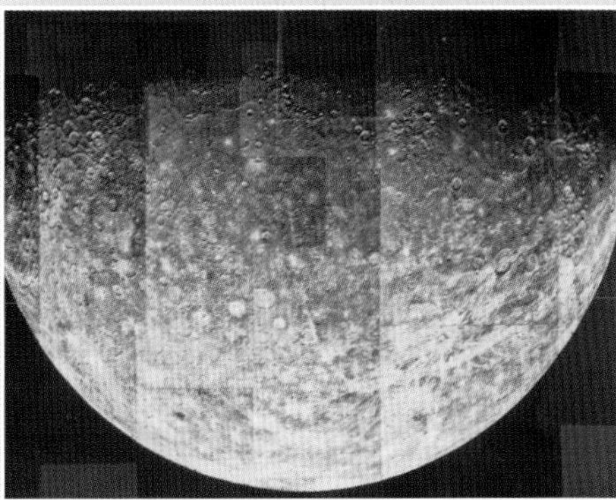

▲ *Mercury is so close to the Sun that it is not easy to see. The first time astronomers had a clear view of it was when the* Mariner 10 *space probe flew past it in 1974.*

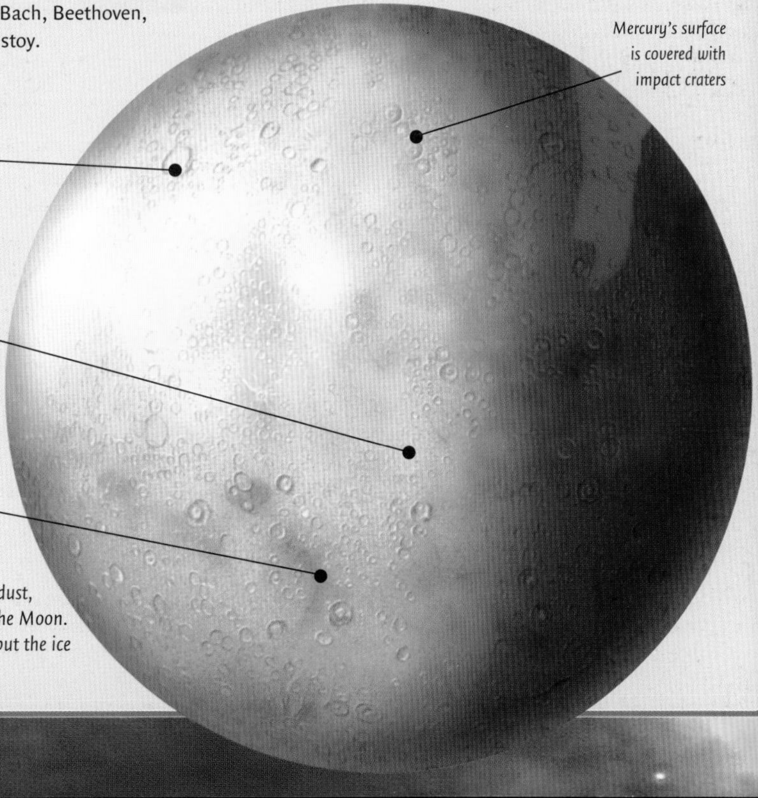

Mercury's surface is covered with impact craters

The largest feature on Mercury is a huge impact crater called the Caloris Basin, which is about 1,300 km across and 2 km deep

Most of the craters were formed by the impact of debris left over from the birth of the solar system, about 4 billion years ago

The surface is wrinkled by long, low ridges which probably formed as the core cooled and shrunk

▶ *Mercury is a planet of yellow dust, as deeply dented with craters as the Moon. It does have small polar icecaps, but the ice is pure acid.*

Copernicus

- **Until the 16th century** most people thought the Earth was the centre of the Universe and that everything – the Moon, Sun, planets and stars – revolved around it.
- **Nicolaus Copernicus** was the astronomer who first suggested that the Sun was the centre, and that the Earth went round the Sun. This is called the heliocentric view.
- **Copernicus was born** on 19 February 1473 at Torun in Poland, and died on 24 May 1547.
- **Copernicus was the nephew** of a prince bishop who spent most of his life as a canon at Frauenberg Cathedral in East Prussia (today Germany).
- **Copernicus described his ideas** in a book called *De revolutionibus orbium coelestium* ('On the revolutions of the heavenly spheres').
- **The Roman Catholic Church** banned Copernicus's book for almost 300 years.
- **Copernicus's ideas** came not from looking at the night sky but from studying ancient astronomy.
- **Copernicus's main clue** came from the way the planets, every now and then, seem to perform a backward loop through the sky.
- **The first proof** of Copernicus's theory came in 1609, when Galileo saw (through a telescope) moons revolving around Jupiter .
- **The change in ideas** that was brought about by Copernicus is known as the Copernican Revolution.

▶ 'The Earth,' wrote Copernicus, 'carrying the Moon's path, passes in a great orbit among the other planets in an annual revolution around the Sun.'

Day and night

- **When it is daylight** on the half of the Earth facing towards the Sun, it is night on the half of the Earth facing away from it. As the Earth rotates, so the day and night halves shift gradually around the world.
- **The Earth turns eastwards** – this means that the Sun comes up in the east as our part of the world spins round to face it.

◀ The Sun comes up to bring the dawn, as the Earth turns your part of the world around to face its light. It sets again at dusk, as the Earth goes on revolving, spinning your part of the world away from the sunlight again.

★ STAR FACT ★
One day on Venus lasts 5,832 Earth hours!

- **As the Earth turns**, the stars come back to the same place in the night sky every 23 hours, 56 minutes and 4.09 seconds. This is a sidereal day (star day).
- **It takes 24 hours** for the Sun to come back to the same place in the daytime sky. This is is the solar day, and it is slightly longer than the star day because the Earth moves 1 degree further round the Sun each day.
- **On the other planets**, the length of day and night varies according to how fast each planet rotates.
- **One day on Mercury** lasts 59 Earth days, because Mercury takes almost two months to spin around.
- **A day on Jupiter** lasts less than 10 hours because Jupiter spins so fast.
- **A day on Mars** is 24.6 hours – much the same as ours.
- **A day on the Moon** lasts one Earth month.

Moon landings

- **The first Moon landing** was by the unmanned Soviet probe *Lunar 9*, which touched down on the Moon's surface in 1966.
- **The first men to orbit** the Moon were the astronauts on board the US *Apollo 8* in 1968.
- **On 20 July 1969** the American astronauts Neil Armstrong and Edwin (Buzz) Aldrin became the first men ever to walk on the Moon.
- **When Neil Armstrong** stepped on to the Moon for the first time, he said these famous words: 'That's one small step for a man; one giant leap for mankind.'
- **Twelve men have landed** on the Moon between 1969 and 1972.

◀ *In 1969, Neil Armstrong was the first to walk on the Moon.*

- **The Moon astronauts** brought back 380 kg of Moon rock.
- **A mirror was left on** the Moon's surface to reflect a laser beam which measured the Moon's distance from Earth with amazing accuracy.
- **Laser measurements** showed that, on average, the Moon is 376,275 km away from the Earth.
- **Gravity on the Moon** is so weak that astronauts can leap high into the air wearing their heavy space suits.
- **Temperatures** reach 117°C at midday on the Moon, but plunge to -162°C at night.

Constellations

- **Constellations are patterns of stars** in the sky which astronomers use to help them pinpoint individual stars.
- **Most of the constellations** were identified long ago by the stargazers of Ancient Babylon and Egypt.
- **Constellations are simply patterns** – there is no real link between the stars whatsoever.
- **Astronomers today** recognize 88 constellations.
- **Heroes and creatures of Greek myth**, such as Orion the Hunter and Perseus, provided the names for many constellations, although each name is usually written in its Latin form, not Greek.
- **The stars in each constellation** are named after a letter of the Greek alphabet.
- **The brightest star in each constellation** is called the Alpha star, the next brightest Beta, and so on.
- **Different constellations** become visible at different times of year, as the Earth travels around the Sun.
- **Southern hemisphere constellations** are different from those in the north.
- **The constellation of the Great Bear** – also known by its Latin name Ursa Major – contains an easily recognizable group of seven stars called the Plough or the Big Dipper.

▼ *Constellations are patterns of stars that help astronomers locate stars among the thousands in the night sky.*

Dark matter

- **Dark matter** is space matter we cannot see because, unlike stars and galaxies, it does not give off light.
- **There is much more dark matter** in the Universe than bright. Some scientists think 90% of matter is dark.
- **Astronomers know about dark matter** because its gravity pulls on stars and galaxies, changing their orbits and the way they rotate (spin round).
- **The visible stars in the Milky Way** are only a thin central slice, embedded in a big bun-shaped ball of dark matter.
- **Dark matter** is of two kinds – the matter in galaxies (galactic), and the matter between them (intergalactic).
- **Galactic dark matter** may be much the same as ordinary matter. However, it burnt out (as black dwarf stars do) early in the life of the Universe.
- **Intergalactic dark matter** is made up of WIMPs (Weakly Interacting Massive Particles).
- **Some WIMPs** are called cold dark matter because they are travelling slowly away from the Big Bang.
- **Some WIMPs** are called hot dark matter because they are travelling very fast away from the Big Bang.
- **The future of the Universe** may depend on how much dark matter there is. If there is too much, its gravity will eventually stop the Universe's expansion – and make it shrink again (see the Big Bang).

▼ *A galaxy's bright stars may be only a tiny part of its total matter. Much of the galaxy may be invisible dark matter.*

Orbits

▲ *Space stations are artificial satellites that orbit the Earth. The Moon is the Earth's natural satellite.*

- **Orbit means 'travel round'**, and a moon, planet or other space object may be held within a larger space object's gravitational field and orbit it.
- **Orbits may be circular**, elliptical (oval) or parabolic (conical). The orbits of the planets are elliptical.
- **An orbiting space object** is called a satellite.
- **The biggest-known orbits** are those of the stars in the Milky Way Galaxy, which can take 200 million years.
- **Momentum** is what keeps a satellite moving through space. Just how much momentum a satellite has depends on its mass and its speed.
- **A satellite orbits** at the height where its momentum exactly balances the pull of gravity.
- **If the gravitational pull** is greater than a satellite's momentum, it falls in towards the larger space object.
- **If a satellite's momentum** is greater than the pull of gravity, it flies off into space.
- **The lower a satellite orbits**, the faster it must travel to stop it falling in towards the larger space object.
- **Geostationary orbit** for one of Earth's artificial satellites is 35,786 km over the Equator. At this height, it must travel around 11,000km/h to complete its orbit in 24 hours. Since Earth also takes 24 hours to rotate, the satellite spins with it and so stays in the same place over the Equator.

Venus

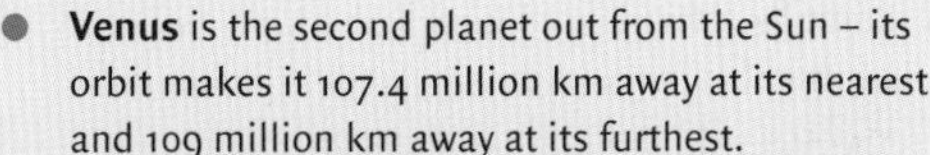

- **Venus** is the second planet out from the Sun – its orbit makes it 107.4 million km away at its nearest and 109 million km away at its furthest.
- **Venus shines like a star** in the night sky because its thick atmosphere reflects sunlight amazingly well. This planet is the brightest thing in the sky, after the Sun and the Moon.
- **Venus is called the Evening Star** because it can be seen from Earth in the evening, just after sunset. It can also be seen before sunrise, though. It is visible at these times because it is quite close to the Sun.
- **Venus's cloudy atmosphere** is a thick mixture of carbon dioxide gas and sulphuric acid, which are belched out by the planet's volcanoes.
- **Venus is the hottest planet** in the solar system, with a surface temperature of over 470°C.
- **Venus is so hot** because the carbon dioxide in its atmosphere works like the panes of glass in a greenhouse to trap the Sun's heat. This overheating is called a runaway greenhouse effect.

★ **STAR FACT** ★
Pressure on the surface of Venus is 90 times greater than that on Earth!

- **Venus's thick clouds** hide its surface so well that until the Russian *Venera 13* probe landed on the planet in 1982, some people thought there might be jungles beneath the clouds.
- **Venus's day** (the time it takes to spin round once) lasts 243 Earth days – longer than its year, which lasts 224.7 days. But because Venus rotates backwards, the Sun actually comes up twice during the planet's yearly orbit – once every 116.8 days.
- **Venus is the nearest** of all the planets to Earth in size, measuring 12,102 km across its diameter.

▼ *Venus's thick clouds of carbon dioxide gas and sulphuric acid reflect sunlight and make it shine like a star, but none of its atmosphere is transparent like the Earth's. This makes it very hard to see what is happening down on its surface.*

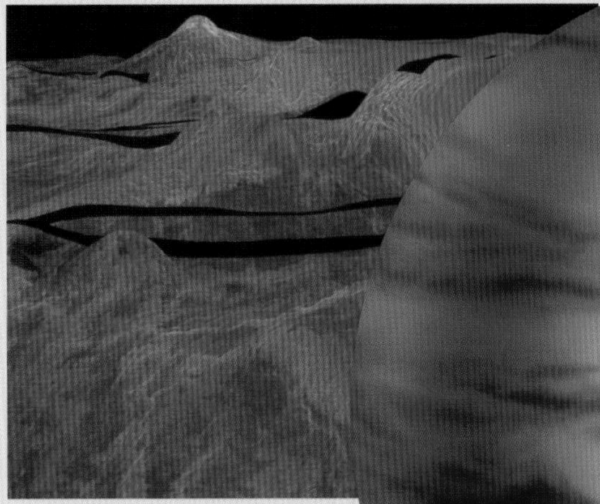

▲ *This is a view of a 6km-high volcano on Venus' surface called Maat Mons. It is not an actual photograph, but was created on computer from radar data collected by the Magellan orbiter which reached Venus in the 1980s. The colours are what astronomers guess them to be from their knowledge of the chemistry of Venus.*

Galileo

- **Galileo Galilei** (1564-1642) was a great Italian mathematician and astronomer.
- **Galileo was born** in Pisa on 15 February 1564, in the same year as William Shakespeare.
- **The pendulum clock** was invented by Galileo after watching a swinging lamp in Pisa Cathedral in 1583.
- **Galileo's experiments** with balls rolling down slopes laid the basis for our understanding of how gravity makes things accelerate (speed up).
- **Learning of the telescope's invention**, Galileo made his own to look at the Moon, Venus and Jupiter.

★ STAR FACT ★
Only on 13 October 1992 was the sentence of the Catholic Church on Galileo retracted.

◀ *One of the most brilliant of scientists of all time, Galileo ended his life imprisoned (in his villa near Florence) for his beliefs.*

- **Galileo described his observations** of space in a book called *The Starry Messenger*, published in 1613.
- **Through his telescope** Galileo saw that Jupiter has four moons (see Jupiter's Galilean moons). He also saw that Venus has phases (as our Moon does).
- **Jupiter's moon and Venus's phases** were the first visible evidence of Copernicus' theory that the Earth moves round the Sun. Galileo also believed this.
- **Galileo was declared a heretic** in 1616 by the Catholic Church, for his support of Copernican theory. Later, threatened with torture, Galileo was forced to deny that the Earth orbits the Sun. Legend has it he muttered '*eppur si muove*' ('yet it does move') afterwards.

Earth's formation

▲ *Earth and the Solar System formed from a cloud of gas and dust.*

- **The Solar System** was created when the gas cloud left over from a giant supernova explosion started to collapse in on itself and spin.
- **About 4.55 billion years ago** there was just a vast, hot cloud of dust and gas circling a new star, our Sun.
- **The Earth probably began** when tiny pieces of space debris (called planetesimals) began to clump together, pulled together by each other's gravity.
- **As the Earth formed**, more space debris kept on smashing into it, adding new material. This debris included ice from the edges of the solar system.
- **About 4.5 billion years ago**, a rock the size of Mars crashed into the Earth. The splashes of material from this crash clumped together to form the Moon.
- **The collision** that formed the Moon made the Earth very hot.
- **Radioactive decay** heated the Earth even further.
- **For a long time** the surface of the Earth was a mass of erupting volcanoes.
- **Iron and nickel melted** and sank to form the core.
- **Lighter materials** such as aluminium, oxygen and silicon floated up and cooled to form the crust.

Distances

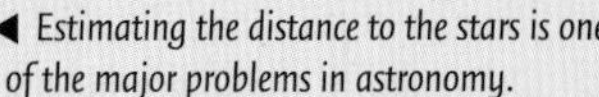

◀ *Estimating the distance to the stars is one of the major problems in astronomy.*

- **The distance to the Moon** is measured with a laser beam.
- **The distance to the planets** is measured by bouncing radar signals off them and timing how long the signals take to get there and back.
- **The distance to nearby stars** is worked out by measuring the slight shift in the angle of each star in comparison to stars far away, as the Earth orbits the Sun. This is called parallax shift.
- **Parallax shift** can only be used to measure nearby stars, so astronomers work out the distance to faraway stars and galaxies by comparing how bright they look with how bright they actually are.
- **For middle distance stars**, astronomers compare colour with brightness using the Hertzsprung-Russell (H-R) diagram. This is called main sequence fitting.
- **Beyond 30,000 light-years,** stars are too faint for main sequence fitting to work.
- **Distances to nearby galaxies** can be estimated using 'standard candles' – stars whose brightness astronomers know, such as Cepheid variables (see variable stars), supergiants and supernovae.
- **The expected brightness of a galaxy** too far away to pick out its stars may be worked out using the Tully-Fisher technique, based on how fast galaxies spin.
- **Counting planetary nebulae** (the rings of gas left behind by supernova explosions) is another way of working out how bright a distant galaxy should be.
- **A third method** of calculating the brightness of a distant galaxy is to gauge how mottled it looks.

Spacecraft

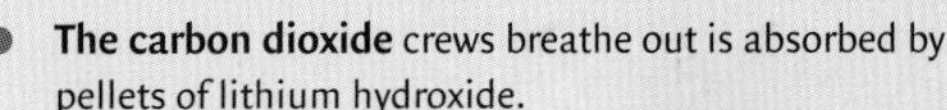

- **There are three kinds of spacecraft** – artificial satellites, unmanned probes and manned spacecraft.
- **Spacecraft** have double hulls (outer coverings) to protect against other space objects that crash into them.
- **Manned spacecraft** must also protect the crew from heat and other dangerous effects of launch and landing.
- **Spacecraft windows** have filters to protect astronauts from the Sun's dangerous ultraviolet rays.
- **Radiators** on the outside of the spacecraft lose heat, to stop the crew's body temperatures overheating the craft.
- **Manned spacecraft** have life-support systems that provide oxygen to breathe, usually mixed with nitrogen (as in ordinary air). Charcoal filters out smells.

★ STAR FACT ★

The weightlessness of space means that most astronauts sleep floating in the air, held in place by a few straps.

- **The carbon dioxide** crews breathe out is absorbed by pellets of lithium hydroxide.
- **Spacecraft toilets** have to get rid of waste in low gravity conditions. Astronauts have to sit on a device which sucks away the waste. Solid waste is dried and dumped in space, but the water is saved.
- **To wash**, astronauts have a waterproof shower which sprays them with jets of water from all sides and also sucks away all the waste water.

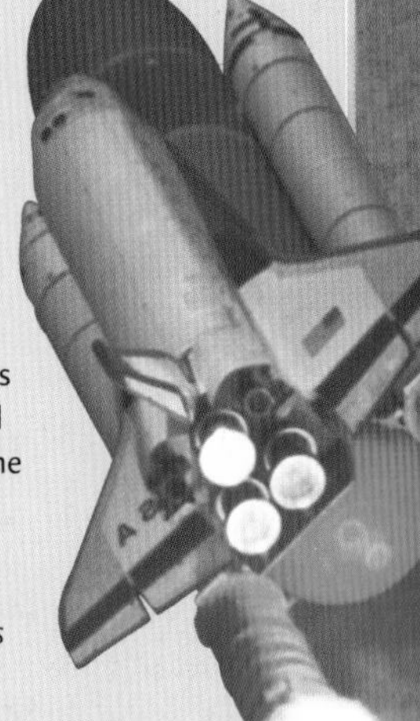

▶ *The US space shuttle, the first reusable spacecraft, has made manned space flights out into Earth's orbit and back almost a matter of routine.*

The Earth

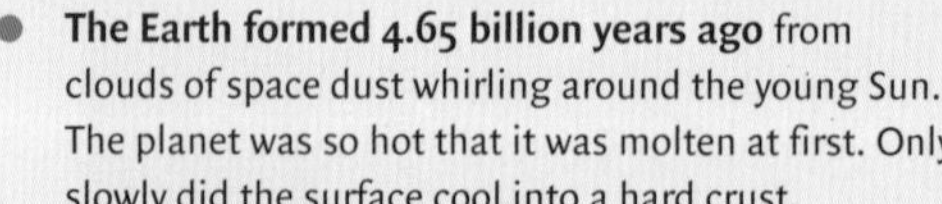

- **The Earth is the third planet** out from the Sun, 149.6 million km away on average. On 3 January, at the nearest point of its orbit (called the perihelion), the Earth is 147,097,800 km away from the Sun. On 4 July, at its furthest (the aphelion), it is 152,098,200 km away.
- **The Earth is the fifth largest planet** in the solar system, with a diameter of 12,756 km and a circumference of 40,024 km at the Equator.
- **The Earth is one of four rocky planets,** along with Mercury, Venus and Mars. It is made mostly of rock, with a core of iron and nickel.
- **No other planet in the solar system** has liquid water on its surface, so Earth is uniquely suitable for life. Over 70% of Earth's surface is under water.
- **The Earth's atmosphere** is mainly harmless nitrogen and life-giving oxygen, and it is over 700 km deep. The oxygen has been made and maintained by plants over billions of years.
- **The Earth formed 4.65 billion years ago** from clouds of space dust whirling around the young Sun. The planet was so hot that it was molten at first. Only slowly did the surface cool into a hard crust.
- **The Earth's orbit** around the Sun is 939,886,400 km long and takes 365.242 days.
- **The Earth is tilted** at an angle of 23.5°. Even so, it orbits the Sun in a level plane, called the plane of the ecliptic.
- **The Earth is made up** of the same basic materials as meteorites and the other rocky planets – mostly iron (35%), oxygen (28%), magnesium (17%), silicon (13%) and nickel (2.7%).

★ **STAR FACT** ★
The Earth is protected from the Sun's radiation by a magnetic field which stretches 60,000 km out into space.

▼ *The Earth looks mostly bright blue from space – this is due to the unique presence of water on its surface.*

▲ *Most of the Earth's rocky crust is drowned beneath oceans, formed from steam belched out by volcanoes early in the planet's history. The Earth is just the right distance from the Sun for surface temperatures to stay an average 15°C, and keep most of its water liquid.*

Comets

▲ *Comet Kahoutek streaks through the night sky.*

- **Comets are bright objects** with long tails, which we sometimes see streaking across the night sky.
- **They may look spectacular**, but a comet is just a dirty ball of ice a few kilometres across.
- **Many comets orbit the Sun**, but their orbits are very long and they spend most of the time in the far reaches of the solar system. We see them when their orbit brings them close to the Sun for a few weeks.
- **A comet's tail** is made as it nears the Sun and begins to melt. A vast plume of gas millions of kilometres across is blown out behind by the solar wind. The tail is what you see, shining as the sunlight catches it.
- **Comets called periodics** appear at regular intervals.
- **Some comets reach speeds** of 2 million km/h as they near the Sun.
- **Far away from the Sun**, comets slow down to 1,000 km/h or so – that is why they stay away for so long.
- **The visit of the comet Hale-Bopp** in 1997 gave the brightest view of a comet since 1811, visible even from brightly lit cities.
- **The Shoemaker-Levy 9 comet** smashed into Jupiter in July 1994, with the biggest crash ever witnessed.
- **The most famous comet** of all is Halley's comet.

Giant stars

- **Giant stars** are 10 to 100 times as big as the Sun, and 10 to 1,000 times as bright.
- **Red giants** are stars that have swollen 10 to 100 times their size, as they reach the last stages of their life and their outer gas layers cool and expand.
- **Giant stars have burned** all their hydrogen, and so burn helium, fusing (joining) helium atoms to make carbon.
- **The biggest stars** go on swelling after they become red giants, and grow into supergiants.
- **Supergiant stars** are up to 500 times as big as the Sun, with absolute magnitudes of -5 to -10 (see star brightness).
- **Pressure in the heart** of a supergiant is enough to fuse carbon atoms together to make iron.

★ STAR FACT ★
The biggest-known star is the hypergiant Cygnus OB2 No.12, which is 810,000 times as bright as the Sun.

- **All the iron in the Universe** was made in the heart of supergiant stars.
- **There is a limit to the brightness** of supergiants, so they can be used as distance markers by comparing how bright they look to how bright they are (see distances).
- **Supergiant stars** eventually collapse and explode as supernovae.

▶ *The constellation of Cygnus, the Swan, contains the very biggest star in the known Universe – a hypergiant which is almost a million times as big as the Sun.*

Eclipses

- **An eclipse** is when the light from a star such as the Sun is temporarily blocked off by another space object.
- **A lunar eclipse** is when the Moon travels behind the Earth, and into the Earth's shadow (Earth is between the Moon and the Sun).
- **Lunar eclipses happen once or twice** every year and last only a few hours.
- **In a total lunar eclipse**, the Moon turns rust red.
- **There will be lunar eclipses** on 16 May and 9 November 2003 and on 4 May and 28 October 2004.
- **A solar eclipse** is when the Moon comes between the Sun and the Earth, casting a shadow a few kilometres wide on to the Earth's surface.
- **In a total eclipse of the Sun**, the Moon passes directly in front of the Sun, completely covering it so that only its corona can be seen (see the Sun).
- **There are one or two solar eclipses every year**, but they are visible only from a narrow strip of the world.

▲ *During a total solar eclipse of the Sun, the Moon blocks out everything but the Sun's corona.*

- **There will be total solar eclipses** on 23 November 2003, and 29 March 2006.
- **Solar eclipses are possible** because the Moon is 400 times smaller than the Sun, and is also 400 times closer to the Earth. This means the Sun and the Moon appear to be the same size in the sky.

Star brightness

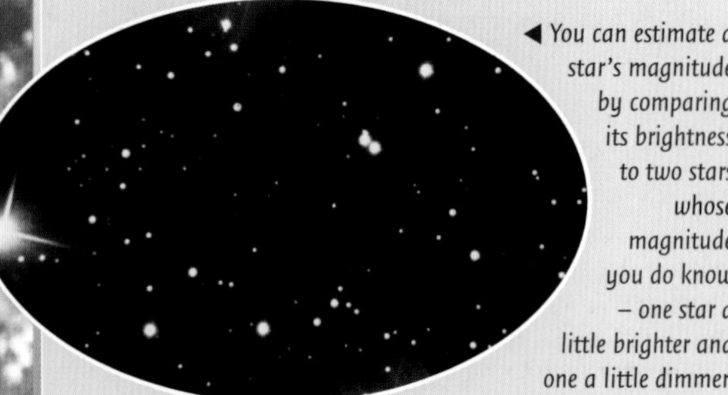

◀ *You can estimate a star's magnitude by comparing its brightness to two stars whose magnitude you do know – one star a little brighter and one a little dimmer.*

- **Star brightness** is worked out on a scale of magnitude (amount) that was first devised in 150 BC by the Ancient Greek astronomer Hipparchus.
- **The brightest star** Hipparchus could see was Antares, and he described it as magnitude 1. He described the faintest star he could see as magnitude 6.
- **Using telescopes and binoculars**, astronomers can now see much fainter stars than Hipparchus could.

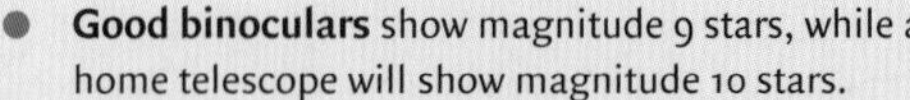

- **Good binoculars** show magnitude 9 stars, while a home telescope will show magnitude 10 stars.
- **Brighter stars than Antares** have been identified with magnitudes of less than 1, and even minus numbers. Betelgeuse is 0.8, Vega is 0.0, and the Sun is -26.7.
- **The brightest-looking star** from Earth is Sirius, the Dog Star, with a magnitude of -1.4.
- **The magnitude scale only** describes how bright a star looks from Earth compared to other stars. This is its relative magnitude.
- **The further away a star is,** the dimmer it looks and the smaller its relative magnitude is, regardless of how bright it really is.
- **A star's absolute magnitude** describes how bright a star really is.
- **The star Deneb** is 60,000 times brighter than the Sun. But because it is 1,800 light-years away, it looks dimmer than Sirius.

Herschel

- **William Herschel** (1738-1822) was an amateur astronomer who built his own, very powerful telescope in his home in Bath, England.
- **Until Herschel's time**, astronomers assumed there were just seven independent objects in the sky – the Moon, the Sun, and five planets.
- **The five known planets** were Mercury, Venus, Mars, Jupiter and Saturn.
- **Uranus**, the sixth planet, was discovered by William Herschel in 1781.
- **At first, Herschel** had thought that the dot of light he could see through his telescope was a star. But when he looked more closely, he saw a tiny disc instead of a point of light. When he looked the next night, the 'star' had moved – this meant that it had to be a planet.

◀ *William Herschel was one of the greatest astronomers. With the help of his sister Caroline, he discovered Uranus in 1781. He later identified two of the moons of Uranus and Saturn.*

- **Herschel wanted to name** the planet George, after King George III, but Uranus was eventually chosen.
- **Herschel's partner** in his discoveries was his sister Caroline (1750-1848), another great astronomer, who catalogued (listed) all the stars of the northern hemisphere.
- **Herschel's son John** catalogued the stars of the southern hemisphere.
- **Herschel himself added** to the catalogue of nebulae.
- **Herschel was also the first** to explain that the Milky Way is our view of a galaxy shaped 'like a grindstone'.

Rockets

- **Rockets** provide the huge thrust needed to beat the pull of Earth's gravity and launch a spacecraft into space.
- **Rockets burn propellant** (propel means 'push'), to produce hot gases that drive the rocket upwards.
- **Rocket propellant** comes in two parts – a solid or liquid fuel, and an oxidizer.
- **Solid fuel** is a rubbery substance that contains hydrogen, and it is usually used in additional, booster rockets.
- **Liquid fuel** is usually liquid hydrogen, and it is typically used on big rockets.
- **There is no oxygen in space**, and the oxidizer supplies the oxygen needed to burn fuel. It is usually liquid oxygen (called 'lox' for short).
- **The first rockets** were made 1,000 years ago in China.

★ **STAR FACT** ★

The most powerful rocket ever was the *Saturn 5* that sent astronauts to the Moon.

- **Robert Goddard** launched the very first liquid-fuel rocket in 1926.
- **The German V2 war rocket**, designed by Werner von Braun, was the first rocket capable of reaching space.

▶ *Unlike other spacecraft, the space shuttle can land like an aeroplane ready for another mission. But even the shuttle has to be launched into space on the back of huge rockets. These soon fall back to Earth where they are collected for reuse.*

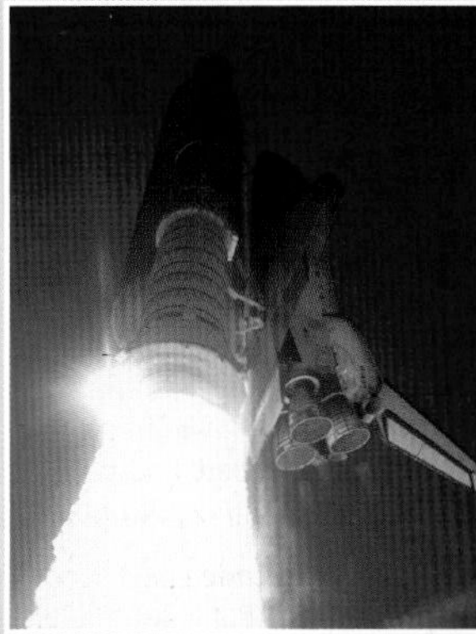

Satellites

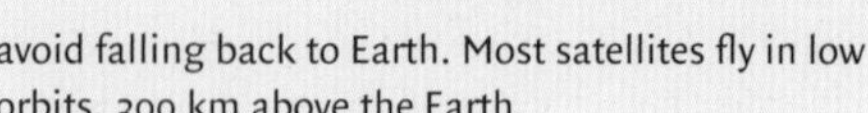

- **Satellites are objects** that orbit planets and other space objects. Moons are natural satellites. Spacecraft sent up to orbit the Earth and the Sun are artificial satellites.
- **The first artificial satellite** was *Sputnik 1*, launched on 4 October 1957.
- **Over 100 artificial satellites** are now launched every year. A few of them are space telescopes.
- **Communications satellites** beam everything from TV pictures to telephone calls around the world.
- **Observation satellites** scan the Earth and are used for purposes such as scientific research, weather forecasting and spying.
- **Navigation satellites** such as the Global Positioning System (GPS) are used by people such as airline pilots to work out exactly where they are.
- **Satellites are launched** at a particular speed and trajectory (path) to place them in just the right orbit.
- **The lower a satellite's orbit**, the faster it must fly to avoid falling back to Earth. Most satellites fly in low orbits, 300 km above the Earth.
- **A geostationary orbit** is 35,786 km up. Satellites in geostationary orbit over the Equator always stay in exactly the same place above the Earth.
- **Polar orbiting satellites** circle the Earth from pole to pole about 850 km up, covering a different strip of the Earth's surface on each orbit.

▼ *One of the many hundreds of satellites now in Earth's orbit.*

Hipparchus

▲ *Some of Hipparchus' knowledge of stars came from the Sumerians who wrote on clay tablets*

- **Hipparchus of Nicaea** was a Greek astronomer who lived in the 2nd century BC, dying in 127 BC.
- **Hipparchus created the** framework for astronomy.
- **Hipparchus's ideas** were almost lost until rescued by roman astronomer Ptolemy and developed into a system that lasted 1500 years until they were overthrown by the ideas of Copernicus.
- **Ancient Babylonian records** brought back by Alexander the Great from his conquests helped Hipparchus to make his observations of the stars.
- **Hipparchus was the first astronomer** to try to work out how far away the Sun is.
- **The first star catalogue**, listing 850 stars, was put together by Hipparchus.
- **Hipparchus was also the first** to identify the constellations systematically and to assess stars in terms of magnitude (see star brightness).
- **Hipparchus discovered** that the positions of the stars on the equinoxes (21 March and 21 December) slowly shift round, taking 26,000 years to return to their original place. This is the 'precession of the equinoxes'.
- **The mathematics of trigonometry** is also thought to have been invented by Hipparchus.

Mars

- **Mars** is the nearest planet to Earth after Venus, and it is the only planet to have either an atmosphere or a daytime temperature close to ours.
- **Mars is called the red planet** because of its rusty red colour. This comes from oxidized (rusted) iron in its soil.
- **Mars is the fourth planet** out from the Sun, orbiting it at an average distance of 227.9 million km. It takes 687 days to complete its orbit.
- **Mars is 6,786 km** in diameter and spins round once every 24.62 hours – almost the same time as the Earth takes to rotate.
- **Mars's volcano Olympus Mons** is the biggest in the solar system. It covers the same area as Ireland and is three times higher than Mount Everest.
- **In the 1880s**, the American astronomer Percival Lowell was convinced that the dark lines he could see on Mars's surface through his telescope were canals built by Martians.

★ STAR FACT ★

The 1997 Mars Pathfinder mission showed that many of the rocks on Mars's surface were dumped in their positions by a huge flood at least 2 billion years ago.

- **The Viking probes** found no evidence of life on Mars, but the discovery of a possible fossil of a micro-organism in a Mars rock (see life) means the hunt for life on Mars is on. Future missions to the planet will hunt for life below its surface.
- **The evidence is growing** that Mars was warmer and wetter in the past, although scientists cannot say how much water there was, or when and why it dried up.
- **Mars has two tiny moons** called Phobos and Deimos. Phobos is just 27 km across, while Deimos is just 15 km across and has so little gravity that you could reach escape velocity (see take off) riding a bike up a ramp!

▼ Mars's surface is cracked by a valley called the Vallis Marineris – so big it makes the Grand Canyon look tiny.

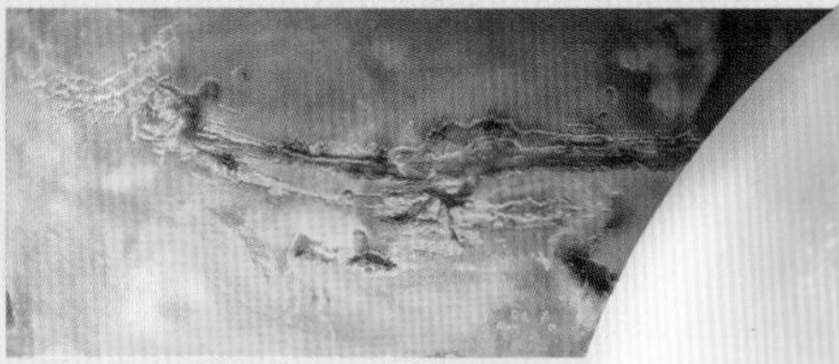

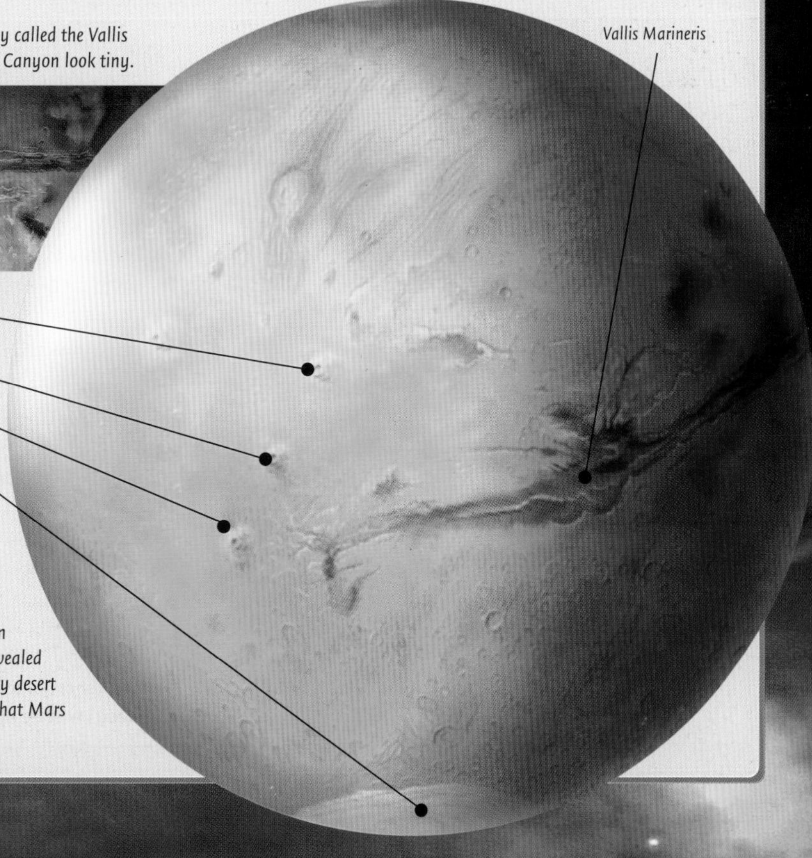

Vallis Marineris

Ascraeus Mons volcano

Pavonis Mons volcano

Arsia Mons volcano

Polar icecap

▶ Mars is the best known planet besides Earth, studied by countless astronomers through powerful telescopes, scanned by orbiting space probes, and landed on more times than any other planet. All this effort has revealed a planet with a surface like a red, rocky desert – but there is also plenty of evidence that Mars wasn't always so desert-like.

Light

- **Light is the fastest thing** in the Universe, travelling at 299,792,458 metres per second.
- **Light rays always travel** in straight lines.
- **Light rays change direction** as they pass from one material to another. This is called refraction.
- **Colours** are different wavelengths of light.
- **The longest light waves** you can see are red, and the shortest are violet.
- **Light is a form** of electromagnetic radiation (see magnetism and radiation), and a light ray is a stream of tiny energy particles called photons.
- **Photons of light** travel in waves just 380 to 750 nanometres (millionths of a millimetre) long.
- **Faint light** from very distant stars is often recorded by sensors called CCDs (see observatories). These count photons from the star as they arrive and build up a picture of the star bit by bit over a long period.
- **The electromagnetic spectrum** (range) includes ultraviolet light and X-rays, but light is the only part of the spectrum our eyes can see.
- **All light is given out by atoms**, and atoms give out light when 'excited' – for example, in a nuclear reaction.

▼ *Stars send out huge amounts of light and other radiation as they are heated within by stupendously big nuclear reactions.*

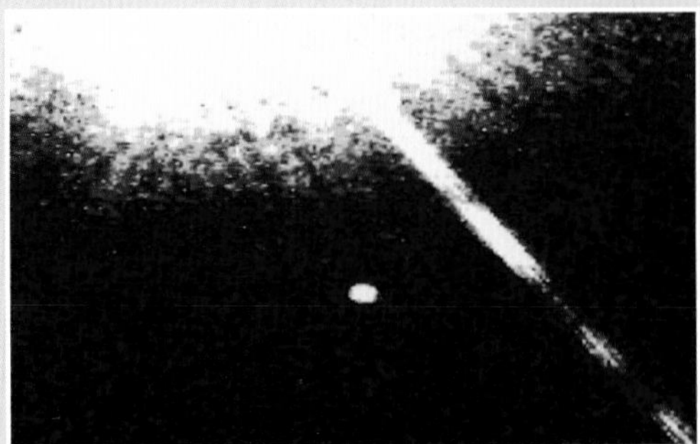

Magnetism

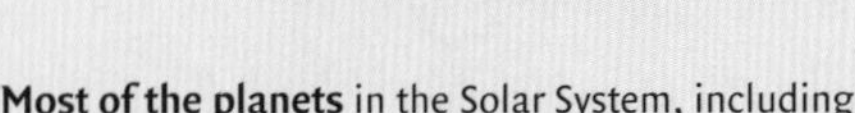

- **Magnetism is a force** that either pulls magnetic materials together or pushes them apart.
- **Iron and nickel** are the most common magnetic materials. Electricity is also magnetic.
- **Around every magnet** there is a region in which its effects are felt, called its magnetic field.
- **The magnetic field** around a planet or a star is called the magnetosphere.

◀ *The planet Jupiter is one of the most powerful magnets in the Solar System. It was first detected by 'synchrotron radiation' – the radiation from tiny electrons accelerating as they fall into a magnetic field.*

- **Most of the planets** in the Solar System, including the Earth, have a magnetic field.
- **Planets have magnetic fields** because of the liquid iron in their cores. As the planets rotate, so the iron swirls, generating electric currents that create the magnetic field.
- **Jupiter's magnetic field** is 30 times stronger than that of the Earth, because Jupiter is huge and spins very quickly.
- **Neptune and Uranus** are unusual because, unlike other planets' magnetic fields, theirs are at right angles to their axis of rotation (the angle at which they spin).
- **Magnetism is linked** to electricity, and together they make up the force called electromagnetism.
- **Electromagnetism** is one of the four fundamental forces in the Universe, along with gravity and the two basic forces of the atomic nucleus.

Atmosphere

- **An atmosphere** is the gases held around a planet by its gravity.
- **Every planet in the Solar System** has an atmosphere.
- **Each atmosphere** is very different. Earth's atmosphere is the only one humans can breathe.
- **Atmospheres** are not fixed, but can change rapidly.

▼ *Earth's unique atmosphere shields us from the Sun's dangerous rays, as well as giving us oxygen and water.*

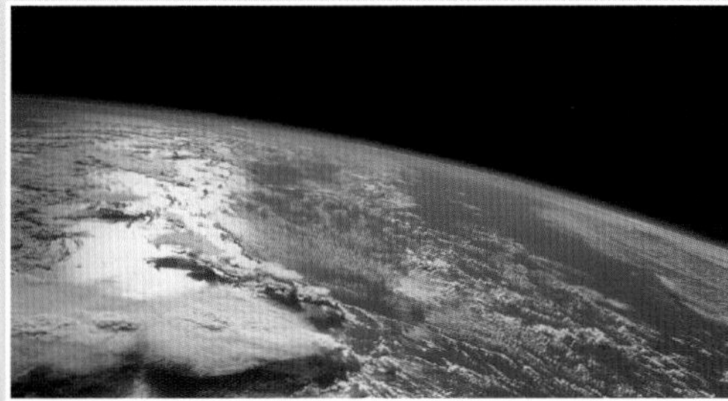

★ **STAR FACT** ★
The oxygen in Earth's atmosphere was formed entirely by microscopic plants.

- **Moons** are generally too small and their gravity is too weak to hold on to an atmosphere. But some moons in the Solar System have one, including Saturn's moon Titan.
- **The primordial (earliest) atmospheres** came from the cloud of gas and dust surrounding the young Sun.
- **If Earth and the other rocky planets** had primordial atmospheres, they were stripped away by the solar wind (see solar eruptions).
- **Earth's atmosphere** was formed first from gases pouring out of volcanoes.
- **Jupiter's atmosphere** is partly primordial, but it has been altered by the Sun's radiation, and the planet's own internal heat and lightning storms.

Cosmic rays

- **Cosmic rays** are streams of high-energy particles that strike Earth's atmosphere.
- **The lowest-energy cosmic rays** come from the Sun, or are Galactic Cosmic Rays (GCRs) from outside the Solar System.
- **Medium-energy cosmic rays** come from sources within our own Milky Way, including powerful supernova explosions.
- **Collisions** between cosmic rays and the hydrogen gas clouds left by supernovae create a kind of radiation called synchrotron radiation, which can be picked up from places such as the Crab nebula by radio telescopes.
- **The highest-energy cosmic rays** may come from outside our galaxy.
- **About 85% of GCRs** are the nuclei of hydrogen atoms, stripped of their electron (see atoms).

◀ *Because Earth's magnetic field makes cosmic rays spiral into our atmosphere, it is not always easy to identify where they have come from. However, many are from the surface of the Sun.*

- **Most other GCRs** are helium and heavier nuclei, but there are also tiny positrons, electrons and neutrinos.
- **Neutrinos** are so small that they pass almost straight through the Earth without stopping.
- **The study of cosmic rays** provided scientists with most of their early knowledge about high-energy particles – every subatomic particle apart from electrons, protons and neutrons.
- **Most cosmic rays** are deflected (pushed aside) by the Earth's magnetic field or collide with particles in the atmosphere long before they reach the ground.

Jupiter

- **Jupiter** is the biggest planet in the Solar System – twice as heavy as all the other planets put together.
- **Jupiter has no surface** for a spacecraft to land on because it is made mostly from helium gas and hydrogen. The massive pull of Jupiter's gravity squeezes the hydrogen so hard that it is liquid.
- **Towards Jupiter's core**, immense pressure turns the hydrogen to solid metal.
- **The Ancient Greeks** originally named the planet Zeus, after the king of their gods. Jupiter was the Romans' name for Zeus.
- **Jupiter spins right round** in less than 10 hours, which means that the planet's surface is moving at nearly 50,000 km/h.

! NEWS FLASH !
The Galileo space probe reached Jupiter and its moons in the year 1995.

- **Jupiter's speedy spin makes** its middle bulge out. It also churns up the planet's metal core until it generates a hugely powerful magnetic field (see magnetism), ten times as strong as the Earth's.
- **Jupiter has a Great Red Spot** – a huge swirl of red clouds measuring more than 40,000 km across. The scientist Robert Hooke first noticed the spot in 1644.
- **Jupiter's four biggest moons** were first spotted by Galileo in the 17th century (see Jupiter's Galilean moons). Their names are Io, Europa, Callisto and Ganymede.
- **Jupiter also has 17 smaller moons** – Metis, Adastrea, Amalthea, Thebe, Leda, Himalia, Lysithea, Elkar, Ananke, Carme, Pasiphaë and Sinope and 5 recent discoveries.
- **Jupiter is so massive** that the pressure at its heart makes it glow very faintly with invisible infrared rays. Indeed, it glows as brightly as 4 million billion 100-watt light bulbs. But it is not quite big enough for nuclear reactions to start, and make it become a star.

◄ *Jupiter is a gigantic planet, 142,984 km across. Its orbit takes 11.86 years and varies between 740.9 and 815.7 million km from the Sun. Its surface is often rent by huge lightning flashes and thunderclaps, and temperatures here plunge to -150°C. Looking at Jupiter's surface, all you can see is a swirling mass of red, brown and yellow clouds of ammonia, including the Great Red Spot.*

Space probes

- **Space probes** are automatic, computer-controlled unmanned spacecraft sent out to explore space.
- **The first successful** planetary probe was the USA's *Mariner 2*, which flew past Venus in 1962.
- ***Mariner 10*** reached Mercury in 1974.
- ***Vikings 1* and *2* landed** on Mars in 1976.
- ***Voyager 2*** has flown over 6 billion km and is heading out of the Solar System after passing close to Jupiter (1979), Saturn (1980), Uranus (1986) and Neptune (1989).
- **Most probes** are 'fly-bys' which spend just a few days passing their target and beaming back data to Earth.
- **To save fuel** on journeys to distant planets, space probes may use a nearby planet's gravity to catapult them on their way. This is called a slingshot.

! NEWS FLASH !
NASA' s Terrestrial Planet Finder (TPF) may set off to visit planets circling nearby stars in 2009.

- **In the next decade**, more than 50 space probes will be sent off to visit planets, asteroids and comets, as well as to observe the Moon and the Sun.
- **Space probes** will bring back samples from Mars, comets and asteroids early in the next few years.

▼ *Probes are equipped with a wealth of equipment for recording data and beaming it back to Earth.*

Hubble

▲ *One of Hubble's earliest achievements was to show that some 'nebulae' were really other galaxies.*

- **Edwin Hubble** (1889-1953) was an American who trained in law at Chicago and Oxford, and was also a great boxer before he turned to astronomy.
- **Until the early 20th century**, astronomers thought that our galaxy was all there was to the Universe.

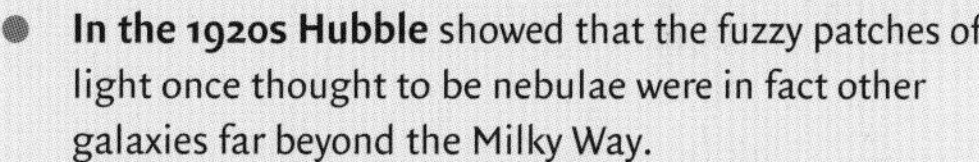

- **In the 1920s Hubble** showed that the fuzzy patches of light once thought to be nebulae were in fact other galaxies far beyond the Milky Way.
- **In 1929 Hubble** measured the red shift of 18 galaxies, and showed that they were all moving away from us.
- **Red shift showed Hubble** that the further away a galaxy is, the faster it is moving.
- **The ratio of a galaxy's distance** to the speed it is moving away from us is now known as Hubble's Law.
- **Hubble's Law** showed that the Universe is getting bigger – and so must have started very small. This led to the idea of the Big Bang.
- **The figure given** by Hubble's law is Hubble's constant and is about 40 to 80 km/sec per megaparsec.
- **In the 1930s Hubble** showed that the Universe is isotropic (the same in all directions).
- **Hubble space telescope** is named after Edwin Hubble.

Meteors

▲ *This crater in Arizona is one of the few large meteorite crater's visible on Earth. The Moon is covered in them.*

- **Meteors** are space objects that crash into Earth's atmosphere. They may be stray asteroids, tiny meteoroids, or the grains of dust from the tails of dying comets.
- **Meteoroids** are the billions of tiny lumps of rocky material that hurtle around the solar system. Most are no bigger than a pea.
- **Most meteors** are very small and burn up as they enter the atmosphere.
- **Shooting stars** may look like stars shooting across the night sky, but they are actually meteors burning up as they hit Earth's atmosphere.
- **Meteor showers** are bursts of dozens of shooting stars which arrive as Earth hits the tail of a comet.
- **Although meteors are not stars**, meteor showers are named after the constellations they seem to come from.
- **The heaviest showers** are the Perseids (12 Aug), the Geminids (13 Dec) and the Quadrantids (3 Jan).
- **Meteorites** are larger meteors that penetrate right through Earth's atmosphere and reach the ground.
- **A large meteorite** could hit the Earth at any time.

★ **STAR FACT** ★

The impact of a large meteorite may have chilled the Earth and wiped out the dinosaurs.

Pulsars

- **A pulsar** is a neutron star that spins rapidly, beaming out regular pulses of radio waves – rather like an invisible cosmic lighthouse.
- **The first pulsar** was detected by a Cambridge astronomer called Jocelyn Bell Burnell in 1967.

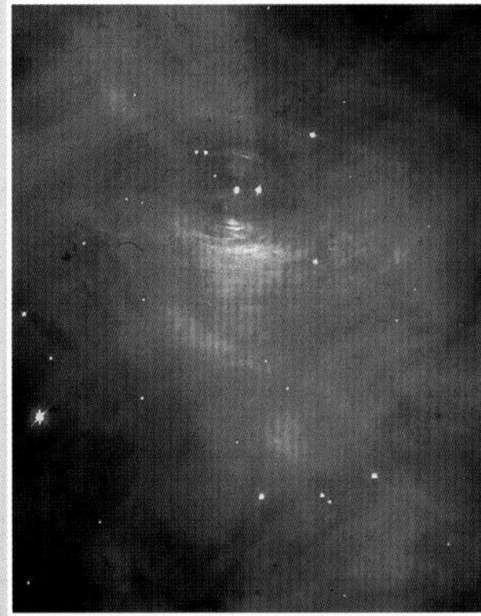

▶ *The Crab nebula contains a pulsar also known as NP0532. It is the youngest pulsar yet discovered and it probably formed after the supernova explosion seen in the Crab nebula in AD 1054. It has a rotation period of 0.0331 seconds, but it is gradually slowing down.*

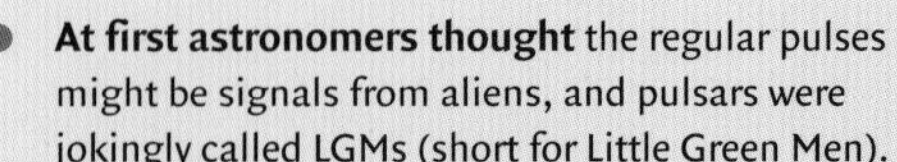

- **At first astronomers thought** the regular pulses might be signals from aliens, and pulsars were jokingly called LGMs (short for Little Green Men).
- **Most pulsars** send their radio pulse about once a second. The slowest pulse only every 4 seconds, and the fastest every 1.6 milliseconds.
- **The pulse rate** of a pulsar slows down as it gets older.
- **The Crab pulsar** slows by a millionth each day.
- **More than 650 pulsars** are now known, but there may be 100,000 active in our galaxy.
- **Pulsars probably result** from a supernova explosion – that is why most are found in the flat disc of the Milky Way, where supernovae occur.
- **Pulsars are not found** in the same place as supernovae because they form after the debris from the explosion has spread into space.
- **We know** they come from tiny neutron stars often less than 10 km across, because they pulse so fast.

Elements

- **Elements** are the basic chemicals of the Universe. There are no simpler substances, and they cannot be broken down into other substances.
- **Elements are formed** entirely of atoms that contain the same number of protons in their nuclei (see atoms). All hydrogen atoms have one proton, for instance.
- **More than 100 elements** are known.
- **The simplest and lightest elements** – hydrogen and helium – formed very early in the history of the Universe (see the Big Bang).
- **Other elements** formed as the nuclei of the atoms of the light elements joined in a process called nuclear fusion.
- **Nuclear fusion of element atoms** happens deep inside stars because of the pressure of their gravity.

★ STAR FACT ★
Massive atoms like uranium and thorium are formed by the shock waves from supernovae.

- **Lighter elements** like oxygen and carbon formed first.
- **Helium nuclei** fused with oxygen and neon atoms to form atoms like silicon, magnesium and calcium.
- **Heavy atoms** like iron formed when massive supergiant stars neared the end of their life and collapsed, boosting the pressure of the gravity in their core hugely. Even now iron is forming inside dying supergiants.

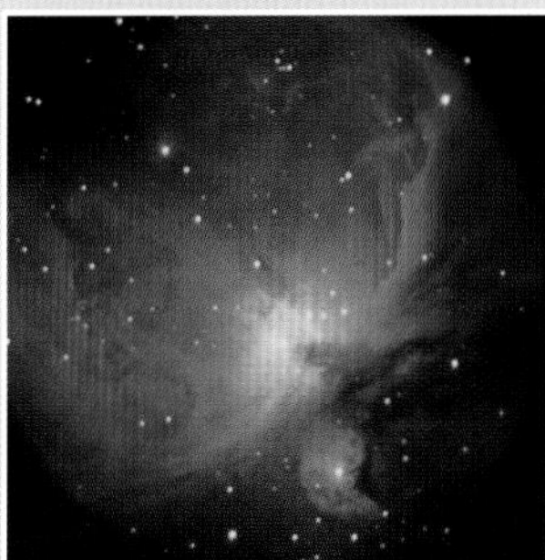

▶ *Nebulae like this one, Orion, contain many elements. Some (such as oxygen, silicon and carbon) formed in their stars, but their hydrogen and helium formed in deep space very long ago.*

Kepler

▶ *Despite almost losing his eyesight and the use of his hands through smallpox at the age of three, Johannes Kepler became an assistant to the great Danish astronomer Tycho Brahe, and took over his work when Brahe died.*

- **Johannes Kepler** (1571-1630) was the German astronomer who discovered the basic rules about the way the planets move.
- **Kepler got his ideas** from studying Mars' movement.
- **Before Kepler's discoveries**, people thought that the planets moved in circles.
- **Kepler discovered** that the true shape of the planets' orbits is elliptical (oval). This is Kepler's first law.

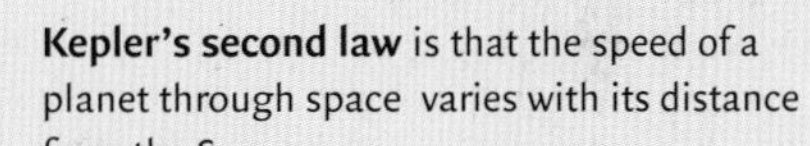

- **Kepler's second law** is that the speed of a planet through space varies with its distance from the Sun.
- **A planet moves fastest** when its orbit brings it nearest to the Sun (called its perihelion). It moves slowest when it is furthest from the Sun (called its aphelion).
- **Kepler's third law** is that a planet's period – the time it takes to complete its yearly orbit of the Sun – depends on its distance from the Sun.
- **Kepler's third law states** that the square of a planet's period is proportional to the cube of its average distance from the Sun.
- **Kepler believed** that the planets made harmonious music as they moved – 'the music of the spheres'.
- **Kepler also wrote a book** about measuring how much wine there was in wine casks, which proved to be important for the mathematics of calculus.

Space shuttle

- **The space shuttle** is a reusable spacecraft, made up of a 37.2m-long orbiter, two big Solid Rocket Boosters (SRBs), three main engines and a tank.
- **The shuttle orbiter is launched** into space upright on the SRBs, which fall away to be collected for reuse. When the mission is over the orbiter lands like a glider.
- **The orbiter can only go** as high as a near-Earth orbit, some 300 km above the Earth.
- **The maximum crew** is eight, and a basic mission is seven days, during which the crew work in shirtsleeves.
- **Orbiter toilets** use flowing air to suck away waste.
- **The orbiter can carry** a 25,000kg-load in its cargo bay.
- **The first four orbiters** were named after old sailing ships – *Columbia*, *Challenger*, *Discovery* and *Atlantis*.
- **The three main engines** are used only for lift off. In space, the small Orbital Manoeuvring System (OMS) engines take over. The Reaction Control System (RCS) makes small adjustments to the orbiter's position.
- **The shuttle programme** was brought to a temporary halt in 1986, when the *Challenger* exploded shortly after launch, killing its crew of seven.
- **In 1994 the crew of *Discovery*** mended the Hubble space telescope in orbit.

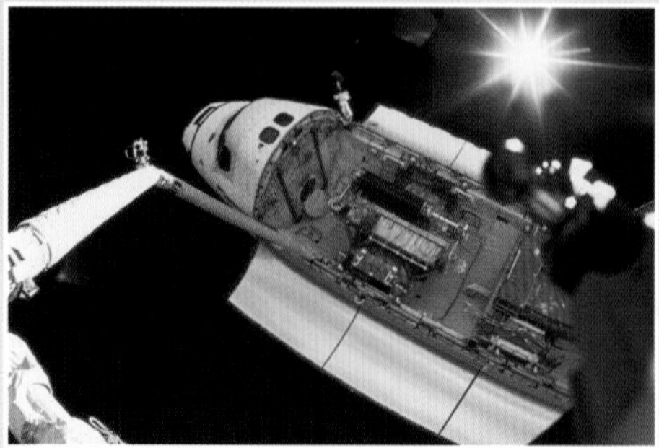

▲ *The entire centre section of the orbiter is a cargo bay which can be opened in space so satellites can be placed in orbit.*

Moons

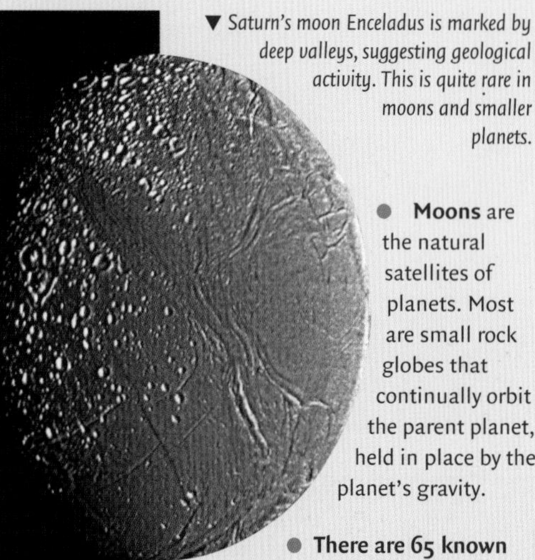

▼ *Saturn's moon Enceladus is marked by deep valleys, suggesting geological activity. This is quite rare in moons and smaller planets.*

- **Moons** are the natural satellites of planets. Most are small rock globes that continually orbit the parent planet, held in place by the planet's gravity.
- **There are 65 known** moons in the Solar System.

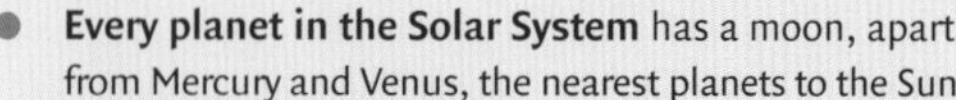

- **Every planet in the Solar System** has a moon, apart from Mercury and Venus, the nearest planets to the Sun.
- **New moons are frequently discovered**, as space probes such as the *Voyagers* reach distant planets.
- **Three moons** have atmospheres – Saturn's moon Titan, Jupiter's Io, and Neptune's Triton.
- **The largest moon** in the Solar System is Jupiter's moon Ganymede.
- **The second largest** is Saturn's moon Titan. This moon is rather like a small frozen Earth, with a rocky core beneath a cold, nitrogen atmosphere.
- **The smallest moons** are rocky lumps just a few kilometres across, rather like asteroids.
- **Saturn's moon Iapetus** is white on one side and black on the other.
- **Saturn's moon Enceladus** is only 500 km across, and glistens because it is covered in beads of ice.

Saturn

- **Saturn is the second biggest planet** in the Solar System – 815 times as big in volume as the Earth, and measuring 120,000 km around its equator.
- **Saturn takes 29 and a half years** to travel round the Sun, so Saturn's year is 29.46 Earth years. The planet's complete orbit is a journey of more than 4.5 billion km.
- **Winds ten times stronger than** a hurricane on Earth swirl around Saturn's equator, reaching up to 1,100 km/h – and they never let up, even for a moment.
- **Saturn is named after Saturnus**, the Ancient Roman god of seed-time and harvest. He was celebrated in the Roman's wild, Christmas-time festival of Saturnalia.
- **Saturn is not solid**, but is made almost entirely of gas – mostly liquid hydrogen and helium. Only in the planet's very small core is there any solid rock.
- **Because Saturn is so massive**, the pressure at its heart is enough to turn hydrogen solid. That is why there is a layer of metallic hydrogen around the planet's inner core of rock.

★ **STAR FACT** ★
Saturn is so low in density that if you could find a bath big enough, you would be able to float the planet in the water.

- **Saturn is one of the fastest spinning** of all the planets. Despite its size, it rotates in just 11.5 hours – which means it turns round at over 10,000 km/h.
- **Saturn's surface appears** to be almost completely smooth, though *Voyager 1* and *2* did photograph a few small, swirling storms when they flew past.
- **Saturn has a very powerful magnetic field** (see magnetism) and sends out strong radio signals.

Saturn's rings are made of many millions of tiny, ice-coated rock fragments

◄ Saturn is the queen of the planets. Almost as big as Jupiter, and made largely of liquid hydrogen and helium, Saturn is stunningly beautiful, with its smooth, pale-butterscotch surface (clouds of ammonia) and its shimmering halo of rings. But it is a very secretive planet. Telescopes have never pierced its upper atmosphere, and data from the fly-bys of the Voyager probes focussed on its rings and moons. But the Cassini probe, launched in 1997, may change this when it eventually descends into Saturn's atmosphere.

Space stations

- **The first space station** was the Soviet *Salyut 1* launched in April 1971. Its low orbit meant it stayed up only five months.
- **The first US space station** was *Skylab*. Three crews spent 171 days in it in 1973-74.
- **The longest serving station** was the Soviet *Mir* – launched in 1986, it made more than 76,000 orbits of the Earth. The last crew left in late 1999.
- ***Mir* was built in stages.** It weighed 125 tonnes and had six docking ports and two living rooms, plus a bathroom and two small individual cabins.
- **There is neither an up nor a down** in a space station, but *Mir* had carpets on the 'floor', pictures on the 'wall' and lights on the 'ceiling'.

! NEWS FLASH !
The living space on the ISS will be bigger than the passenger space on two jumbo jets.

- **The giant International Space Station (ISS)** is being built in stages and should be complete in 2004.
- **The first crew** went on board the ISS in January 2000.
- **The ISS** will be 108 m long and 90 m wide, and weigh 450 tonnes.
- **In April 2001,** Dennis Tito became the first space tourist, ferried up to the ISS by the Russian Soyuz space shutle.

▶ Mir *space station, photographed from the space shuttle* Discovery *in February 1995.*

Gravity

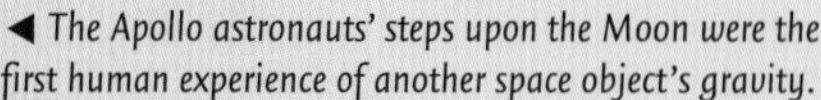

◀ *The Apollo astronauts' steps upon the Moon were the first human experience of another space object's gravity.*

- **Gravity** is the attraction, or pulling force, between all matter.
- **Gravity** is what holds everything on Earth on the ground and stops it flying off into space. It holds the Earth together, keeps the Moon orbiting the Earth, and the Earth and all the planets orbiting the Sun.
- **Gravity** makes stars burn by squeezing their matter together.
- **The force of gravity** is the same everywhere.

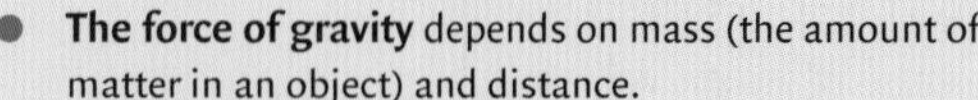

- **The force of gravity** depends on mass (the amount of matter in an object) and distance.
- **The more mass an object has**, and the closer it is to another object, the more strongly its gravity pulls.
- **Black holes** have the strongest gravitational pull in the entire Universe.
- **The basic laws of gravity** can be used for anything from detecting an invisible planet by studying the flickers in another star's light, to determining the flight of a space probe.
- **Einstein's theory of general relativity** shows that gravity not only pulls on matter, but also bends space and even time itself (see Einstein).
- **Orbits are the result** of a perfect balance between the force of gravity on an object (which pulls it inward towards whatever it is orbiting), and its forward momentum (which keeps it flying straight onwards).

Light-years

- **Distances in space** are so vast that the fastest thing in the Universe – light – is used to measure them.
- **The speed of light** is about 300,000 km per second.
- **A light-second** is the distance light travels in a second – 299 million metres.
- **A light-year** is the distance light travels in one year – 9.46 trillion km. Light-years are one of the standard distance measurements in astronomy.
- **It takes about 8 minutes** for light from the Sun to reach us on Earth.
- **Light takes 5.46 years** to reach us from the Sun's nearest star, Proxima Centauri. This means the star is 5.46 light-years away – more than 51 trillion km.
- **We see Proxima Centauri** as it was 5.46 years ago, because its light takes 5.46 years to reach us.
- **The star Deneb** is 1,800 light-years away, which means we see it as it was when the emperor Septimus Severius was ruling in Rome (AD 200).

▲ *Distances in space are so vast that they are measured in light-years, the distance light travels in a year.*

- **With powerful telescopes**, astronomers can see galaxies 2 billion light-years away. This means we see them as they were when the only life forms on Earth were bacteria.
- **Parsecs** may also be used to measure distances. They originally came from parallax shift measurements (see distances). A light-year is 0.3066 parsecs.

Rotation

▶ *Rotating galaxies are just part of the spinning, moving Universe.*

- **Rotation is the normal motion** (movement) of most space objects. Rotate means 'spin'.
- **Stars spin**, planets spin, moons spin and galaxies spin – even atoms spin.
- **Moons rotate** around planets, and planets rotate around stars.
- **The Earth rotates** once every 23.93 hours. This is called its rotation period.
- **We do not feel the Earth's rotation** – that it is hurtling around the Sun, while the Sun whizzes around the galaxy – because we are moving with it.
- **Things rotate because** they have kinetic (movement) energy. They cannot fly away because they are held in place by gravity, and the only place they can go is round.
- **The fastest rotating planet** is Saturn, which turns right around once every 10.23 hours.
- **The slowest rotating planet** is Venus, which takes 243.01 days to turn around.
- **The Sun takes 25.4 days** to rotate, but since the Earth is going around it too, it seems to take 27.27 days.

★ STAR FACT ★

The fastest spinning objects in the Universe are neutron stars – these can rotate 500 times in just one second!

Uranus

▼ *Uranus is the third largest planet in the Solar System – 51,118 km across and with a mass 14.54 times that of the Earth's. The planet spins round once every 17.24 hours, but because it is lying almost on its side, this has almost no effect on the length of its day. Instead, this depends on where the planet is in its orbit of the Sun. Like Saturn, Uranus has rings, but they are much thinner and were only detected in 1977. They are made of the darkest material in the Solar System.*

The planet's surface of liquid methane gives it a stunning blue colour

Uranus has an atmosphere of hydrogen and helium gas

Uranus has its own, very faint set of rings

- **Uranus is the seventh planet** out from the Sun. Its orbit keeps it 1,784 million km away on average and takes 84 years to complete.
- **Uranus tilts so far on its side** that it seems to roll around the Sun like a gigantic bowling ball. The angle of its tilt is 98°, in fact, so its equator runs top to bottom. This tilt may be the result of a collision with a meteor or another planet a long time ago.
- **In summer on Uranus**, the Sun does not set for 20 years. In winter, darkness lasts for over 20 years. In autumn, the Sun rises and sets every 9 hours.
- **Uranus has over 20 moons**, all named after characters in William Shakespeare's plays. There are five large moons – Ariel, Umbriel, Titania, Oberon and Miranda. The ten smaller ones were discovered by the *Voyager 2* space probe in 1986.
- **Uranus's moon Miranda** is the weirdest moon of all. It seems to have been blasted apart, then put itself back together again!
- **Because Uranus is so far from the Sun**, it is very, very cold, with surface temperatures dropping to -210°C. Sunlight takes just 8 minutes to reach Earth, but 2.5 hours to reach Uranus.
- **Uranus's icy atmosphere** is made of hydrogen and helium. Winds whistle around the planet at over 2,000 km/h – ten times as fast as hurricanes on Earth.
- **Uranus's surface** is an ice-cold ocean of liquid methane (natural gas), thousands of kilometres deep, which gives the planet its beautiful colour. If you fell into this ocean even for a fraction of a second, you would freeze so hard that you would shatter like glass.
- **Uranus is only faintly visible** from Earth. It looks no bigger than a star through a telescope, and was not identified until 1781 (see Herschel).
- **Uranus was named** after Urania, the Ancient Greek goddess of astronomy.

★ **STAR FACT** ★

On Uranus in spring, the Sun sets every 9 hours – backwards!

Solar eruptions

- **Solar flares** are sudden eruptions on the Sun's surface. They flare up in just a few minutes, then take more than half an hour to die away again.
- **Solar flares reach temperatures** of 10 million °C and have the energy of a million atom bombs.
- **Solar flares not only send out** heat and radiation, but also streams of charged particles.
- **The solar wind** is the stream of charged particles that shoots out from the Sun in all directions at speeds of over a million km/h. It reaches the Earth in 21 hours, but also blows far throughout the Solar System.
- **Every second** the solar wind carries away over a million tonnes of charged particles from the Sun.
- **Earth is shielded** from the lethal effects of the solar wind by its magnetic field (see magnetism).
- **Solar prominences** are gigantic, flame-like tongues of hot hydrogen that sometimes spout out from the Sun.
- **Solar prominences** reach temperatures of 10,000°C.
- **Coronal mass ejections** are gigantic eruptions of charged particles from the Sun, creating gusts in the solar wind which set off magnetic storms on Earth.
- **Magnetic storms** are massive hails of charged particles that hit the Earth every few years or so, setting the atmosphere buzzing with electricity.

▼ *Solar prominences can loop as far as 100,000 km out from the Sun's surface.*

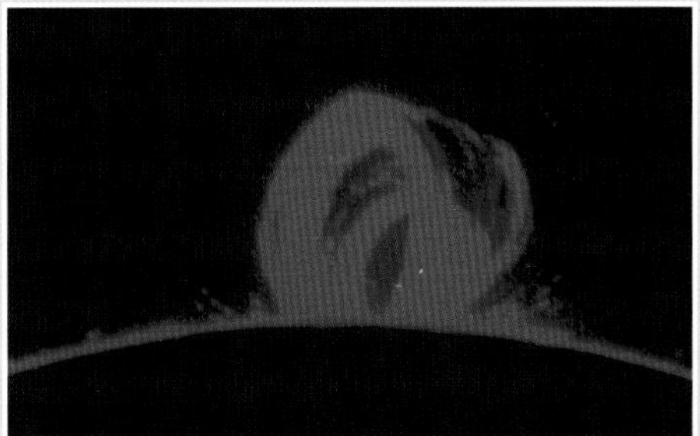

Jupiter's Galilean moons

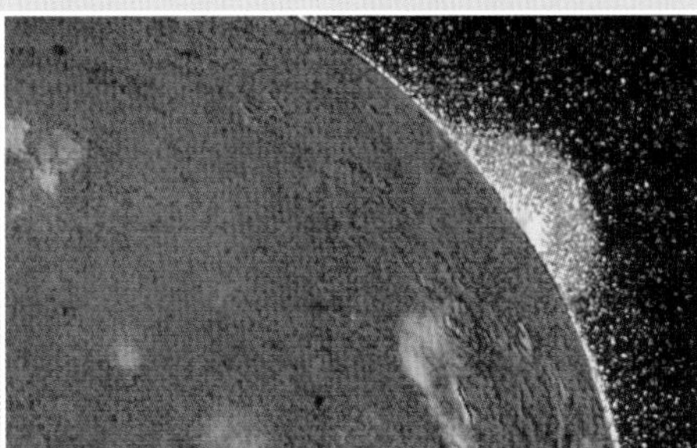

▲ *Io's yellow glow comes from sulphur, which is spewed as far as 300 km upwards by the moon's volcanoes.*

- **The Galilean moons** are the four biggest of Jupiter's 21 moons. They were discovered by Galileo, centuries before astronomers identified the other, smaller ones.
- **Ganymede is the biggest** of the Galilean moons – at 5,268 km across, it is larger than the planet Mercury.
- **Ganymede looks hard** but under its shell of solid ice is 900 km of slushy, half-melted ice and water.
- **Callisto is the second biggest**, at 4,806 km across.
- **Callisto is scarred** with craters from bombardments early in the Solar System's life.
- **Io is the third biggest**, at 3,642 km across.
- **Io's surface is a mass of volcanoes**, caused by it being stretched and squeezed by Jupiter's massive gravity.
- **The smallest** of the Galilean moons is Europa, at 3,138 km across.
- **Europa is covered in ice** and looks like a shiny, honey-coloured billiard ball from a distance – but a close-up view reveals countless cracks in its surface.

★ STAR FACT ★

A crater called Valhalla on Callisto is so big it makes the moon look like a giant eyeball.

Tides

- **Ocean tides** are the twice daily rise and fall of the water level in the Earth's oceans.
- **Ocean tides on Earth are created** by the gravitational pull of the Moon and the Sun.
- **The Moon's pull** creates two bulges in the oceans – one beneath it and one on the opposite side of the Earth.
- **As the Earth spins,** the tidal bulges seem to move around the world, creating two high tides every day.
- **Spring tides** are very high tides that happen when the Sun and Moon are in line, and combine their pull.
- **Neap tides** are small tides that happen when the Sun and Moon are at right angles to the Earth and their pulls are weakened by working against one another.
- **The solid Earth has tides too,** but they are very slight and the Earth moves only about 0.5 m.
- **Tides are also any upheaval** created by the pull of gravity, as one space object orbits another.
- **Moons orbiting** large planets undergo huge tidal pulls. Jupiter's moon Io is stretched so much that its interior is heated enough to create volcanoes.
- **Whole galaxies** can be affected by tidal pulls, making them stretch this way and that as they are tugged by the gravitational pull of other, passing galaxies.

▼ *As the Earth spins beneath the Moon, its oceans and seas are lifted by the Moon's gravity into tides.*

Binary stars

◀ *In the middle of this picture is the constellation of Cygnus, the Swan, which contains an optical binary star called Albireo – a pair of stars that only appear to be partners, but which are in fact quite some way apart.*

- **Our Sun is alone** in space, but most stars have one, two or more starry companions.
- **Binaries are double stars,** and there are various kinds.
- **True binary stars** are two stars held together by one another's gravity, which spend their lives whirling around together like a pair of dancers.
- **Optical binaries** are not really binaries at all. They are simply two stars that look as if they are together because they are in roughly the same line of sight from the Earth.
- **Eclipsing binaries** are true binary stars that spin round in exactly the same line of sight from Earth. This means they keep blocking out one another's light.
- **Spectroscopic binaries** are true binaries that spin so closely together that the only way we can tell there are two stars is by changes in colour.
- **The star Epsilon** in the constellation of Lyra is called the Double Double, because it is a pair of binaries.
- **Mizar, in the Great Bear,** was the first binary star to be discovered.
- **Mizar's companion Alcor** is an optical binary star.
- **Albireo in Cygnus** is an optical binary visible to the naked eye – one star looks gold, the other, blue.

Halley's comet

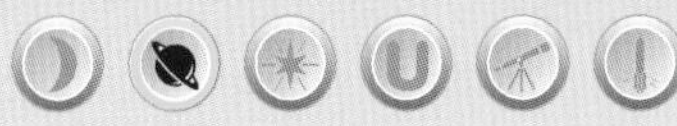

▲ *This photograph of Halley's comet was taken in 1986, when it last came close to the Earth.*

- **Halley's comet** is named after the British scientist Edmund Halley (1656-1742).
- **Halley predicted** that this particular comet would return in 1758, 16 years after his death. It was the first time a comet's arrival had been predicted.
- **Halley's comet** orbits the Sun every 76 years.
- **Its orbit** loops between Mercury and Venus, and stretches out beyond Neptune.
- **Halley's comet last** came in sight in 1986. Its next visit will be in 2062.
- **The Chinese** described a visit of Halley's comet as long ago as 240 BC.
- **When Halley's comet** was seen in AD 837, Chinese astronomers wrote that its head was as bright as Venus and its tail stretched right through the sky.
- **Harold, King of England,** saw the comet in 1066. When he was defeated by William the Conqueror a few months later, people took the comet's visit as an evil omen.
- **Halley's comet** was embroidered on the Bayeux tapestry, which shows Harold's defeat by William.

★ **STAR FACT** ★
Halley's comet was seen in about 8 BC, so some say it was the Bible's Star of Bethlehem.

Asteroids

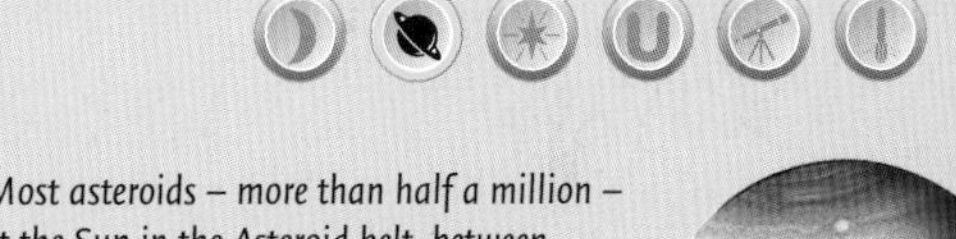

- **Asteroids** are lumps of rock that orbit the Sun. They are sometimes called the minor planets.
- **Most asteroids** are in the Asteroid belt, which lies between Mars and Jupiter.
- **Some distant asteroids** are made of ice and orbit the Sun beyond Neptune.
- **A few asteroids** come near the Earth. These are called Near Earth Objects (NEOs).
- **The first asteroid to be discovered** was Ceres in 1801. It was detected by Giuseppi Piazzi, one of the Celestial Police whose mission was to find a 'missing' planet.
- **Ceres** is the biggest asteroid – 940 km across, and 0.0002% the size of the Earth.

★ **STAR FACT** ★
Every 50 million years, the Earth is hit by an asteroid measuring over 10 km across.

▼ *Most asteroids – more than half a million – orbit the Sun in the Asteroid belt, between Mars and Jupiter.*

- **The *Galileo* space probe** took close-up pictures of the asteroids Ida and Gaspra in 1991 and 1993.
- **There are half a million or so** asteroids bigger than 1 km across. More than 200 asteroids are over 100 km across.
- **The Trojan asteroids** are groups of asteroids that follow the same orbit as Jupiter. Many are named after warriors in the Ancient Greek tales of the Trojan wars.

Solar changes

- **The Sun is about 5 billion years old** and half way through its life – as a medium-sized star it will probably live for around 10 billion years.
- **Over the next few billion years** the Sun will brighten and swell until it is twice as bright and 50% bigger.
- **In 5 billion years**, the Sun's hydrogen fuel will have burned out, and its core will start to shrink.

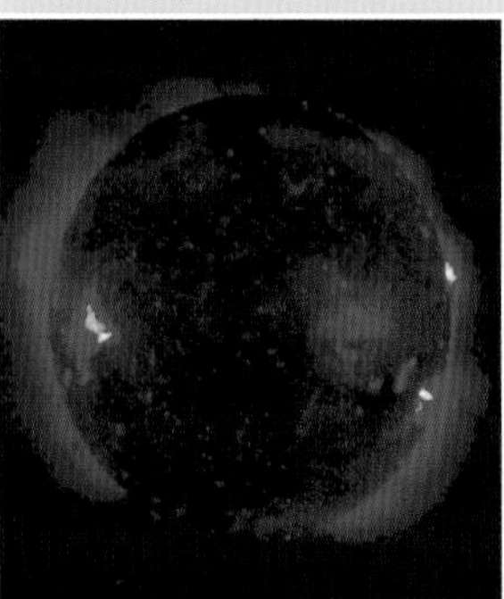

◀ *The Sun seems to burn so steadily that we take for granted that it will be equally bright and warm all the time. In the short term, however, its brightness does seem to vary very slightly all the time, and over the next 5 billion years it will probably burn more and more ferociously.*

- **As its core shrinks**, the rest of the Sun will swell up with gases and its surface will become cooler and redder. It will be a red giant star.
- **The Earth will have been burned** to a cinder long before the Sun is big enough to swallow it up completely.
- **The Sun will end** as a white dwarf.
- **The Sun's brightness varies**, but it was unusually dim and had no sunspots between 1645 and 1715 – this period is called the Maunder minimum. The Earth suffered the Little Ice Age at this time.
- **More of the chemical carbon-14** is made on Earth when the Sun is more active. The carbon-14 is taken into trees, which means scientists can work out changes in solar activity in the past by measuring carbon-14 in old wood.
- **The SOHO space observatory** is stationed between the Earth and the Sun, monitoring the Sun to find out about changes in solar activity.

Star birth

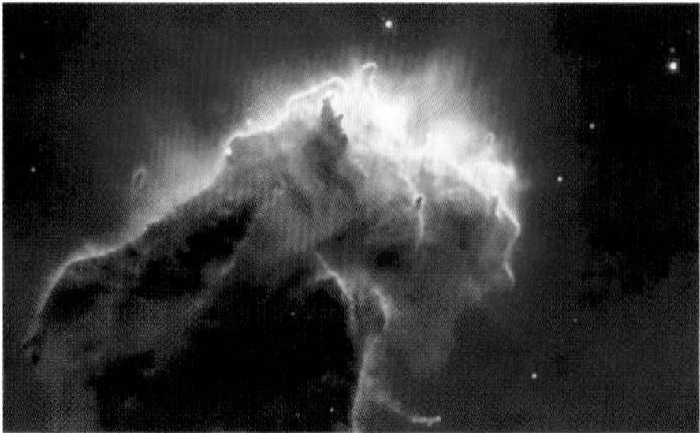

▲ *Stars are born in vast clouds of dust and gas, like this, an eagle nebula.*

- **Stars are being born** and dying all over the Universe, and by looking at stars in different stages of their life, astronomers have worked out their life stories.
- **Medium-sized stars** last for about 10 billion years. Small stars may last for 200 billion years.
- **Big stars** have short, fierce lives of 10 million years.
- **Stars start life** in clouds of gas and dust called nebulae.
- **Inside nebulae**, gravity creates dark clumps called dark nebulae, each clump containing the seeds of a family of stars.
- **As gravity squeezes** the clumps in dark nebulae, they become hot.
- **Smaller clumps** never get very hot and eventually fizzle out. Even if they start burning, they lose surface gas and shrink to wizened, old white dwarf stars.
- **If a larger clump** reaches 10 million °C, hydrogen atoms in its core begin to join together in nuclear reactions, and the baby star starts to glow.
- **In a medium-sized star** like our Sun, the heat of burning hydrogen pushes gas out as fiercely as gravity pulls inwards, and the star becomes stable (steady).
- **Medium-sized stars** burn steadily until all of their hydrogen fuel is used up.

Neptune

★ **STAR FACT** ★

Neptune's moon Triton is the coldest place in the Solar System, with surface temperatures of -236°C.

- **Neptune is the eighth** planet out from the Sun, varying in distance from 4,456 to 4,537 million km.
- **Neptune was discovered** in 1846 because two mathematicians, John Couch Adams in England and Urbain le Verrier in France, worked out that it must be there because of the effect of its gravity on the movement of Uranus.
- **Neptune is so far** from the Sun that its orbit lasts 164.79 Earth years. Indeed, it has not yet completed one orbit since it was discovered in 1846.

▼ Neptune is the fourth largest planet. At 49,528 km across, it is slightly smaller than Uranus – but it is actually a little heavier. Like Uranus, its oceans of incredibly cold liquid methane make it a beautiful shiny blue, although Neptune's surface is a deeper blue than that of Uranus. Again like Uranus, Neptune has a thin layer of rings. But Neptune's are level, and not at right angles to the Sun. Neptune has a Great Dark Spot, like Jupiter's Great Red Spot, where storms whip up swirling clouds.

Great Dark Spot

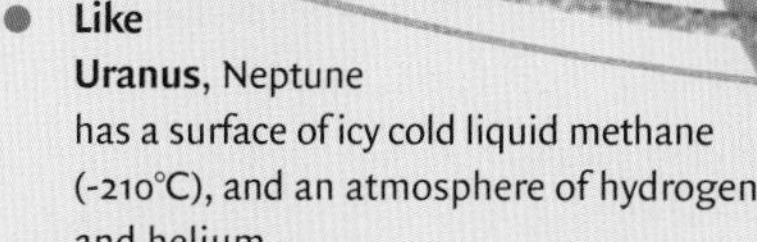

- **Like Uranus**, Neptune has a surface of icy cold liquid methane (-210°C), and an atmosphere of hydrogen and helium.
- **Unlike Uranus**, which is almost perfectly blue, Neptune has white clouds, created by heat inside the planet.
- **Neptune has the strongest winds** in the solar system, blowing at up to 700 m per second.
- **Neptune has eight moons**, each named after characters from Ancient Greek myths – Naiad, Thalassa, Despoina, Galatea, Larissa, Proteus, Triton and Nereid.
- **Neptune's moon Triton** looks like a green melon, while its icecaps of frozen nitrogen look like pink ice cream. It also has volcanoes that erupt fountains of ice.
- **Triton is the only moon** to orbit backwards.

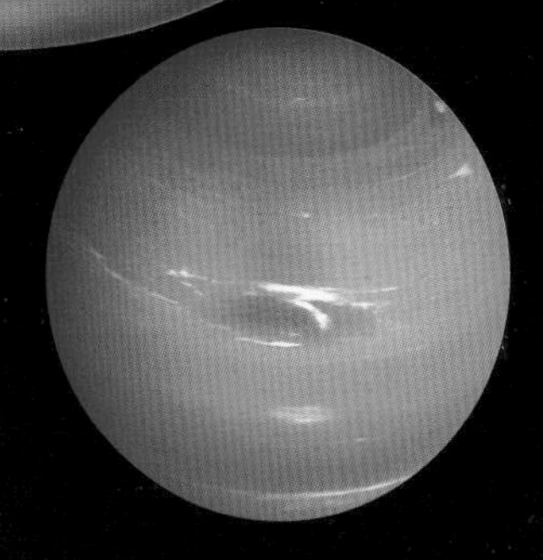

▶ This photo of Neptune was taken by the Voyager 2 spacecraft in 1989. The Great Dark Spot, and the little white tail of clouds named Scooter by astronomers, are both clearly visible.

Atoms

- **Atoms are the building blocks** of the Universe, the invisibly small particles from which matter is made.
- **Atoms are so small** that you could fit a billion on the full stop at the end of this sentence.
- **Atoms** are the very smallest identifiable piece of a chemical element (see elements).
- **There are** as many different atoms as elements.
- **Atoms are mostly empty space** dotted with tiny sub-atomic particles (subatomic is 'smaller than an atom').
- **The core of an atom** is a nucleus made of a cluster of two kinds of subatomic particle – protons and neutrons.
- **Whizzing around the nucleus** are even tinier particles called electrons.

★ STAR FACT ★
Quarks came into existence in the very first few seconds of the Universe.

- **Electrons have** a negative electrical charge, and protons have a positive charge, so electrons are held to the nucleus by electrical attraction.
- **Under certain conditions** atoms can be split into over 200 kinds of short-lived subatomic particle. The particles of the nucleus are made from various even tinier particles called quarks.

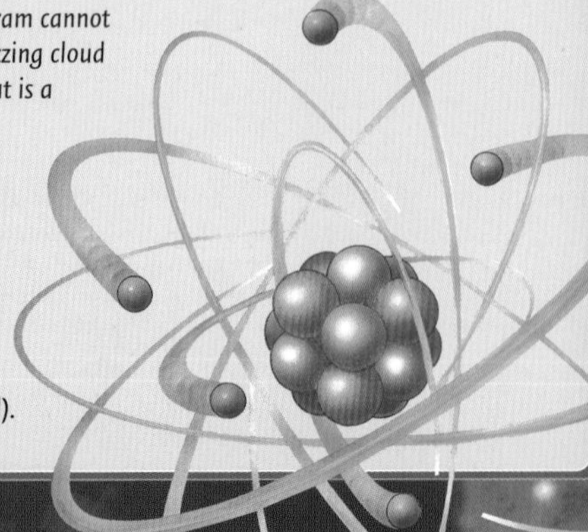

▶ *This diagram cannot show the buzzing cloud of energy that is a real atom! Electrons (blue) whizz around the nucleus, made of protons (green) and neutrons (red).*

Observatories

- **Observatories** are special places where astronomers study space and, to give the best view of the night sky, most are built on mountain tops far from city lights.
- **One of the largest observatory complexes** is 4,200 m above sea level, in the crater of the extinct Hawaiian volcano, Mauna Kea.
- **In most observatories**, telescopes are housed in a dome-roofed building which turns around so they can keep aiming at the same stars while the Earth rotates.

▶ *The Kitt Peak National Observatory in Arizona, USA.*

- **The oldest existing observatory** is the Tower of the Winds in Athens, Greece, which dates from 100 BC.
- **In the imperial observatory** in Beijing, China, there are 500-year-old, bronze astronomical instruments.
- **One of the oldest** working observatories is London's Royal Greenwich Observatory, founded in 1675.
- **The highest observatory** on the Earth is 4,300 m above sea level, at Denver, Colorado, in the USA.
- **The lowest observatory** is 1.7 km below sea level, in Homestake Mine, Dakota, USA. Its 'telescope' is actually tanks of cleaning fluid which trap neutrinos from the Sun (see cosmic rays) .
- **The first photographs** of the stars were taken in 1840. Nowadays, most observatories rely on photographs rather than on the eyes of astronomers.
- **Observatory photographs are made** using sensors called Charge-Coupled Devices (CCDs) which give off an electrical signal when struck by light.

Voyagers 1 and 2

▲ *Voyager 2 reached Neptune in 1989, revealing a wealth of new information about this distant planet.*

- **The *Voyagers*** are a pair of unmanned US space probes, launched to explore the outer planets.
- ***Voyager 1*** was launched on 5 September 1977. It flew past Jupiter in March 1979 and Saturn in November 1980, then headed onwards on a curved path that will take it out of the Solar System altogether.
- ***Voyager 2*** travels more slowly. Although launched two weeks earlier than *Voyager 1*, it did not reach Jupiter until July 1979 and Saturn until August 1981.
- **The *Voyagers*** used the 'slingshot' of Jupiter's gravity (see space probes) to hurl them on towards Saturn.
- **While *Voyager 1* headed out** of the Solar System, *Voyager 2* flew past Uranus in January 1986.
- ***Voyager 2* also passed** Neptune on 24 August 1989. It took close-up photographs of the two planets.
- **The *Voyagers*** revealed volcanoes on Io, one of Jupiter's Galilean moons.
- ***Voyager 2*** found ten unknown moons around Uranus.
- ***Voyager 2*** found six unknown moons and three rings around Neptune.

! NEWS FLASH !
Voyager 2 will beam back data until 2020 as it travels beyond the edges of the Solar System.

Space exploration

- **Space is explored** in two ways – by studying it from Earth using powerful telescopes, and by launching spacecraft to get a closer view.
- **Most space exploration** is by unmanned space probes.
- **The first pictures** of the far side of the Moon were sent back by the *Luna 3* space probe in October 1959.
- **Manned missions** have only reached as far as the Moon, but there may be a manned mission to Mars in 2005.
- **Apollo astronauts** took three days to reach the Moon.
- **No space probe** has ever come back from another planet.
- **Travel to the stars** would take hundreds of years, but one idea is that humans might go there inside gigantic spaceships made from hollowed-out asteroids.

! NEWS FLASH !
NASA may fund research on spacecraft that jump to the stars through wormholes (see black holes).

- **Another idea is that spacecraft** on long voyages of exploration may be driven along by pulses of laser light.
- **The *Pioneer 10* and *11* probes** carry metal plaques with messages for aliens telling them about us.

▼ *Most space exploration is by unmanned probes, guided by on-board computers and equipped with various devices which feed data back to Earth via radio signals.*

Pluto

- **Pluto was the last** of all the planets to be discovered, and it was only found because it has a slight effect on the orbits of Neptune and Uranus.
- **Pluto is the furthest out** of all the planets, varying from 4,730 to 7,375 million km from the Sun.
- **The Sun is so far from Pluto** that if you could stand on the planet's surface, the Sun would look no bigger than a star in Earth's sky and shine no more brightly than the Moon does.
- **Pluto's orbit** is so far from the Sun that it takes 248.54 years just to travel right around once. This means that a year on Pluto lasts almost three Earth centuries. A day, however, lasts just under a week.
- **Pluto has a strange elliptical (oval) orbit** which actually brings it closer to the Sun than Neptune for a year or two every few centuries.
- **Unlike all the other planets** which orbit on exactly the same plane (level) as the Earth, Pluto's orbit cuts across diagonally.
- **While studying** a photo of Pluto in 1978, American astronomer James Christy noticed a bump. This turned out to be a large moon, which was later named Charon.

★ **STAR FACT** ★

Pluto was discovered on 18 February 1930 by young American astronomer Clyde Tombaugh.

- **Charon** is about half the size of Pluto and they orbit one another, locked together like a weightlifter's dumbbells.
- **Charon** always stays in the same place in Pluto's sky, looking three times as big as our Moon.
- **Unlike the other outer planets**, Pluto is made from rock. But the rock is covered in water, ice and a thin layer of frozen methane.

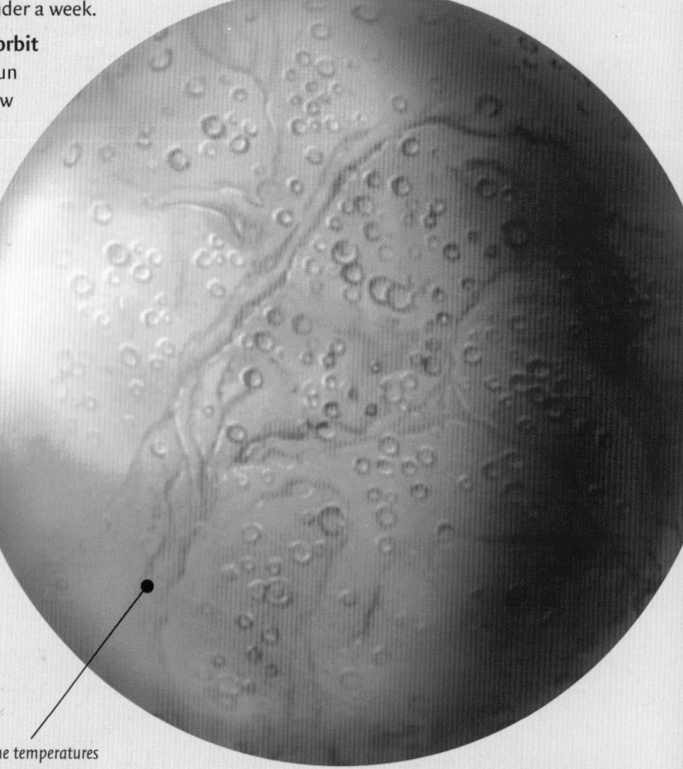

Daytime temperatures on Pluto's surface are -220°C or less, so the surface is thought to be coated in frozen methane.

▲ This picture of Pluto is entirely imaginary, since it is so small and so far away that even photographs from the Hubble space telescope show no more detail on Pluto's surface than you could see on the surface of a billiard ball. However, a twinkling of starlight around the edge of the planet shows that it must have some kind of atmosphere.

▼ Pluto is tiny in comparison to the Earth, which is why it was so hard to find. Earth is five times bigger and 500 times as heavy. This illustration shows the relative sizes of the Earth and Pluto.

Einstein

▲ *Einstein's theory of general relativity was proved right in 1919, when light rays from a distant star just grazing the Sun were measured during an eclipse and shown to be slightly bent.*

- **The great scientist Albert Einstein** (1879-1955) is most famous for creating the two theories of relativity.
- **Special relativity** (1905) shows that all measurements are relative, including time and speed. In other words, time and speed depend on where you measure them.
- **The fastest thing in the Universe**, light, is the same speed everywhere and always passes at the same speed – no matter where you are or how fast you are going.
- **Special relativity** shows that as things travel faster, they seem to shrink in length and get heavier. Their time stretches too – that is, their clocks seem to run slower.
- **The theory of general relativity** (1915) includes the idea of special relativity, but also shows how gravity works.
- **General relativity** shows that gravity's pull is acceleration (speed) – gravity and acceleration are the same.
- **When things are falling** their acceleration cancels out gravity, which is why astronauts in orbit are weightless.
- **If gravity and acceleration** are the same, gravity must bend light rays simply by stretching space (and time).
- **Gravity works by bending space** (and time). 'Matter tells space how to bend; space tells matter how to move.'
- **General relativity** predicts that light rays from distant stars will be bent by the gravitational pull of stars they pass.

Space telescopes

- **Space telescopes** are launched as satellites so we can study the Universe without interference from Earth's atmosphere.
- **The first space telescope** was Copernicus, sent up in 1972.
- **The most famous** is the Hubble space telescope, launched from a space shuttle in 1990.
- **Different space telescopes** study all the different forms of radiation that make up the electromagnetic spectrum (see light).
- **The COBE satellite** picks up microwave radiation which may be left over from the Big Bang.
- **The IRAS satellite** studied infrared radiation from objects as small as space dust.
- **Space telescopes** that have studied ultraviolet rays from the stars include the International Ultraviolet Explorer (IUE), launched in 1978.
- **Helios** was one of many space telescopes studying the Sun.
- **X-rays** can only be picked up by space telescopes such as the Einstein, ROSAT and SXTE satellites.
- **Gamma rays** can only be picked up by space telescopes like the Compton Gamma-Ray Observatory.

▼ *The Hubble space telescope's main mirror was faulty when it was launched, but a replacement was fitted by shuttle astronauts in 1994.*

Radio telescopes

- **Radio telescopes** are telescopes that pick up radio waves instead of light waves.
- **Radio telescopes**, like reflecting telescopes (see telescopes), have a big dish to collect and focus data.
- **At the centre of its dish**, a radio telescope has an antenna which picks up radio signals.
- **Because radio waves** are much longer than light waves, radio telescope dishes are very big – often as much as 100 m across.
- **Instead of one big dish**, some radio telescopes use an array (collection) of small, linked dishes. The further apart the dishes are, the sharper the image.
- **The Very Long Baseline Array** (VLBA) is made of ten dishes scattered all the way across the USA.

◀ *Many radio telescopes use an array of dishes linked by a process called interferometry.*

- **Radio astronomy** led to the discovery of pulsars and background radiation from the Big Bang.
- **Radio galaxies** are very distant and only faintly visible (if at all), but they can be detected because they give out radio waves.
- **Radio astronomy** proved that the Milky Way is a disc-shaped galaxy with spiralling arms.

★ **STAR FACT** ★

At 305 m across, the Arecibo radio telescope in Puerto Rico is the largest dish telescope in the world.

Astronauts

▼ *To cope with the demands of space missions and to help them deal with weightlessness, astronauts undergo tough physical training. They also spend long hours in simulators and jet aircraft.*

- **The very first astronauts** were jet pilots.
- **Astronauts** must be extremely fit and also have very good eyesight.
- **The American** space agency NASA trains its astronauts at the Johnson Space Center near Houston, Texas.
- **The US space shuttle** carries three kinds of astronaut – pilots, mission specialists and payload specialists.
- **The pilot or commander's job** is to head the mission and control the spacecraft.
- **Mission specialists** are crew members who carry out specific jobs, such as running experiments or going on space walks.
- **Payload specialists** are not NASA astronauts, but scientists and other on-board guests.
- **Astronauts learn** SCUBA diving to help them deal with space walks.
- **During training**, astronauts experience simulated (imitation) weightlessness – first in a plunging jet aircraft, and then in a water tank. They are also exposed to very high and very low atmospheric pressure.
- **Weightlessness** makes astronauts grow several centimetres during a long mission.

Space catalogues

- **Astronomers list the stars** in each constellation according to their brightness, using the Greek alphabet (see constellations). So the brightest star in the constellation of Pegasus is Alpha Pegasi.

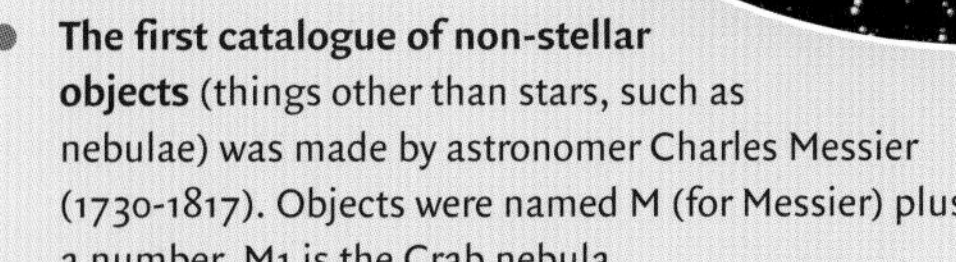

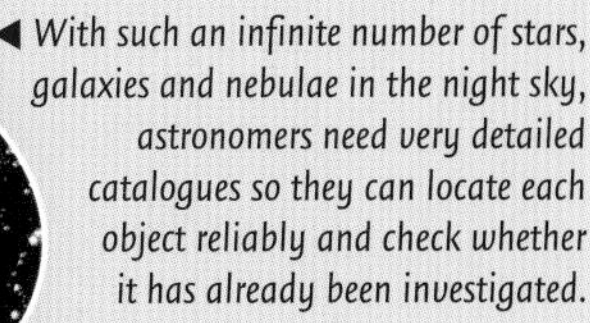

◀ *With such an infinite number of stars, galaxies and nebulae in the night sky, astronomers need very detailed catalogues so they can locate each object reliably and check whether it has already been investigated.*

- **The first catalogue of non-stellar objects** (things other than stars, such as nebulae) was made by astronomer Charles Messier (1730-1817). Objects were named M (for Messier) plus a number. M1 is the Crab nebula.
- **Messier published a list** of 103 objects in 1781, and by 1908 the catalogue had grown to 15,000 entries.
- **Many of the objects** originally listed by Messier as nebulae are now known to be galaxies.
- **Today the standard list of non-stellar objects** is the New General Catalogue of nebulae and star clusters (NGC). First published in 1888, this soon ran to over 13,000 entries.
- **Many objects** are in both the Messier and the NGC and therefore have two numbers.
- **The Andromeda galaxy** is M31 and NGC224.
- **Radio sources** are listed in similar catalogues, such as Cambridge University's 3C catalogue.
- **The first quasar** to be discovered was 3c 48.
- **Many pulsars** are now listed according to their position by right ascension and declination (see celestial sphere).

Space travel

- **The first artificial satellite**, the Soviet *Sputnik 1*, was launched into space in 1957.
- **The first living creature** in space was the dog Laika on-board *Sputnik 2* in 1957. Sadly, she died when the spacecraft's oxygen supply ran out.
- **The first manned space flight** was made in April 1961 by the Soviet cosmonaut Yuri Gagarin, in *Vostok 1*.
- **The first controlled Moon landing** was made by the Soviet *Luna 9*, in February 1966.
- **In 1970, the Soviet *Venera 7*** was the first probe to touch down on another planet.
- **The Soviet robot vehicles**, the Lunokhods, were driven 47 km across the Moon in the early 1970s.

! NEWS FLASH !
The Lockheed Martin X33 was to make trips into space almost as easy as aeroplane flights, but the project has recently been cancelled.

- **The coming of the space shuttle** in 1981 made working in orbit much easier.
- **Some cosmonauts** have spent over 12 continuous months in space on-board the Mir space station.
- **Cosmonaut Valeri Poliakov** spent 437 days on-board the Mir space station.

▶ *One problem facing a spacecraft returning to Earth is the heat produced by friction as it re-enters the Earth's atmosphere. Here you can see scorched, heatproof tiles on the underside of the shuttle.*

Astronomy

- **Astronomy is the study of the night sky** – from the planets and moons to the stars and galaxies.
- **Astronomy** is the most ancient of all the sciences, dating back tens of thousands of years.
- **The Ancient Egyptians** used their knowledge of astronomy to work out their calendar and to align the pyramids.
- **The word astronomy** comes from the Ancient Greek words *astro* meaning 'star' and *nomia* meaning 'law'.
- **Astronomers** use telescopes to study objects far fainter and smaller than can be seen with the naked eye.
- **Space objects** give out other kinds of radiation besides light, and astronomers have special equipment to detect this (see radio and space telescopes).
- **Professional astronomers** usually study photographs and computer displays instead of staring through telescopes, because most faint space objects only show up on long-exposure photographs.
- **Astronomers can spot** new objects in the night sky by laying a current photograph over an old one and looking for differences.
- **Professional astronomy** involves sophisticated equipment, but amateurs with binoculars can still occasionally make some important discoveries.

▶ *Most astronomers work in observatories far from city lights, where they can get a very clear view of the night sky.*

Stars

▲ *The few thousand stars visible to the naked eye are just a tiny fraction of the trillions in the Universe.*

- **Stars are balls** of mainly hydrogen and helium gas.
- **Nuclear reactions** in the heart of stars, like those in atom bombs, generate heat and light.
- **The heart of a star** reaches 16 million°C. A grain of sand this hot would kill someone 150 km away.
- **The gas in stars** is in a special hot state called plasma, which is made of atoms stripped of electrons.
- **In the core of a star**, hydrogen nuclei fuse (join together) to form helium. This nuclear reaction is called a proton-proton chain.
- **Stars twinkle** because we see them through the wafting of the Earth's atmosphere.
- **Astronomers work out how big a star is** from its brightness and its temperature.
- **The size and brightness** of a star depends on its mass – that is, how much gas it is made of. Our Sun is a medium-sized star, and no star has more than 100 times the Sun's mass or less than 6-7% of its mass.
- **The coolest stars**, such as Arcturus and Antares, glow reddest. Hotter stars are yellow and white. The hottest are blue-white, like Rigel and Zeta Puppis.
- **The blue supergiant Zeta Puppis** has a surface temperature of 40,000°C, while Rigel's is 10,000°C.

The Sun

- **The Sun** is a medium-sized star measuring 1,392,000 km across – 100 times the diameter of the Earth.
- **The Sun weighs** 2,000 trillion trillion tonnes – about 300,000 times as much as the Earth – even though it is made almost entirely of hydrogen and helium, the lightest gases in the Universe.
- **The Sun's interior** is heated by nuclear reactions to temperatures of 15 million°C.
- **The visible surface layer of the Sun** is called the photosphere. This sea of boiling gas sends out the light and heat we see and feel on Earth.
- **Above the photosphere** is the chromosphere, a thin layer through which dart tongues of flame called spicules, making the chromosphere look like a flaming forest.
- **Above the chromosphere** is the Sun's halo-like corona.
- **The heat from the Sun's interior** erupts on the surface in patches called granules, and gigantic, flame-like tongues of hot gases called solar prominences (see solar eruptions).
- **The Sun gets hot** because it is so big that the pressure in its core is tremendous – enough to force the nuclei of hydrogen atoms to fuse (join together) to make helium atoms. This nuclear fusion reaction is like a gigantic atom bomb and it releases huge amounts of heat.
- **Halfway out from its centre** to its surface, the Sun is about as dense as water. Two-thirds of the way out, it is as dense as air.
- **The nuclear fusion reactions** in the Sun's core send out billions of light photons every minute (see light) – but they take 10 million years to reach its surface.

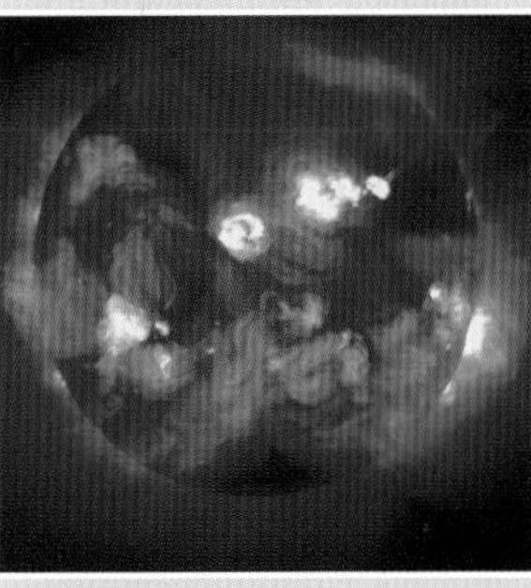

▶ *This artificially coloured photo was taken by a space satellite and shows the Sun's surface to be a turbulent mass of flames and tongues of hot gases – very different from the even, yellowish ball we see from Earth.*

★ **STAR FACT** ★

The temperature of the Sun's surface is 6,000°C. Each centimetre burns with the brightness of 250,000 candles!

▶ *The Sun is not a simple ball of burning gases. It is made mostly of hydrogen and helium, but has many layers. It has a core, where most heat is made, then a number of layers building to the flaming chromosphere on its surface. Space observatories like SOHO (Solar and Heliospheric Observatory) have revealed a great deal about the Sun to astronomers.*

Nuclear energy

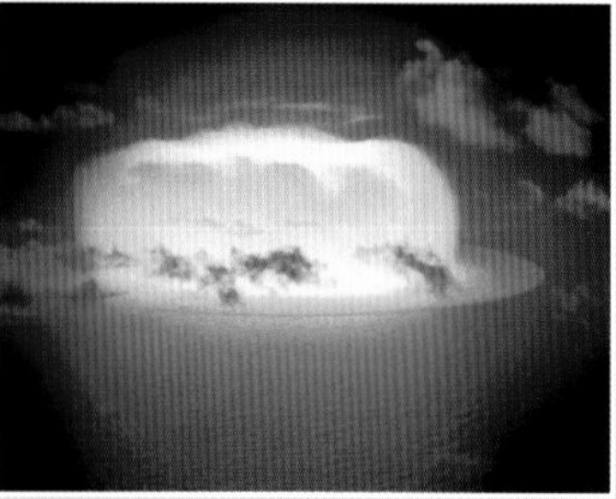

◀ The extraordinary power locked in the nucleus of atoms is shown when the explosion of an atom bomb releases some of the energy.

- **Nuclear energy** is the huge amount of energy that holds together the nucleus of every single atom.
- **Nuclear energy** fuels atom bombs and power stations – and every star in the Universe. It can be released either by fisson or fusion.
- **Nuclear fusion** is when nuclear energy is released by the joining together of nuclei – as inside stars, where they are squeezed together by gravity, and in hydrogen bombs.
- **Usually only tiny nuclei** such as those of hydrogen and helium fuse (join). Only under extreme pressure in huge, collapsing stars do big nuclei like iron fuse.
- **Nuclear fission** is when nuclear energy is released by the splitting of nuclei. This is the method used in most power stations and in atom bombs.
- **Nuclear fission** involves splitting big nuclei like Uranium-235 and plutonium.
- **When a nucleus splits**, it shoots out gamma rays, neutrons (see atoms) and intense heat.
- **In an atom bomb** the energy is released in one second.
- **In a power station**, control rods make sure nuclear reactions are slowed and energy released gradually.

★ STAR FACT ★
The Hiroshima bomb released 84 trillion joules of energy. A supernova releases 125,000 trillion trillion times as much.

Supernova

- **A supernova** (plural supernovae) is the final, gigantic explosion of a supergiant star at the end of its life.
- **A supernova** lasts for just a week or so, but shines as bright as a galaxy of 100 billion ordinary stars.
- **Supernovae happen** when a supergiant star uses up its hydrogen and helium fuel and shrinks, boosting pressure in its core enough to fuse heavy elements such as iron (see nuclear energy).
- **When iron begins to fuse** in its core, a star collapses instantly – then rebounds in a mighty explosion.
- **Seen in 1987, supenova 1987A** was the first viewed with the naked eye since Kepler's 1604 sighting.
- **Supernova remnants** (leftovers) are the gigantic, cloudy shells of material swelling out from supernovae.

★ STAR FACT ★
Many of the elements that make up your body were forged in supernovae.

- **A supernova** seen by Chinese astronomers in AD 184 was thought to be such a bad omen that it sparked off a palace revolution.
- **A dramatic supernova** was seen by Chinese astronomers in AD 1054 and left the Crab nebula.
- **Elements heavier** than iron were made in supernovae.

▼ Seeing a supernova is rare, but at any moment in time there is one happening somewhere in the Universe.

Red shift

- **When distant galaxies** are moving away from us, the very, very, fast light waves they give off are stretched out behind them – since each bit of the light wave is being sent from a little bit further away.
- **When the light waves** from distant galaxies are stretched out in this way, they look redder. This is called red shift.
- **Red shift** was first described by Czech mathematician Christian Doppler in 1842.
- **Edwin Hubble** showed that a galaxy's red shift is proportional to its distance. So the further away a galaxy is, the greater its red shift – and the faster it must be zooming away from us. This is Hubble's Law.

★ STAR FACT ★
The most distant galaxies (quasars) have red shifts so big that they must be moving away from us at speeds approaching the speed of light!

▶ *Massive red shifts reveal that the most distant objects in the Universe are flying away from us at absolutely astonishing speeds – often approaching the speed of light.*

- **The increase of red shift** with distance proved that the Universe is growing bigger.
- **Only nearby galaxies** show no red shift at all.
- **The record red shift** is 4.25, from the quasar 8C 1435 + 63. It is 96% of the speed of light.
- **Red shift** can be caused by the expansion of the Universe, gravity or the effect of relativity (see Einstein).
- **Black holes** may create large red shifts.

Auroras

- **Auroras** are bright displays of shimmering light that appear at night over the North and South poles.
- **The Aurora Borealis** is the Northern Lights, the aurora that appears above the North Pole.
- **The Aurora Australis** is the Southern Lights, the aurora that appears above the South Pole.

▲ *The Northern Lights above the Arctic Circle are among nature's most beautiful sights. Shimmering, dancing curtains of colour – bright green rays flashing with red, and streamers of white – blaze into the darkness of the polar night.*

- **Auroras are caused** by streams of charged particles from the Sun known as the solar wind (see solar eruptions) crashing into the gases of the Earth's atmosphere.
- **Oxygen gas glows yellow-green** when it is hit low in the atmosphere, and orange higher up.
- **Nitrogen gas glows** bright red when hit normally, and bright blue when ionized.
- **Auroras form a halo of light** over the poles all the time, but they are usually too faint to see. They flare up brightly when extra bursts of energy reach the Earth's atmosphere from the Sun.
- **Auroras appear at the poles** and nowhere else in the world because there are deep cracks here in the Earth's magnetic field (see magnetism).
- **Auroras are more spectacular** when the solar wind is blowing strongly.
- **New York and Edinburgh** get an average of ten aurora displays every year.

The Moon

▼ *Unlike the Earth's surface, which changes by the hour, the Moon's dusty, crater-pitted surface has remained much the same for billions of years. The only change happens when a meteorite smashes into it and creates a new crater.*

▲ *The Moon is the only other world that humans have ever set foot on. Because the Moon has no atmosphere or wind, the footprints planted in its dusty surface in 1969 by the Apollo astronauts are still there today, perfectly preserved.*

- **Only the side of the Moon** lit by the Sun is bright enough to see. And because we see more of this side each month as the Moon orbits the Earth, and then less again, the Moon seems to change shape. These changes are called the Moon's phases.
- **During the first half of each monthly cycle**, the Moon waxes (grows) from a crescent-shaped new moon to a full moon. During the second half, it wanes (dwindles) back to a crescent-shaped old moon.
- **The Moon** is 384,400 km from the Earth and about 25% of Earth's size.
- **The Moon** orbits the Earth once every month, with each orbit taking 27.3 days. It spins round once on its axis every 720 hours.
- **The Moon** is the brightest object in the night sky, but it does not give out any light itself. It shines only because its light-coloured surface reflects sunlight.

★ **STAR FACT** ★

The Moon's gravity is 17% of the Earth's, so astronauts in space suits can jump 4 m high!

- **A lunar month** is the time between one full moon and the next. This is slightly longer than the time the Moon takes to orbit the Earth because the Earth is also moving.
- **The Moon has no atmosphere** and its surface is simply white dust, pitted with craters created by meteorites smashing into it early in its history.
- **On the Moon's surface** are large, dark patches called seas – because that is what people once believed they were. They are, in fact, lava flows from ancient volcanoes.
- **One side of the Moon** is always turned away from us and is called its dark side. This is because the Moon spins round on its axis at exactly the same speed that it orbits the Earth.

Quasars

- **Quasars** are the most intense sources of light in the Universe. Although no bigger than the Solar System, they glow with the brightness of 100 galaxies.
- **Quasars are the most distant** known objects in the Universe. Even the nearest is billions of light-years away.
- **The most distant quasar** is on the very edges of the known Universe, 12 billion light-years away.
- **Some quasars** are so far away that we see them as they were when the Universe was still in its infancy – 20% of its current age.
- **Quasar** is short for Quasi-Stellar (star-like) Radio Object. This comes from the fact that the first quasars were detected by the strong radio signals they give out, and also because quasars are so small and bright that at first people thought they looked like stars.
- **Only one of the 200 quasars** now known actually beams out radio signals, so the term Quasi-Stellar Radio Object is in fact misleading!
- **The brightest** quasar is 3C 273, 2 billion light-years away.
- **Quasars** are at the heart of galaxies called 'active galaxies'.
- **Quasars** may get their energy from a black hole at their core, which draws in matter ferociously.
- **The black hole** in a quasar may pull in matter with the same mass as 100 million Suns.

▲ *The Hubble space telescope's clear view of space has given the best-ever photographs of quasars. This is a picture of the quasar PKS2349, billions of light-years away.*

Space walks

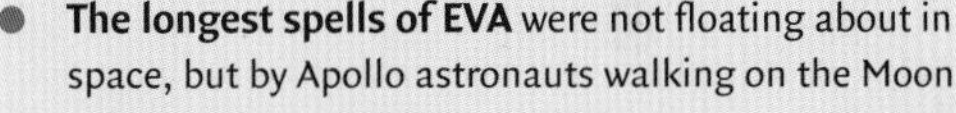

▲ *An astronaut wearing an MMU can move completely independently in space.*

- **The technical name** for going outside a spacecraft is Extra-Vehicular Activity (EVA).
- **In 1965** Soviet cosmonaut Alexei Leonov was the first person ever to walk in space.
- **The longest spells of EVA** were not floating about in space, but by Apollo astronauts walking on the Moon.
- **The first space walkers** were tied to their spacecraft by life-support cables.
- **Nowadays, most space walkers** use a Manned Manoeuvering Unit (MMU) – a huge, rocket-powered backpack that lets them move about freely.
- **In 1984**, US astronaut Bruce McCandless was the first person to use an MMU in space.
- **Damages to the *Mir* space station** and other satellites have been repaired by space-walking astronauts.
- **Russian and US astronauts** will perform more than 1,700 hours of space walks when building the International Space Station.

! NEWS FLASH !
Astronauts on space walks will be aided by a flying robot camera the size of a beach ball.

The night sky

- **The night sky** is brightened by the Moon and twinkling points of light.
- **Most lights** in the sky are stars. But moving, flashing lights may be satellites.
- **The brightest 'stars'** in the night sky are not actually stars at all, but the planets Jupiter, Venus, Mars and Mercury.
- **You can see** about 2,000 stars with the naked eye.
- **The pale band across** the middle of the sky is a side-on view of our own galaxy, the Milky Way.

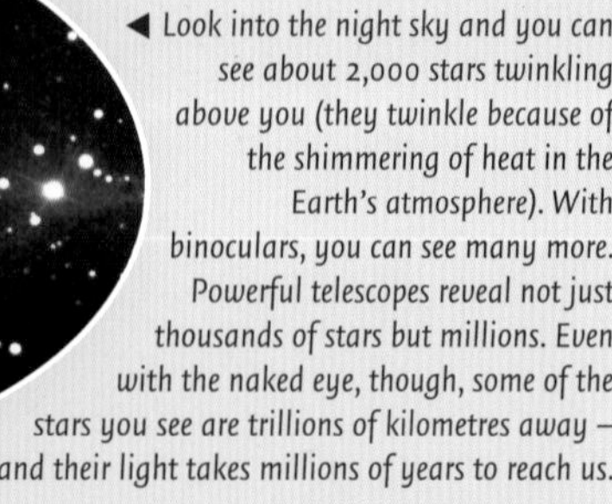

◀ *Look into the night sky and you can see about 2,000 stars twinkling above you (they twinkle because of the shimmering of heat in the Earth's atmosphere). With binoculars, you can see many more. Powerful telescopes reveal not just thousands of stars but millions. Even with the naked eye, though, some of the stars you see are trillions of kilometres away – and their light takes millions of years to reach us.*

★ **STAR FACT** ★
You can see another galaxy besides the Milky Way with the naked eye – the Andromeda galaxy, over 2.2 million light-years away.

- **The pattern of stars** in the sky is fixed, but seems to rotate (turn) through the night sky as the Earth spins.
- **It takes 23 hours 56 minutes** for the star pattern to return to the same place in the sky.
- **As Earth orbits the Sun**, our view of the stars changes and the pattern starts in a different place each night.
- **Different patterns of stars** are seen in the northern hemisphere and the southern hemisphere.

Water

- **Water is the only substance** on Earth which is commonly found as a solid, a liquid and a gas.
- **Over 70% of the Earth's surface** is covered in water.
- **Water is fundamental** (basic) to all life – 70% of our bodies is water.
- **Earth is the only planet** in the Solar System to have liquid water on its surface.
- **Neptune has a deep ocean** of ionized water beneath its icy surface of helium and hydrogen.

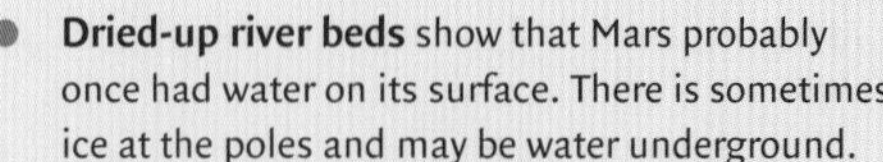

▼ *There is a little water on the Moon, but Earth's blue colour shows it to be the real water planet of the solar system.*

- **Dried-up river beds** show that Mars probably once had water on its surface. There is sometimes ice at the poles and may be water underground.
- **Jupiter's moon Europa** may have oceans of water beneath its icy surface, and it is a major target in the search for life in the Solar System.
- **In 1998** a space probe found signs of frozen water on the Moon, but they proved false.
- **Water is a compound** of the elements hydrogen and oxygen, with the chemical formula H_2O.
- **Water** is the only substance less dense (heavy) as a solid than as a liquid, which is why ice floats.

Galaxies

- **Galaxies are giant groups** of millions or even trillions of stars. Our own local galaxy is the Milky Way.
- **There may be 20 trillion** galaxies in the Universe.
- **Only three galaxies** are visible to the naked eye from Earth besides the Milky Way – the Large and Small Magellanic clouds, and the Andromeda galaxy.
- **Although galaxies are vast**, they are so far away that they look like fuzzy clouds. Only in 1916 did astronomers realize that they are huge star groups.
- **Spiral galaxies** are spinning, Catherine-wheel-like galaxies with a dense core and spiralling arms.
- **Barred spiral galaxies** have just two arms. These are linked across the galaxy's middle by a bar from which they trail like water from a spinning garden sprinkler.

> ★ STAR FACT ★
> Galaxies like the Small Magellanic Cloud may be the debris of mighty collisions between galaxies.

- **Elliptical galaxies** are vast, very old, egg-shaped galaxies, made up of as many as a trillion stars.
- **Irregular galaxies** are galaxies with no obvious shape. They may have formed from the debris of galaxies that crashed into each other.
- **Galaxies are often** found in groups called clusters. One cluster may have 30 or so galaxies in it.

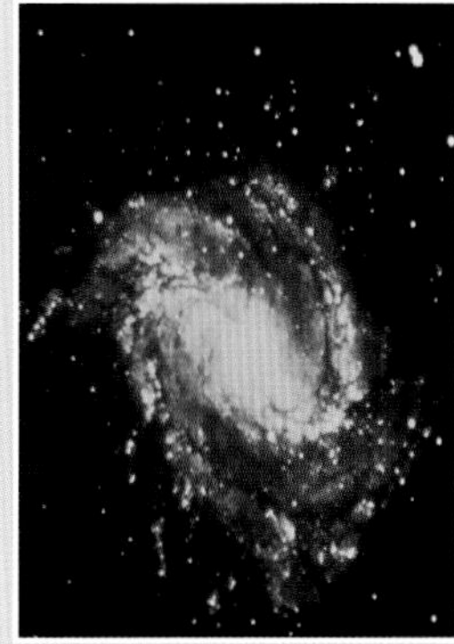

▲ *Like our own Milky Way and the nearby Andromeda galaxy, many galaxies are spiral in shape, with a dense core of stars and long, whirling arms made up of millions of stars.*

Radiation

- **Radiation** is energy shot out at high speed by atoms. There are two main forms – radioactivity and electromagnetic radiation.
- **Radiation either travels as waves** or as tiny particles called photons (see light).
- **Radioactivity** is when an atom decays (breaks down) and sends out deadly energy such as gamma rays.
- **Nuclear radiation** is the radiation from the radioactivity generated by atom bombs and power stations. In large doses, this can cause radiation sickness and death.
- **Electromagnetic radiation** is electric and magnetic fields (see magnetism) that move together in tiny bursts of waves or photons.
- **There are different kinds** of electromagnetic radiation, each one with a different wavelength.
- **Gamma rays** are a very short-wave, energetic and dangerous form of electromagnetic radiation.
- **Radio waves** are a long-wave, low-energy radiation.
- **In between these come** X-rays, ultraviolet rays, visible light, infrared rays and microwaves.
- **Together these forms of electromagnetic radiation** are called the electromagnetic spectrum. Visible light is the only part of the spectrum we can see with our eyes.
- **All electromagnetic rays** move at the speed of light – 300,000 km per second.
- **Everything we detect in space** is picked up by the radiation it gives out (see astronomy, the Big Bang and radio telescopes).

◀ *The Sun throws out huge quantities of radiation of all kinds. Fortunately, our atmosphere protects us from the worst.*

Mars landings

- **In the 1970s** the US *Vikings* 1 and 2 and the Soviet *Mars 3* and 5 probes all reached the surface of Mars.
- ***Mars 3*** was the first probe to make a soft landing on Mars, on 2 December 1971, and sent back data for 20 seconds before being destroyed by a huge dust-storm.
- ***Viking 1*** sent back the first colour pictures from Mars, on 26 July 1976.
- **The aim of the *Viking* missions** was to find signs of life, but there were none. Even so, the *Viking* landers sent back plenty of information about the geology and atmosphere of Mars.
- **On 4 July 1997**, the US *Mars Pathfinder* probe arrived on Mars and at once began beaming back 'live' TV pictures from the planet's surface.
- ***Mars Pathfinder*** used air bags to cushion its landing on the planet's surface.
- **Two days after** the *Pathfinder* landed, it sent out a wheeled robot vehicle called the *Sojourner* to survey the surrounding area.
- **The *Sojourner*** showed a rock-strewn plain which looks as if it were once swept by floods.
- ***Pathfinder* and *Sojourner*** operated for 83 days and took more than 16,000 photos.
- **Missions to Mars** early in the 21st century will include the first return flight in 2010.

▶ *The Mars Pathfinder mission provided many stunning images of the surface of the 'red planet', many taken by the* Sojourner *as it motored over the surface.*

Telescopes

▶ *This is the kind of reflecting telescope that many amateur astronomers use.*

- **Optical telescopes** magnify distant objects by using lenses or mirrors to refract (bend) light rays so they focus (come together).
- **Other telescopes** detect radio waves (see radio telescopes), X-rays (see X-ray astronomy), or other kinds of electromagnetic radiation (see radiation).
- **Refracting telescopes** are optical telescopes that use lenses to refract the light rays.
- **Reflecting telescopes** are optical telescopes that refract light rays by reflecting them off curved mirrors.
- **Because the light rays** are folded, reflecting telescopes are shorter and fatter than refracting ones.
- **Most professional astronomers** do not gaze at the stars directly, but pick up what the telescope shows with light sensors called CCDs (see observatories).
- **Most early discoveries** in astronomy were made with refracting telescopes.
- **Modern observatories** use gigantic reflector dishes made up of hexagons of glass or coated metal.
- **Large telescope dishes** are continually monitored and tweaked by computers to make sure that the reflector's mirrored surface stays completely smooth.

★ STAR FACT ★
Telescope dishes have to be made accurate to within 2 billionths of a millimetre.

Star charts

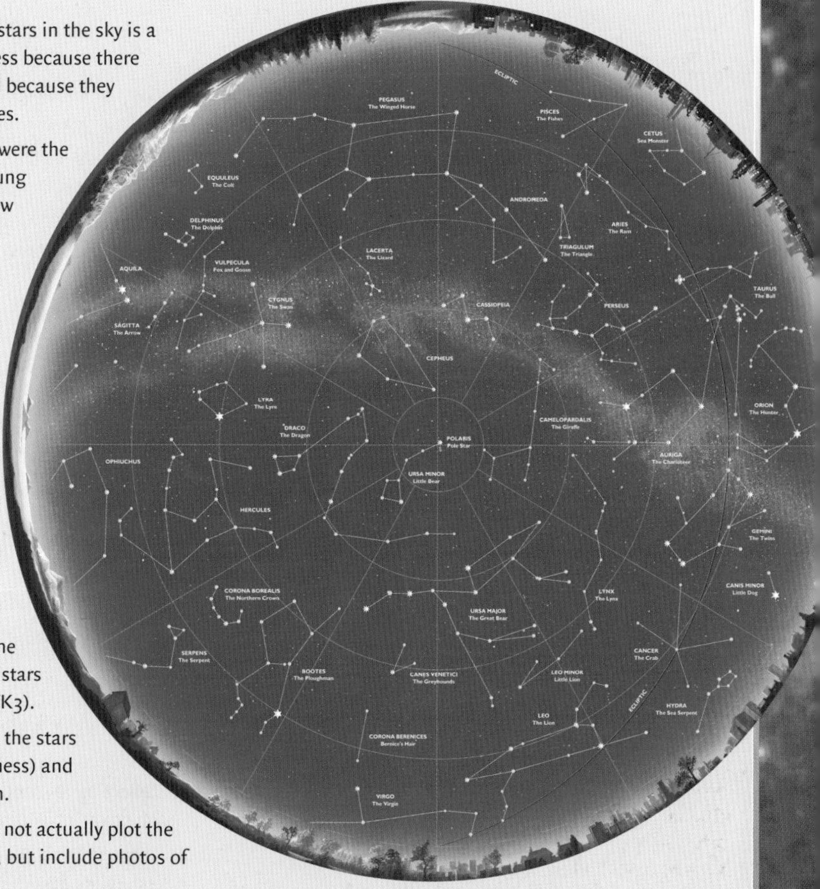

- **Plotting the positions** of the stars in the sky is a phenomenally complex business because there are a vast number of them and because they are at hugely different distances.
- **The first modern star charts** were the German Bonner Durchmusterung (BD) charts of 1859, which show the positions of 324,189 stars. The German word *durchmusterung* means 'scanning through'.
- **The AGK1 chart** of the German Astronomical was completed in 1912 and showed 454,000 stars.
- **The AGK charts** are now on version AGK3 and remain the standard star chart. They are compiled from photographs.
- **The measurements** of accurate places for huge numbers of stars depends on the careful determination of 1,535 stars in the Fundamental Catalog (FK3).
- **Photometric catalogues** map the stars by magnitude (see star brightness) and colour, as well as their position.
- **Photographic star atlases** do not actually plot the position of every star on paper, but include photos of them in place instead.
- **Three main atlases** are popular with astronomers – *Norton's Star Atlas*, which plots all stars visible to the naked eye; the *Tirion Sky Atlas*; and the photographic *Photographischer Stern-Atlas*.
- **Celestial coordinates** are the figures that plot a star's position on a ball-shaped graph (see celestial sphere). The altazimuth system of coordinates gives a star's position by its altitude (its angle in degrees from the horizon) and its azimuth (its angle in degrees clockwise around the horizon, starting from north). The ecliptic system does the same, using the ecliptic rather than the horizon as a starting point. The equatorial system depends on the celestial equator, and gives figures called right ascensions and declination, just like latitude and longitude on Earth.

▲ *The basic map of the sky shows the 88 constellations that are visible at some time during the year from each hemisphere (half) of the world. This picture shows the northern constellations visible in December.*

★ **STAR FACT** ★

The star patterns we call constellations were the basis of the first star charts, dating back to the 2nd millennium BC. Even today astronomers divide the sky into 88 constellations, whose patterns are internationally recognized – even though the names of many constellations are the mythical ones given to them by the astronomers of Ancient Greece.

Planets

▲ *Most of the nine planets in our Solar System have been known since ancient times, but in the last few years planets have been found orbiting other, faraway stars.*

- **Planets** are globe-shaped space objects that orbit a star such as the Sun.
- **Planets begin life** at the same time as their star, from the leftover clouds of gas and dust.
- **Planets are never** more than 20% of the size of their star. If they were bigger, they would have become stars.
- **Some planets,** called terrestrial planets, have a surface of solid rock. Others, called gas planets, have a surface of liquid or airy gas.
- **The solar system** has nine planets including Pluto. But Pluto may be an escaped moon or an asteroid, not a planet.
- **Over 80 planets** have now been detected orbiting stars other than the Sun. These are called extra-solar planets.
- **Extra-solar planets** are too far away to see, but can be detected because they make their star wobble.
- **Most known extra-solar planets** are giants bigger than Jupiter and orbit rapidly as close to their stars as Mercury to the Sun.
- **Improved detection techniques** may reveal smaller planets orbiting further out which might support life.
- **The Kepler space telescope** to be launched in 2006 will scan 100,000 stars for signs of Earth-sized planets.

Clusters

▲ *Space looks like a formless collection of stars and clouds, but all matter tends to cluster together.*

- **The Milky Way** belongs to a cluster of 30 galaxies called the Local Group, which is 7 million light-years across.
- **The Local Group** is 7 million light years across.
- **There are 3 giant spiral galaxies** in the Local Group, plus 15 ellipticals and 13 irregulars, such as the Large Magellanic Cloud.

★ **STAR FACT** ★

One film of superclusters makes up a vast structure called the Great Wall. It is the largest structure in the Universe – over 700 million light-years long, but just 30 million thick.

- **Beyond the Local Group** are many millions of similar star clusters.
- **The Virgo cluster** is 50 million light-years away and is made up of over 1,000 galaxies.
- **The Local Group plus millions** of other clusters make up a huge group called the Local Supercluster.
- **Other superclusters** are Hercules and Pegasus.
- **Superclusters** are separated by huge voids (empty space), which the superclusters surround like the film around a soap bubble.
- **The voids between superclusters** measure 350 to 400 million light-years across.

Variable stars

- **Variable stars** are stars that do not burn steadily like our Sun, but which flare up and down.
- **Pulsating variables** are stars that pulse almost as if they were breathing. They include the kinds of star known as Cepheid variables and RR Lyrae variables.
- **Cepheid variables** are big, bright stars that pulse with energy, flaring up regularly every 1 to 50 days.

▼ *The constellation of Cygnus, containing a vanishing star.*

- **Cepheid variables** are so predictable in brightness that they make good distance markers (see distances).
- **RR Lyrae variables** are yellow, supergiant stars near the end of their life, which flicker as their fuel runs down.
- **Mira-type variables** are similar to Mira in Cetus, the Whale, and vary regularly over months or years.
- **RV Tauri variables** are very unpredictable, flaring up and down over changing periods of time.
- **Eclipsing variables** are really eclipsing binaries (see binary stars). They seem to flare up and down, but in fact are simply one star getting in the way of the other.
- **The Demon Star** is Algol in Perseus. It seems to burn fiercely for 59 hours, become dim, then flare up again 10 hours later. It is really an eclipsing binary.
- **The vanishing star** is Chi in Cygnus, the Swan. It can be seen with the naked eye for a few months each year, but then becomes so dim that it cannot be seen, even with a powerful telescope.

Take off

- **The biggest problem** when launching a spacecraft is overcoming the pull of Earth's gravity.
- **To escape Earth's gravity**, a spacecraft must be launched at a particular velocity (speed and direction).
- **The mininum velocity** needed for a spacecraft to combat gravity and stay in orbit around the Earth is called the orbital velocity.
- **When a spacecraft** reaches 140% of the orbital velocity, it is going fast enough to break free of Earth's gravity. This is called the escape velocity.
- **The thrust (push)** that launches a spacecraft comes from powerful rockets called launch vehicles.
- **Launch vehicles** are divided into sections called stages, which fall away as their task is done.

> ★ STAR FACT ★
> To stay in orbit 200 km up, a spacecraft has to fly at over 8 km per second.

- **The first stage** lifts everything off the ground, so its thrust must be greater than the weight of launch vehicle plus spacecraft. It falls away a few minutes after take off.
- **A second stage** is then needed to accelerate the spacecraft towards escape velocity.
- **After the two launch stages** fall away, the spacecraft's own, less powerful rocket motors start.

▶ *A spacecraft cannot use wings to lift it off the ground, as wings only work in the lower atmosphere. Instead, launch rockets must develop a big enough thrust to power them straight upwards, overcoming gravity with a mighty blast of heat.*

Saturn's rings

▲ *Saturn's rings are one of the wonders of the solar system, and many people think they make it the most beautiful planet.*

- **Saturn's rings** are sets of thin rings of ice, dust and tiny rocks, which orbit the planet around its equator.
- **The rings shimmer** as their ice is caught by sunlight.
- **The rings** may be fragments of a moon that was torn apart by Saturn's gravity before it formed properly.

★ STAR FACT ★
Saturn's rings measure over 270,000 km across, but are very thin – just 100 m or less.

- **Galileo was first** to see Saturn's rings, in 1610. But it was Dutch scientist Christian Huygens (1629-95) who first realized they were rings, in 1659.
- **There are two** main sets of rings – the A and the B rings.
- **The A and B rings** are separated by a gap called the Cassini division after Italian astronomer Jean Cassini (1625-1712), who spotted it in 1675.
- **A third large ring** called the C or *crepe* ring was spotted closer to the planet in 1850.
- **In the 1980s**, space probes revealed many other rings and 10,000 or more ringlets, some just 10 m wide.
- **The rings are** (in order out from the planet) D, C, B, Cassini division, A, F, G and E. The A ring has its own gap called the Encke division.

Neutron stars

- **Neutron stars** are incredibly small, super-dense stars made mainly of neutrons (see atoms), with a solid crust made of iron and similar elements.
- **Neutron stars** are just 20 km across on average, yet weigh as much as the Sun.
- **A tablespoon** of neutron star would weigh about 10 billion tonnes.
- **Neutron stars** form from the central core of a star that has died in a supernova explosion.
- **A star must be more than** 1.4 times as big as a medium-sized star like our Sun to produce a neutron star. This is the Chandrasekhar limit.
- **A star more than three times** as big as the Sun would collapse beyond a neutron star to form a black hole. This is called the Oppenheimer-Volkoff limit.
- **The first evidence** of neutron stars came when pulsars were discovered in the 1960s.
- **Some stars giving out X-rays**, such as Hercules X-1, may be neutron stars. The X-rays come from material from nearby stars squeezed on to their surfaces by their huge gravity.
- **Neutron stars** have very powerful magnetic fields (see magnetism), over 2,000 times stronger than Earth's, which stretch the atoms out into frizzy 'whiskers' on the star's surface.

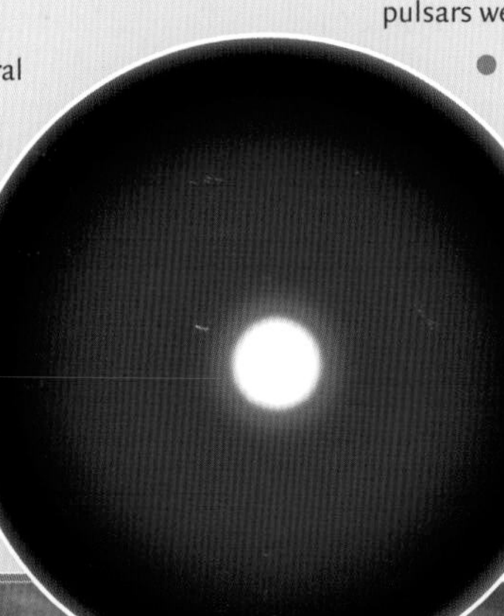

▶ *Neutron stars are tiny, super-dense stars that form in supernova explosions, as a star's core collapses within seconds under the huge force of its own immense gravity.*

Years

▶ *Our years come from the time the Earth takes to go once round the Sun, so that the Sun appears at the same height in the sky again. But this journey actually takes not an exact number of days but 365 and a fraction. So the calendar gives a year as 365 days, and compensates with leap years and century years.*

- **A calendar year is roughly the time** the Earth takes to travel once around the Sun – 365 days.
- **The Earth** actually takes 365.24219 days to orbit the Sun. This is called a solar year.
- **To compensate** for the missing 0.242 days, the western calendar adds an extra day in February every fourth (leap) year, but misses out three leap years every four centuries (century years).
- **Measured by the stars** not the Sun, Earth takes 365.25636 days to go round the Sun, because the Sun also moves a little relative to the stars. This is called the sidereal year.
- **Earth's perihelion** is the day its orbit brings it closest to the Sun, 3 January.
- **Earth's aphelion** is the day it is furthest from the Sun, 4 July.
- **The planet with the shortest year** is Mercury, which whizzes around the Sun in just 88 days.
- **The planet with the longest year** is Pluto, which takes 249 years to orbit the Sun.
- **The planet with the year** closest to Earth's in length is Venus, whose year lasts 225 days.
- **A year on Earth** is the time the Sun takes to return to the same height in the sky at noon.

Zodiac

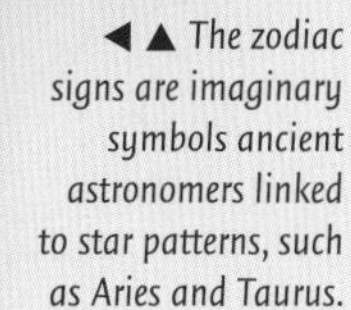

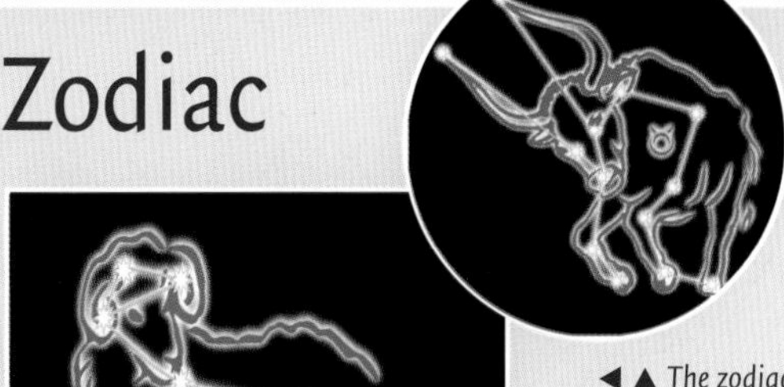

◀ ▲ *The zodiac signs are imaginary symbols ancient astronomers linked to star patterns, such as Aries and Taurus.*

- **The zodiac** is the band of constellations the Sun appears to pass in front of during the year, as the Earth orbits the Sun. It lies along the ecliptic.
- **The ecliptic** is the plane (level) of the Earth's orbit around the Sun. The Moon and all planets but Pluto lie in the same plane.
- **The Ancient Greeks** divided the zodiac into 12 parts, named after the constellation they saw in each part. These are the signs of the zodiac.

★ **STAR FACT** ★

A 13th constellation, Ophiuchus, now lies within the zodiac; astrologers ignore it.

- **The 12 constellations of the zodiac** are Aries, Taurus, Gemini, Cancer, Leo, Virgo, Libra, Scorpio, Sagittarius, Capricorn, Aquarius and Pisces.
- **Astrologers** believe the movements of the planets and stars in the zodiac affect people's lives, but there is no physical connection.
- **For astrologers** all the constellations of the zodiac are equal in size. The ones used by astronomers are not.
- **The Earth has tilted** slightly since ancient times and the constellations no longer correspond to the zodiac.
- **The orbits of the Moon** and all the planets (except Pluto) lie within the zodiac.
- **The dates that the Sun** seems to pass in front of each constellation no longer match the dates astrologers use.

Celestial sphere

- **Looking at the stars**, they seem to move across the night sky as though they were painted on the inside of a slowly turning, giant ball. This is the celestial sphere.
- **The northern tip** of the celestial sphere is called the North Celestial Pole.
- **The southern tip** is the South Celestial Pole.
- **The celestial sphere rotates** on an axis which runs between its two celestial poles.
- **There is an equator** around the middle of the celestial sphere, just like Earth's.
- **Stars are positioned** on the celestial sphere by their declination and their right ascension.
- **Declination** is like latitude. It is measured in degrees and shows a star's position between pole and equator.
- **Right ascension** is like longitude. It is measured in hours, minutes and seconds, and shows how far a star is from a marker called the First Point of Aries.
- **The Pole Star**, Polaris, lies very near the North Celestial Pole.
- **The zenith** is the point on the sphere directly above your head as you look at the night sky.

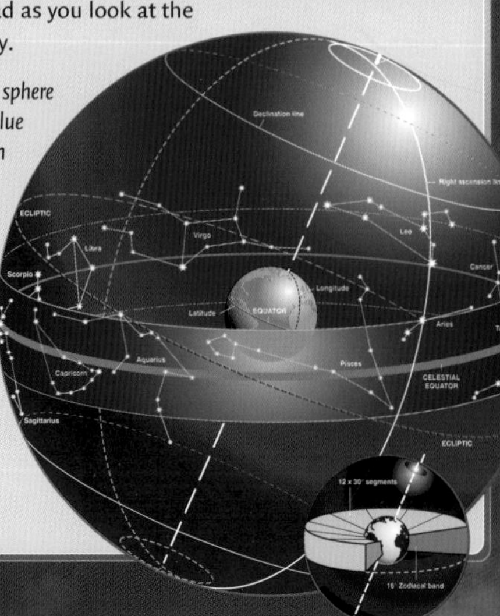

▶ *The celestial sphere is like a great blue ball dotted with stars, with the Earth in the middle. It is imaginary, but makes it easy to locate stars and constellations. The zodiac is shown on the inset.*

X-rays

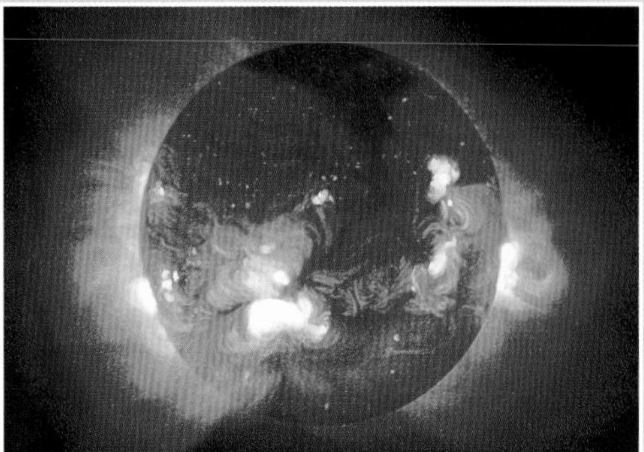

▲ *The Sun was the first X-ray source to be discovered.*

- **X-rays** are electromagnetic rays whose waves are shorter than ultraviolet rays and longer than gamma rays (see radiation).
- **X-rays in space** may be produced by very hot gases well over 1 million °C.
- **X-rays are also made** when electrons interact with a magnetic field in synchrotron radiation (see cosmic rays).
- **X-rays cannot get through** Earth's atmosphere, so astronomers can only detect them using space telescopes such as ROSAT.
- **X-ray sources** are stars and galaxies that give out X-rays.
- **The first and brightest X-ray source** found (apart from the Sun) was the star Scorpius X-1, in 1962. Now tens of thousands are known, although most are weak.
- **The remnants of supernovae** such as the Crab nebula are strong sources of X-rays.
- **The strongest sources of X-rays** in our galaxy are X-ray binaries like Scorpius X-1 and Cygnus X-1 (see binary stars). Some are thought to contain black holes.
- **X-ray binaries** pump out 1,000 times as much X-ray radiation as the Sun does.
- **X-ray galaxies** harbouring big black holes are powerful X-ray sources outside our galaxy.

Sunspots

- **Sunspots are dark spots** on the Sun's photosphere (surface), 2,000°C cooler than the rest of the surface.
- **The dark centre** of a sunspot is the umbra, the coolest bit of a sunspot. Around it is the lighter penumbra.

▼ *Infrared photographs reveal the dark sunspots that appear on the surface of the Sun.*

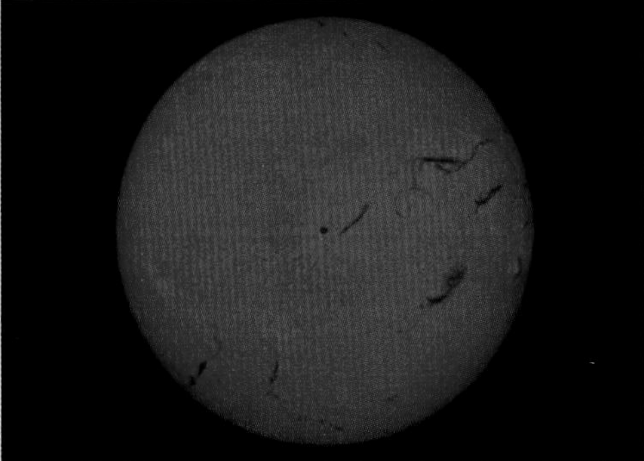

★ STAR FACT ★
The SOHO satellite confirmed that sunspots move faster on the Sun's equator.

- **Sunspots appear in groups** which seem to move across the Sun over two weeks, as the Sun rotates.
- **Individual sunspots** last less than a day.
- **The number of sunspots** reaches a maximum every 11 years. This is called the solar or sunspot cycle.
- **The next sunspot maximum** will be in the year 2012.
- **Earth's weather** may be warmer and stormier when sunspots are at their maximum.
- **Long-term sunspot cycles** are 76 and 180 years, and are almost like the Sun breathing in and out.
- **Observations of the Sun** by satellites such as *Nimbus-7* showed that less heat reaches the Earth from the Sun when sunspots are at a minimum.

The Big Bang

- **The Big Bang explosion** is how scientists think the Universe began some 15 billion years ago.
- **First there was a hot ball** tinier than an atom. This cooled to 10 billion billion °C as it grew to football size.
- **A split second later**, a super-force swelled the infant Universe a thousand billion billion billion times. Scientists call this inflation.
- **As it mushroomed out**, the Universe was flooded with energy and matter, and the super-force separated into basic forces such as electricity and gravity.
- **There were no atoms at first**, just tiny particles such as quarks in a dense soup a trillion trillion trillion trillion trillion times denser than water.
- **There was also antimatter**, the mirror image of matter. Antimatter and matter destroy each other when they meet, so they battled it out. Matter just won – but the Universe was left almost empty.
- **After 3 minutes**, quarks started to fuse (join) to make the smallest atoms, hydrogen. Then hydrogen gas atoms fused to make helium gas atoms.
- **After 1 million years** the gases began to curdle into strands with dark holes between them.
- **After 300 million years**, the strands clumped into clouds, and then the clouds clumped together to form stars and galaxies.
- **The afterglow of the Big Bang** can still be detected as microwave background radiation coming from all over space (see below).

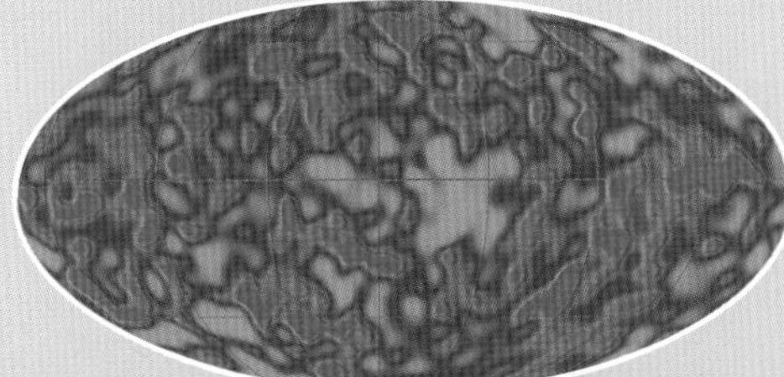

1000
THINGS
YOU SHOULD KNOW ABOUT
PLANET
EARTH

KEY

 Planet Earth

 Volcanoes and earthquakes

 Shaping the land

 Weather and climate

 Continents

 Oceans

Air moisture

▲ *Clouds are the visible, liquid part of the moisture in the air. They form when the water vapour in the air cools and condenses.*

- **Up to 10 km** above the ground, the air is always moist because it contains an invisible gas called water vapour.
- **There is enough water vapour** in the air to flood the entire globe to a depth of 2.5 m.
- **Water vapour** enters the air when it evaporates from oceans, rivers and lakes.
- **Water vapour** leaves the air when it cools and condenses (turns to drops of water) to form clouds. Most clouds eventually turn to rain, and the water falls back to the ground. This is called precipitation.
- **Like a sponge,** the air soaks up evaporating water until it is saturated (full). It can only take in more water if it warms up and expands.
- **If saturated air cools,** it contracts and squeezes out the water vapour, forcing it to condense into drops of water. The point at which this happens is called the dew point.
- **Humidity** is the amount of water in the air.
- **Absolute humidity** is the weight of water in grams in a particular volume of air.
- **Relative humidity,** which is written as a percentage, is the amount of water in the air compared to the amount of water the air could hold when saturated.

The lithosphere

- **The lithosphere** is the upper, rigid layer of the Earth. It consists of the crust and the top of the mantle (see core and mantle). It is about 100 km thick.
- **The lithosphere** was discovered by 'seismology', which means listening to the pattern of vibrations from earthquakes.
- **Fast earthquake waves** show that the top of the mantle is as rigid as the crust, although chemically it is different.
- **Lithosphere** means 'ball of stone'.
- **The lithosphere** is broken into 20 or so slabs, called tectonic plates. The continents sit on top of these plates (see continental drift).
- **Temperatures** increase by 35°C for every 1,000 m you move down through the lithosphere.
- **Below the lithosphere,** in the Earth's mantle, is the hot, soft rock of the asthenosphere (see Earth's interior).
- **The boundary between the lithosphere** and the asthenosphere occurs at the point where temperatures climb above 1,300°C.
- **The lithosphere** is only a few kilometres thick under the middle of the oceans. Here, the mantle's temperature just below the surface is 1,300°C.
- **The lithosphere is thickest** – 120 km or so – under the continents.

◀ *The hard rocky surface of the Earth is made up of the 20 or so strong rigid plates of the lithosphere.*

Earthquake waves

- **Earthquake waves** are the vibrations sent out through the ground by earthquakes (see earthquakes). They are also called seismic waves.
- **There are two kinds** of deep earthquake wave: primary (P) waves and secondary (S) waves.
- **P waves** travel at 5 km per second and move by alternately squeezing and stretching rock.
- **S waves** travel at 3 km per second and move the ground up and down or from side to side.
- **There are two kinds** of surface wave: Love waves and Rayleigh waves.
- **Love, or Q, waves** shake the ground from side to side in a jerky movement that can often destroy very tall buildings.

★ STAR FACT ★
Some earthquake waves travel at 20 times the speed of sound.

- **Rayleigh, or R, waves** shake the ground up and down, often making it seem to roll.
- **In solid ground** earthquake waves travel too fast to be seen. However, they can turn loose sediments into a fluid-like material so that earthquake waves can be seen rippling across the ground like waves in the sea.
- **When waves ripple** across loose sediment they can uproot tall buildings.

▼ Surface waves travel much slower than deep waves, but they are usually the ones that cause the most damage.

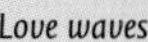

Rayleigh waves

Love waves

Caves

★ STAR FACT ★
The Sarawak Chamber is big enough to hold the world's biggest sports stadium 3 times over.

- **Caves** are giant holes that run horizontally underground. Holes that plunge vertically are called potholes.
- **The most spectacular caves,** called caverns, are found in limestone. Acid rainwater trickles through cracks in the rock and wears away huge cavities.
- **The world's largest known** single cave is the Sarawak Chamber in Gunung Mulu in Sarawak, Malaysia.
- **The deepest** cave gallery yet found is the Pierre St Martin system, 800 m down in the French Pyrenees.
- **The longest** cave system is the Mammoth Cave in Kentucky, USA, which is 560 km long.
- **Many caverns** contain fantastic deposits called speleothems. They are made mainly from calcium carbonate deposited by water trickling through the cave.
- **Stalactites** are icicle-like speleothems that hang from cave ceilings. Stalagmites poke upwards from the floor.
- **The world's longest** stalactite is 6.2 m long. It is in the Poll an Ionain in County Clare, Ireland.
- **The world's tallest column** is the Flying Dragon Pillar in the Nine Dragons Cave, Guizhou, China.

▼ Caverns can be subterranean palaces filled with glistening pillars.

Africa

- **Africa is the world's second largest** continent. It stretches from the Mediterranean in the north to the Cape of Good Hope in the south. Area: 30,131,536 sq km.
- **Africa is the world's warmest** continent, lying almost entirely within the tropics or subtropics.
- **Temperatures in the Sahara** Desert are the highest on Earth, often soaring over 50°C.
- **The Sahara** in the north of Africa, and the Kalahari in the south, are the world's largest deserts. Most of the continent in between is savannah (grassland) and bush. In the west and centre are lush rainforests.
- **Much of Africa** consists of vast plains and plateaux, broken in places by mountains such as the Atlas range in the northwest and the Ruwenzori in the centre.

★ STAR FACT ★
The River Nile is perhaps the second longest river in the world, measuring 6673 km long.

- **The Great Rift Valley** runs 7,200 km from the Red Sea. It is a huge gash in the Earth's surface opened up by the pulling apart of two giant tectonic plates.
- **Africa's largest lake** is Victoria, 69,484 sq km.
- **Africa's highest mountain** is Kilimanjaro, 5,895 m high.
- **The world's** biggest sand dune is 430 m high – Erg Tifernine in Algeria.

▶ *Africa is a vast, warm, fairly flat continent covered in savannah, desert and tropical forest.*

Ocean deeps

▲ *Huge numbers of sea creatures live in the pelagic zone – the surface waters of the open ocean beyond the continental shelf.*

- **The oceans** are over 2,000 m deep on average.
- **Along the edge** of the ocean is a ledge of land – the continental shelf. The average sea depth here is 130 m.
- **At the edge of the continental shelf** the sea-bed plunges thousands of metres steeply down the continental slope.
- **Underwater avalanches** roar down the continental slope at over 60 km/h. They carve out deep gashes called submarine canyons.
- **The gently** sloping foot of the continental slope is called the continental rise.
- **Beyond the continental rise** the ocean floor stretches out in a vast plain called the abyssal plain. It lies as deep as 5,000 m below the water's surface.
- **The abyssal plain** is covered in a thick slime called ooze. It is made partly from volcanic ash and meteor dust and partly from the remains of sea creatures.
- **The abyssal plain** is dotted with huge mountains, thousands of metres high, called seamounts.
- **Flat-topped seamounts** are called guyots. They may be volcanoes that once projected above the surface.
- **The deepest places** in the ocean floor are ocean trenches – made when tectonic plates are driven down into the mantle. The Mariana Trench is 10,863 m deep.

Earthquake damage

- **Many of the world's** major cities are located in earthquake zones, such as Los Angeles, Mexico City and Tokyo.
- **Severe earthquakes** can shake down buildings and rip up flyovers.
- **When freeways collapsed** in the 1989 San Francisco quake, some cars were crushed to just 0.5 m thick.
- **The 1906 earthquake** in San Francisco destroyed 400 km of railway track around the city.
- **Some of the worst** earthquake damage is caused by fire, often set off by the breaking of gas pipes and electrical cables.
- **In 1923** 200,000 died in the firestorm that engulfed Tokyo as an earthquake upset domestic charcoal stoves.

▲ *The complete collapse of overhead freeways is a major danger in severe earthquakes.*

- **In the Kobe** earthquake of 1995 and the San Francisco earthquake of 1989 some of the worst damage was to buildings built on landfill – loose material piled in to build up the land.
- **The earthquake** that killed the most people was probably the one that hit Shansi in China in 1556. It may have claimed 830,000 lives.
- **The most fatal** earthquake this century destroyed the city of Tangshan in China in 1976. It killed an estimated 255,000 people.
- **The worst earthquake** to hit Europe centred on Lisbon, Portugal, in 1755. It destroyed the city, killing 100,000 or more people. It probably measured 9.0 on the Richter scale (see earthquake measurement) and was felt in Paris.

Changing landscapes

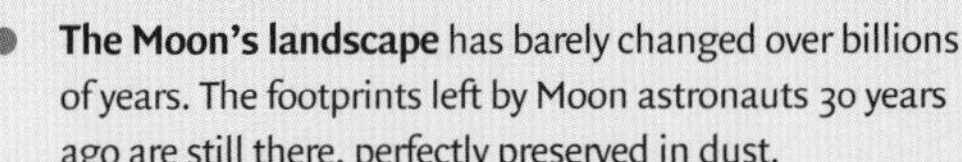

- **The Moon's landscape** has barely changed over billions of years. The footprints left by Moon astronauts 30 years ago are still there, perfectly preserved in dust.
- **The Earth's surface** changes all the time. Most changes take millions of years. Sometimes the landscape is reshaped suddenly by an avalanche or a volcano.
- **The Earth's surface** is distorted and re-formed from below by the huge forces of the Earth's interior.
- **The Earth's surface** is moulded from above by weather, water, waves, ice, wind and other 'agents of erosion'.
- **Most landscapes,** except deserts, are moulded by running water, which explains why hills have rounded slopes. Dry landscapes are more angular, but even in deserts water often plays a major shaping role.
- **Mountain peaks** are jagged because it is so cold high up that the rocks are often shattered by frost.
- **An American scientist** W. M. Davis (1850–1935) thought landscapes are shaped by repeated 'cycles of erosion'.
- **Davis's cycles of erosion** have three stage: vigorous 'youth', steady 'maturity' and sluggish 'old age'.
- **Observation** has shown that erosion does not become more sluggish as time goes on, as Davis believed.
- **Many landscapes** have been shaped by forces no longer in operation, such as moving ice during past Ice Ages.

▼ *Rivers are one of the most powerful agents of erosion.*

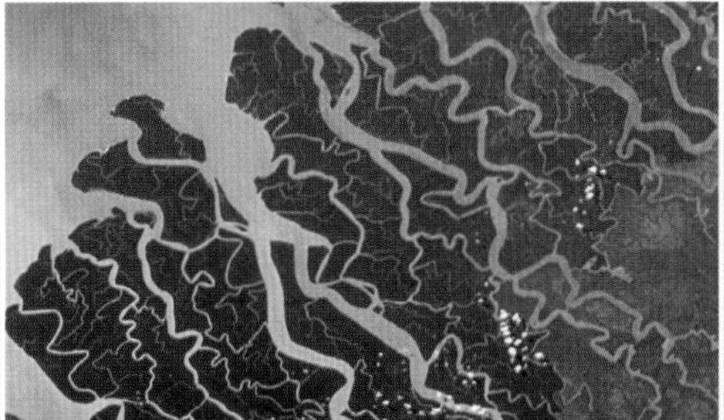

Continental drift

- **Continental drift** is the slow movement of the continents around the world.
- **About 220 million years ago** all the continents were joined together in one supercontinent, which geologists call Pangaea.
- **Pangaea** began to break up about 200 million years ago. The fragments slowly drifted apart to form the continents we know today.
- **South America** used to be joined to Africa. North America used to be joined to Europe.
- **The first hint** that the continents were once joined was the discovery by German explorer Alexander von Humboldt (1769–1859) that rocks in Brazil (South America) and the Congo (Africa) are very similar.
- **When German meteorologist** Alfred Wegener (1880–1930) first suggested the idea of continental drift in 1923, many scientists laughed. The chairman of the American Philosophical Society described the idea as 'Utter damned rot!'.
- **Strong evidence** of continental drift has come from similar ancient fossils found in separate continents, such as the *Glossopteris* fern found in both Australia and India; the *Diadectid* insect found in Europe and North America; and *Lystrosaurus*, a tropical reptile from 200 million years ago, found in Africa, India, China and Antarctica.

★ STAR FACT ★
New York is moving about 2.5 cm farther away from London every year.

- **Satellites** provide such incredibly accurate ways of measuring that they can actually measure the slow movement of the continents. The main method is satellite laser ranging (SLR), which involves bouncing a laser beam off a satellite from ground stations on each continent. Other methods include using the Global Positioning System (GPS) and Very Long Baseline Interferometry (VLBI).
- **Rates of continental drift** vary. India drifted north into Asia very quickly. South America is moving 20 cm farther from Africa every year. On average, continents move at about the same rate as a fingernail grows.

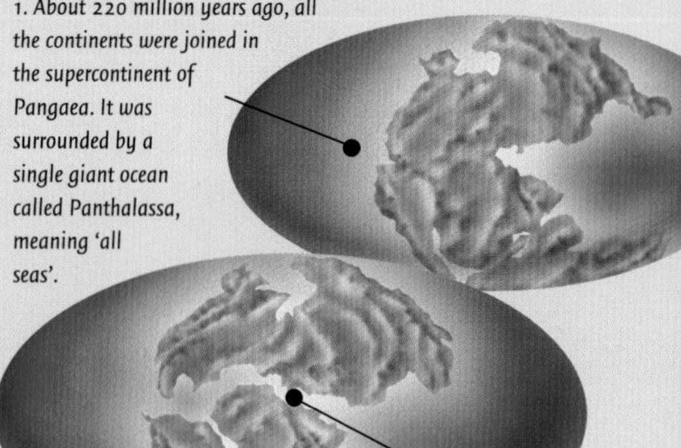

1. About 220 million years ago, all the continents were joined in the supercontinent of Pangaea. It was surrounded by a single giant ocean called Panthalassa, meaning 'all seas'.

2. By 200 million years ago Pangaea had split into two huge landmasses called Laurasia and Gondwanaland, separated by the Tethys Sea. About 135 million years ago these landmasses also began to divide.

3. About 110 million years ago North and South America finally began to link up. Later, Australia and Antarctica separated. India broke off from Africa and drifted rapidly north into Asia. Europe and North America began to move apart about 60 million years ago, at about the same time that the dinosaurs died out.

4. The continents have not stopped moving. North America is still moving farther away from Europe – and closer to Asia.

▶ It is hard to believe that the continents move, but they do. Over tens of millions of years they move huge distances. The drifting of the continents has changed the map of the world very, very slowly over the past 200 million years, and will continue to do so in the future.

Earthquake measurement

- **Earthquakes** are measured with a device called a seismograph.
- **The Richter scale** measures the magnitude (size) of an earthquake on a scale of 1 to 10 using a seismograph. Each step in the scale indicates a tenfold increase in the energy of the earthquake.
- **The Richter scale** was devised in the 1930s by an American geophysicist called Charles Richter (1900–1985).
- **The most powerful** earthquake ever recorded was an earthquake in Chile in 1960, which registered 9.5 on the Richter scale. The 1976 Tangshan earthquake registered 7.8.
- **Between 10 and 20** earthquakes each year reach 7 on the Richter scale.
- **The Modified Mercalli scale** assesses an earthquake's severity according to its effects on a scale of 1 to 12 in Roman numerals (I–XII).

▶ *The Richter scale tells us how much energy an earthquake has – but the damage it does to somewhere depends on how far the place is from the centre.*

- **The Mercalli scale** was devised by the Italian scientist Guiseppe Mercalli (1850–1914).
- **A Mercalli scale I** earthquake is one that is only detectable with special instruments.
- **A Mercalli scale XII** earthquake causes almost total destruction of cities and reshapes the landscape.
- **The Moment-magnitude** scale combines Richter readings with observations of rock movements.

Waterfalls

▲ *The spectacular Iguacu Falls in Brazil are made up from 275 individual falls cascading 82 m into the gorge below.*

- **Waterfalls** are places where a river plunges vertically.
- **Waterfalls** may form where the river flows over a band of hard rock, such as a volcanic sill. The river erodes the soft rock below but it has little effect on the hard band.
- **Waterfalls** can also form where a stream's course has been suddenly broken, for example where it flows over a cliff into the sea, over a fault (see faults) or over a hanging valley (see glaciated landscapes).

> ★ **STAR FACT** ★
> The world's highest falls are the Angel Falls in Venezuela, which plunge 979 m.

- **Boulders often swirl** around at the foot of a waterfall, wearing out a deep pool called a plunge pool.
- **Angel Falls** are named after American pilot Jimmy Angel who flew over them in 1935.
- **Victoria Falls** in Zimbabwe are known locally as *Mosi oa Tunya*, which means the 'smoke that thunders'.
- **The roar** from Victoria Falls can be heard 40 km away.
- **Niagara Falls** on the US/Canadian border developed where the Niagara River flows out of Lake Erie.
- **Niagara Falls** has two falls: Horseshoe Falls, 54 m high, and American Falls, 55 m high.

Antarctica

- **Antarctica** is the ice-covered continent at the South Pole. It covers an area of 14 million square km and is larger than Australia.
- **It is the coldest place** on Earth. Even in summer, temperatures rarely climb over −25°C. On July 21, 1983, the air at the Vostok science station plunged to −89.2°C .
- **Antarctica** is one of the driest places on Earth, with barely any rain or snow. It is also very windy.
- **Until about 80 million years ago** Antarctica was joined to Australia.
- **Glaciers began to form** in Antarctica 38 million years ago, and grew rapidly from 13 million years ago. For the past five million years 98% of the continent has been covered in ice.

◀ Antarctica does not belong to any one nation. Under the Antarctic Treaty of 1959, 12 countries agreed to use it only for scientific research.

- **The Antarctic ice cap** contains 70% of the world's fresh water.
- **The ice cap** is thickest – up to 4,800 m deep – in deep sea basins dipping far below the surface. Here it is thick enough to bury the Alps.
- **Antarctica** is mountainous. Its highest point is the Vinson Massif, 5,140 m high, but there are many peaks over 4,000 m in the Transarctic Range.
- **The magnetic South Pole** – the pole to which a compass needle points – moves 8 km a year.
- **Fossils of tropical plants** and reptiles show that Antarctica was at one time in the tropics.

Formation of the Earth

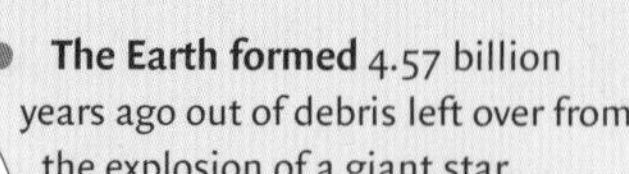

- **The Earth formed** 4.57 billion years ago out of debris left over from the explosion of a giant star.
- **The Earth began to form** as star debris spun round the newly formed Sun and clumped into rocks called planetesimals.
- **Planetesimals** were pulled together by their own gravity to form planets such as Earth and Mars.

◀ When the Earth formed from a whirling cloud of stardust, the pieces rushed together with such force that the young planet turned into a fiery ball. It slowly cooled down, and the continents and oceans formed.

- **At first** the Earth was a seething mass of molten rock.
- **After 50 million years** a giant rock cannoned into the newborn Earth. The impact melted the rock into a hot splash, which cooled to become our Moon.
- **The shock of the impact** that formed the Moon made iron and nickel collapse towards the Earth's centre. They formed a core so dense that its atoms fuse in nuclear reactions that have kept the inside of the Earth hot ever since.
- **The molten rock** formed a thick mantle about 3,000 km thick around the metal core. The core's heat keeps the mantle warm and churning, like boiling porridge.
- **After about 100 million years** the surface of the mantle cooled and hardened to form a thin crust.
- **Steam and gases** billowing from volcanoes formed the Earth's first, poisonous atmosphere.
- **After 200 million years** the steam had condensed to water. It fell in huge rain showers to form the oceans.

Fog and mist

- **Like clouds,** mist is billions of tiny water droplets floating on the air. Fog forms near the ground.
- **Mist forms** when the air cools to the point where the water vapour it contains condenses to water.
- **Meteorologists** define fog as a mist that reduces visibility to less than 1 km.
- **There are four main kinds** of fog: radiation fog, advection fog, frontal fog and upslope fog.
- **Radiation fog** forms on cold, clear, calm nights. The ground loses heat that it absorbed during the day, and so cools the air above.
- **Advection fog** forms when warm, moist air flows over a cold surface. This cools the air so much that the moisture it contains condenses.

★ STAR FACT ★
Smog is a thick fog made when fog combines with polluted air.

▲ *Huge amounts of moisture transpire from the leaves of forest trees. It condenses on cool nights to form a thick morning mist.*

- **Sea fog** is advection fog that forms as warm air flows out over cool coastal waters and lakes.
- **Frontal fog** forms along fronts (see weather fronts).
- **Upslope fog** forms when warm, moist air rises up a mountain and cools.

Earthquake prediction

◀ *Modern earthquake prediction methods detect minute distortions of the ground that indicate the rock is under stress. Seismologists use the latest survey techniques, with precision instruments like this laser rangefinder.*

- **One way to predict earthquakes** is to study past quakes.
- **If there has been no earthquake** in an earthquake zone for a while, there will be one soon. The longer it has been since the last quake, the bigger the next one will be.
- **Seismic gaps** are places in active earthquake zones where there has been no earthquake activity. This is where a big earthquake will probably occur.
- **Seismologists** make very accurate surveys with ground instruments and laser beams bounced off satellites (see earthquake measurement). They can spot tiny deformations of rock that show strain building up.
- **A linked network** of four laser-satellite stations called Keystone is set to track ground movements in Tokyo Bay, Japan, so that earthquakes can be predicted better.
- **The level of water** in the ground may indicate stress as the rock squeezes groundwater towards the surface. Chinese seismologists check water levels in wells.
- **Rising surface levels** of the underground gas radon may also show that the rock is being squeezed.
- **Other signs of strain** in the rock may be changes in the ground's electrical resistance or its magnetism.
- **Before an earthquake** dogs are said to howl, pandas moan, chickens flee their roosts, rats and mice scamper from their holes and fish thrash about in ponds .
- **Some people** claim to be sensitive to earthquakes.

Mineral resources

- **The Earth's surface** contains an enormous wealth of mineral resources, from clay for bricks to precious gems such as rubies and diamonds.
- **Fossil fuels** are oil, coal and natural gas.
- **Fossil fuels were made** from the remains of plant and animals that lived millions of years ago. The remains were changed into fuel by intense heat and pressure.
- **Coal** is made from plants that grew in huge warm swamps during the Carboniferous Period 300 million years ago.
- **Oil and natural gas** were made from the remains of tiny plants and animals that lived in warm seas.
- **Ores** are the minerals from which metals are extracted. Bauxite is the ore for aluminium; chalcopyrite for copper; galena for lead; hematite for iron; sphalerite for zinc.
- **Veins** are narrow pipes of rock that are rich in minerals such as gold and silver. They are made when hot liquids made from volcanic material underground seep upwards through cracks in the rock.

▶ *Bulk materials such as cement, gravel and clay are taken from the ground in huge quantities for building.*

- **Mineral resources** can be located by studying rock strata, (layers), often by satellite and by taking rock samples.
- **Geophysical prospecting** is hunting for minerals using physics – looking for variations in the rock's electrical conductivity, magnetism, gravity or moisture content.

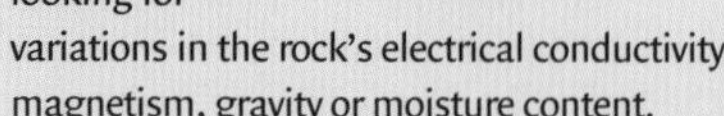

- **Seismic surveys** try to locate minerals using sound vibrations, often generated by underground explosions.

Deserts

▲ *Water erosion over millions of years has created these dramatic pillar-like mesas and buttes in Monument Valley in Utah, USA.*

- **Deserts are dry places** where it rarely rains. Many are hot, but one of the biggest deserts is Antarctica. Deserts cover about one-fifth of the Earth's land.
- **Hamada** is desert that is strewn with boulders. Reg is desert that is blanketed with gravel.
- **About one-fifth** of all deserts are seas of sand dunes. These are known as ergs in the Sahara.
- **The type of sand dune** depends on how much sand there is, and how changeable the wind is.
- **Barchans** are moving, crescent-shaped dunes that form in sparse sand where the wind direction is constant.
- **Seifs** are long dunes that form where sand is sparse and the wind comes from two or more directions.
- **Most streams** in deserts flow only occasionally, leaving dry stream beds called wadis or arroyos. These may suddenly fill with a flash flood after rain.
- **In cool, wet regions**, hills are covered in soil and rounded in shape. In deserts, hills are bare rock with cliff faces footed by straight slopes.
- **Mesas and buttes** are pillar-like plateaux that have been carved gradually by water in deserts.

★ **STAR FACT** ★

In the western Sahara, two million dry years have created sand ridges over 300 m high.

Earthquakes

- **Earthquakes** are a shaking of the ground. Some are slight tremors that barely rock a cradle. Others are so violent they can tear down mountains and cities.
- **Small earthquakes** may be set off by landslides, volcanoes or even just heavy traffic. Big earthquakes are set off by the grinding together of the vast tectonic plates that make up the Earth's surface.
- **Tectonic plates** are sliding past each other all the time, but sometimes they stick. The rock bends and stretches for a while and then snaps. This makes the plates jolt, sending out the shock waves that cause the earthquake's effects to be felt far away.
- **Tectonic plates** typically slide 4 or 5 cm past each other in a year. In a slip that triggers a major quake they can slip more than 1 m in a few seconds.
- **In most quakes** a few minor tremors (foreshocks) are followed by an intense burst lasting just 1 or 2 minutes. A second series of minor tremors (aftershocks) occurs over the next few hours.
- **The starting point** of an earthquake below ground is called the hypocentre, or focus.The epicentre of an earthquake is the point on the surface directly above the hypocentre.
- **Earthquakes are strongest** at the epicentre and become gradually weaker farther away.
- **Certain regions** called earthquake zones are especially prone to earthquakes. Earthquake zones lie along the edges of tectonic plates.
- **A shallow earthquake** originates 0–70 km below the ground. These are the ones that do the most damage. An intermediate quake begins 70–300 km down. Deep quakes begin over 300 km down. The deepest ever recorded earthquake began over 720 km down.

★ **STAR FACT** ★

The longest recorded earthquake, in Alaska on March 21, 1964, lasted just 4 minutes.

▶ During an earthquake, shock waves radiate in circles outwards and upwards from the focus of the earthquake. The damage caused is greatest at the epicentre, where the waves are strongest, but vibrations may be felt 400 km away.

Epicentre

As two tectonic plates jolt past each other, they send out shock waves.

Isoseismic lines show where the quake's intensity is equal.

The quake's intensity is reduced away from the epicentre.

Hypocentre where the quake begins

Climate

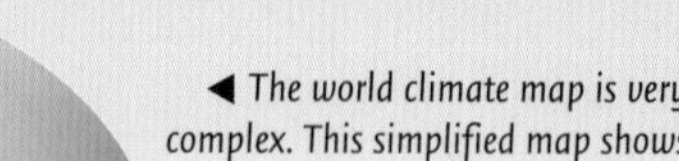

- **Climate is the typical weather** of a place over a long time.
- **Climates are warm** near the Equator, where the Sun climbs high in the sky.
- **Tropical climates** are warm climates in the tropical zones on either side of the Equator. Average temperatures of 27°C are typical.
- **The climate is cool** near the Poles, where the Sun never climbs high in the sky. Average temperatures of –30°C are typical.
- **Temperate climates** are mild climates in the temperate zones between the tropics and the polar regions. Summer temperatures may average 23°C. Winter temperatures may average 12°C.

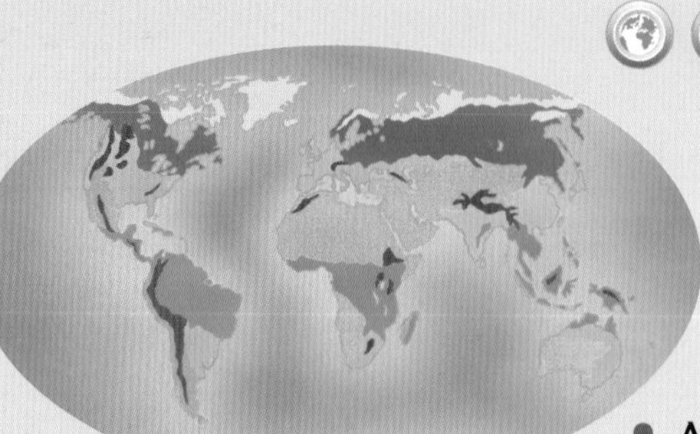

◀ *The world climate map is very complex. This simplified map shows some of the main climate zones.*

Moist temperate
Tropical
Desert
Polar
Continental temperate
Mountain

- **A Mediterranean climate** is a temperate climate with warm summers and mild winters. It is typical of the Mediterranean, California, South Africa and South Australia.
- **A monsoon climate** is a climate with one very wet and one very dry season – typical of India and SE Asia.
- **An oceanic climate** is a wetter climate near oceans, with cooler summers and warmer winters.
- **A continental climate** is a drier climate in the centre of continents, with hot summers and cold winters.
- **Mountain climates** get colder and windier with height.

Weathering

- **Weathering** is the gradual breakdown of rocks when they are exposed to the air.
- **Weathering affects** surface rocks the most, but water trickling into the ground can weather rocks 200 m down.
- **The more extreme** the climate, the faster weathering takes place, whether the climate is very cold or very hot.

▼ *The desert heat means that both the chemical and the mechanical weathering of the rocks is intense.*

★ STAR FACT ★

At –22°C, ice can exert a pressure of 3,000 kg on an area of rock the size of a postage stamp.

- **In tropical Africa** the basal weathering front (the lowest limit of weathering underground) is often 60 m down.
- **Weathering** works chemically (through chemicals in rainwater), mechanically (through temperature changes) and organically (through plants and animals).
- **Chemical weathering** is when gases dissolve in rain to form weak acids that corrode rocks such as limestone.
- **The main form of mechanical weathering** is frost shattering – when water expands as it freezes in cracks in the rocks and so shatters the rock.
- **Thermoclastis** is when desert rocks crack as they get hot and expand in the day, then cool and contract at night.
- **Exfoliation** is when rocks crack in layers as a weight of rock or ice above them is removed.

Gems and crystals

- **Gems** are mineral crystals that are beautifully coloured or sparkling.
- **There are over 3,000 minerals** but only 130 are gemstones. Only about 50 of these are commonly used.
- **The rarest gems** are called precious gems and include diamonds, emeralds and rubies.
- **Less rare gems** are known as semi-precious gems.
- **Gems** are weighed in carats. A carat is one-fifth of a gram. A 50-carat sapphire is very large and very valuable.

◀ *Quartz is a very common mineral. Occasionally it forms beautiful purple amethyst. Minute traces of iron in the rock turn the quartz to amethyst.*

- **In the ancient world** gems were weighed with carob seeds. The word 'carat' comes from the Arabic for seed.
- **Gems** often form in gas bubbles called geodes in cooling magma. They can also form when hot magma packed with minerals seeps up through cracks in the rock to form a vein.
- **When magma** cools, minerals with the highest melting points crystallize first. Unusual minerals are left behind to crystallize last, forming rocks called pegmatites. These rocks are often rich in gems such as emeralds, garnets, topazes and tourmalines.
- **Some gems** with a high melting point and simple chemical composition form directly from magma, such as diamond, which is pure carbon, and rubies.

★ **STAR FACT** ★

Diamonds are among the oldest mineral crystals, over 3,000 million years old.

Deep ocean currents

- **Ocean surface currents** (see ocean currents) affect only the top 100 m or so of the ocean. Deep currents involve the whole ocean.
- **Deep currents** are set in motion by differences in the density of sea water. They move only a few metres a day.
- **Most deep currents** are called thermohaline circulations because they depend on the water's temperature ('thermo') and salt content ('haline').
- **If sea water** is cold and salty, it is dense and sinks.
- **Typically, dense water** forms in the polar regions. Here the water is cold and weighed down by salt left behind when sea ice forms.
- **Dense polar water** sinks and spreads out towards the Equator deep below the surface.
- **Oceanographers** call dense water that sinks and starts deep ocean currents 'deep water'.
- **In the Northern Hemisphere** the main area for the formation of deep water is the North Atlantic.
- **Dense salty water** from the Mediterranean pours deep down very fast – 1 m per second – through the Straits of Gibraltar to add to the North Atlantic deep water.
- **There are three levels** in the ocean: the 'epilimnion' (the surface waters warmed by sunlight, up to 100–300 m down); the 'thermocline', where it becomes colder quickly with depth; and the 'hypolimnion', the bulk of deep, cold ocean water.

▼ *This satellite picture shows variations in ocean surface temperature.*

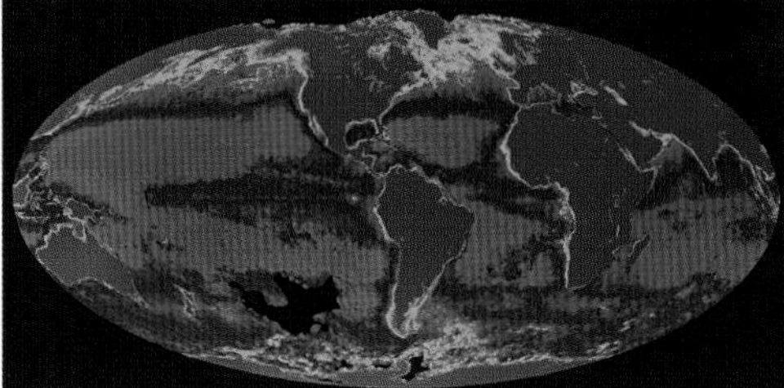

Glaciers

- **Glaciers** are rivers of slowly moving ice. They form in mountain regions when it is too cold for snow to melt. They flow down through valleys, creeping lower until they melt in the warm air lower down.
- **Glaciers** form when new snow, or névé, falls on top of old snow. The weight of the new snow compacts the old snow into denser snow called firn.
- **In firn snow**, all the air is squeezed out so it looks like white ice. As more snow falls, firn gets more compacted and turns into glacier ice that flows slowly downhill.
- **Nowadays** glaciers form only in high mountains and towards the North and South Poles. In the Ice Ages glaciers were widespread and left glaciated landscapes in many places that are now free of ice.
- **As glaciers** move downhill, they bend and stretch, opening up deep cracks called crevasses. Sometimes these occur where the glacier passes over a ridge of rock.

◀ The dense ice in glaciers is made from thousands of years of snow. As new snow fell, the old snow beneath it became squeezed more and more in a process called firnification.

- **The biggest crevasse** is often a crevasse called the bergschrund. It forms when the ice pulls away from the back wall of the hollow where the glacier starts.
- **Where the underside** of a glacier is warmish (about 0°C), it moves by gliding over a film of water that is made as pressure melts the glacier's base. It is called basal slip.
- **Where the underside** of a glacier is coldish (well below 0°C), it moves as if layers were slipping over each other like a pack of cards. This is called internal deformation.
- **Valley glaciers** are glaciers that flow in existing valleys.
- **Cirque glaciers** are small glaciers that flow from hollows high up. Alpine valley glaciers form when several cirque glaciers merge. Piedmont glaciers form where valley glaciers join as they emerge from the mountains.

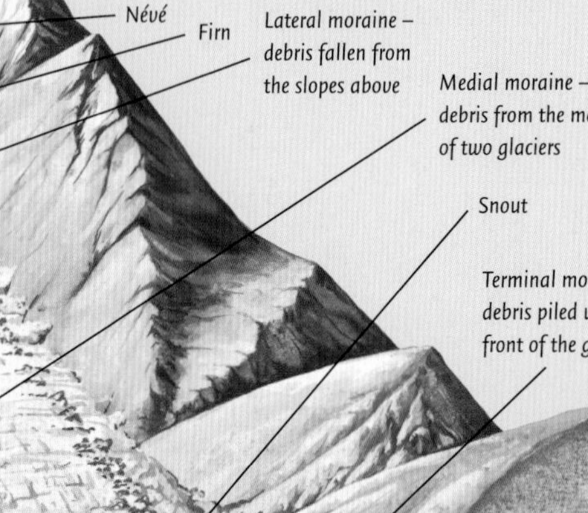

▲ Glaciers begin in small hollows in the mountain called cirques, or corries. They flow downhill, gathering huge piles of debris called moraine on the way.

Ocean currents

- **Ocean surface currents** are like giant rivers, often tens of kilometres wide, 100 m deep and flowing at 15 km/h.
- **The major currents** are split on either side of the Equator into giant rings called gyres.
- **In the Northern Hemisphere** the gyres flow round clockwise; in the south they flow anticlockwise.
- **Ocean currents** are driven by a combination of winds and the Earth's rotation.
- **Near the Equator** water is driven by easterly winds (see wind) to make westward-flowing equatorial currents.
- **When equatorial currents** reach continents, the Earth's rotation deflects them polewards as warm currents.
- **As warm currents flow** polewards, westerly winds drive them east back across the oceans. When the currents reach the far side, they begin to flow towards the Equator along the west coasts of continents as cool currents.

★ STAR FACT ★
The West Wind Drift around Antarctica moves 2,000 times as much water as the Amazon.

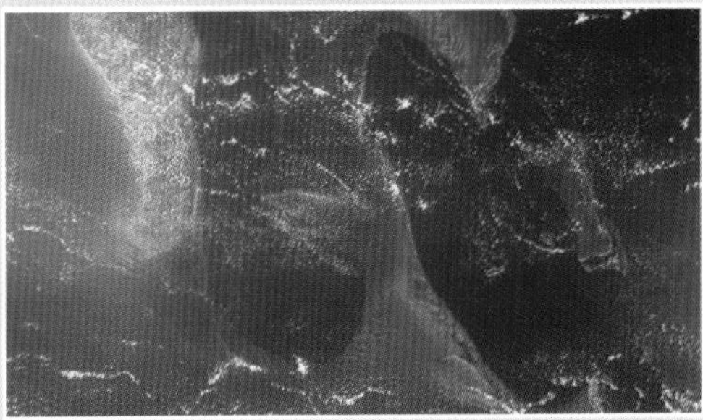

▲ *Ocean currents start as wind blows across the water's surface.*

- **The North Atlantic Drift** brings so much warm water from the Caribbean to SW England that it is warm enough to grow palm trees, yet it is as far north as Newfoundland.
- **By drying out the air** cool currents can create deserts, such as California's Baja and Chile's Atacama deserts.

Climate change

- **The world's climate** is changing all the time, getting warmer, colder, wetter or drier. There are many theories why this happens.
- **One way to see** how climate changed before weather records were kept is to look at the growth rings in old trees. Wide rings show the good growth of a warm summer.
- **Another way** of working out past climate is to look in ancient sediments for remains of plants and animals that only thrive in certain conditions.
- **One cause of climate change** may be shifts in the Earth's orientation to the Sun. These shifts are called Milankovitch cycles.
- **One Milankovitch cycle** is the way the Earth's axis wobbles round like a top every 21,000 years. Another is the way its axis tilts like a rolling ship every 40,000 years. A third is the way its orbit gets more or less oval shaped every 96,000 years.

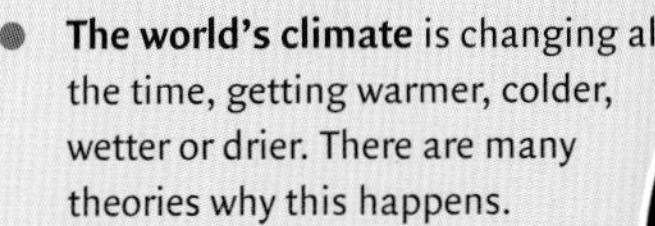

◀ *When more sunspots form on the Sun's surface, the weather on the Earth may be stormier.*

- **Climate** may also be affected by dark patches on the Sun called sunspots. These flare up and down every 11 years.
- **Sunspot activity** is linked to stormy weather on the Earth.
- **Climates may cool** when the air is filled with dust from volcanic eruptions or meteors hitting the Earth.
- **Climates** may get warmer when levels of certain gases in the air increase (see global warming).
- **Local climates** may change as continents drift around. Antarctica was once in the tropics, while the New York area once had a tropical desert climate.

Clouds

- **Clouds** are dense masses of water drops and ice crystals that are so tiny they float high in the air.
- **Cumulus clouds** are fluffy white clouds. They pile up as warm air rises and cools to the point where water vapour condenses.
- **Strong updraughts** create huge cumulonimbus, or thunder, clouds.
- **Stratus clouds** are vast shapeless clouds that form when a layer of air cools to the point where moisture condenses. They often bring long periods of light rain.

▲ *Cumulus clouds build up in fluffy piles as warm, moist air rises. Once it reaches about 2,000 m, the air cools enough for clouds to form.*

★ STAR FACT ★
Cumulonimbus thunder clouds are the tallest clouds, often over 10 km high.

- **Cirrus clouds** are wispy clouds that form so high up they are made entirely of ice. Strong winds high up blow them into 'mares' tails.
- **Low clouds** lie below 2,000 m above the ground. They include stratus and stratocumulus clouds (the spread tops of cumulus clouds).
- **Middle clouds** often have the prefix 'alto' and lie from 2,000 m to 6,000 m up. They include rolls of altocumulus cloud, and thin sheets called altostratus.
- **High-level clouds** are ice clouds up to 11,000 m up. They include cirrus, cirrostratus and cirrocumulus.
- **Contrails** are trails of ice crystals left by jet aircraft.

Hot-spot volcanoes

- **About 5% of volcanoes** are not near the margins of tectonic plates. Instead they are over especially hot places in the Earth's interior called hot spots.
- **Hot spots** are created by mantle plumes – hot currents that rise all the way from the core through the mantle.
- **When mantle plumes** come up under the crust, they burn their way through to become hot-spot volcanoes.
- **Famous hot-spot volcanoes** include the Hawaiian island volcanoes and Réunion Island in the Indian Ocean.
- **Hot-spot volcanoes** ooze runny lava that spreads out to create shield volcanoes (see kinds of volcano).
- **Lava** from hot-spot volcanoes also creates plateaux, such as the Massif Central in France.
- **The geysers, hot springs and bubbling mud pots** of Yellowstone National Park, USA, indicate a hot spot below.
- **Yellowstone** has had three huge eruptions in the past two million years. The first produced over 2,000 times as much lava as the 1980 eruption of Mt St Helens.
- **Hot spots** stay in the same place while tectonic plates slide over the top of them. Each time the plate moves, the hot spot creates a new volcano.
- **The movement** of the Pacific plate over the Hawaiian hot spot has created a chain of old volcanoes 6,000 km long. It starts with the Meiji seamount under the sea north of Japan, and ends with the Hawaiian islands.

▼ *Hot spots pump out huge amounts of lava.*

Glaciated landscapes

- **Glaciers** move slowly but their sheer weight and size give them enormous power to shape the landscape.
- **Over tens of thousands of years** glaciers carve out winding valleys into huge, straight U-shaped troughs.
- **Glaciers** may truncate (slice off) tributary valleys to leave them 'hanging', with a cliff edge high above the main valley. Hill spurs (ends of hills) may also be truncated.
- **Cirques, or corries,** are armchair-shaped hollows carved out where a glacier begins high up in the mountains.
- **Arêtes** are knife-edge ridges that are left between several cirques as the glaciers in them cut backwards.
- **Drift** is a blanket of debris deposited by glaciers. Glaciofluvial drift is left by the water made as the ice melts. Till is left by the ice itself.
- **Drumlins** are egg-shaped mounds of till. Eskers are snaking ridges of drift left by streams under the ice.
- **Moraine** is piles of debris left by glaciers.
- **Proglacial lakes** are lakes of glacial meltwater dammed up by moraine.

★ STAR FACT ★

After the last Ice Age, water from the huge Lake Agassiz submerged over 500,000 sq km of land near Winnipeg, in Canada.

◀ *After an Ice Age, glaciers leave behind a dramatically altered landscape of deep valleys and piles of debris.*

Rocks

- **The oldest known rocks** are 3,900 million years old – they are the Acasta gneiss rocks from Canada.
- **There are three main kinds of rock**: igneous rock, sedimentary rock and metamorphic rock.
- **Igneous rocks** (igneous means 'fiery') are made when hot molten magma or lava cools and solidifies.
- **Volcanic rocks,** such as basalt, are igneous rocks that form from lava that has erupted from volcanoes.
- **Plutonic rocks** are igneous rocks made when magma solidifies underground, like granite.
- **Metamorphic rocks** are rocks formed when other rocks are changed by extreme heat and pressure, such as limestone which hot magma turns to marble.
- **Sedimentary rocks** are made from the slow hardening of sediments into layers, or strata.
- **Many sedimentary rocks,** like sandstone, are formed when sand, silt and other fragments of rocks are broken down by weathering and erosion.
- **Most sediments** form on the sea-bed. Sand is washed down onto the sea-bed by rivers.
- **Limestone and chalk** are sedimentary rocks made mainly from the remains of sea creatures.

▶ *Rocks are continually recycled. Whether they form from volcanoes or sediments, all rocks are broken down into sand by weathering and erosion.The sand is deposited on sea-beds and river-beds where it hardens to form new rock. This process is the rock cycle.*

Famous eruptions

- **One of the biggest eruptions** ever occurred 2.2 million years ago in Yellowstone, USA. It poured out enough magma to build half a dozen Mt Fujiyamas.
- **In 1645 BC** the Greek island of Thera erupted, destroying the Minoan city of Akoteri. It may be the origin of the Atlantis myth.
- **On August 24, AD79** the volcano Mt Vesuvius in Italy erupted. It buried the Roman town of Pompeii in ash.
- **The remains** of Pompeii were discovered in the 18th century, wonderfully preserved under metres of ash. They provide a remarkable snapshot of ancient Roman life.
- **The eruption** of the volcanic island of Krakatoa near Java in 1883 was heard a quarter of the way round the world.
- **In 1815** the eruption of Tambora in Indonesia was 60–80 times bigger than the 1980 eruption of Mt St Helens.

◀ *The eruption of Mt St Helens in Washington, USA on May 18, 1980 blew away the side of the mountain. It sent out a blast of gas that flattened trees for 30 km around.*

- **Ash from Tambora** filled the sky, making the summer of 1816 cool all around the world.
- **J. M. W. Turner's paintings** may have been inspired by fiery sunsets caused by dust from Tambora.
- **During the eruption of Mt Pelée** on Martinique on May 8, 1902, all but two of the 29,000 townspeople of nearby St Pierre were killed in a few minutes by a scorching flow of gas, ash and cinders.
- **The biggest eruption** in the past 50 years was that of Mt Pinatubo in the Philippines in April 1991.

Ice Ages

- **Ice Ages** are periods lasting millions of years when the Earth is so cold that the polar ice caps grow huge. There are various theories about why they occur (see climate change).
- **There have been four Ice Ages** in the last 1,000 million years, including one which lasted 100 million years.

▼ *California may have looked something like this 18,000 years ago when it was on the fringes of an ice sheet.*

- **The most recent Ice Age** – called the Pleistocene Ice Age – began about 2 million years ago.
- **In an Ice Age** the weather varies between cold spells called glacials and warm spells called interglacials.
- **There have been** 17 glacials and and interglacials in the last 1.6 million years of the Pleistocene Ice Age.
- **The last glacial,** called the Holocene glacial, peaked about 18,000 years ago and ended 10,000 years ago.
- **Ice covered 40% of the world** 18,000 years ago.
- **Glaciers spread** over much of Europe and North America 18,000 years ago. Ice caps grew in Tasmania and New Zealand.
- **About 18,000 years ago** there were glaciers in Hawaii.

★ **STAR FACT** ★

Where Washington and London are today, the ice was 1.5 km thick 18,000 years ago.

Atmosphere

- **The atmosphere** is a blanket of gases about 1,000 km deep around the Earth. It can be divided into five layers: troposphere (the lowest), stratosphere, mesosphere, thermosphere and exosphere.
- **The atmosphere** is: 78% nitrogen, 21% oxygen, 1% argon and carbon dioxide with tiny traces of neon, krypton, zenon, helium, nitrous oxide, methane and carbon monoxide.
- **The atmosphere** was first created by the fumes pouring out from the volcanoes that covered the early Earth 4,000 million years ago. But it was changed as rocks and seawater absorbed carbon dioxide, and then algae in the sea built up oxygen levels over millions and millions of years.
- **The troposphere** is just 12 km thick yet it contains 75% of the weight of gases in the atmosphere. Temperatures drop with height from 18°C on average to about –60°C at the top, called the tropopause.
- **The stratosphere** contains little water. Unlike the troposphere, which is heated from below, it is heated from above as the ozone in it is heated by ultraviolet light from the Sun. Temperatures rise with height from –60°C to 10°C at the top, about 50 km up.

★ **STAR FACT** ★

The stratosphere glows faintly at night because sodium from salty sea spray reacts chemically in the air.

- **The stratosphere** is completely clear and calm, which is why jet airliners try to fly in this layer.
- **The mesosphere** contains few gases but it is thick enough to slow down meteorites. They burn up as they hurtle into it, leaving fiery trails in the night sky. Temperatures drop from 10°C to –120°c 80 km up.
- **In the thermosphere** temperatures are very high, but there is so little gas that there is little real heat. Temperatures rise from –120°C to 2,000°C 700 km up.
- **The exosphere** is the highest level of the atmosphere where it fades into the nothingness of space.

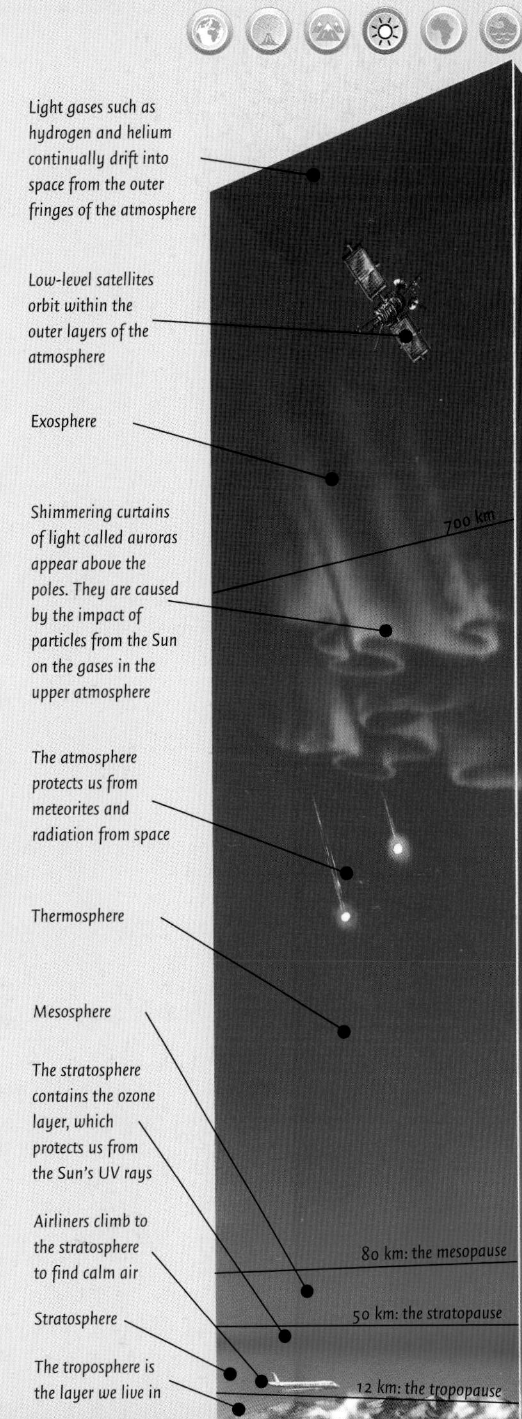

▶ *The atmosphere is a sea of colourless, tasteless, odourless gases, mixed with moisture and fine dust particles. It is about 800 km deep but has no distinct edge, simply fading away into space. As you move up, each layer contains less and less gas. The topmost layers are very rarefied, which means that gas is very sparse.*

Waves

- **Waves in the sea** are formed when wind blows across the sea and whips the surface into ripples.
- **Water particles** are dragged a short way by the friction between air and water, which is known as wind stress.
- **If the wind continues to blow** long and strong enough in the same direction, moving particles may build up into a ridge of water. At first this is a ripple, then a wave.
- **Waves seem to move** but the water in them stays in the same place, rolling around like rollers on a conveyor belt.

★ **STAR FACT** ★
A wave over 40 m high was recorded by the USS *Ramapo* in the Pacific in 1933.

- **The size of a wave** depends on the strength of the wind and how far it blows over the water (the fetch).
- **If the fetch is short,** the waves may simply be a chaotic, choppy 'sea'. If the fetch is long, they may develop into a series of rolling waves called a swell.
- **One in 300,000 waves** is four times bigger than the rest.
- **The biggest waves** occur south of South Africa.
- **When waves** move into shallow water, the rolling of the water is impeded by the sea-bed. The water piles up, then spills over in a breaker.

◀ *When waves enter shallow water, the water in them piles up until eventually they spill over at the top and break.*

Ecosystems

- **An ecosystem** is a community of living things interacting with each other and their surroundings.
- **An ecosystem** can be anything from a piece of rotting wood to a huge swamp. In every ecosystem each organism depends on the others.

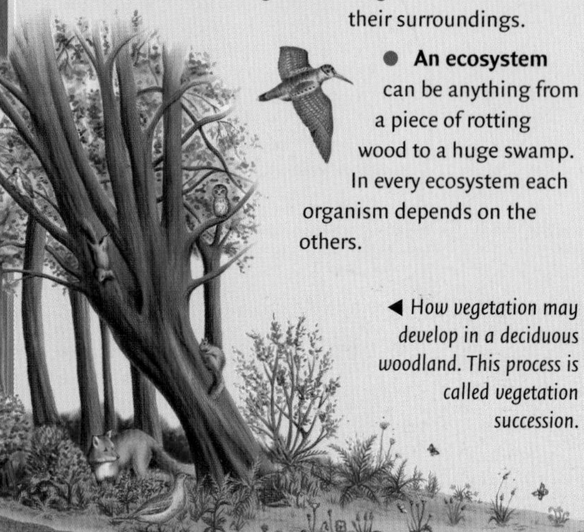

◀ *How vegetation may develop in a deciduous woodland. This process is called vegetation succession.*

- **When vegetation** colonizes an area, the first plants to grow there are small and simple, such as mosses and lichens. Grass and sedges appear next.
- **The simple plants** stabilize the soil so that bigger and more complex plants can move in. This is called vegetation succession.
- **Rainforest ecosystems** cover only 8% of the world's land, yet they include 40% of all the world's plant and animal species.
- **Farming has a huge effect** on natural ecosystems, reducing the number of species dramatically.
- **Green plants** are autotrophs, or producers, which means they make their own food (from sunlight).
- **Animals** are heterotrophs, or consumers, which means they get their food from other living things.
- **Primary consumers** are herbivores that eat plants.
- **Secondary consumers** are carnivores that eat herbivores or each other.

Asia

- **Asia is the world's largest continent**, stretching from Europe in the west to Japan in the east. It has an area of 44,680,718 sq km.
- **Asia has huge climate extremes,** from a cold polar climate in the north to a hot tropical one in the south.
- **Verkhoyansk** in Siberia has had temperatures as high as 37°C and as low as –68°C.

◀ *Asia is a vast continent of wide plains and dark forests in the north, separated from the tropical south by the Himalayas.*

★ STAR FACT ★
Lake Baikal is the world's deepest lake – 1,743 m – and it holds 20% of the world's fresh water.

- **The Himalayas** are the highest mountains in the world, with 14 peaks over 8,000 m high. To the north are vast empty deserts, broad grasslands and huge coniferous forests. To the south are fertile plains and valleys and steamy tropical jungles.
- **Northern Asia** sits on one giant tectonic plate.
- **India** is on a separate plate that crashed into the north Asia plate 50 million years ago. It is piling up the Himalayas as it ploughs on northwards.
- **Asia's longest river** is China's Yangtze, 5,520 km long.
- **Asia's** highest mountain is the world's highest – Mt Everest, or Sagarmatha, in Nepal at 8,848 m.
- **The Caspian Sea** bewteen Azerbaijan and Kazakhstan is the world's largest lake, covering 378,400 sq km.

Cold

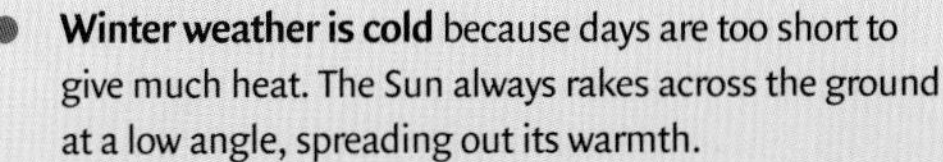

- **Winter weather is cold** because days are too short to give much heat. The Sun always rakes across the ground at a low angle, spreading out its warmth.
- **The coldest places** in the world are the North and South Poles. Here the Sun shines at a low angle even in summer, and winter nights last almost 24 hours.
- **The average temperature** at Polus Nedostupnosti (Pole of Cold) in Antarctica is –58°C.
- **The coldest temperature** ever recorded was –89.2°C at Vostok in Antarctica on July 21, 1983.
- **The interiors of the continents** can get very cold in winter because land loses heat rapidly.
- **When air cools** below freezing point (0°C), water vapour in the air may freeze without turning first to dew. It covers the ground with white crystals of ice or frost.
- **Fern frost** is feathery tails of ice that form on cold glass as dew drops freeze bit by bit.
- **Hoar frost** is spiky needles of frost that form when damp air blows over very cold surfaces and freezes onto them.
- **Rime** is a thick coating of ice that forms when drops of water in clouds and fogs stay liquid well below freezing point. The drops freeze hard when they touch a surface.
- **Black ice** forms when rain falls on a very cold road.

▼ *Rime is a thick coating of ice that forms when moisture cools well below 0°C before freezing onto surfaces.*

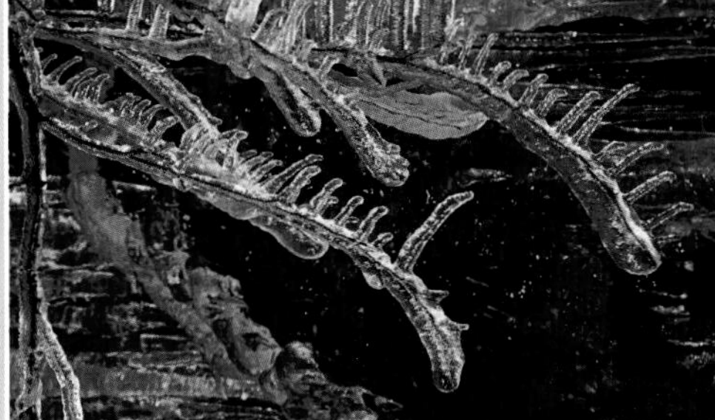

Converging plates

- **In many places** around the world, the tectonic plates that make up the Earth's crust, or outer layer, are slowly crunching together with enormous force.
- **The Atlantic** is getting wider, pushing the Americas further west. Yet the Earth is not getting any bigger because as the American plates crash into the Pacific plates, the thinner, denser ocean plates are driven down into the Earth's hot mantle and are destroyed.
- **The process** of driving an ocean plate down into the Earth's interior is called subduction.
- **Subduction** creates deep ocean trenches typically 6–7 km deep at the point of collision. One of these, the Mariana Trench, could drown Mt Everest with 2 km to spare on top.

★ STAR FACT ★
Subduction creates a ring of volcanoes around the Pacific Ocean called the 'Ring of Fire'.

- **As an ocean plate** bends down into the Earth's mantle, it cracks. The movement of these cracks sets off earthquakes originating up to 700 km down. These earthquake zones are called Benioff–Wadati zones after Hugo Benioff, who discovered them in the 1950s.
- **As an ocean plate** slides down, it melts and makes blobs of magma. This magma floats up towards the surface, punching its way through to create a line of volcanoes along the edge of the continental plate.

▲ *Volcanoes in subduction zones are usually highly explosive. This is because the magma becomes contaminated as it burns its way up through the continental crust.*

- **If volcanoes in subduction zones** emerge in the sea, they form a curving line of volcanic islands called an island arc. Beyond this arc is the back-arc basin, an area of shallow sea that slowly fills up with sediments.
- **As a subducting plate sinks,** the continental plate scrapes sediments off the ocean plate and piles them in a great wedge. Between this wedge and the island arc there may be a fore-arc basin, which is a shallow sea that slowly fills with sediment.
- **Where two continental plates collide,** the plate splits into two layers: a lower layer of dense mantle rock and an upper layer of lighter crustal rock, which is too buoyant to be subducted. As the mantle rock goes down, the crustal rock peels off and crumples against the other to form fold mountains (see mountain ranges).

▼ *This is a cross-section through the top 1,000 km or so of the Earth's surface. It shows a subduction zone, where an ocean plate is bent down beneath a continental plate.*

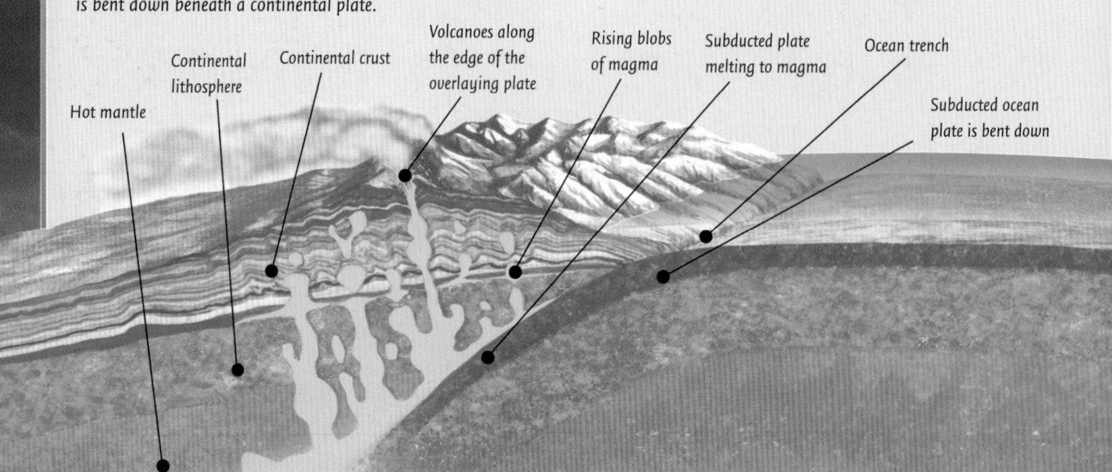

Great lakes

- **Most of the world's great lakes** lie in regions that were once glaciated. The glaciers carved out deep hollows in the rock in which water collected. The Great Lakes of the USA and Canada are partly glacial in origin.
- **In Minnesota, USA** 11,000 lakes were formed by glaciers.
- **The world's deepest lakes** are often formed by faults in the Earth's crust, such as Lake Baikal in Siberia (see Asia) and Lake Tanganyika in East Africa.
- **Most lakes** last only a few thousand years before they are filled in by silt or drained by changes in the landscape.
- **The world's oldest great lake** is Lake Baikal in Siberia, which is over 2 million years old.
- **The Great Lakes** include three of the world's five largest lakes: Superior, Huron and Michigan.
- **The world's largest lake** is the Caspian Sea (see Asia), which is a saltwater lake.
- **The world's highest great lake** is Titicaca in South America, which is 3,812 m above sea level.
- **The world's lowest great lake** is the Dead Sea between Israel and Jordan. It is 399 m below sea level and getting lower all the time.
- **The largest underground lake** in the world is Drauchenhauchloch, which is inside a cave in Namibia.

▼ *Many of the world's great lakes were formed by glaciation, and will eventually disappear.*

Beaches

▲ *The little bays in this beach have been scooped out as waves strike the beach at an angle.*

- **Beaches** are sloping bands of sand, shingle or pebbles along the edge of a sea or lake.
- **Some beaches** are made entirely of broken coral or shells.
- **On a steep beach,** the backwash after each wave is strong. It washes material down the beach and so makes the beach gentler sloping.

★ **STAR FACT** ★

The world's largest pleasure beach is Virginia Beach, Virginia, USA, over 45 km long.

- **On a gently sloping beach,** each wave runs in powerfully and falls back gently. Material gets washed up the beach, making it steeper.
- **The slope of a beach** matches the waves, so the slope is often gentler in winter when the waves are stronger.
- **A storm beach** is a ridge of gravel and pebbles flung high above the normal high-tide mark during a storm.
- **At the top of each beach** a ridge, or berm, is often left at the high-tide mark.
- **Beach cusps** are tiny bays in the sand that are scooped out along the beach when waves strike it at an angle.
- **Many scientists** believe that beaches are only a temporary phenomena caused by the changes in sea levels after the last Ice Age.

Seasons

- **Seasons** are periods of similar weather that occur at certain times of year.
- **Outside the tropics** there are four seasons each year. Each one lasts about three months.
- **The changes in the seasons** occur because the tilt of the Earth's axis is always the same as it circles the Sun.
- **When the Earth** is on one side of the Sun, the Northern Hemisphere (half of the world) is tilted towards the Sun. It is summer in the north of the world and winter in the south.
- **As the Earth moves** a quarter way round the Sun, the northern half begins to tilt away. This brings cooler autumn weather to the north and spring to the south.
- **When the Earth** moves another quarter round to the far side of the Sun, the Northern Hemisphere is tilted away from the Sun. It is winter in the north of the world, and summer in the south.
- **As the Earth moves** three-quarters of the way round the Sun, the north begins to tilt towards the Sun again. This brings the warmer weather of spring to the north, and autumn to the south.
- **Around March 21** and September 21, the night is exactly 12 hours long all over the world. These times are called the vernal (spring) equinox and the autumnal equinox.
- **The day when** nights begin to get longer again is called the summer solstice. This is around June 21 in the north and December 21 in the south.
- **Many places** in the tropics have just two six-month seasons: wet and dry.

▲ *In autumn, the leaves of deciduous trees change colour then drop off ready for winter. Nights grow cooler, and a mist will often develop by morning.*

Global warming

- **Global warming** is the general increase in average temperatures around the world. This increase has been between 0.3°C and 0.8°C over the last hundred years.
- **Most scientists** now think that global warming is caused by human activities, which have resulted in an increase in the Earth's natural greenhouse effect.
- **The greenhouse effect** is the way that certain gases in the air – notably carbon dioxide – trap some of the Sun's warmth, like the panes of glass in a greenhouse.
- **The greenhouse effect** keeps the Earth pleasantly warm – but if it increases, the Earth may become hot.
- **Many experts** expect a 4°C rise in average temperatures over the next 100 years.
- **Humans** boost the greenhouse effect by burning fossil fuels, such as coal and oil, that produce carbon dioxide.
- **Emission of the greenhouse gas** methane from the world's cattle has added to global warming.
- **Global warming** is bringing stormier weather by trapping more energy inside the atmosphere.
- **Global warming** may melt much of the polar ice caps, flooding low-lying countries such as Bangladesh.

▼ *Could global warming make the Mediterranean look like this?*

! NEWS FLASH !
Recent observations show global warming could be much worse than we thought.

Black smokers

- **Black smokers** are natural chimneys on the sea-bed. They billow black fumes of hot gases and water.
- **Black smokers** are technically known as hydrothermal vents. They are volcanic features.
- **Black smokers** form along mid-ocean ridges where the tectonic plates are moving apart.
- **Black smokers** begin when seawater seeps through cracks in the sea floor. The water is heated by volcanic magma, and it dissolves minerals from the rock.
- **Once the water is superheated,** it spews from the vents in scalding, mineral-rich black plumes.
- **The plume cools** rapidly in the cold sea, leaving behind thick deposits of sulphur, iron, zinc and copper in tall, chimney-like vents.
- **The tallest vents** are 50 m high.
- **Water jetting** from black smokers can reach 662°C.
- **Smokers** are home to a community of organisms that thrive in the scalding waters and toxic chemicals. The organisms include giant clams and tube worms.

★ STAR FACT ★
Each drop of sea water in the world circulates through a smoker every ten million years.

◀ *Black smokers were first discovered less than 30 years ago.*

Australasia

- **Australasia** is a vast region that includes islands spread over much of the Pacific Ocean. The land area is 8,508,238 sq km, but the sea area is much, much bigger.
- **Australia** is the only country in the world which is a continent in its own right.
- **The largest island** is New Guinea, 787,878 sq km.
- **Fraser Island,** off Queensland, Australia, is the world's largest sand island with a sand dune 120 km long.
- **Australasia** is mostly tropical, with temperatures averaging 30°C in the north of Australia, and slightly lower on the islands where the ocean keeps the land cool.
- **New Zealand** is only a few thousand kilometres from the Antarctic Circle at its southern tip. As a result New Zealand has only mild summers and cold winters.
- **Australasia's highest peak** is Mt Wilhelm on Papua New Guinea, 4,300 m high.
- **The Great Barrier Reef** is the world's largest living thing, 2,027 km long. It is the only structure built by animals, that is visible from space.
- **Australia** was the first modern continent to break off from Pangaea (see continental drift) about 200 million years ago, and so has developed its own unique wildlife.
- **Australia sits** on the Indian-Australian plate, which is moving very slowly north away from Antarctica. New Zealand sits astride the boundary (see converging plates) with the Pacific plate.

▶ *Apart from the landmass of Australia, much of Australasia is open water.*

Kinds of volcano

- **Each volcano and each eruption** are slightly different.
- **Shield volcanoes** are shaped like upturned shields. They form where lava is runny and spreads over a wide area.
- **Fissure volcanoes** are found where floods of lava pour out of a long crack in the ground.
- **Composite volcanoes** are cone shaped. They build up in layers from a succession of explosive eruptions.
- **Cinder cones** are built up from ash, with little lava.
- **Strombolian eruptions** are eruptions from sticky magma. They spit out sizzling clots of red-hot lava.
- **Vulcanian eruptions** are explosive eruptions from sticky magma. The magma clogs the volcano's vent between cannon-like blasts of ash clouds and thick lava flows.
- **Peléean eruptions** eject glowing clouds of ash and gas called *nuée ardente* (see famous eruptions).
- **Plinian eruptions** are the most explosive kind of eruption. They are named after Pliny who witnessed the eruption of Vesuvius in AD 79 (see famous eruptions).
- **In Plinian eruptions** boiling gases blast clouds of ash and volcanic fragments up into the stratosphere.

▼ *Fissure volcanoes shoot lava fountains in the air. This happens when gases in the lava boil suddenly as they reach the surface.*

Thunderstorms

◀ *Few places have more spectacular lightning displays than Nevada, USA. The energy in clouds piled up during hot afternoons is unleashed at night.*

- **Thunderstorms** begin when strong updraughts build up towering cumulonimbus clouds.
- **Water drops** and ice crystals in thunderclouds are buffeted together. They become charged with static electricity.
- **Negative charges** in a cloud sink; positive ones rise. Lightning is a rush of negative charge towards the positive.
- **Sheet lightning** is a flash within a cloud. Fork lightning flashes from a cloud to the ground.
- **Forked lightning** begins with a fast, dim flash from a cloud to the ground, called the leader stroke. It prepares the air for a huge, slower return stroke a split second later.
- **Thunder is the sound** of the shock wave as air expands when heated instantly to 25,000°C by the lightning.
- **Sound travels** more slowly than light, so we hear thunder 3 seconds later for every 1 km between us and the storm.
- **At any moment** there are 2,000 thunderstorms around the world, each generating the energy of a hydrogen bomb. Every second, 100 lightning bolts hit the ground.
- **A flash of lightning** is brighter than 10 million 100-watt light bulbs. For a split second it has more power than all the power stations in the USA put together. Lightning travels at up to 100,000 km per second down a path that is the width of a finger but up to 14 km long. Sheet lightning can be 140 km long.
- **Lightning** can fuse sand under the ground into hard root-like strands called fulgurites.

Coasts

- **Coastlines** are changing all the time as new waves roll in and out and tides rise and fall every six hours or so. Over longer periods coastlines are reshaped by the action of waves and the corrosion of salty water.
- **On exposed coasts** where waves strike the high rocks, they undercut the slope to create steep cliffs and headlands. Often waves can penetrate into the cliff to open up sea caves or blast through arches. When a sea arch collapses, it leaves behind tall pillars called stacks which may be worn away to stumps.
- **Waves work** on rocks in two ways. First, the rocks are pounded with a huge weight of water filled with stones. Second, the waves force air into cracks in the rocks with such force that the rocks split apart.
- **The erosive power** of waves is focused in a narrow band at wave height. So as waves wear away sea cliffs, they leave the rock below wave height untouched. As cliffs retreat, the waves slice away a broad shelf of rock called a wave-cut platform. Water left behind in dips when the tide falls forms rockpools.
- **On more sheltered coasts,** the sea may pile up sand into beaches (see beaches). The sand has been washed down by rivers or worn away from cliffs.
- **When waves hit** a beach at an angle, they fall straight back down the beach at a right angle. Any sand and shingle that the waves carry fall back slightly farther along the beach. In this way sand and shingle are moved along the beach in a zig-zag fashion. This is called longshore drift.
- **On beaches** prone to longshore drift, low fences called groynes are often built to stop the sand being washed away along the beach.
- **Longshore drift** can wash sand out across bays and estuaries to create sand bars called spits.
- **Bays** are broad indents in the coast with a headland on each side. Waves reach the headlands first, focusing their energy here. Material is worn away from the headlands and washed into the bay, forming a bay-head beach.
- **A cove is a small bay.** A bight is a huge bay, such as the Great Australian Bight. A gulf is a long narrow bight. The world's biggest bay is Hudson Bay, Canada, which has a shoreline 12,268 km long. The Bay of Bengal in India is larger in area.

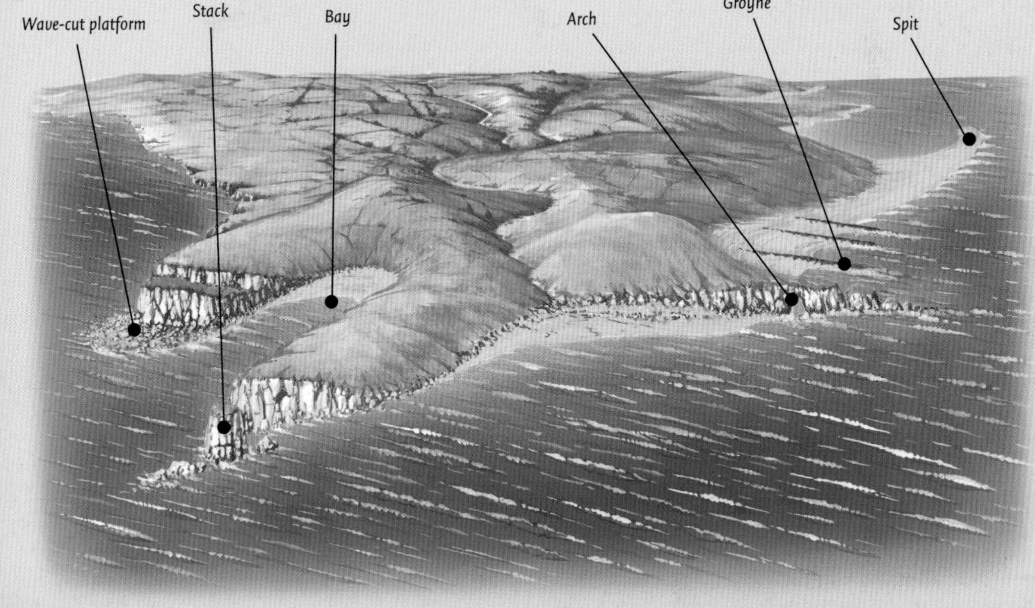

Europe

- **Europe** is the smallest continent, with an area of just 10,400,000 sq km. For for its size Europe has an immensely long coastline.
- **In the north** are the ancient glaciated mountains of Scandinavia and Scotland, which were once much, much higher.
- **Across the centre** are the lowlands of the North European Plain, stretching from the Urals in Russia to France in the west.
- **Much of southern Europe** has been piled up into young mountain ranges, as Africa drifts slowly north.
- **The highest point** in Europe is Mt Elbrus in the Russian Caucasus, 5,642 m high.

◀ *Europe is a small continent but its peninsulas and inlets give it a long coast.*

- **Northwest Europe** was once joined to Canada. The ancient Caledonian mountains of eastern Canada, Greenland, Scandinavia and Scotland were formed together as a single mountain chain 360–540 million years ago.
- **Mediterranean Europe** has a Mediterranean climate with warm summers and mild winters.
- **NW Europe** is often wet and windy. It has very mild winters because it is bathed by the warm North Atlantic Drift (see ocean currents).
- **The Russian islands** of Novaya Zimlya are far into the Arctic Circle and are icebound in winter.
- **The largest lake** is Ladoga in Russia, 18,389 sq km.

Floods

- **A flood** is when a river or the sea rises so much that it spills over the surrounding land.
- **River floods** may occur after a period of prolonged heavy rain or after snow melts in spring.

◀ *Even when no one drowns, a flood can destroy homes and wash away soil from farmland, leaving it barren.*

- **Small floods** are common; big floods are rare. So flood size is described in terms of frequency.
- **A 2-year flood** is a smallish flood that is likely to occur every two years. A 100-year flood is a big flood that is likely to occur once a century.
- **A flash flood** occurs when a small stream changes to a raging torrent after heavy rain during a dry spell.
- **The 1993 flood** on the Mississippi–Missouri caused damage of $15,000 million and made 75,000 homeless, despite massive flood control works in the 1930s.
- **The Hwang Ho river** is called 'China's sorrow' because its floods are so devastating.
- **Not all floods** are bad. Before the Aswan Dam was built, Egyptian farmers relied on the yearly flooding of the River Nile to enrich the soil.
- **After the Netherlands** was badly flooded by a North Sea surge in 1953, the Dutch embarked on the Delta project, one of the biggest flood control schemes in history.

★ STAR FACT ★

In 1887, one million people were killed when the Hwang Ho river in China flooded.

Core and mantle

- **The mantle** makes up the bulk of the Earth's interior. It reaches from about 10–90 km to 2,890 km down.
- **Temperatures** in the mantle climb steadily as you move through the mantle, reaching 3,000°C.
- **Mantle rock** is so warm that it churns slowly round like very, very thick treacle boiling on a stove. This movement is known as mantle convection currents.

▲ *Every now and then, mantle rock melts into floods of magma, which collects along the edges of tectonic plates. It then rises to the surface and erupts as a volcano.*

! NEWS FLASH !
Scientists have found 'anti-continents' on the CMB that match with continents on the surface.

- **Mantle rock moves** about 10,000 times more slowly than the hour hand on a kitchen clock. Cooler mantle rock takes about 200 million years to sink all the way to the core.
- **Near the surface,** mantle rock may melt into floods of magma. These may gush through the upper layers like oil that is being squeezed from a sponge.
- **The boundary** between the mantle and the core (see Earth's interior) is called the core–mantle boundary (CMB).
- **The CMB** is about 250 km thick. It is an even more dramatic change than between the ground and the air.
- **Temperatures jump by 1,500°C** at the CMB.
- **The difference** in density between the core and the mantle at the CMB is twice as great as the difference between air and rock.

The Arctic Ocean

- **Most of the Arctic Ocean** is permanently covered with a vast floating raft of sea ice.
- **Temperatures** are low all year round, averaging −30°C in winter and sometimes dropping to −70°C.
- **During the long winters,** which last more than four months, the Sun never rises above the horizon.
- **The Arctic** gets its name from *arctos*, the Greek word for 'bear', because the Great Bear constellation is above the North Pole.
- **There are three kinds of sea ice** in the Arctic: polar ice, pack ice and fast ice.
- **Polar ice** is the raft of ice that never melts through.
- **Polar ice** may be as thin as 2 m in places in summer, but in winter it is up to 50 m thick.
- **Pack ice** forms around the edge of the polar ice and only freezes completely in winter.
- **The ocean swell** breaks and crushes the pack ice into chunky ice blocks and fantastic ice sculptures.

▲ *The seal is one of the few creatures that can survive the bitter cold of the Arctic winter.*

- **Fast ice** forms in winter between pack ice and the land around the Arctic Ocean. It gets its name because it is held fast to the shore. It cannot move up and down with the ocean as the pack ice does.

Diverging plates

▲ *Unlike subduction zones, which create explosive volcanoes, diverging plates create volcanoes that ooze lava gently. For this to happen above the ocean surface is rare.*

- **Deep down on the ocean floor**, some of the tectonic plates of the Earth's crust are slowly pushing apart. New molten rock wells up from the mantle into the gap between them and freezes onto their edges. As plates are destroyed at subduction zones (see converging plates), so new plate spreads the ocean floor wider.
- **The spreading of the ocean floor** centres on long ridges down the middle of some oceans, called mid-ocean ridges. Some of these ridges link up to make the world's longest mountain range, winding over 60,000 km beneath the oceans.
- **The Mid-Atlantic ridge** stretches through the Atlantic from North Pole to South Pole. The East Pacific Rise winds under the Pacific Ocean from Mexico to Antarctica.
- **Along the middle** of a mid-ocean ridge is a deep canyon. This is where molten rock from the mantle wells up through the sea-bed.
- **Mid-ocean ridges** are broken by the curve of the Earth's surface into short stepped sections. Each section is marked off by a long sideways crack called a transform fault. As the sea floor spreads out from a ridge, the sides of the fault rub together setting off earthquakes.
- **As molten rock wells** up from a ridge and freezes, its magnetic material sets in a certain way to line up with the Earth's magnetic field. Because the field reverses every now and then, bands of material set in alternate directions. This means that scientists can see how the sea floor has spread in the past.
- **Rates of sea floor spreading** vary from 1 cm to 20 cm a year. Slow-spreading ridges such as the Mid-Atlantic Ridge are much higher, with seamounts often topping the ridge. Fast-spreading ridges such as the East Pacific Rise are lower, and magma oozes from these just like fissure volcanoes on the surface (see kinds of volcano).

★ **STAR FACT** ★

About 10 cubic km of new crust is created at the mid-ocean ridges every year.

- **Hot magma** bubbling up through a mid-ocean ridge emerges as hot lava. As it comes into contact with the cold seawater it freezes into blobs called pillow lava.
- **Mid-ocean ridges** may begin where a mantle plume (see hot-spot volcanoes) rises through the mantle and melts through the sea-bed. Plumes may also melt through continents to form Y-shaped cracks, which begin as rift valleys (see faults) and then widen into new oceans.

▼ *This is a cross-section of the top 50 km or so of the Earth's surface. It shows where the sea floor is spreading away from the mid-ocean ridge.*

Rain

- **Rain falls** from clouds filled with large water drops and ice crystals. The thick clouds block out the sunlight.
- **The technical name** for rain is precipitation, which also includes snow, sleet and hail.
- **Drizzle** is 0.2–0.5 mm drops falling from nimbostratus clouds. Rain from nimbostratus is 1–2 mm drops. Drops from thunderclouds can be 5 mm. Snow is ice crystals. Sleet is a mix of rain or snow, or partly melted snow.
- **Rain starts** when water drops or ice crystals inside clouds grow too large for the air to support them.
- **Cloud drops grow** when moist air is swept upwards and cools, causing lots of drops to condense. This happens when pockets of warm, rising air form thunderclouds – at weather fronts or when air is forced up over hills.
- **In the tropics** raindrops grow in clouds by colliding with each other. In cool places, they also grow on ice crystals.
- **The world's rainiest place** is Mt Wai-'ale-'ale in Hawaii, where it rains 350 days a year.
- **The wettest place** is Tutunendo in Colombia, which gets 11,770 mm of rain every year. (London gets about 70 mm).
- **La Réunion in the Indian Ocean** received 1,870 mm of rain in one day in 1952.
- **Guadeloupe in the West Indies** received 38.1 mm of rain in one minute in 1970.

▼ *Rain starts when moist air is lifted up dramatically. Water drops and ice crystals inside the cloud grow so big that it turns dark.*

Great rivers

▲ *All great rivers develop the same horseshoe-shaped meanders in their lower reaches (see river channels).*

- **Measurements** of river lengths vary according to where the river is said to begin. So some people say that Africa's Nile is the world's longest river; others say that South America's Amazon is longer.
- **The source** of the Amazon was only discovered in 1971, in snowbound lakes high in the Andes. It is named Laguna McIntyre after the American who found it.

> ★ **STAR FACT** ★
> The Amazon in flood could fill the world's biggest sports stadium with water in 13 seconds.

- **If the full length** of the Amazon is counted, it is 6,750 km long compared with the Nile at 6,673 km.
- **The Amazon basin** covers more than 7 million sq km.
- **China's Yangtse** is the third longest river, at 6,300 km.
- **The world's longest tributary** is the Madeira flowing into the Amazon. At 3,380 km long it is the 18th longest river in the world.
- **The world's longest estuary** is that of the Ob' in Russia, which is up to 80 km wide and 885 km long.
- **The Ob'** is the biggest river to freeze solid in winter.
- **The shortest official river** is the North Fork Roe River in Montana, USA, which is just 17.7 m long.

Hills

- **One definition** of a hill is high ground up to 307 m high. Above that height it is a mountain.
- **Mountains are solid rock**; hills can be solid rock or piles of debris built up by glaciers or the wind.
- **Hills that are solid rock** are either very old, having been worn down from mountains over millions of years, or they are made from soft sediments that were low hills.
- **In moist climates** hills are often rounded by weathering and by water running over the land.
- **As solid rock is weathered**, the hill is covered in a layer of debris called regolith. This material either creeps slowly downhill or slumps suddenly in landslides.

▲ *The contours of hills in damp places have often been gently rounded over long periods by a combination of weathering and erosion by running water.*

- **Hills** often have a shallow S-shaped slope. Geologists call this kind of slope 'convexo-concave' because there is a short rounded convex section at the top, and a long dish-shaped concave slope lower down.
- **Hill slopes** may become gentler as they are worn away, because the top is worn away faster. This is called decline.
- **Some hill slopes** may stay equally steep, but are simply warn back. This is called retreat
- **Some hill slopes** may wear backwards, as gentler sections get longer and steeper sections get shorter. This is called replacement
- **Decline** may take place in damp places; retreat happens in dry places.

Snow

- **Snow** is crystals of ice. They fall from clouds in cold weather when the air is too cold to melt ice to rain.
- **Outside the tropics** most rain starts to fall as snow but melts on the way down.

- **More snow falls** in the northern USA than falls at the North Pole because it is too cold to snow at the North Pole.
- **The heaviest** snow falls when the air temperature is hovering around freezing.

◀ *Fresh snow can contain up to 90% air, which is why snow can actually insulate the ground and keep it warm, protecting plants.*

- **Snow can be hard to forecast** because a rise in temperature of just 1°C or so can turn snow into rain.
- **All snow flakes** have six sides. They usually consist of crystals that are flat plates, but occasionally needles and columns are found.
- **W. A. Bentley** was an American farmer who photographed thousands of snowflakes through microscopes. He never found two identical flakes.
- **In February 1959** the Mt Shaska Ski Bowl in California had 4,800 mm of snow in just six days.
- **In March 1911** Tamarac in California was buried in 11,460 mm of snow. The Antarctic is buried in over 4,000 m of snow.
- **The snowline** is the lowest level on a mountain where snow remains throughout the summer. It is 5,000 m in the tropics, 2,700 m in the Alps, 600 m in Greenland and at sea level at the Poles.

Folds

     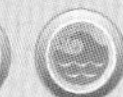

- **Rocks usually form** in flat layers called strata. Tectonic plates can collide (see converging plates) with such force that they crumple up these strata.
- **Sometimes the folds** are just tiny wrinkles a few centimetres long. Sometimes they are gigantic, with hundreds of kilometres between crests (the highest points on a fold).

▼ *The main features of a fold.*

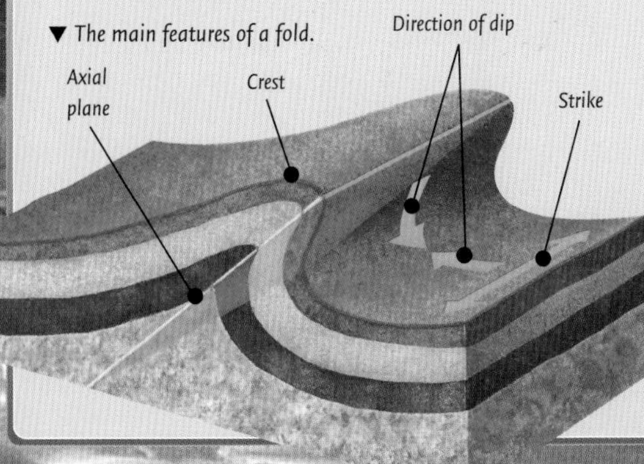

★ STAR FACT ★
Most of the world's oil comes from reservoirs that are trapped in anticlines.

- **The shape of a fold** depends on the force that is squeezing it and on the resistance of the rock.
- **The slope of a fold** is called the dip. The direction of the dip is the direction in which it is sloping.
- **The strike of the fold** is at right angles to the dip. It is the horizontal alignment of the fold.
- **Some folds turn right over** on themselves to form upturned folds called nappes.
- **As nappes fold on top of other nappes,** the crumpled strata may pile up into mountains.
- **A downfold** is called a syncline; an upfolded arch of strata is called an anticline.
- **The axial plane** of a fold divides the fold into halves.

Biomes

- **A biome** is a community of plants and animals adapted to similar conditions in certain parts of the world.
- **Biomes** are also known as 'major life zones' or 'biogeographical regions'.
- **The soil** and animal life of a region are closely linked to its vegetation. Biomes are usually named after the dominant vegetation, e.g. grassland or coniferous forest.
- **Vegetation** is closely linked to climate, so biomes correspond to climate zones.
- **Major biome types** include: tundra, boreal (cold) coniferous forests, temperate deciduous forests, temperate grasslands, savannahs (tropical grasslands), tropical rainforests and deserts.
- **Most types of biome** are found across several different continents.
- **Species within a biome type** vary from continent to continent, but they share the same kind of vegetation.
- **Many plants and animals** have features that make them especially suited to a particular biome .
- **Polar bears** are adapted to life in the Arctic; cacti are well equipped to survive in the desert.
- **Biomes also exist in the sea,** for example coral reefs.

▼ *Extreme conditions, such as flooding in a swamp, can create different kinds of communities within the same biome.*

Sunshine

▲ *Without sunshine, the Earth would be cold, dark and dead.*

- **Half of the Earth** is exposed to the Sun at any time. Radiation from the Sun is the Earth's main source of energy, providing huge amounts of heat and light.
- **Solar** means anything to do with the Sun
- **About 41% of solar radiation** is light; 51% is long-wave radiation that our eyes cannot see, such as infrared light. The other 8% is short-wave radiation, such as UV rays.
- **Only 47%** of the solar radiation that strikes the Earth actually reaches the ground; the rest is soaked up or reflected by the atmosphere.
- **The air is not warmed** much by the Sun directly. Instead, it is warmed by heat reflected from the ground.
- **Solar radiation** reaching the ground is called insolation.
- **The amount of heat reaching** the ground depends on the angle of the Sun's rays. The lower the Sun in the sky, the more its rays are spread out and give off less heat.
- **Insolation is at a peak** in the tropics and during the summer. It is lowest near the Poles and in winter.
- **The tropics** receive almost two and a half times more heat per day than the Poles do.
- **Some surfaces** reflect the Sun's heat and warm the air better than others. The percentage they reflect is called the albedo. Snow and ice have an albedo of 85–95% and so they stay frozen even as they warm the air. Forests have an albedo of 12%, so they soak up a lot of the Sun's heat.

River channels

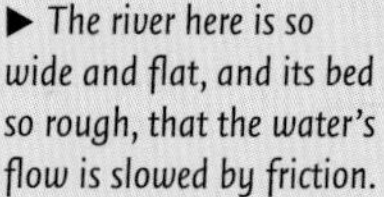

▶ *The river here is so wide and flat, and its bed so rough, that the water's flow is slowed by friction.*

- **A channel** is the long trough along which a river flows.
- **When a river's channel** winds or has a rough bed, friction slows the river down.
- **A river flows faster** through a narrow, deep channel than a wide, shallow one because there is less friction.
- **All river channels** tend to wind, and the nearer they are to sea level, the more they wind. They form remarkably regular horseshoe-shaped bends called meanders.
- **Meanders** seem to develop because of the way in which a river erodes and deposits sediments.
- **One key factor** in meanders is the ups and downs along the river called pools (deeps) and riffles (shallows).
- **The distance between pools and riffles,** and the size of meanders, are in close proportion to the river's width.
- **Another key factor** in meanders is the tendency of river water to flow not only straight downstream but also across the channel. Water spirals through the channel in a corkscrew fashion called helicoidal flow.
- **Helicoidal flow** makes water flow faster on the outside of bends, wearing away the bank. It flows more slowly on the inside, building up deposits called slip-off slopes.

★ STAR FACT ★

Meanders can form almost complete loops with only a neck of land separating the ends.

Volcanoes

- **Volcanoes** are places where magma (red-hot liquid rock from the earth's interior) emerges through the crust and onto the surface.
- **The word 'volcano'** comes from Vulcano Island in the Mediterranean. Here Vulcan, the ancient Roman god of fire and blacksmith to the gods, was supposed to have forged his weapons in the fire beneath the mountain.
- **There are many types** of volcano (see kinds of volcano). The most distinctive are the cone-shaped composite volcanoes, which build up from alternating layers of ash and lava in successive eruptions.
- **Beneath a composite volcano** there is typically a large reservoir of magma called a magma chamber. Magma collects in the chamber before an eruption.
- **From the magma chamber** a narrow chimney, or vent, leads up to the surface. It passes through the cone of debris from previous eruptions.
- **When a volcano erupts,** the magma is driven forcefully up the vent by the gases within it. As the magma nears the surface, the pressure drops, allowing the gases dissolved in the magma to boil out. The expanding gases – mostly carbon dioxide and steam – push the molten rock upwards and out of the vent.
- **If the level of magma** in the magma chamber drops, the top of the volcano's cone may collapse into it, forming a giant crater called a caldera. *Caldera* is Spanish for 'boiling pot'. The world's largest caldera is Toba on Sumatra, Indonesia, which is 1,775 sq km.

★ **STAR FACT** ★

At Urgüp, Turkey, volcanic ash has been blown into tall cones by gas fumes bubbling up. The cones have hardened like huge salt cellars. People have dug them out to make homes.

- **When a volcano** with a caldera subsides, the whole cone may collapse into the old magma chamber. The caldera may fill with water to form a crater lake, such as Crater Lake in Oregon, USA.
- **All the magma** does not gush up the central vent. Some exits through branching side vents, often forming their own small 'parasitic' cones on the side of the main one.

Volcanic bombs, or tephra, are fragments of the shattered volcanic plug flung out far and wide.

Before each eruption, the vent is clogged by old volcanic material from previous eruptions. The explosion blows the plug into tiny pieces of ash and cinder, and blasts them high into the air

Central vent

Side vent

Magma chamber where magma collects before an eruption

Air pollution

- **Air pollution** comes mainly from car, bus and truck exhausts, waste burners, factories, power stations and the burning of oil, coal and gas in homes.
- **Air pollution** can also come from farmers' crop sprays, farm animals, mining and volcanic eruptions.
- **Some pollutants,** such as soot and ash, are solid, but many more pollutants are gases.
- **Air pollution** can spread huge distances. Pesticides, for instance, have been discovered in Antarctica where they have never been used.
- **Most fuels** are chemicals called hydrocarbons. Any hydrocarbons that are left unburned in car exhausts, for example, can react in sunlight to form toxic ozone.
- **When exhaust gases** react in strong sunlight to form ozone, they may create a photochemical smog.

★ STAR FACT ★
Factories in the Chinese city of Benxi make so much smoke the city is invisible to satellites.

▲ *Factories pour out a range of fumes that pollute the air.*

- **Air pollution** is probably a major cause of global warming (see global warming).
- **Air pollution** may destroy the ozone layer inside the Earth's atmosphere (see the ozone hole).
- **Breathing the air** in Mexico City is thought to be as harmful as smoking 40 cigarettes a day.

Hurricanes

- **Hurricanes** are powerful, whirling tropical storms. They are also called willy-willies, cyclones or typhoons.
- **Hurricanes develop** in late summer as clusters of thunderstorms build up over warm seas (at least 27°C).
- **As hurricanes grow,** they tighten into a spiral with a calm ring of low pressure called the 'eye' at the centre.
- **Hurricanes** move westwards at about 20 km/h. They strike east coasts, bringing torrential rain and winds gusting up to 360 km/h.
- **Officially** a hurricane is a storm with winds exceeding 119 km/h.
- **Hurricanes last,** on average, 3–14 days. They die out as they move towards the Poles into cooler air.
- **Each hurricane** is given a name in alphabetical order each year, from a list issued by the World Meteorological Organization. The first storm of the year might be, for instance, Hurricane Andrew.
- **The most fatal cyclone ever** was the one that struck Bangladesh in 1970. It killed 266,000 with the flood from the storm surge – the rapid rise in sea level created as winds drive ocean waters ashore.
- **A hurricane** generates the same energy every second as a small hydrogen bomb.
- **Each year** 35 tropical storms reach hurricane status in the Atlantic Ocean, and 85 around the world.

◀ *A satellite view of a hurricane approaching Florida, USA. Notice the yellow eye in the centre of the storm.*

Tsunamis

- **Tsunamis** are huge waves that begin when the sea floor is violently shaken by an earthquake, a landslide or a volcanic eruption.
- **In deep water** tsunamis travel almost unnoticeably below the surface. However, once they reach shallow coastal waters they rear up into waves 30 m or higher.
- **Tsunamis** are often mistakenly called 'tidal waves', but they are nothing to do with tides. The word *tsunami* (soon-army) is Japanese for 'harbour wave'.
- **Tsunamis** usually come in a series of a dozen or more – anything from five minutes to one hour apart.
- **Before a tsunami arrives,** the sea may recede dramatically, like water draining from a bath.
- **Tsunamis can travel** along the sea-bed as fast as a jet plane, at 700 km/h or more.
- **Tsunamis** arrive within 15 minutes from a local quake.
- **A tsunami** generated by an earthquake in Japan might swamp San Francisco, USA, 10 hours later .
- **The biggest tsunami** ever recorded was an 85-m high wave which struck Japan on April 24, 1771.
- **Tsunami warnings** are issued by the Pacific Tsunami Warning Centre in Honolulu.

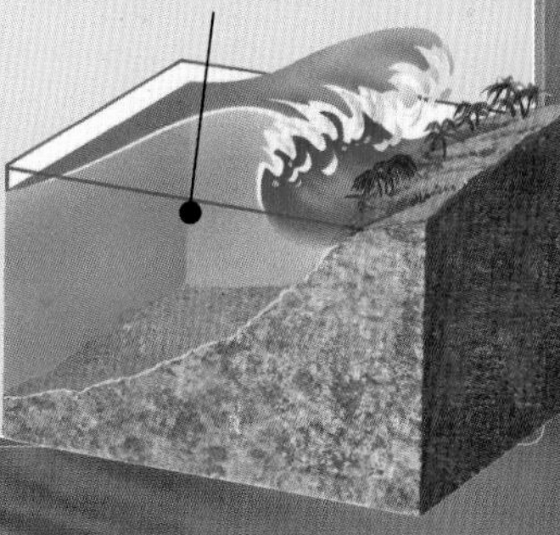

▶ *Tsunamis may be generated underwater by an earthquake, then travel far along the seabed before emerging to swamp a coast.*

The Indian Ocean

▲ *Many of the Indian Ocean's islands have shining coral beaches.*

- **The Indian Ocean** is the third largest ocean. It is about half the size of the Pacific and covers one-fifth of the world's ocean area. Area: 73,426,000 sq km.
- **The average depth** of the Indian Ocean is 3,890 m.
- **The deepest point** is the Java Trench off Java, in Indonesia, which is 7,450 m deep. It marks the line where the Australian plate is being subducted (see converging plates) under the Eurasian plate.
- **The Indian Ocean** is 10,000 km across at its widest point, between Africa and Australia.
- **Scientists believe** that the Indian Ocean began to form about 200 million years ago when Australia broke away from Africa, followed by India.
- **The Indian Ocean** is getting 20 cm wider every year.
- **The Indian Ocean** is scattered with thousands of tropical islands such as the Seychelles and Maldives.
- **The Maldives** are so low lying that they may be swamped if global warming melts the polar ice.
- **Unlike in other oceans,** currents in the Indian Ocean change course twice a year. They are blown by monsoon winds towards Africa in winter, and then in the other direction towards India in summer.
- **The Persian Gulf** is the warmest sea in the world; the Red Sea is the saltiest.

Rivers

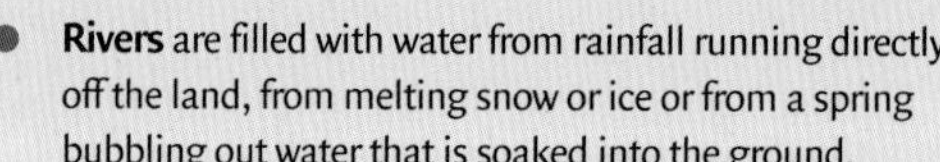

- **Rivers** are filled with water from rainfall running directly off the land, from melting snow or ice or from a spring bubbling out water that is soaked into the ground.
- **High up in mountains** near their source (start), rivers are usually small. They tumble over rocks through narrow valleys which they carved out over thousands of years.
- **All the rivers** in a certain area, called a catchment area, flow down to join each other, like branches on a tree. The branches are called tributaries. The bigger the river, the more tributaries it is likely to have.
- **As rivers flow downhill**, they are joined by tributaries and grow bigger. They often flow in smooth channels made not of big rocks but of fine debris washed down from higher up. River valleys are wider and gentler lower down, and the river may wind across the valley floor.
- **In its lower reaches** a river is often wide and deep. It winds back and forth in meanders (see river channels) across broad floodplains made of silt from higher up.

▲ *A river typically tumbles over boulders high up near its source.*

- **Rivers flow fast** over rapids in their upper reaches. On average, they flow as fast in the lower reaches where the channel is smoother because there is less turbulence.
- **Rivers wear away** their banks and beds, mainly by battering them with bits of gravel and sand and by the sheer force of the moving water.
- **Every river** carries sediment, which consists of large stones rolled along the river bed, sand bounced along the bed and fine silt that floats in the water.
- **The discharge of a river** is the amount of water flowing past a particular point each second (in cubic m per sec).
- **Rivers that flow** only after heavy rainstorms are 'intermittent'. Rivers that flow all year round are 'perennial' – they are kept going between rains by water flowing from underground.

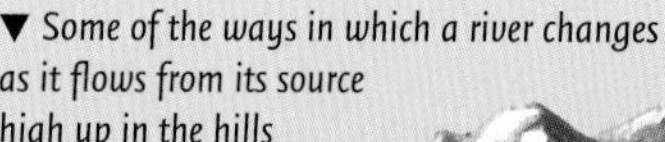

▼ *Some of the ways in which a river changes as it flows from its source high up in the hills downwards to the sea.*

The neck of a meander may in time be worn through to leave an oxbow lake

In its lower reaches, a river winds broadly and smoothly across flat floodplains

In its upper reaches, a river tumbles over rocks through steep valleys

In its middle reaches, a river winds through broad valleys

Over flat land, a river may split into branches

Tornadoes

- **Tornadoes,** or twisters, are long funnels of violently spiralling winds beneath thunderclouds.
- **Tornadoes** roar past in just a few minutes, but they can cause severe damage.
- **Wind speeds** inside tornadoes are difficult to measure, but they are believed to be over 400 km/h.
- **Tornadoes develop** beneath huge thunderclouds, called supercells, which develop along cold fronts.
- **England** has more tornadoes per square kilometre than any other country, but they are usually mild.
- **Tornado Alley** in Kansas, USA, has 1,000 tornadoes a year. Some of them are immensely powerful.
- **A tornado** may be rated on the Fujita scale, from F zero (gale tornado) to F6 (inconceivable tornado).

★ STAR FACT ★
In 1879, a Kansas tornado tore up an iron bridge and sucked dry the river beneath it.

- **An F5 tornado** (incredible tornado) can lift a house and carry a bus hundreds of metres.
- **In 1990** a Kansas tornado lifted an 88-car train from the track and then dropped it in piles four cars high.

▶ *A tornado starts deep inside a thundercloud, where a column of strongly rising warm air is set spinning by high winds roaring through the cloud's top. As air is sucked into this column, or mesocyclone, it corkscrews down to the ground.*

Crust

▶ *The Horn of Africa and the Red Sea is one of the places where the Earth's thin oceanic crust is cracked and moving. It is gradually widening the Red Sea.*

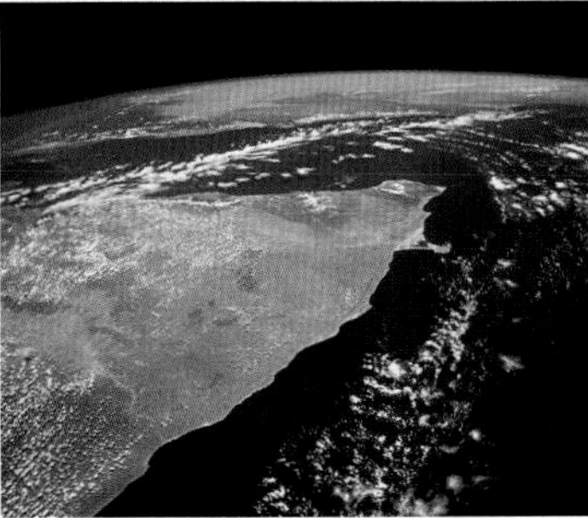

- **The Earth's crust** is its hard outer shell.
- **The crust** is a thin layer of dense solid rock that floats on the mantle. It is made mainly of silicate minerals (minerals made of silicon and oxygen) such as quartz.
- **There are two kinds of crust:** oceanic and continental.
- **Oceanic crust** is the crust beneath the oceans. It is much thinner – just 7 km thick on average. It is also young, with none being over 200 million years old.
- **Continental crust** is the crust beneath the continents. It is up to 80 km thick and mostly old.
- **Continental crust** is mostly crystalline 'basement' rock up to 3,800 million years old. Some geologists think at least half of this rock is over 2,500 million years old.
- **One cubic kilometre** of new continental crust is probably being created each year.
- **The 'basement' rock** has two main layers: an upper half of silica-rich rocks such as granite, schist and gneiss, and a lower half of volcanic rocks such as basalt which have less silica. Ocean crust is mostly basalt.
- **Continental crust** is created in the volcanic arcs above subduction zones (see converging plates). Molten rock from the subducted plate oozes to the surface over a period of a few hundred thousand years.
- **The boundary** between the crust and the mantle beneath it is called the Mohorovicic discontinuity.

Tectonic plates

- **The Earth's surface** is divided into thick slabs called tectonic plates. Each plate is a fragment of the Earth's rigid outer layer, or lithosphere (see the lithosphere).
- **There are 16 large plates** and several smaller ones.
- **The biggest plate** is the Pacific plate, which underlies the whole of the Pacific Ocean.
- **Tectonic plates** are moving all the time – by about 10 cm a year. Over hundreds of millions of years they move vast distances. Some have moved halfway round the globe.
- **The continents** are embedded within most of the plates and move with them.
- **The Pacific plate** is the only large plate with no part of a continent situated on it.
- **The movement** of tectonic plates accounts for many things, including the pattern of volcanic and earthquake activity around the world.
- **There are three kinds** of boundary between plates: convergent, divergent and transform.
- **Tectonic plates** are probably driven by convection currents of molten rock that circulate within the Earth's mantle (see core and mantle).
- **The lithosphere** was too thin for tectonic plates until 500 million years ago.

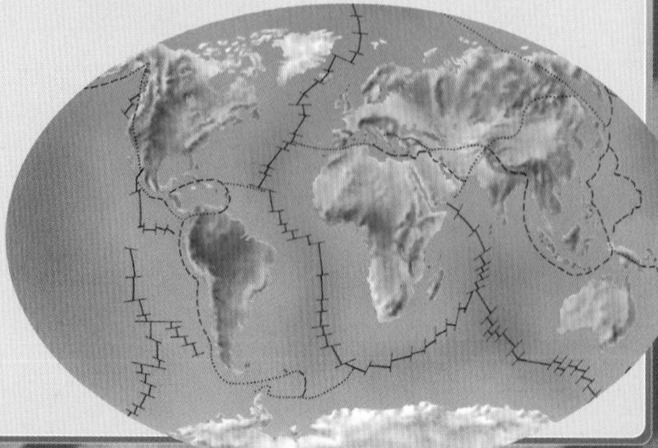

▶ *This map shows some of the jagged boundaries between plates.*

The ozone hole

▲ *The loss of ozone was first spotted by scientists in the Antarctic.*

- **Life on Earth** depends on the layer of ozone gas in the air (see atmosphere), which shields the Earth from the Sun's ultraviolet (UV) rays. Ozone molecules are made from three atoms of oxygen, not two like oxygen.
- **In 1982** scientists in Antarctica noticed a 50% loss of ozone over the Antarctic every spring. This finding was confirmed in 1985 by the *Nimbus-7* satellite.
- **The ozone hole** is a patch where the ozone layer becomes very thin.

! NEWS FLASH !
In 1996 an ozone hole appeared over the Arctic for the first time – and it is now getting bigger.

- **The ozone hole** appears over Antarctica every spring.
- **The ozone hole** is monitored all the time by the TOMS (Total Ozone Mapping Spectrometer) satellite.
- **The loss of ozone** is caused by manufactured gases, notably chlorofluorocarbons (CFCs), which drift up through the air and combine with the ozone.
- **CFCs** are used in many things, from refrigerators and aerosol sprays to forming the foam for fast-food cartons.
- **CFCs** were banned in 1996, but it may be at least 100 years before the ban takes effect. The hole is still growing.
- **UV rays** from the Sun come in three kinds: UVA, UVB and UVC. Both oxygen and ozone soak up UVA and UVC rays, but only ozone absorbs UVB. For every 1% loss of ozone, 1% more UVB rays reach the Earth's surface.

Minerals

- **Minerals** are the natural chemicals from which rocks are made.
- **All but a few minerals** are crystals.
- **Some rocks are made** from crystals of just one mineral; many are made from half a dozen or more minerals.
- **Most minerals** are combinations of two or more chemical elements. A few minerals, such as gold and copper, are made of just one element.
- **There are over 2,000** minerals, but around 30 of these are very common.
- **Most of the less common** minerals are present in rocks in minute traces. They may become concentrated in certain places by geological processes.

▲ *The rich range of colours in each layer is evidence of traces of different minerals within the rocks.*

- **Silicate minerals** are made when metals join with oxygen and silicon. There are more silicate minerals than all the other minerals together.
- **The most common** silicates are quartz and feldspar, the most common rock-forming minerals. They are major constituents in granite and other volcanic rocks.
- **Other common minerals** are oxides such as haematite and cuprite, sulphates such as gypsum and barite, sulphides such as galena and pyrite, and carbonates such as calcite and aragonite.
- **Some minerals** form as hot, molten rock from the Earth's interior, some from chemicals dissolved in liquids underground, and some are made by changes to other minerals.

The Pacific Ocean

- **The Pacific** is the world's largest ocean. It is twice as large as the Atlantic and covers over one third of the world, with an area of 181 million sq km.
- **It is over 24,000 km** across from Panama to the Malay Peninsula – more than halfway round the world.
- **The word 'pacific'** means calm. The ocean got its name from the 16th-century Portuguese explorer Magellan who was lucky enough to find gentle winds.
- **The Pacific is dotted** with thousands of islands. Some are the peaks of undersea volcanoes. Others are coral reefs sitting on top of the peaks.
- **The Pacific** has some of the greatest tides in the world (over 9 m off Korea). Its smallest tide (just 0.3 m) is on Midway Island in the middle of the Pacific.
- **On average,** the Pacific Ocean is 4,200 m deep.
- **Around the rim** there are deep ocean trenches including the world's deepest, the Mariana Trench.
- **A huge** undersea mountain range called the East Pacific Rise stretches from Antarctica up to Mexico.
- **The floor of the Pacific** is spreading along the East Pacific Rise at the rate of 12–16 cm per year.
- **The Pacific** has more seamounts (undersea mountains) than any other ocean.

▼ *The huge expanse of the Pacific means that waves breaking on the coast are often enormous – and popular with surfers.*

Volcanic eruptions

- **Volcanic eruptions** are produced by magma, the hot liquid rock under the Earth's surface. Magma is less dense than the rock above, and so it tries to bubble to the surface.
- **When magma** is runny, eruptions are 'effusive', which means they ooze lava gently all the time.
- **When magma** is sticky, eruptions are explosive. The magma clogs the volcano's vent until so much pressure builds up that the magma bursts out , like a popping champagne cork.

▲ *There are about 60 major volcanic eruptions a year round the world, including two or three huge, violent eruptions.*

★ STAR FACT ★
Pressure of the magma below a volcano is 10 times greater than pressure on the surface.

- **The explosion** shatters the plug of hard magma that blocks the volcano's vent, reducing it to ash and cinder.
- **Explosive eruptions** are driven by expanding bubbles of carbon dioxide gas and steam inside the magma.
- **An explosive eruption** blasts globs of hot magma, ash, cinder, gas and steam high up into the air.
- **Volcanoes** usually erupt again and again. The interval between eruptions, called the repose time, varies from a few minutes to thousands of years.
- **Magma near subduction zones** contains 10 times more gas, so the volcanic eruptions here are violent.
- **The gas inside magma** can expand hundreds of times in just a few seconds.

Mountain ranges

- **Great mountain ranges** such as the Andes in South America usually lie along the edges of continents.
- **Most mountain ranges** are made by the folding of rock layers (see folds) as tectonic plates move slowly together.
- **High ranges** are geologically young because they are soon worn down. The Himalayas are 25 million years old.
- **Many ranges** are still growing. The Himalayas grow a few centimetres each year as the Indian plate pushes into Asia.

- **Mountain** building is very slow because rocks flow like thick treacle. Rock is pushed up like the bow wave in front of a boat as one tectonic plate pushes into another.
- **Satellite techniques** show that the central peaks of the Andes and Himalayas are rising. The outer peaks are sinking as the rock flows slowly away from the 'bow wave'.
- **Mountain building** is very active during orogenic (mountain- forming) phases that last millions of years.
- **Different orogenic phases** occur in different places, for example the Caledonian, Hercynian and Alpine in Europe and the Huronian, Nevadian and Pasadenian in North America. The Caledonian was about 550 million years ago.
- **Mountain building** makes the Earth's crust especially thick under mountains, giving them very deep 'roots'.
- **As mountains** are worn down, their weight reduces and the 'roots' float upwards. This is called isostasy.

◀ *Mountain ranges are thrown up by the crumpling of rock strata (layers) as the tectonic plates of the Earth's surface crunch together.*

Weather fronts

▼ *This illustration shows two short sections through the cold and warm weather fronts that are linked to depressions in the mid-latitudes.*

- **A weather front** is where a big mass of warm air meets a big mass of cold air.
- **At a warm front,** the mass of warm air is moving faster than the cold air. The warm air slowly rises over the cold air in a wedge. It slopes gently up to 1.5 km over 300 km.
- **At a cold front,** the mass of cold air is moving faster. It undercuts the warm air, forcing it to rise sharply and creating a steeply sloping front . The front climbs to 1.5 km over about 100 km.
- **In the mid-latitudes,** fronts are linked to vast spiralling weather systems called depressions, or lows. These are centred on a region of low pressure where warm, moist air rises. Winds spiral into the low – anticlockwise in the Northern Hemisphere, clockwise in the Southern.
- **Lows start** along the polar front, which stretches round the world. Here, cold air spreading out from the Poles meets warm, moist air moving up from the subtropics.
- **Lows develop** as a kink in the polar front. They then grow bigger as strong winds in the upper air drag them eastwards, bringing rain, snow and blustery winds. A wedge of warm air intrudes into the heart of the low, and the worst weather occurs along the edges of the wedge. One edge is a warm front, the other is a cold front.
- **The warm front arrives first,** heralded by feathery cirrus clouds of ice high in the sky. As the front moves over, the sky fills with slate-grey nimbostratus clouds that bring steady rain. As the warm front passes away, the weather becomes milder and skies may briefly clear.
- **After a few hours,** a build-up of thunderclouds and gusty winds warn that the cold front is on its way. When it arrives, the clouds unleash short, heavy showers, and sometimes thunderstorms or even tornadoes.
- **After the cold front passes,** the air grows colder and the sky clears, leaving just a few fluffy cumulus clouds.
- **Meteorologists** think that depressions are linked to strong winds, called jet streams, which circle the Earth high above the polar front. The depression may begin with Rossby waves, which are giant kinks in the jet stream up to 2,000 km long.

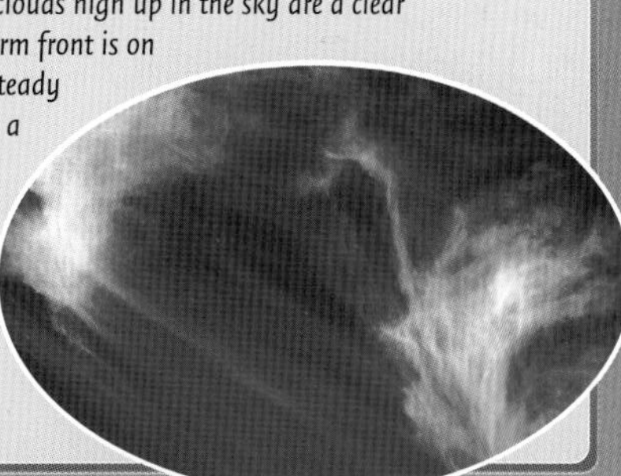

▶ *Feathery cirrus clouds high up in the sky are a clear warning that a warm front is on its way, bringing steady rain. When there is a warm front, a cold front is likely to follow, bringing heavy rain, strong winds and perhaps even a thunderstorm.*

The Southern Ocean

- **The Southern Ocean** is the world's fourth largest ocean. It stretches all the way round Antarctica, and has an area of 35,000,000 sq km.
- **It is the only ocean** that stretches all around the world.
- **In winter** over half the Southern Ocean is covered with ice and icebergs that break off the Antarctic ice sheet.
- **The East Wind Drift** is a current that flows anticlockwise around Antarctica close to the coast.

★ STAR FACT ★

The circumpolar current could fill the Great Lakes in North America in just 48 hours.

- **Further out** from the coast of Antarctica, the Antarctic circumpolar current flows in the opposite direction – clockwise from west to east.
- **The circumpolar current** carries more water than any other current in the world.
- **The 'Roaring Forties'** is the band between 40° and 50° South latitude. Within this band strong westerly winds blow unobstructed around the world.
- **The waves in the 'Roaring Forties'** are the biggest in the world, sometimes higher than a ten-storey building.
- **Sea ice** forms in round pieces called pancake ice.

◀ *Many penguins such as the emperor, the world's largest penguin, live on the ice floes of the Southern Ocean.*

North America

- **North America** is the world's third largest continent. It has an area of 24,230,000 sq km.
- **North America** is a triangle, with its long side bounded by the icy Arctic Ocean and its short side by the tropical Caribbean Sea.
- **The north** of North America lies inside the Arctic Circle and is icebound for much of the year. Death Valley, in the southwestern desert in California and Nevada, is one of the hottest places on the Earth.
- **Mountain ranges** run down each side of North America – the ancient, worn-down Appalachians in the east and the younger, higher Rockies in the west.
- **In between** the mountains lie vast interior plains. These plains are based on very old rocks, the oldest of which are in the Canadian Shield in the north.
- **North America** is the oldest continent on the Earth. It has rocks that are almost 4,000 million years old.
- **The Grand Canyon** is one of the world's most spectacular gorges. It is 440 km long, and 1,800 m deep in places.
- **The longest river** in North America is the Mississippi–Missouri, at 6,019 km long.
- **The highest mountain** is Mt McKinley in Alaska, 6,194 m high.
- **The Great Lakes** contain one-fifth of the world's freshwater.

▶ *North America broke away from Europe about 100 million years ago. It is still moving 2.5 cm farther every year.*

Weather forecasting

- **Weather forecasting** relies partly on powerful computers, which analyse the Earth's atmosphere.
- **One kind of weather prediction** divides the air into parcels. These are stacked in columns above grid points spread throughout the world.
- **There are over one million** grid points, each with a stack of at least 30 parcels above it.

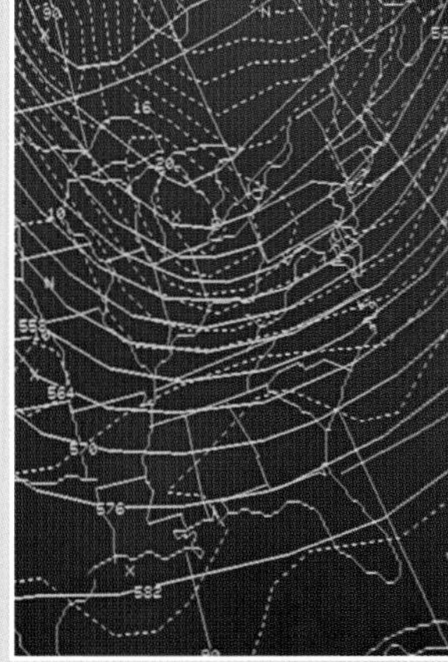

▶ *This weather map shows isobars – lines of equal air pressure – over North America. It has been compiled from millions of observations.*

- **Weather observatories** take millions of simultaneous measurements of weather conditions at regular intervals each day.
- **Every 3 hours** 10,000 land-based weather stations record conditions on the ground. Every 12 hours ballooons fitted with radiosondes go into the atmosphere to record conditions high up.
- **Satellites in the sky** give an overview of developing weather patterns.
- **Infrared satellite images** show temperatures on the Earth's surface.
- **Cloud motion winds** show the wind speed and wind direction from the way in which the clouds move.
- **Supercomputers** allow the weather to be predicted accurately 3 days in advance, and for up to 14 days in advance with some confidence.
- **Astrophysicist** Piers Corbyn has developed a forecasting system linked to variations in the Sun's activity.

River valleys

- **Rivers** carve out valleys as they wear away their channels.
- **High up in the mountains,** much of a river's energy goes into carving into the river bed. The valleys there are deep, with steep sides.
- **Farther down** towards the sea, more of a river's erosive energy goes into wearing away its banks. It carves out a broader valley as it winds back and forth.
- **Large meanders** normally develop only when a river is crossing broad plains in its lower reaches.
- **Incised meanders** are meanders carved into deep valleys. The meanders formed when the river was flowing across a low plain. The plain was lifted up and the river cut down into it, keeping its meanders.
- **The Grand Canyon** is made of incised meanders. They were created as the Colorado River cut into the Colorado Plateau after it was uplifted 17 million years ago.
- **The shape of a river valley** depends partly on the structure of the rocks over which it is flowing.

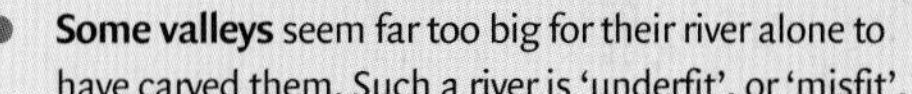

- **Some valleys** seem far too big for their river alone to have carved them. Such a river is 'underfit', or 'misfit'.
- **Many large valleys** with misfit rivers were carved out by glaciers or glacial meltwaters.
- **The world's rivers** wear the entire land surface down by an average of 8 cm every 1,000 years.

▼ *Rivers carve out valleys over hundreds of thousands of years as they grind material along their beds.*

Earth's interior

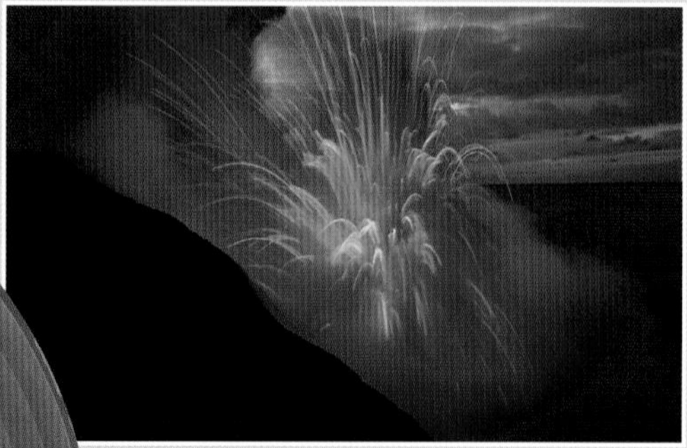

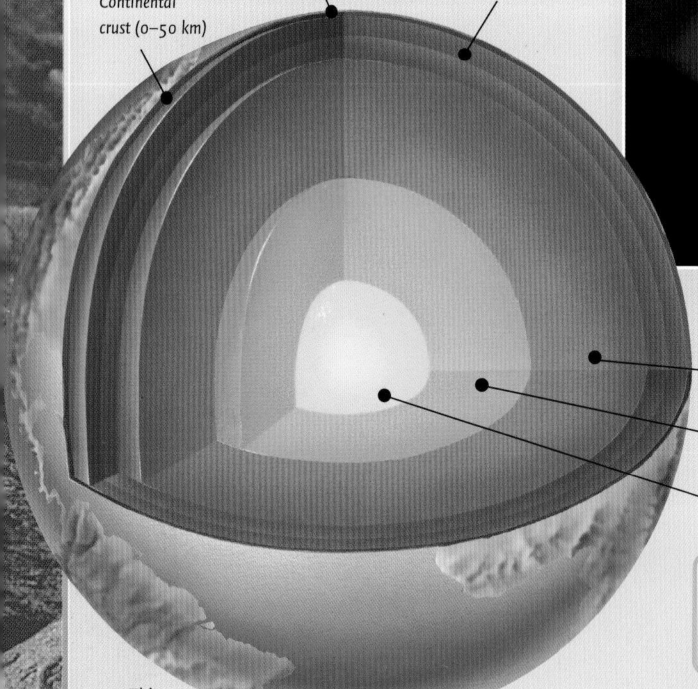

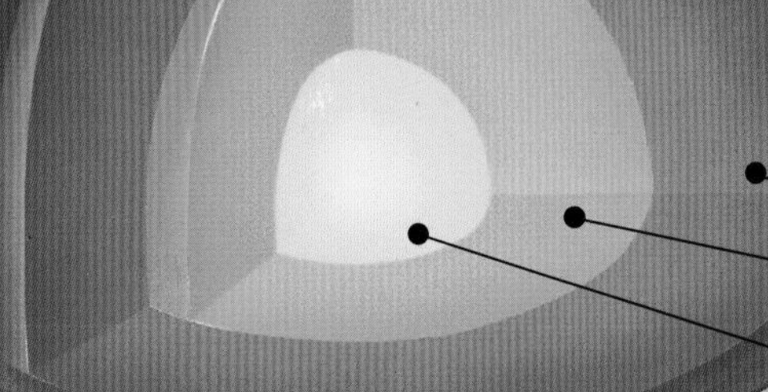

▲ Hot material from the Earth's interior often bursts on to the surface from volcanoes.

▲ This illustration shows the main layers inside the Earth.

★ **STAR FACT** ★

The deepest drill into the Earth is on the Kola Peninsula in Arctic Russia. It has penetrated just 12 km into the crust.

- **The Earth's crust** (see crust) is a thin hard outer shell of rock which is a few dozen kilometres thick. Its thickness in relation to the Earth is about the same as the skin on an apple.
- **Under the crust**, there is a deep layer of hot soft rock called the mantle (see core and mantle).
- **The crust and upper mantle** can be divided into three layers according to their rigidity: the lithosphere, the asthenosphere and the mesosphere.
- **Beneath the mantle** is a core of hot iron and nickel. The outer core is so hot – climbing from 4,500°C to 6,000°C – that it is always molten. The inner core is even hotter (up to 7,000°C) but it stays solid because the pressure is 6,000 times greater than on the surface.
- **The inner core** contains 1.7% of the Earth's mass, the outer core 30.8%; the core–mantle boundary 3%; the lower mantle 49%; the upper mantle 15%; the ocean crust 0.099% and the continental crust 0.374%.
- **Satellite measurements** are so accurate they can detect slight lumps and dents in the Earth's surface. These indicate where gravity is stronger or weaker because of differences in rock density. Variations in gravity reveal things such as mantle plumes (see hot-spot volcanoes).
- **Our knowledge of the Earth's interior** comes mainly from studying how earthquake waves vibrate right through the Earth.
- **Analysis of how earthquake waves** are deflected reveals where different materials occur in the interior. S (secondary) waves pass only through the mantle. P (primary) waves pass through the core as well. P waves passing through the core are deflected, leaving a shadow zone where no waves reach the far side of the Earth.
- **The speed of earthquake waves** reveals how dense the rocky materials are. Cold, hard rock transmits waves more quickly than hot, soft rock.

High mountains

- **A few high mountains** are lone volcanoes, such as Africa's Kilimanjaro, which are built by many eruptions.
- **Some volcanic mountains** are in chains in volcanic arcs (see volcano zones), such as Japan's Fujiyama.
- **Most high mountains** are part of great mountain ranges stretching hundreds of kilometres.
- **Some mountain ranges** are huge slabs of rock called fault blocks (see faults). They were forced up by quakes.
- **The biggest mountain ranges,** such as the Himalayas and the Andes, are fold mountains.
- **The height of mountains** used to be measured from the ground, using levels and sighting devices to measure angles. Now mountains are measured more accurately using satellite techniques.
- **Satellite measurements** in 1999 raised the height of the world's highest peak, Mt Everest in Nepal in the Himalayas, from 8,848 m to 8,850 m.
- **All 14 of the world's peaks** over 8,000 m are in the Himalayas – in Nepal, China and Kashmir.
- **Temperatures drop 0.6°C** for every 100 m you climb, so mountain peaks are very cold and often covered in snow.
- **The air** is thinner on mountains, so the air pressure is lower. Climbers may need oxygen masks to breathe.

▼ *High peaks are jagged because massive folding fractures the rock and makes it very vulnerable to the sharp frosts high up.*

Limestone weathering

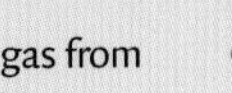
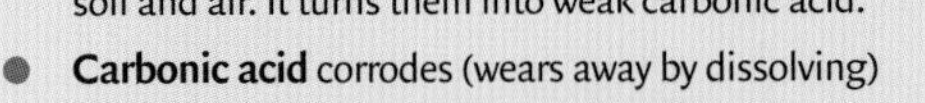

- **Streams and rainwater** absorb carbon dioxide gas from soil and air. It turns them into weak carbonic acid.
- **Carbonic acid** corrodes (wears away by dissolving) limestone in a process called carbonation.
- **When limestone rock** is close to the surface, carbonation can create spectacular scenery.
- **Corroded limestone scenery** is often called karst, because the best example of it is the Karst Plateau near Dalmatia, in Bosnia.

- **On the surface,** carbonation eats away along cracks to create pavements, with slabs called clints. The slabs are separated by deeply etched grooves called grykes.
- **Limestone rock** does not soak up water like a sponge. It has massive cracks called joints, and streams and rainwater trickle deep into the rock through these cracks.
- **Streams** drop down into limestone through swallow-holes, like bathwater down a plughole. Carbonation eats out such holes to form giant shafts called potholes.
- **Some potholes** are eaten out to create great funnel-shaped hollows called dolines, up to 100 m across.
- **Where water** streams out along horizontal cracks at the base of potholes, the rock may be etched out into caverns.
- **Caverns** may be eaten out so much that the roof collapses to form a gorge or a large hole called a polje.

◀ *Corrosion by underground streams in limestone can eat out huge caverns, often filled with spectacular stalactites (see caves).*

Icebergs

- **Icebergs** are big lumps of floating ice that calve, or break off, from the end of glaciers or polar ice caps. This often occurs when tides and waves move the ice up and down.
- **Calving of icebergs occurs** mostly during the summer when the warm conditions partially melt the ice.
- **Around 15,000 icebergs a year** calve in the Arctic.
- **Arctic icebergs** vary from car-sized ones called growlers to mansion-sized blocks.The biggest iceberg, 11 km long, was spotted off Baffin Island in 1882.
- **The Petterman and Jungersen** glaciers in northern Greenland form big table-shaped icebergs called ice islands. They are like the icebergs found in Antarctica.
- **Antarctic icebergs** are much, much bigger than Arctic ones. The biggest iceberg, which was 300 km long, was spotted in 1956 by the icebreaker USS *Glacier*.
- **Antarctic icebergs** last for ten years on average; Arctic icebergs last for about two years.
- **The ice** that makes Arctic icebergs is 3,000–6,000 years old.
- **Each year 375 or so icebergs** drift from Greenland into the shipping lanes off Newfoundland. They are a major hazard to shipping in that area.
- **The International Ice Patrol** was set up in 1914 to monitor icebergs after the great liner *Titanic* was sunk. The liner hit an iceberg off Newfoundland in 1912.

▼ *Icebergs are big chunks of floating ice that break off glaciers.*

The Atlantic Ocean

- **The Atlantic Ocean** is the world's second largest ocean, with an area of 82 million sq km. It covers about one-fifth of the world's surface.
- **At its widest point,** between Spain and Mexico, the Atlantic is 9,600 km across.
- **The Atlantic** was named by the ancient Romans after the Atlas Mountains of North Africa. The Atlas were at the limit of their known world.

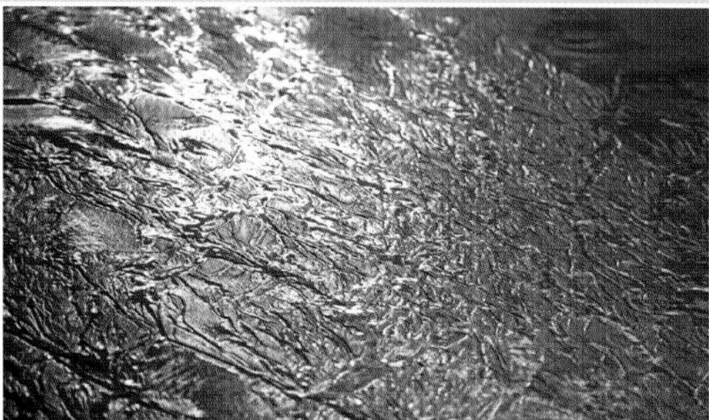

- **There are very few islands** in the main part of the Atlantic Ocean. Most lie close to the continents.
- **On average,** the Atlantic is about 3,660 m deep.
- **The deepest point** in the Atlantic is the Puerto Rico Trench off Puerto Rico, which is 8,648 m deep.
- **The Mid-Atlantic Ridge** is a great undersea ridge which splits the sea-bed in half. Along this ridge, the Atlantic is growing wider by 2–4 cm every year.
- **Islands** in the mid-Atlantic are volcanoes that lie along the Mid-Atlantic Ridge, such as the Azores and Ascension Island.
- **The Sargasso Sea** is a huge area of water in the western Atlantic. It is famous for its floating seaweed.
- **The Atlantic** is a youngish ocean, about 150 million years old.

◀ *The damp, cool climate of the northern Atlantic frequently turns its waters steely grey.*

Wind

- **Wind is moving air.** Strong winds are fast-moving air; gentle breezes are air that moves slowly.
- **Air moves** because the Sun warms some places more than others, creating differences in air pressure.
- **Warmth makes** air expand and rise, lowering air pressure. Cold makes air heavier, raising pressure.
- **Winds blow** from areas of high pressure to areas of low pressure, which are called lows.

▲ *The more of the Sun's energy there is in the air, the windier it is. This is why the strongest winds may blow in the warm tropics.*

★ **STAR FACT** ★
The world's windiest place is George V in Antarctica, where 320 km/h winds are usual.

- **The sharper the pressure difference,** or gradient, the stronger the winds blow.
- **In the Northern Hemisphere,** winds spiral in a clockwise direction out of highs, and anticlockwise into lows. In the Southern Hemisphere, the reverse is true.
- **A prevailing wind** is a wind that blows frequently from the same direction. Winds are named by the direction they blow from. A westerly wind blows from the west.
- **In the tropics** the prevailing winds are warm, dry trade winds. They blow from the northeast and the southeast towards the Equator.
- **In the mid-latitudes** the prevailing winds are warm, moist westerlies.

South America

- **South America** is the world's fourth largest continent. It has an area of 17,814,000 sq km.
- **The Andes Mountains,** which run over 4,500 km down the west side, are the world's longest mountain range.
- **The heart of South America** is the vast Amazon rain-forest around the Amazon River and its tributaries.
- **The southeast** is dominated by the huge grasslands of the Gran Chaco, the Pampas and Patagonia.
- **No other continent** reaches so far south. South America extends to within 1,000 km of the Antarctic Circle.
- **Three-quarters of South America** is in the tropics. In the high Andes are large zones of cool, temperate climate.
- **Quito, in Ecuador,** is called the 'Land of Eternal Spring' because its temperature never drops below 8°C at night, and never climbs above 22°C during the day.
- **The highest volcanic peak** is Aconcagua, 6,960 m high.
- **Eastern South America** was joined to western Africa until the Atlantic began to open up 90 million years ago.

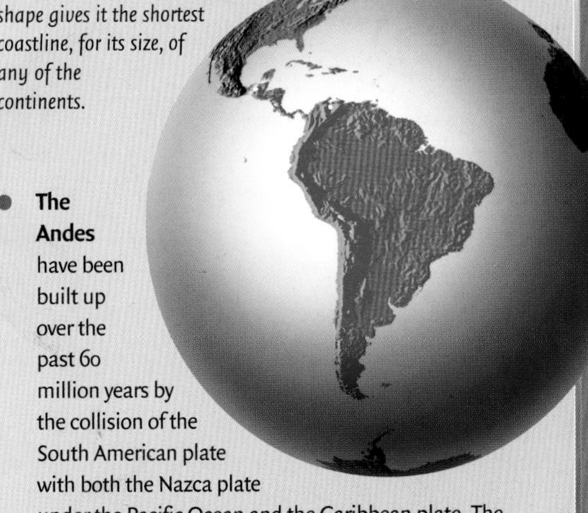

▶ *South America's triangular shape gives it the shortest coastline, for its size, of any of the continents.*

- **The Andes** have been built up over the past 60 million years by the collision of the South American plate with both the Nazca plate under the Pacific Ocean and the Caribbean plate. The subduction of the Nazca plate has created the world's highest active volcanoes in the Andes.

Cold landscapes

▲ *Cold conditions have a dramatic effect on the landscape.*

- **'Periglacial'** used to describe conditions next to the ice in the Ice Ages. It now means similar conditions found today.
- **Periglacial conditions** are found on the tundra of northern Canada and Siberia and on nunataks, which are the hills that protrude above ice sheets and glaciers.
- **In periglacial areas** ice only melts in spring at the surface. Deep down under the ground it remains permanently frozen permafrost.
- **When the ground** above the permafrost melts, the soil twists into buckled layers called involutions.
- **When frozen soil melts** it becomes so fluid that it can creep easily down slopes, creating large tongues and terraces.
- **Frost heave** is the process when frost pushes stones to the surface as the ground freezes.
- **After frost heave,** large stones roll down leaving the fine stones on top. This creates intricate patterns on the ground.
- **On flat ground,** quilt-like patterns are called stone polygons. On slopes, they stretch into stone stripes.
- **Pingos** are mounds of soil with a core of ice. They are created when groundwater freezes beneath a lake.

> ★ **STAR FACT** ★
> In periglacial conditions temperatures never ever climb above freezing in winter.

Tides

- **Tides are the way** in which the sea rises a little then falls back every 12 hours or so.
- **When the tide is flowing** it is rising. When the tide is ebbing it is falling.
- **Tides are caused** by the pull of gravity between the Earth, the Moon and the Sun.
- **The mutual pull** of the Moon's and the Earth's gravity stretches the Earth into an egg shape.
- **The solid Earth** is so rigid that it stretches only 20 cm.
- **Ocean waters** can flow freely over the Earth to create two tidal bulges (high tides) of water. One bulge is directly under the Moon, the other is on the far side of the Earth.
- **As the Earth rotates** every 24 hours the tidal bulges stay in the same place under the Moon. Each place on the ocean has high tide twice a day. The Moon is moving as well as the Earth, making high tides occur not once every 12 hours but once every 12 hours 25 minutes.

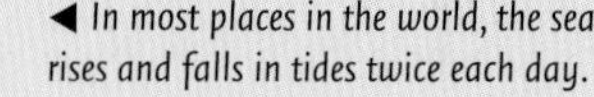

◀ *In most places in the world, the sea rises and falls in tides twice each day.*

- **The continents** get in the way, making the tidal bulges slosh about in a complex way. As a result the timing and height of tides vary enormously. In the open ocean tides rise only 1 m or so, but in enclosed spaces such as the Bay of Fundy, in Nova Scotia, Canada they rise over 15 m.
- **The Sun is much farther away** than the Moon, but it is so big that its gravity has an effect on the tides.
- **The Moon and the Sun** line up at a Full and a New Moon, creating high spring tides twice a month. When the Moon and the Sun pull at right angles at a Half Moon, they cause neap tides which are lower than normal tides.

The Ages of the Earth

- **The Earth formed 4,570 million years ago (mya)** but the first animals with shells and bones appeared less than 600 mya. It is mainly with the help of their fossils that geologists have learned about the Earth's history since then. We know very little about the 4,000 million years before, known as Precambrian Time.
- **Just as days are divided** into hours and minutes, so geologists divide the Earth's history into time periods. The longest are eons, thousands of millions of years long. The shortest are chrons, a few thousand years along. In between come eras, periods, epochs and ages.
- **The years since Precambrian Time** are split into three eras: Palaeozoic, Mesozoic and Cenozoic.
- **Different plants and animals** lived at different times, so geologists can tell from the fossils in rocks how long ago the rocks formed. Using fossils, they have divided the Earth's history since Precambrian Time into 11 periods.
- **Layers of rock** form on top of each other, so the oldest rocks are usually at the bottom and the youngest at the top, unless they have been disturbed. The order of layers from top to bottom is known as the geological column.
- **By looking for certain fossils** geologists can tell if one layer of rock is older than another, and so place it within the geological column.
- **Fossils can only show** if a rock is older or younger than another; they cannot give a date in years. Also, many rocks such as igneous rocks contain no fossils. To give an absolute date, geologists may use radiocarbon dating.
- **Radiocarbon dating** allows the oldest rocks on Earth to be dated. After certain substances, such as uranium and rubidium, form in rocks, their atoms slowly break down into different atoms. As atoms break down they send out rays, or radioactivity. By assessing how many atoms in a rock have changed, geologists work out the rock's age.
- **Breaks in the sequence** of the geological column are called unconformities. They help to create a picture of the geological history of an area.

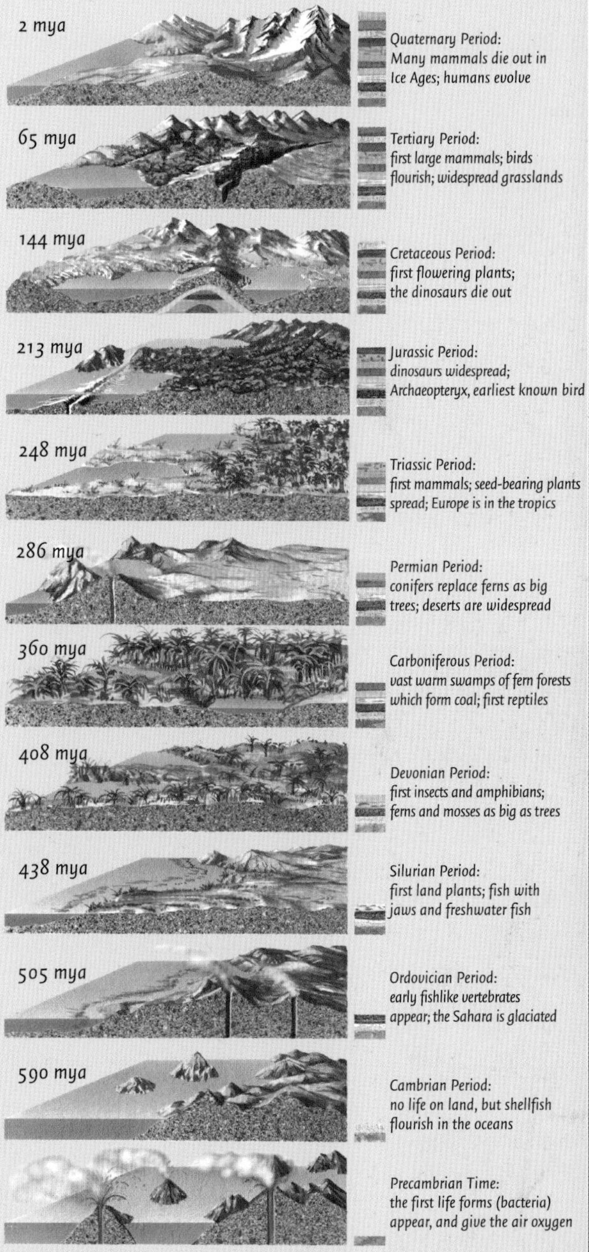

2 mya
Quaternary Period: Many mammals die out in Ice Ages; humans evolve

65 mya
Tertiary Period: first large mammals; birds flourish; widespread grasslands

144 mya
Cretaceous Period: first flowering plants; the dinosaurs die out

213 mya
Jurassic Period: dinosaurs widespread; Archaeopteryx, earliest known bird

248 mya
Triassic Period: first mammals; seed-bearing plants spread; Europe is in the tropics

286 mya
Permian Period: conifers replace ferns as big trees; deserts are widespread

360 mya
Carboniferous Period: vast warm swamps of fern forests which form coal; first reptiles

408 mya
Devonian Period: first insects and amphibians; ferns and mosses as big as trees

438 mya
Silurian Period: first land plants; fish with jaws and freshwater fish

505 mya
Ordovician Period: early fishlike vertebrates appear; the Sahara is glaciated

590 mya
Cambrian Period: no life on land, but shellfish flourish in the oceans

Precambrian Time: the first life forms (bacteria) appear, and give the air oxygen

Lava and ash

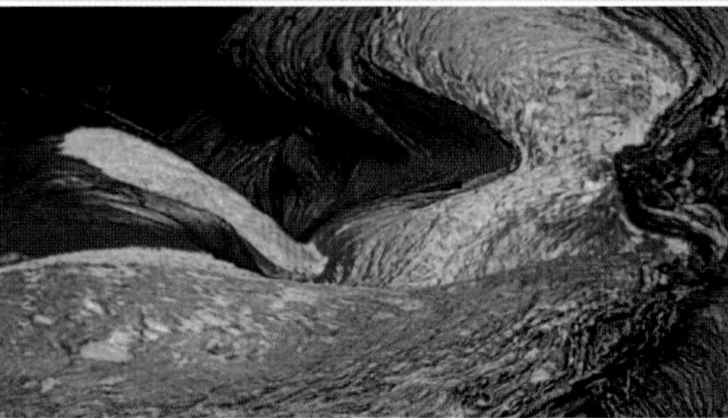

▲ *Runny lava flows in rivers of red-hot molten rock, but sticky lava from subduction zones creeps a few metres a day.*

- **When a volcano erupts** it sends out a variety of hot materials, including lava, tephra, ash and gases.
- **Lava is hot molten rock** from the Earth's interior. It is called magma while it is still underground.
- **Tephra** is material blasted into the air by an eruption. It includes pyroclasts (solid lava) and volcanic bombs.
- **Pyroclasts** are big chunks of volcanic rock that are thrown out by explosive volcanoes when the plug in the volcano's vent shatters. 'Pyroclast' means fire broken. Pyroclasts are usually 0.3 –1 m across.
- **Big eruptions** can blast pyroclasts weighing 1 tonne or more up into the air at the speed of a jet plane.
- **Cinders and lapilli** are small pyroclasts. Cinders are 6.4–30 cm in diameter; lapilli are 0.1–6.4 cm.
- **Volcanic bombs** are blobs of molten magma that cool and harden in flight.
- **Breadcrust bombs** are bombs that stretch into loaf shapes in flight; gases inside them create a 'crust'.
- **Around 90% of the material** ejected by explosive volcanoes is not lava, but tephra and ash.

> **★ STAR FACT ★**
> Pumice rock is made from hardened lava froth – it is so full of air bubbles that it floats.

Fossils

- **Fossils** are the remains of living things preserved for millions of years, usually in stone.
- **Most fossils** are the remains of living things such as bones, shells, eggs, leaves and seeds.
- **Trace fossils** are fossils of signs left behind by creatures, such as footprints and scratch marks.
- **Paleontologists** (scientists who study fossils) tell the age of a fossil from the rock layer in which it is found in. Also, they measure how the rock has changed radioactively since it was formed (radiocarbon dating).
- **The oldest fossils** are called stromatolites. They are fossils of big, pizza-like colonies of microscopic bacteria over 3,500 million years old.

1. A trilobite dies on the ocean floor long ago.

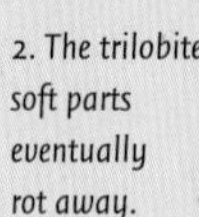

2. The trilobite's soft parts eventually rot away.

3. The shell is slowly buried by mud.

4. Mineral-rich waters dissolve the shell.

5. New minerals fill the mould to form a fossil.

◀ *When an animal dies, its soft parts rot away quickly. If its bones or shell are buried quickly in mud, they may turn to stone. When a shellfish such as this ancient trilobite dies and sinks to the sea-bed, its shell is buried. Over millions of years, water trickling through the mud may dissolve the shell, but minerals in the water fill its place to make a perfect cast.*

- **The biggest fossils** are conyphytons, 2,000-million-year-old stromatolites over 100 m high.
- **Not all fossils** are stone. Mammoths have been preserved by being frozen in the permafrost (see cold landscapes) of Siberia.
- **Insects** have been preserved in amber, the solidified sap of ancient trees.
- **Certain widespread, short-lived fossils** are very useful for dating rock layers. These are known as index fossils.
- **Index fossils** include ancient shellfish such as trilobites, graptolites, crinoids, beleminites, ammonites and brachiopods.

Air pressure

- **Although air is light,** there is so much of it that air can exert huge pressure at ground level. Air pressure is the constant bombardment of billions of air molecules as they zoom about.
- **Air pushes** in all directions at ground level with a force of over 1 kg per sq cm – that is the equivalent of an elephant standing on a coffee table.
- **Air pressure varies** constantly from place to place and from time to time as the Sun's heat varies.
- **Air pressure** is measured with a device called a barometer in units called millibars (mb for short).
- **Normal air pressure** at sea level is 1,013 mb, but it can vary between 800 mb and 1,050 mb.
- **Air pressure** is shown on weather maps with lines called isobars, which join together places of equal pressure.
- **High-pressure zones** are called anticyclones; low-pressure zones are called cyclones, or depressions.
- **Barometers** help us to forecast weather because changes in air pressure are linked to changes in weather.
- **A fall in air pressure** warns that stormy weather is on its way, because depressions are linked to storms.
- **Steady high pressure** indicates clear weather, because sinking air in a high means that clouds cannot form.

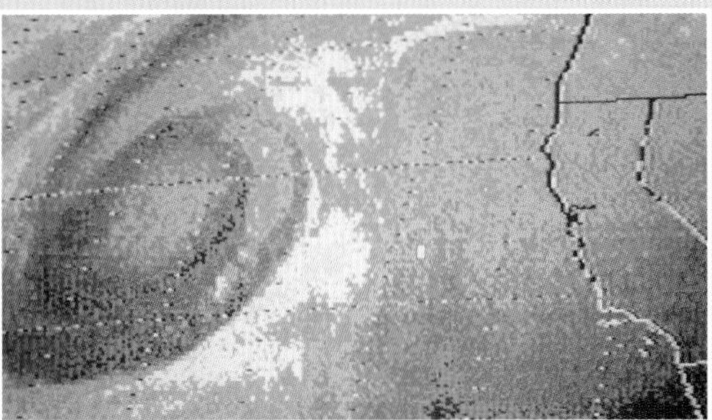

◀ *In this satellite picture, a spiral of clouds indicates that stormy weather in a depression is heading for California, USA.*

The Earth's chemistry

- **The bulk of the Earth** is made from iron, oxygen, magnesium and silicon.
- **More than 80 chemical elements** occur naturally in the Earth and its atmosphere.
- **The crust** is made mostly from oxygen and silicon, with aluminium, iron, calcium, magnesium, sodium, potassium, titanium and traces of 64 other elements.
- **The upper mantle** is iron and magnesium silicates; the lower is silicon and magnesium sulphides and oxides.
- **The core** is mostly iron, with a little nickel and traces of sulphur, carbon, oxygen and potassium.
- **Evidence for the Earth's chemistry** comes from analysing densities with the help of earthquake waves, and from studying stars, meteorites and other planets.
- **When the Earth** was still semi-molten, dense elements such as iron sank to form the core. Lighter elements such as oxygen floated up to form the crust.
- **Some heavy elements, such as uranium,** ended up in the crust because they easily make compounds with oxygen and silicon.
- **Large blobs of elements** that combine easily with sulphur, such as zinc and lead, spread through the mantle.
- **Elements that combine easily with iron,** such as gold and nickel, sank to the core.

▼ *This diagram shows the percentages of the chemical elements that make up the Earth.*

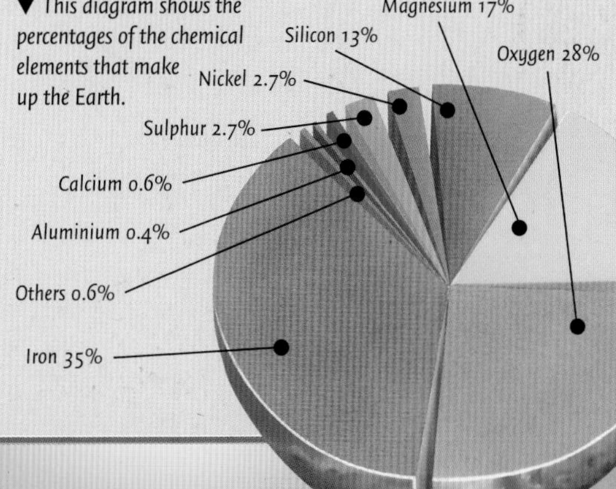

Volcano zones

▶ *One of many volcanoes in the Ring of Fire is Mt Rainier, in Washington State, USA.*

- **Worldwide** there are over 1,500 volcanoes; 500 of these are active. A volcano can have a lifespan of a million years and not erupt for several centuries.
- **Volcanoes** are said to be active if they have erupted recently. The official Smithsonian Institute list of active volcanoes includes any that have erupted in the past 10,000 years. Extinct volcanoes will never erupt again.

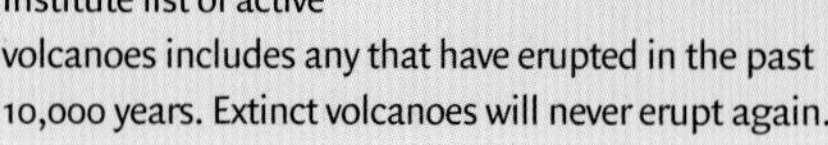

- **Volcanoes** occur either along the margins of tectonic plates, or over hot spots in the Earth's interior.
- **Some volcanoes** erupt where the plates are pulling apart, such as under the sea along mid-ocean ridges.
- **Some volcanoes** lie near subduction zones, forming either an arc of volcanic islands or a line of volcanoes on land, called a volcanic arc.
- **Subduction zone volcanoes** are explosive, because the magma gets contaminated and acidic as it burns up through the overlying plate. Acidic magma is sticky and gassy. It clogs up volcanic vents then blasts its way out.
- **Around the Pacific** there is a ring of explosive volcanoes called the Ring of Fire. It includes Mt Pinatubo in the Philippines, and Mt St Helens in Washington State, USA.
- **Away from subduction zones** magma is basaltic. It is runny and low in gas, so the volcanoes here gush lava.
- **Effusive volcanoes** pour out lava frequently but gently.
- **3D radar interferometry** from satellites may pick up the minutest swelling on every active volcano in the world. In this way it helps to predict eruptions.

Shape of the Earth

- **The study of the shape of the Earth** is called geodesy. In the past, geodesy depended on ground-based surveys. Today, satellites play a major role.
- **The Earth is not a perfect sphere.** It is a unique shape called a geoid, which means 'Earth shaped'.
- **The Earth spins** faster at the Equator than at the Poles, because the Equator is farther from the Earth's spinning axis.

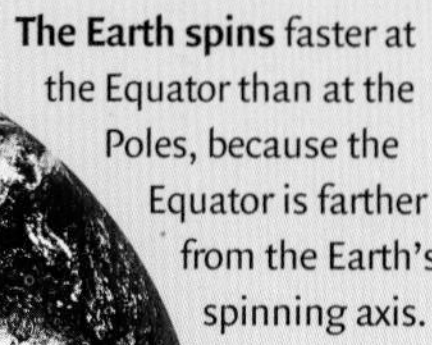

◀ *The ancient Greeks realized that the Earth is a globe. Satellite measurements show that it is not quite perfectly round.*

- **The extra speed** of the Earth at the Equator flings it out in a bulge, while it is flattened at the Poles.
- **Equatorial bulge** was predicted in 1687 by Isaac Newton.
- **The equatorial bulge** was confirmed 70 years after Newton – by French surveys in Peru by Charles de La Condamine, and in Lapland by Pierre de Maupertuis.
- **The Earth's diameter** at the Equator is 12,758 km. This is larger – by 43 km – than the vertical diameter from North Pole to South Pole.
- **The official measurement** of the Earth's radius at the Equator is 6,376,136 m, plus or minus 1 m.
- **The Lageos** (Laser Geodynamic) satellite launched in 1976 has measured gravitational differences with extreme precision. It has revealed bumps up to 100 m high, notably just south of India.
- **The Seasat** satellite confirmed the ocean surfaces are geoid. It took millions of measurements of the height of the ocean surface, accurate to within a few centimetres.

Seas

- **Seas** are small oceans, enclosed or partly enclosed by land.
- **Seas** are shallower than oceans and have no major currents flowing through them.
- **In the Mediterranean** and other seas, tides can set up a seiche – a standing wave that sloshes back and forth like a ripple running up and down a bath.
- **If the natural** wave cycle of a seiche is different from the ocean tides, the tides are cancelled out.

★ **STAR FACT** ★
The Dead Sea is the lowest sea on Earth, 400 m below sea level.

- **If the natural** wave cycle of a seiche is similar to the ocean tides, the tides are magnified.
- **Scientists thought that** the Mediterranean was a dry desert six million years ago. They believed it was 3,000 m lower than it is today, and covered in salts.
- **Recent evidence** from microfossils suggests that the Mediterranean was never completely dry.
- **Warm seas such as the Mediterranean** lose much more water by evaporation than they gain from rivers. So a current of water flows in steadily from the ocean.
- **Warm seas** lose so much water by evaporation that they are usually much saltier than the open ocean.

◀ *Waves in enclosed seas tend to be much smaller than those in the open ocean, because there is less space for them to develop.*

Drought

- **A drought** is a long period when there is too little rain.
- **During a drought** the soil dries out, streams stop flowing, groundwater sinks and plants die.
- **Deserts** suffer from permanent drought. Many tropical places have a seasonal drought, with long dry seasons.
- **Droughts** are often accompanied by high temperatures, which increase water loss through evaporation.
- **Between 1931 and 1938** drought reduced the Great Plains of the USA to a dustbowl, as the soil dried out and turned to dust. Drought came again from 1950 to 1954.
- **Desertification** is the spread of desert conditions into surrounding grassland. It is caused either by climate changes or by pressure from human activities.
- **Drought,** combined with increased numbers of livestock and people, have put pressure on the Sahel, south of the Sahara in Africa, causing widespread desertification.
- **Drought** has brought repeated famine to the Sahel, especially the Sudan and Ethiopia.
- **Drought** in the Sahel may be partly triggered off by El Niño – a reversal of the ocean currents in the Pacific Ocean, off Peru, which happens every 2–7 years.
- **The Great Drought** of 1276–1299 destroyed the cities of the ancient Indian civilizations of southwest USA. It led to the cities being abandoned.

▶ *Drought bakes the soil so hard it shrinks and cracks. It will no longer absorb water even when rain comes.*

Faults

- **A fault** is a fracture in rock along which large blocks of rock have slipped past each other.
- **Faults usually occur** in fault zones, which are often along the boundaries between tectonic plates. Faults are typically caused by earthquakes.
- **Single earthquakes** rarely move blocks more than a few centimetres. Repeated small earthquakes can shift blocks hundreds of kilometres.
- **Compression faults** are faults caused by rocks being squeezed together, perhaps by converging plates.
- **Tension faults** are faults caused by rocks being pulled together, perhaps by diverging plates.
- **Normal, or dip-slip, faults** are tension faults where the rock fractures and slips straight down.
- **A wrench, or tear, fault** occurs when plates slide past each other and make blocks slip horizontally.
- **Large wrench faults,** such as the San Andreas in California, USA, are called transcurrent faults.
- **Rift valleys** are huge, trough-shaped valleys created by faulting, such as Africa's Great Rift Valley. The floor is a thrown-down block called a graben. Some geologists think they are caused by tension, others by compression.
- **Horst blocks** are blocks of rock thrown up between normal faults, often creating a high plateau.

▼ *Geologists who study faults describe the movement of a fault using the terms illustrated here.*

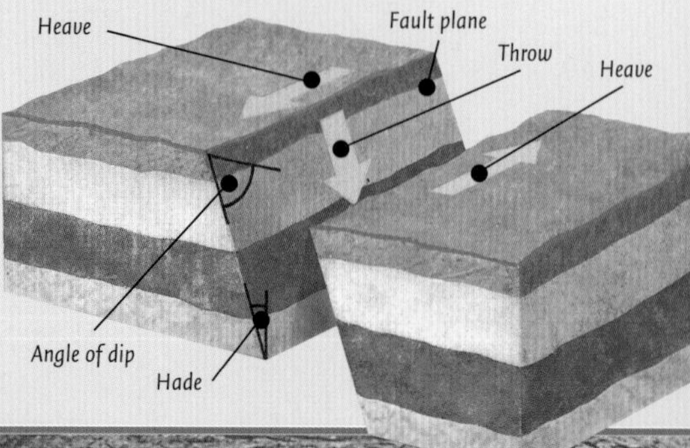

Famous earthquakes

◀ *The San Fransisco earthquake was so strong that its effects were detected thousands of miles away. More than two thirds of its population were left homeless.*

- **In 1906** San Francisco in California, USA was shaken by an earthquake that lasted three minutes. The earthquake started fires that burned the city almost flat.
- **The palaces** of the Minoan people on Crete were destroyed by an earthquake in about 1750 BC.
- **The earliest documented earthquake** hit the ancient Greek town of Sparta in 464 BC, killing 20,000 people.
- **In AD 62** the musical debut of the Roman Emperor Nero in Naples was ended by an earthquake.

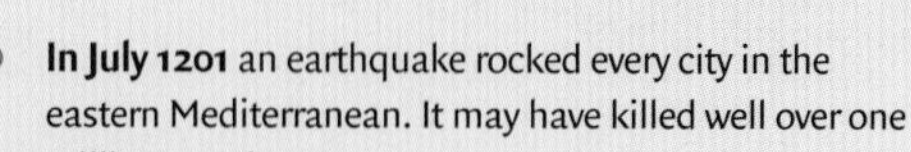

- **In July 1201** an earthquake rocked every city in the eastern Mediterranean. It may have killed well over one million people.
- **In 1556** an earthquake, which is thought to have been about 8.3 on the Richter scale, hit the province of Shansi in China (see earthquake damage).
- **The 1923** earthquake which devastated Tokyo and Yokohama (see earthquake damage) also made the sea-bed in nearby Sagami Bay drop over 400 m.
- **The 1755 Lisbon earthquake** (see earthquake damage) prompted the French writer Voltaire to write *Candide*, a book that inspired the French and American revolutions.
- **The Michoacán earthquake** of 1985 killed 35,000 in Mexico City 360 km away. Silts (fine soils) under the city amplified the ground movements 75 times.
- **The 1970 earthquake** in Peru shook 50 million cu m of rock and ice off the peak Huascaran. They roared down at 350 km/h and swept away the town of Yungay.

Swamps and marshes

- **Wetlands** are areas of land where the water level is mostly above the ground.
- **The main types** of wetland are bogs, fens, swamps and marshes.
- **Bogs and fens** occur in cold climates and contain plenty of partially rotted plant material called peat.
- **Marshes and swamps** are found in warm and cold places. They have more plants than bogs and fens.
- **Marshes** are in permanently wet places, such as shallow lakes and river deltas. Reeds and rushes grow in marshes.
- **Swamps** develop where the water level varies – often along the edges of rivers in the tropics where they are flooded, notably along the Amazon and Congo rivers. Trees such as mangroves grow in swamps.
- **Half the wetlands** in the USA were drained before most people appreciated their value. Almost half of Dismal Swamp in North Carolina has been drained.

▲ *In the past, wetlands were seen simply as dead areas, ripe for draining. Now their value both for wildlife and for water control is beginning to be realized.*

- **The Pripet Marshes** on the borders of Belorussia are the biggest in Europe, covering 270,000 sq km.
- **Wetlands act** like sponges and help to control floods.
- **Wetlands help** to top up supplies of groundwater.

Acid rain

- **All rain** is slightly acidic, but air pollution can turn rain into harmful acid rain.
- **Acid rain** forms when sunlight makes sulphur dioxide and nitrogen oxide combine with oxygen and moisture in the air.
- **Sulphur dioxide and nitrogen oxides** come from burning fossil fuels such as coal, oil and natural gas.

▲ *Cuts in emissions are essential to reduce acid rain, but installing 'scrubbers' that soak up sulphur and nitrous oxide are expensive.*

! NEWS FLASH !
Sulphur emissions from ships may double by 2010, counteracting cuts in power station emissions.

- **Acidity** is measured in terms of pH. The lower the pH, the more acid the rain is. Normal rain has a pH of 6.5. Acid rain has a pH of 5.7 or less.
- **A pH** of 2–3 has been recorded in many places in the eastern USA and central Europe.
- **Acid fog** is ten times more acid than acid rain.
- **Acid rain** washes aluminium from soil into lakes and streams, and so poisons fish. Limestone helps to neutralize the acid, but granite areas are vulnerable. Spring meltwaters are especially acid and damaging.
- **Acid rain** damages plants by removing nutrients from leaves and blocking the plants' uptake of nitrogen.
- **Acid rain has damaged** 20% of European trees; in Germany 60% of trees have been damaged.

1000
THINGS
YOU SHOULD KNOW ABOUT
WILD
ANIMALS

KEY

 Mammals

 Birds

 Reptiles and amphibians

 Sea creatures

 Insects, spiders and creepy crawlies

 How animals live

Monkeys

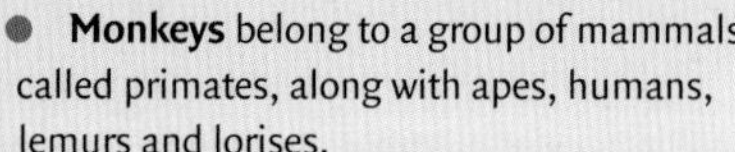

- **Monkeys** belong to a group of mammals called primates, along with apes, humans, lemurs and lorises.
- **Monkeys** live mostly in trees, and their hands have fingers and their feet have toes for gripping branches. Most monkeys also have tails.
- **There are about 150** species of monkey, and they live in tropical forests in Asia, Africa and the Americas.
- **New World monkeys** (from the Americas) live in trees and often have muscular tails that can grip like a hand. These tails are described as prehensile.

◀ Baboons such as the Hamadryas (sacred) baboon are large, dog-like monkeys which are well adapted to living on the ground in African bush country.

- **New World monkeys** include howler monkeys, spider monkeys, woolly monkeys and capuchins, as well as marmosets, and tamarins such as the golden lion tamarin, one of the world's most colourful mammals.
- **Old World monkeys** (from Africa and Asia) live on grasslands as well as in forests. They include baboons, colobus monkeys, langurs and macaques.
- **Old World monkeys** do not have a prehensile tail, but their thumbs and fingers can point together, like ours can, so they can grasp things well.
- **The proboscis monkey** gets its name from its huge nose (proboscis is another word for nose).
- **Most monkeys** eat anything from fruit to birds' eggs, but baboons may also catch and eat baby antelopes.

★ STAR FACT ★
Howler monkeys can howl so loud that a pair of them can be heard over 3 km away.

Rays

- **Rays** are a huge group of over 300 species of fish, which includes skates, stingrays, electric rays, manta rays, eagle rays and guitar fish.
- **Many rays** have flat, almost diamond-shaped bodies, with pectoral fins elongated into broad wings. Guitar fish have longer, more shark-like bodies.
- **A ray's gills** are slot-like openings beneath its fins.
- **Rays have no bones.** Instead, like sharks, they are cartilaginous fish – their body framework is made of rubbery cartilage (you have this in your nose and ears).
- **Rays live mostly** on the ocean floor, feeding on seabed creatures such as oysters, clams and other shellfish.
- **Manta rays** live near the surface and feed on plankton.
- **The Atlantic manta ray** is the biggest ray, often over 7 m wide and 6 m long.
- **Stingrays** get their name from their whip-like tail with its poisonous barbs. A sting from a stingray can make humans very ill.

▲ Manta rays often bask near the surface of the oceans, with the tips of their pectoral fins poking out of the water.

- **Electric rays** are tropical rays able to give off a powerful electric charge to defend themselves against attackers.
- **The black torpedo ray** can put out a 220 volt shock – as much as a household electric socket.

Lizards

- **Lizards** are a group of 3,800 scaly-skinned reptiles, varying from a few centimetres long to the 3-m-long Komodo dragon.
- **Lizards cannot** control their own body heat, and so rely on sunshine for warmth. This is why they live in warm climates and bask in the sun for hours each day.
- **Lizards move** in many ways – running, scampering and slithering. Some can glide. Unlike mammals, their limbs stick out sideways rather than downwards.
- **Most lizards** lay eggs, although a few give birth to live young. But unlike birds or mammals, a mother lizard does not nurture (look after) her young.
- **Most lizards** are meat-eaters, feeding on insects and other small creatures.

★ STAR FACT ★
The Basilisk lizard is also known as the Jesus Christ lizard because it can walk on water.

- **The glass lizard** has no legs. Its tail may break off and lie wriggling as a decoy if attacked. It can grow another tail later.
- **The Australian frilled lizard** has a ruff around its neck. To put off attackers, it can spread out its ruff to make itself look much bigger.
- **Horned lizards** can squirt a jet of blood from their eyes almost as far as 1 m to put off attackers.
- **The Komodo dragon** of Sumatra is the biggest lizard, weighing up to 150 kg. It can catch deer and pigs and swallow them whole.

▶ *Lizards have four legs and a long tail. In most lizards, the back legs are much stronger than the front, and are used to drive the animal forwards in a kind of writhing motion.*

Life on the seashore

- **Seashores** contain a huge variety of creatures which can adapt to the constant change from wet to dry as the tide rolls in and out.
- **Crabs, shellfish** and other creatures of rocky shores have tough shells to protect them from pounding waves and the sun's drying heat.
- **Anemones, starfish** and shellfish such as barnacles have powerful suckers for holding on to rocks.
- **Limpets** are the best rock clingers and can only be prised away if caught by surprise.
- **Anemones** may live on a hermit crab's shell, feeding on its leftovers but protecting it with their stinging tentacles.

▲ *Crabs, lugworms, sandhoppers, shellfish and many other creatures live on seashores. Many birds come to feed on them.*

- **Rock pools** are water left behind among the rocks as the tide goes out. They get very warm and salty.
- **Rock pool creatures** include shrimps, hermit crabs, anemones and fish such as blennies and gobies.
- **Sandy shores** are home to burrowing creatures such as crabs, razor clams, lugworms, sea cucumbers and burrowing anemones.
- **Sandhoppers** are tiny shelled creatures that live along the tide line, feeding on seaweed.
- **Beadlet anemones** look like blobs of jelly on rocks when the tide is out. But when the water returns, they open a ring of flower-like tentacles to feed.

Eagles and hawks

▲ *The bald eagle eats fish, snatching them from rivers.*

- **Eagles and hawks** are among 280 species of raptor (bird of prey). The group also includes kestrels, falcons, goshawks, buzzards and vultures.
- **Most birds of prey are hunters** that feed on other birds, fish and small mammals.
- **Most birds of prey** are strong fliers, with sharp eyes, powerful talons (claws) and a hooked beak.
- **Birds of prey lay** only a few eggs at a time. This makes them vulnerable to human egg collectors – one reason why many are endangered species.
- **Eagles** are the biggest of the hunting birds, with wing spans of up to 2.5 m. The harpy eagle of the Amazon catches monkeys and sloths.
- **The American bald eagle** is not really bald, but has white feathers on its head.
- **There are two kinds of hawks**. Accipiters, like the goshawk, catch their prey by lying in wait on perches. Buteos, like the kestrel, hover in the air.
- **Buzzards** are buteo hawks.
- **In the Middle Ages**, merlins and falcons were trained to fly from a falconer's wrist to catch birds and animals.

★ **STAR FACT** ★
The peregrine falcon can reach speeds of 350 km/h when stooping (diving) on prey.

Frogs and toads

◀ *Frogs are superb jumpers, with long back legs to propel them into the air. Most also have suckers on their fingers to help them land securely on slippery surfaces.*

- **Frogs** and toads are amphibians – creatures that live both on land and in the water.
- **There are about 3,500 species** of frog and toad. Most live near water, but some live in trees and others live underground.
- **Frogs** are mostly smaller and better jumpers. Toads are bigger, with thicker, wartier skin which holds on to moisture and allows them to live on land longer.
- **Frogs and toads** are meat-eaters. They catch fast-moving insects by darting out their long, sticky tongues.
- **Frogs and toads begin life** as fish-like tadpoles, hatching in the water from huge clutches of eggs called spawn.
- **After 7 to 10 weeks**, tadpoles grow legs and lungs and develop into frogs ready to leave the water.
- **In midwife toads**, the male looks after the eggs, not the female – winding strings of eggs around his back legs and carrying them about until they hatch.
- **The male Darwin's frog** swallows the eggs and keeps them in his throat until they hatch – and pop out of his mouth.
- **The goliath frog** of West Africa is the largest frog – at over 30 cm long. The biggest toad is the cane toad of Queensland, Australia – one weighed 2.6 kg and measured more than 25 cm in length.
- **The arrow-poison frogs** that live in the tropical rainforests of Central America get their name because natives tip their arrows with deadly poison from glands in the frogs' skin. Many arrow-poison frogs are very colourful, including some that are bright red.

Bats

- **Bats** are the only flying mammals. Their wings are made of leathery skin.
- **Most bats sleep** during the day, hanging upside down in caves, attics and other dark places. They come out at night to hunt.
- **Bats find things** in the dark by giving out a series of high-pitched clicks – the bats tell where they are and locate (find) prey from the echoes (sounds that bounce back to them). This is called echolocation.
- **Bats are not blind** – their eyesight is as good as that of most humans.
- **There are 900 species** of bat, living on all continents except Antarctica.
- **Most bats feed** on insects, but fruit bats feed on fruit.
- **Many tropical flowers** rely on fruit bats to spread their pollen.
- **Frog-eating bats** can tell edible frogs from poisonous ones by the frogs' mating calls.

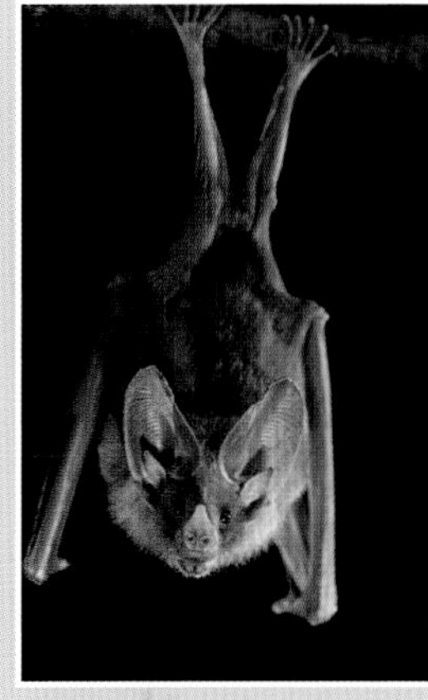

▶ *Bats spend their lives in darkness, finding their way with sounds so high-pitched only a young child can hear them.*

- **The vampire bats** of tropical Latin America feed on blood, sucking it from animals such as cattle and horses. A colony of 100 vampire bats can drink blood from 25 cows or 14,000 chickens in one night.
- **False vampire bats** are bats that do not suck on blood, but feed on other small creatures such as bats and rats. The greater false vampire bat of Southeast Asia is one of the biggest of all bats.

Animal senses

- **Animals** sense the world in a variety of ways, including by sight, hearing, touch, smell and taste. Many animals have senses that humans do not have.
- **Sea creatures** rely on smell and taste, detecting tiny particles drifting in the water. For balance they often rely on simple balance organs called statocysts.
- **Sharks** have a better sense of smell than any other kind of fish. They can detect one part of animal blood in 100 million parts of water.

◀ *The slow loris is nocturnal, and its enormous eyes help it jump safely through forests in the darkness.*

- **For land animals**, sight is usually the most important sense. Hunting animals often have very sharp eyesight. Eagles, for instance, can see a rabbit moving from as far as 5 km away.
- **Owls** can hear sounds ten times softer than any human can.
- **Male gypsy moths** can smell a mate over 11 km away.
- **Pit vipers** have special sensory pits (holes) on their heads which can pinpoint heat. This lets them track warm-blooded prey such as mice in pitch darkness.
- **The forked tongues** of snakes and lizards are used to taste the air and detect prey.
- **Cats' eyes** absorb 50% more light than human eyes, so they can see very well in the dark.

★ **STAR FACT** ★

Many butterflies can smell with special sense organs in their feet.

Lions

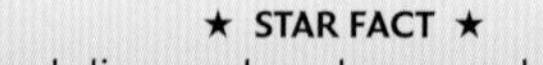

★ STAR FACT ★
A male lion can drag along a 300 kg zebra – it would take at least six men to do this.

- **Lions** (along with tigers) are the biggest members of the cat family, weighing up to 230 kg. Male lions may be 3 m long.
- **Lions used to live** through much of Europe and Asia. Now they are restricted to East and Southern Africa. Around 200 lions also live in the Gir forest in India.
- **Lions usually live** in grassland or scrub, in families called prides.
- **Lions are hunters** and they prey on antelopes, zebras and even young giraffes. The lionesses (females) do most of the hunting.
- **Male lions** are easily recognizable because of their huge manes. There are usually two to five adult males in each pride and they usually eat before the lionesses and cubs.

The mane can be blonde, but gets darker with age

▲ To other lions, a male lion's shaggy mane makes him look even bigger and stronger, and protects him when fighting. A male lion is born without a mane. It starts growing when he is about two or three and is fully grown by the time he is five.

Cubs have very big paws for their size

◀ Lion cubs live on milk at first, and eat their first meat after 50 days.

▲ Female lions are called lionesses. They are slightly smaller than males but usually do most of the hunting, often in pairs. There are typically 4 to 12adult lionesses in each pride, and each one mates with the male when she is about 3 years old.

- **Lions usually catch** something to eat every four days or so. They can eat up to 40 kg in a single meal. Afterwards they rest for 24 hours.
- **The lions in a pride** usually spend about 20 hours a day sleeping and resting, and they walk no farther than 10 km or so a day.
- **Lionesses catch their prey** not by speed, but by stealth and strength. They stalk their prey quietly, creeping close to the ground. Then, when it is about 15 m away, the lionesses make a sudden dash and pull the victim down with their strong forepaws.
- **Lionesses usually hunt** at dusk or dawn, but they have very good night vision, and so will often hunt in the dark.
- **Male lion cubs** are driven out of the pride when they are two years old. When a young male is fully grown, he has to fight an older male to join another pride.

Wading birds

- **Herons** are large wading birds that hunt for fish in shallow lakes and rivers. There are about 60 species.
- **When hunting**, a heron stands alone in the water, often on one leg, apparently asleep. Then it makes a lightning dart with its long beak to spear a fish or frog.
- **Herons** usually nest in colonies called heronries. They build loose stick-nests in trees.
- **Storks** are very large black-and-white water birds with long necks and legs. There are 17 species of stork.
- **The white stork** lives in Eurasia in the summer, and then migrates to Africa, India and southern China in the winter.

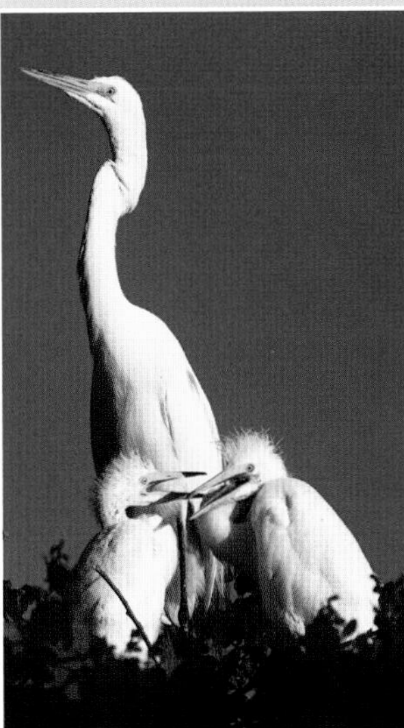

- **White storks** build twig-nests on roofs, and some people think they bring luck to the house they nest on.
- **Flamingoes** are large pink wading birds which live in huge colonies on tropical lakes.
- **Spoonbills and ibises** are wading birds whose bills are sensitive enough to let them feel their prey moving in the water.
- **There are 28 species** of spoonbill and ibis.
- **The spoonbill's name** comes from its spoon-shaped bill, which it swings through the water to scoop up fish.

◀ *Egrets are large wading birds that live in marshy areas, feeding on fish and insects.*

Beetles

- **At least 250,000** species of beetle have been identified. They live everywhere on Earth, apart from in the oceans.
- **Unlike other insects**, adult beetles have a pair of thick, hard, front wings called elytra. These form an armour-like casing over the beetle's body.
- **The goliath beetle** of Africa is the heaviest flying insect, weighing over 100 grams and growing to as much as 13 cm long.
- **Dung beetles** roll away the dung of grazing animals to lay their eggs on. Fresh dung from one elephant may contain 7,000 beetles – they will clear the dung away in little more than a day.
- **A click beetle** can jump 30 cm into the air.

★ STAR FACT ★
The Arctic beetle can survive in temperatures below -60°C.

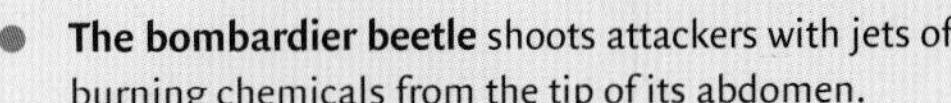

- **The bombardier beetle** shoots attackers with jets of burning chemicals from the tip of its abdomen.
- **The rove beetle** can zoom across water on a liquid given off by glands on its abdomen.
- **The leaf-eating beetle** can clamp on to leaves using the suction of a layer of oil.
- **Stag beetles** have huge jaws which look like a stag's antlers.

▶ *The jewel beetles of tropical South America get their name from the brilliant rainbow colours of their elytra (front wings).*

Surviving the winter

- **Some animals** cope with the cold and lack of food in winter by going into a kind of deep sleep called hibernation.
- **During hibernation**, an animal's body temperature drops and its heart rate and breathing slow, so it needs little energy to survive.
- **Small mammals** such as bats, squirrels, hamsters, hedgehogs and chipmunks hibernate. So do birds such as nighthawks and swifts.
- **Reptiles** such as lizards and snakes go into a state called torpor whenever it gets too cold. They wake up only when the temperature rises again.

★ STAR FACT ★
Macaque monkeys in Japan keep warm in winter by bathing in hot volcanic springs.

◀ *This Arctic fox, which lives in the far north of Asia and North America, can sometimes sleep for days when food is scarce in winter.*

- **Butterflies and other insects** go into a kind of suspended animation called diapause in winter.
- **The pika** (a small lagomorph) makes haystacks from grass in summer to provide food for the winter.
- **Beavers** collect branches in autumn and store them next to their lodges so they can feed on the bark during the winter.
- **Bears** go to sleep during winter, but not all scientists agree that they go into true hibernation.
- **Squirrels** bury dozens of stores of nuts in autumn to feed on during winter. They seem to have a remarkable memory, as they are able to find most of these stores when they need them.

Beavers

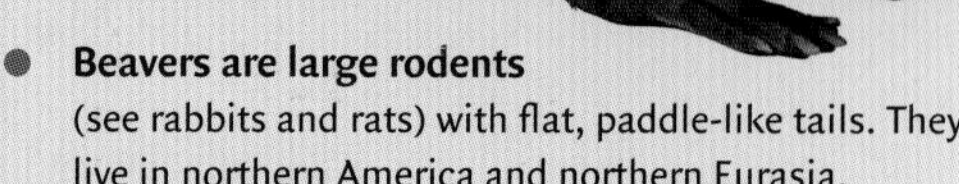

▶ *In North America, beavers were once hunted so much that they were almost wiped out. They are now protected by law in some places.*

- **Beavers are large rodents** (see rabbits and rats) with flat, paddle-like tails. They live in northern America and northern Eurasia.
- **Beavers live** in rivers, streams and lakes near woodlands and they are good swimmers, using their webbed feet as flippers and their tail as a rudder.
- **A beaver can swim underwater** for almost 1 km, holding its breath all the way.
- **Beavers can chop down** quite large trees with their incredibly strong front teeth, gnawing around the tree in a ring until it finally crashes down.
- **Beavers feed on** bark as well as tree roots and shrubs. They are especially fond of poplars and willows.
- **Beavers build dams** across streams from tree branches laid on to a base of mud and stones. Families of beavers often work together on a dam.
- **Beaver dams** are 5 to 30 m long on average, but they can be up to 300 m long.
- **Beavers repair** their dams year after year, and some beaver dams are thought to be centuries old.
- **In the lake** behind the dam, beavers build a shelter called a lodge to live in during winter. Most lodges are like mini-islands made of branches and mud, with only a few underwater tunnels as entrances.
- **Beaver lodges** keep a beaver family so warm that in cold weather steam can often be seen rising from the ventilation hole.

Jellyfish

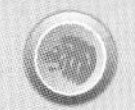     

- **Jellyfish** are sea creatures with bell-shaped, jelly-like bodies, and long stinging tentacles.
- **Biologists** call jellyfish medusa, after the mythical Greek goddess Medusa, who had wriggling snakes for hair.
- **Jellyfish** belong to a large group of sea creatures called cnidarians, which also includes corals and anemones.
- **Unlike anemones**, jellyfish float about freely, moving by squeezing water out from beneath their body. When a jellyfish stops squeezing, it slowly sinks.
- **A jellyfish's tentacles** are covered with stinging cells called nematocysts, which are used to catch fish and for protection. The stinging cells explode when touched, driving tiny poisonous threads into the victim.
- **Jellyfish vary in size** from a few millimetres to over 2 m.

★ **STAR FACT** ★
The box jellyfish has one of the most deadly poisons. It can kill a human in 30 seconds.

- **The bell of one giant jellyfish** measured 2.29 m across. Its tentacles were over 36 m long.
- **The Portuguese man-of-war** is not a true jellyfish, but a collection of hundreds of tiny animals called polyps which live together under a gas-filled float.
- **The purple jellyfish** can be red, yellow or purple.

▼ *Jellyfish are among the world's most ancient animals.*

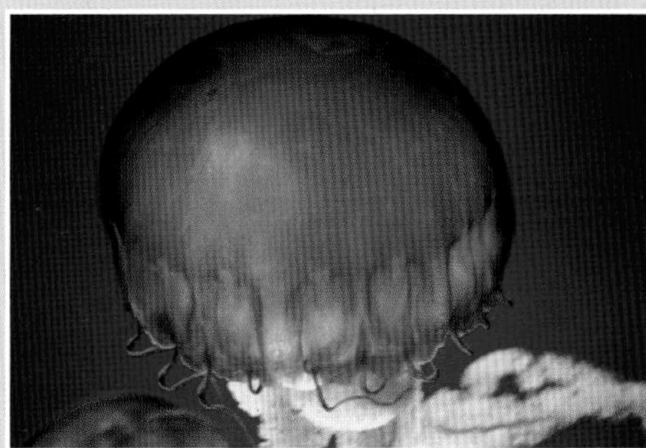

Otters

- **Otters** are small hunting mammals which are related to weasels. They are one of the 65 species of mustelid, along with stoats, skunks and badgers.
- **Otters live** close to water and are brilliant swimmers and divers.
- **Otters can close off** their nostrils and ears, allowing them to remain underwater for 4 or 5 minutes.

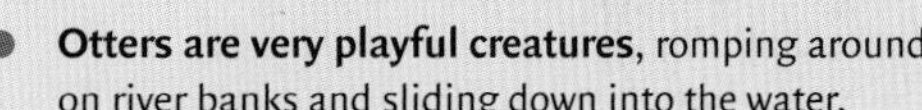

- **Otters are very playful creatures**, romping around on river banks and sliding down into the water.
- **Otters can use their paws** like hands, to play with things such as stones and shellfish.
- **Otters hunt fish**, mostly at night, but they also eat crayfish and crabs, clams and frogs.
- **Otters usually live** in burrows in riverbanks.
- **Sea otters** live on the shores of western North America.
- **Sea otters will float** on their backs for hours, eating or sleeping. Mother sea otters often carry their baby on their stomachs while floating like this.
- **Sea otters eat shellfish.** They will balance a rock on their stomach while floating on their back, and crack the shellfish by banging it on the rock.

◀ *Sea otters float on their backs for hours in the seas off California and Alaska.*

Farm animals

- **Cattle** are descended from a creature called the wild auroch, which was tamed 9,000 years ago. There are now over 200 breeds of domestic cow.
- **Female cows** reared for milk, butter and cheese production are called dairy cows. They give birth to one calf each year, and after it is born they provide milk twice a day.
- **A typical dairy cow** gives 16 litres of milk a day, or almost 6,000 litres a year.
- **Male cattle** are reared mainly for their meat, called beef. Beef breeds are usually heftier than dairy ones.
- **Sheep were first domesticated** over 10,000 years ago. There are now more than 700 million sheep in the world, and 800 different breeds.

◀ *Female cattle are called cows, and males are called bulls. The young are calves. Female calves are also called heifers.*

- **Hairy sheep** are kept for their milk and meat (lamb and mutton). Woolly sheep are kept for their wool.
- **Hens** lay one or two eggs a day – about 350 a year.
- **To keep hens laying**, their eggs must be taken from them every day. Otherwise the hens will try to nest so they can hatch them.
- **Turkeys** may have got their name from the mistaken idea that they came from Turkey.

★ STAR FACT ★
When a cow chews the cud, the cud is food regurgitated from one of its four stomachs.

Colours and markings

▲ *A zebra's stripes may seem to make it easy to see, but when it is moving they actually blur its outline and confuse predators.*

- **Protective colouring** helps an animal hide from its enemies or warns them away.
- **Camouflage** is when an animal is coloured to blend in with its surroundings, making it hard to see.
- **Ground nesting birds** like the nightjar are mottled brown, making them hard to spot among fallen leaves.
- **The fur of wild pig and tapir babies** is striped and spotted to make them hard to see in the jungle light.
- **Squid** can change their colour to blend in with new surroundings.
- **Disruptive colouring** distorts an animal's body so that its real shape is disguised.
- **Bright colours** often warn predators that an animal is poisonous or tastes bad. For example, ladybirds are bright red and the cinnabar moth's caterpillars are black and yellow because they taste nasty.
- **Some creatures** mimic the colours of poisonous ones to warn predators off. Harmless hoverflies, for instance, look just like wasps.
- **Some animals** frighten off predators with colouring that makes them look much bigger. Peacock butterflies have big eyespots on their wings.
- **Courting animals**, especially male birds like the peacock, are often brightly coloured to attract mates.

Crocodiles and alligators

- **Crocodiles, alligators, caimans and gharials** are large reptiles that together form the group known as crocodilians. There are 14 species of crocodile, 7 alligators and caimans, and 1 gharial.
- **Crocodilian species** lived alongside the dinosaurs 200 million years ago, and they are the nearest we have to living dinosaurs today.
- **Crocodilians are hunters** that lie in wait for animals coming to drink at the water's edge. When crocodilians seize a victim they drag it into the water, stun it with a blow from their tail, then drown it.
- **Like all reptiles**, crocodilians get their energy from the Sun. Typically, they bask in the Sun on a sandbar or the river bank in the morning, then slip into the river at midday to cool off.
- **Crocodiles live** in tropical rivers and swamps. At over 5 m long, saltwater crocodiles are the world's largest reptiles – one grew to over 8 m long.
- **Crocodiles** are often said to cry after eating their victims. In fact only saltwater crocodiles cry, and they do it to get rid of salt, not because they are sorry.
- **Crocodiles have thinner snouts** than alligators, and a fourth tooth on the lower jaw which is visible when the crocodile's mouth is shut.

> ★ STAR FACT ★
> Crocodilians often swallow stones to help them stay underwater for long periods. Without this ballast, they might tip over.

- **The female Nile crocodile** lays her eggs in nests which she digs in sandy river banks, afterwards covering the eggs in sand to keep them at a steady temperature. When the babies hatch they make loud piping calls. The mother then digs them out and carries them one by one in her mouth to the river.
- **Alligators** are found both in the Florida Everglades in the United States and in the Yangtze River in China.

▼ *Crocodiles often lurk in rivers, with just their eyes and nostrils visible above the water.*

▶ *Crocodiles are huge reptiles with powerful bodies, scaly skin and great snapping jaws. When a crocodile opens its jaws, it reveals a flash of bright scarlet tongue and throat, as well as rows of very sharp teeth. The bright colour is thought to terrify potential victims.*

A crocodile will often kill its victims with a swipe from its strong tail

The skin on its back has ridges formed by dozens of tiny bones called osteoderms

The crocodile's eyes and nostrils are raised so it can see and breathe while floating under water

The skin on its belly is smooth and was once prized as a material for shoes and handbags

Bears

- **Although bears** are the largest meat-eating land animals, they also eat many other foods, including fruits, nuts and leaves.
- **The biggest bear** is the Alaskan brown bear, which grows to 2.7 m long and weighs up to 770 kg.
- **There are 7 species of bear.** Most live north of the equator. Only two live south of the equator – the spectacled bear of South America and the sun bear of Southeast Asia.
- **Bears do not hug** their prey to death, as is sometimes thought. Instead, they kill their victims with a powerful cuff from their front paws, or with their teeth.

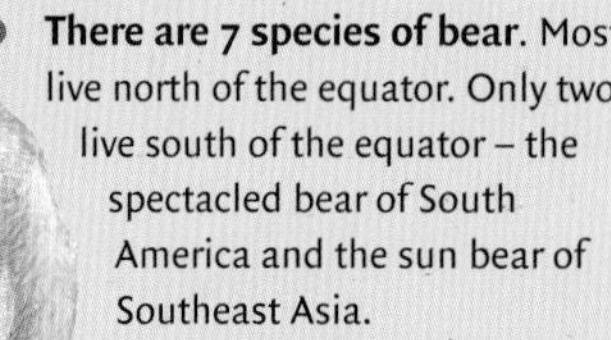

◀ *The polar bear has a white coat to camouflage it against the Arctic snow when it is hunting seals. Sometimes, only its black nose gives it away.*

★ STAR FACT ★
Bears and humans are among the few animals to walk on the soles of their feet.

- **The grizzly bear** is actually a brown bear with white fur on its shoulders. Grizzly bears from Alaska are the biggest brown bears, along with kodiak bears.
- **Polar bears mainly eat** seals and they are the only truly carnivorous bears.
- **Polar bears catch seals** when the seals poke their heads up through breathing holes in the Arctic ice.
- **Polar bears often swim underwater** and come up under an ice floe to tip seals off. They may also chuck huge chunks of ice at seals to stun them.
- **The sun bear** of Southeast Asia is the smallest bear, and a very good climber.

Bees and wasps

▲ *Honey bees and bumble bees feed on pollen. They make honey from flower nectar to feed their young.*

- **Bees and wasps** are narrow-waisted insects (usually with hairy bodies). Many suck nectar from flowers.
- **There are 22,000 species of bee.** Some, like leaf-cutter bees, live alone. But most, like honey bees and bumble bees, live in vast colonies.
- **Honey bees** live in hives, either in hollow trees or in man-made beehive boxes. The inside of the hive is a honeycomb made up of hundreds of six-sided cells.
- **A honey bee colony** has a queen (the female bee that lays the eggs), tens of thousands of female worker bees, and a few hundred male drones.
- **Worker bees** collect nectar and pollen from flowers.
- **Each worker bee** makes ten trips a day and visits 1,000 flowers each trip. It takes 65,000 trips to 65 million flowers to make 1 kg of honey.
- **Honey bees** tell others where to find flowers, rich in pollen or nectar, by flying in a dance-like pattern.
- **Wasps** do not make honey, but feed on nectar and fruit juice. Many species have a nasty sting in their tail.
- **Paper wasps build** huge papier maché nests the size of footballs, containing 15,000 or more cells.
- **Paper wasps make** papier maché for their nest by chewing wood and mixing it with their spit.

Communication

- **Crows** use at least 300 different croaks to communicate with each other. But crows from one area cannot understand crows from another one.
- **When two howler monkey troops** meet, the males scream at each other until one troop gives way.
- **The male orang utan** burps to warn other males to keep away.
- **Dogs** communicate through barks, yelps, whines, growls and howls.
- **Many insects communicate** through the smell of chemicals called pheromones, which are released from special glands.

★ STAR FACT ★
Using sign language, Coco the gorilla took an IQ test and got a score of 95.

◀ *Lone wolves often howl at dusk or in the night to signal their ownership of a particular territory and to warn off rival wolves.*

- **Tropical tree ant species** use ten different pheromones, combining them with different movements to send 50 different kinds of message.
- **A gorilla** named Coco was trained so that she could use over 1,000 different signs to communicate, each sign meaning different words. She called her pet cat 'Soft good cat cat', and herself 'Fine animal gorilla'.
- **Female glow worms** communicate with males by making a series of flashes.
- **Many birds** are mimics and can imitate a whole variety of different sounds, including the human voice and machines like telephones. This is not communication, though, it is simply showing off.

Parrots and budgerigars

▲ *The blue-and-yellow macaw of the Amazon rainforest has been trapped so much for the pet trade, it is now quite rare.*

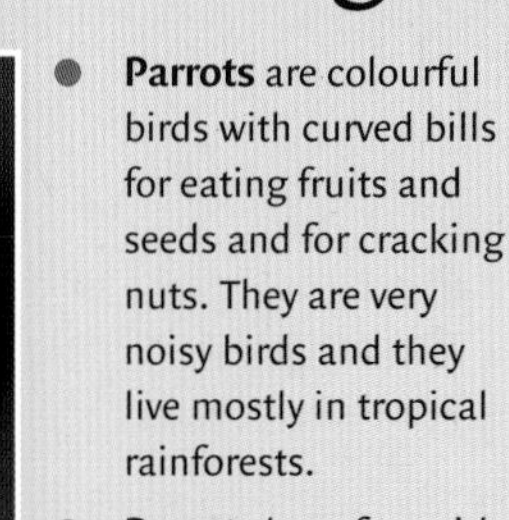

- **Parrots** are colourful birds with curved bills for eating fruits and seeds and for cracking nuts. They are very noisy birds and they live mostly in tropical rainforests.
- **Parrots** have feet with two toes pointing forwards and two backwards, allowing them to grip branches and hold food.
- **There are 330 or so parrot species** divided into three main groups – true parrots, cockatoos and lories.
- **Half of all parrot species**, including macaws, green Amazon parrots and parakeets, live in Latin America.
- **Australia and New Guinea** are home to parrots called cockatoos (which are white with feathered crests on their heads), as well as to lories and lorikeets.
- **The budgerigar** is a small parakeet from central Australia which is very popular as a pet.
- **The hanging parrots** of Southeast Asia get their name because they sleep upside down like bats.
- **The kea** of New Zealand is a parrot that eats meat as well as fruit. It was once wrongly thought to be a sheep killer.
- **Parrots** are well known for their mimicry of human voices. Some have a repertoire of 300 words or more.
- **An African grey parrot** called Alex was trained by scientist Irene Pepperberg to identify at least 50 different objects. Alex could ask for each of these objects in English – and also refuse them.

Ostriches and emus

▶ Ostriches live on the grasslands of Africa and nest in holes scooped out of the ground. The male scoops out the hole and leads several females to it to lay their eggs.

★ STAR FACT ★
The biggest bird ever is now extinct – the flightless elephant bird of Madagascar was truly elephantine, growing up to 4.5 m tall (taller than two grown men).

Bony crest

◀ The cassowary lives in the forests of tropical Australia and New Guinea. It has a crest which it uses like a crash helmet as it charges through the undergrowth.

Two toes with very sharp toenails

- **Ratites are big, but flightless, birds** like the ostrich, emu, cassowary, rhea and kiwi. They are descended from an ancient group of birds, and have lost the ability to fly. Ratites always walk or run, only using their small wings for balance and for show.
- **The ostrich** is the biggest living bird, towering up to 2.75 m in height and weighing over 150 kg.
- **To escape a lion**, the ostrich can hurtle over the African savannah grasslands, where it lives, at speeds of 60 km/h – faster than a racehorse. Even when the ostrich tires, its strong legs can still deliver a massive kick.
- **Ostriches** have only two toes on each foot – unlike the rhea of South America which has three.

◀ Ostriches have soft downy plumage, but their head, neck and legs are almost bare.

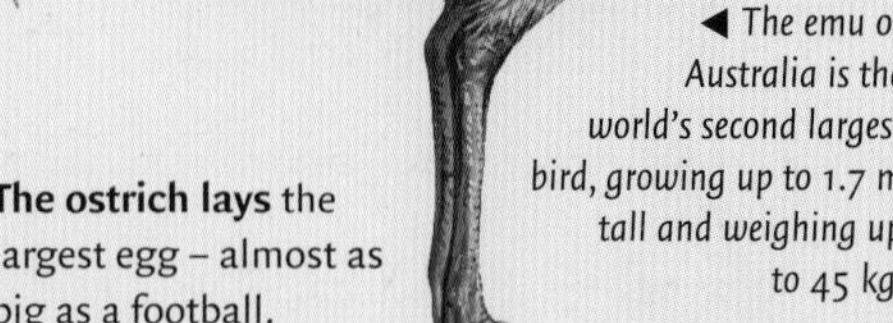

◀ The emu of Australia is the world's second largest bird, growing up to 1.7 m tall and weighing up to 45 kg.

- **The ostrich lays** the largest egg – almost as big as a football.
- **The kiwi of New Zealand** is the smallest ratite, no bigger than a chicken. It has fur-like feathers and is the only bird with nostrils at the tip of its bill, which it uses to sniff out worms and grubs.
- **The rare kakapo parrot** of New Zealand could fly once, but it lost the power of flight because it had no natural predators – until Europeans introduced dogs and cats to New Zealand.
- **The dodo** was a flightless bird that once lived on islands, such as Mauritius in the Indian Ocean. It was wiped out in the 17th century when its eggs were eaten by pigs and monkeys imported by Europeans.
- **The emu** of Australia is the best swimmer of any flightless bird. Ostriches can swim well, too.

Dogs and wolves

- **The dog family** is a large group of four-legged, long-nosed, meat-eating animals. It includes dogs, wolves, foxes, jackals and coyotes.
- **All kinds of dog** have long canine teeth for piercing and tearing their prey. (Canine means 'dog').
- **When hunting**, dogs rely mainly on their good sense of smell and acute hearing.
- **Wolves** are the largest wild dogs. They hunt together in packs to track down animals bigger than themselves, such as moose, deer, caribou and musk oxen.
- **A wolf pack** may have 7 to 20 wolves, led by the eldest male and female.
- **A wolf pack's territory** may be 1,000 square km or more. Wolves can travel vast distances when hunting.
- **Wolves once lived** all over Europe and North America, but are now rare in Europe and are found only in Asia and in remote areas of North America.
- **Foxes** are cunning hunters which prowl at night, alone or in pairs. Typical prey includes rats, mice and rabbits.
- **The red fox** has adapted to the growth of towns and cities and may often be seen at night raiding surburban rubbish bins and dumps.
- **The jackals** of Africa look like small wolves, but they hunt alone for small prey and only meet in packs to grab the leftovers from the kill of a lion.

► *Most wolves are grey wolves – either the timber wolf of cold forest regions, or the tundra wolf of the Arctic plains.*

Poisonous insects

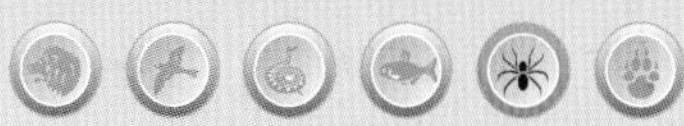

- **Insects are small**, but many have nasty poisons to protect themselves.
- **Most poisonous insects** are brightly coloured – including many caterpillars, wasps and cardinal beetles – to warn off its potential enemies.
- **Ants, bees and wasps** have stings in their tails which they use to inject poison to defend themselves or paralyse prey.
- **Bee and wasp stings** have barbed ends to keep the sting in long enough to inject the poison. Honey bees cannot pull the barb out from human skins, and so tear themselves away and die.
- **Velvet ants** are not really ants at all, but wingless wasps with such a nasty sting that they are called 'cow killers'.
- **Ladybirds** make nasty chemicals in their knees.
- **When attacked**, swallowtail caterpillars whip out a smelly forked gland from a pocket behind their head and hit their attacker with it.

▲ *Wasps poison their victims with the sharp sting in their tail.*

- **The lubber grasshopper** is slow moving, but when attacked it oozes a foul smelling froth from its mouth and thorax.
- **It is not only insects** that are poisonous, but some spiders. The black widow spider is one of the deadliest spiders, with a bite that can kill a human. The funnel-web spider and many bird-eating spiders are also poisonous.

Penguins

- **There are 17 or 18 different species** of penguin, most of them living in huge colonies called rookeries along the coast of Antarctica and nearby islands.
- **Penguins** are superb swimmers, using their wings as flippers to push them through the water, and steering with their webbed feet.
- **Penguins have coats** waterproofed with oil and thick fat so they can survive in temperatures as low as -60°C.
- **The smallest** is the fairy penguin, at 40 cm high.
- **The emperor penguin** is the biggest swimming bird, at up to 1.2 m tall and weighing over 40 kg – twice the weight of any flying bird.
- **Emperor penguins** can dive briefly to depths of 250 m or more chasing fish, their main diet.

★ **STAR FACT** ★
The male emperor penguin keeps the female's egg warm on his feet until it hatches.

▲ *Penguins are sociable birds that live in large colonies.*

- **Penguins** can leap high out of the water to land on an ice bank, but on land they can only waddle clumsily or toboggan along on their bellies.
- **Adélie penguins** waddle more than 320 km across the ice every year to reach their breeding ground.
- **When crossing the ice**, Adélie penguins steer by the sun. They lose their way when the sun goes down.

Iguanas

- **Iguanas** are large lizards that live around the Pacific and in the Americas.
- **Larger iguanas** are the only vegetarian lizards. Unlike other lizards, most eat fruit, flowers and leaves, rather than insects.
- **The common iguana** lives high up in trees, but lays its eggs in a hole in the ground.

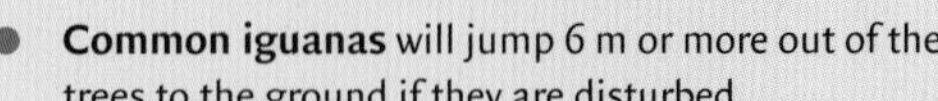

- **Common iguanas** will jump 6 m or more out of the trees to the ground if they are disturbed.
- **The rhinoceros iguana** of the West Indies gets its name from the pointed scales on its snout.
- **The marine iguana** of the Galapagos Islands is the only lizard that spends much of its life in the sea.
- **Marine iguanas** keep their eggs warm ready for hatching in the mouth of volcanoes, risking death to put them there.
- **When in the water**, a marine iguana may dive for 15 minutes or more, pushing itself along with its tail.
- **Although marine iguanas** cannot breathe underwater, their heart rate slows so that they use less oxygen.
- **The chuckwalla** inflates its body with air to wedge itself in a rock crack if it is in danger.

◀ *Before each dive into water, marine iguanas warm themselves in the sun to gain energy.*

Crabs and lobsters

- **Crabs and lobsters** are part of an enormous group of creatures called crustaceans.
- **Most crabs and lobsters** have their own shell, but hermit crabs live inside the discarded shells of other creatures.
- **Crabs and lobsters are decapods**, which means they have ten legs – although the first pair are often strong pincers which are used to hold and tear food.
- **For spotting prey**, crabs and lobsters have two pairs of antennae on their heads and a pair of eyes on stalks.
- **One of a lobster's claws** usually has blunt knobs for crushing victims. The other has sharp teeth for cutting.
- **Male fiddler crabs** have one giant pincer which they waggle to attract a mate.
- **Robber crabs** have claws on their legs which they use to climb up trees to escape from predators.
- **The giant Japanese spider crab** can grow to measure 3 m across between the tips of its outstretched pincers.
- **When American spiny lobsters** migrate, they cling to each others' tails in a long line, marching for hundreds of kilometres along the seabed.
- **Sponge crabs** hide under sponges which they cut to fit. The sponge then grows at the same rate as the crab.

▼ *Lobsters are dark green or blue when alive and only turn red when cooked.*

Life in the desert

▲ *Deserts like this are among the world's toughest environments for animals to survive.*

- **In the Sahara desert**, a large antelope called the addax survives without waterholes because it gets all its water from its food.
- **Many small animals** cope with the desert heat by resting in burrows or sheltering under stones during the day. They come out to feed only at night.
- **Desert animals** include many insects, spiders, scorpions, lizards and snakes.
- **The dwarf puff adder** hides from the sun by burying itself in the sand until only its eyes show.
- **The fennec fox** and the antelope jack rabbit both lose heat through their ears. This way they keep cool.
- **The kangaroo rats** of California's Death Valley save water by eating their own droppings.
- **The Mojave squirrel** survives through long droughts by sleeping five or six days a week.
- **Swarms of desert locusts** can cover an area as big as 5,000 square kilometres.
- **Sand grouse** fly hundreds of kilometres every night to reach watering holes.

★ **STAR FACT** ★

The African fringe-toed lizard dances to keep cool, lifting each foot in turn off the hot sand.

Finding a mate

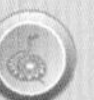

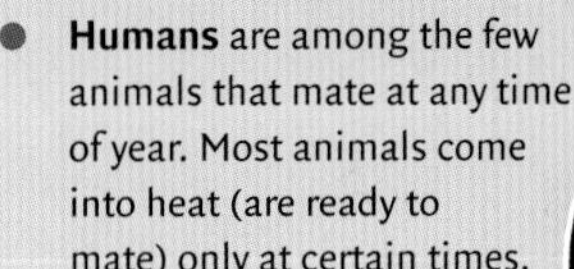

◀ *Prairie dogs live in families called coteries, each made up of a male and several females.*

- **Humans** are among the few animals that mate at any time of year. Most animals come into heat (are ready to mate) only at certain times.
- **Spring** is a common mating time. The warmer weather and longer daylight hours triggers the production of sperm in males and eggs in females.
- **Some mammals**, such as bats, bears and deer, have only one mating time a year. Others, such as rabbits, have many.
- **Many large mammals** pair for a short time, but a few (including beavers and wolves) pair for life. Some animals (including lions and seals) have lots of mates.
- **To attract a mate**, many animals put on courtship displays such as a special colours, songs and dances.
- **The male capercaillies** (turkey-like birds) attract a mate with a loud display that can be heard for miles.
- **Great crested grebes** perform dramatic dances in the water and present water plants to one another.
- **Male bower birds** paint their nests blue with berry juice and line them with blue shells and flowers to attract a mate.
- **Male birds of paradise** flash their bright feathers while strutting and dancing to attract a mate.
- **The male tern** catches a fish as a gift for the female. The male dancefly brings a dead insect which the female eats while mating.

Life in tropical grasslands

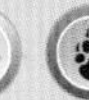

- **Tropical grasslands** are home to vast herds of grazing animals such as antelope and buffalo – and to the lions, cheetahs and other big cats that prey on them.
- **There are few places to hide** on the grasslands, so most grassland animals are fast runners with long legs.

▼ *With their long necks, giraffes can feed on the high branches of the thorn trees that dot the savannah grasslands of Africa.*

★ STAR FACT ★
Cheetahs are the fastest runners in the world, reaching 110 km/h in short bursts.

- **Pronghorns** can manage 67 km/h for 16 km.
- **There are more than 60 species** of antelope on the grasslands of Africa and southern Asia.
- **A century ago in South Africa**, herds of small antelopes called springboks could be as large as 10 million strong and hundreds of kilometres long.
- **The springbok** gets its name from its habit of springing 3 m straight up in the air.
- **Grazing animals** are divided into perissodactyls and artiodactyls, according to how many toes they have.
- **Perissodactyls** have an odd number of toes on each foot. They include horses, rhinos and tapirs.
- **Artiodactyls** have an even number. They include camels, deer, antelope, cattle and buffaloes.

Elephants

- **There are three kinds** of elephant – the African forest elephant, of central and west Africa, the African savanna elephant, of east and south Africa, and the Asian elephant, of India and Southeast Asia.
- **African elephants** are the largest land animals, growing as tall as 4 m and weighing more than 6,000 kg.
- **Asian elephants** are smaller than African elephants, with smaller ears and tusks. They also have one 'finger' on the tip of their trunk, while African elephants have two.
- **The scientific word** for an elephant's trunk is a proboscis. It is used like a hand to put food into the elephant's mouth, or to suck up water to squirt into its mouth or over its body to keep cool.
- **Elephants** are very intelligent animals, with the biggest brain of all land animals. They also have very good memories.
- **Female elephants**, called cows, live with their calves and younger bulls (males) in herds of 20 to 30 animals. Older bulls usually live alone.
- **Once a year**, bull elephants go into a state called musth (said 'must'), when male hormones make them very wild and dangerous.
- **Elephants** usually live for about 70 years.
- **When an elephant dies**, its companions seem to mourn and cry.

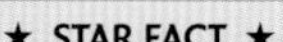

★ STAR FACT ★

Elephants use their trunks like snorkels when crossing deep rivers.

▼ *When the leader of the herd senses danger, she lifts her trunk and sniffs the air – then warns the others by using her trunk to give a loud blast called a trumpet. If an intruder comes too close, she will roll down her trunk, throw back her ears, lower her head and charge at up to 50 km/h.*

▼ *In dry areas, herds may travel vast distances to find food, with the bigger elephants protecting the little ones between their legs.*

Camels

- **Camels** are the biggest desert mammals and they have adapted in many ways to help them live in extremely dry conditions.
- **Dromedary camels** have one hump and live mainly in the Sahara desert and the Middle East. Bactrian camels live in central Asia and have two humps.
- **A camel's hump** is made of fat, but the camel's body can break the fat down into food and water when these are scarce.
- **Camels can go** many days or even months without water. But when water is available, they can drink over 200 litres in a day.

▶ *The Dromedary camel has been the 'ship of the desert', transporting people and baggage, for thousands of years.*

- **Camels sweat** very little, to save moisture. Instead, their body temperature rises by as much as 6°C when it is hot.
- **The camel's feet** have two joined toes to stop them sinking into soft sand (Dromedary camels) or soft snow (Bactrians).
- **The camel's nostrils** can close up completely to block out sand.
- **Camels have** a double row of eyelashes to protect their eyes from sand and sun.
- **The camel's stomach** is huge, with three different sections. Like cows, camels are ruminants – this means they partially digest food, then bring it back into their mouths to chew the cud.

★ **STAR FACT** ★

Camels have by far the worst smelling breath in the entire animal kingdom!

Eating food

▲ *Bears are omnivores, eating fish and other meat, although they will eat berries, leaves and almost anything when hungry.*

- **Herbivores** are animals that usually eat only plants.
- **Carnivores** are animals that eat animal flesh (meat).
- **Omnivores** eat plants and animals. Many primates such as monkeys, apes and humans are omnivorous.
- **Insectivores** eat insects. Some, such as bats, have teeth for breaking through insects' shells. Others, such as anteaters, have long, sticky tongues for licking up ants and termites, but few or no teeth.
- **Herbivores** such as cattle, elephants and horses either graze (eat grass) or browse (eat mainly leaves, bark and the buds of bushes and trees).
- **Herbivores** have tough, crowned teeth to cope with their hard plant food.
- **Carnivores** have pointed canine teeth for tearing meat.
- **Some carnivores**, such as hyenas, do not hunt and instead feed on carrion (the remains of dead animals).
- **Herbivores** eat for much of the time. However, because meat is very nourishing, carnivores eat only occasionally and tend to rest after each meal.
- **Every living thing** is part of a food chain, in which it feeds on the living thing before it in the chain and is in turn eaten by the living thing next to it in the chain.

Dolphins

- **Dolphins** are sea creatures that belong to the same family as whales – the cetaceans.
- **Dolphins are mammals**, not fish. They are warm-blooded, and mothers feed their young on milk.
- **There are two kinds** of dolphin – marine (sea) dolphins (32 species) and river dolphins (5 species).
- **Dolphins usually live** in groups of 20 to 100 animals.
- **Dolphins look after** each other. Often, they will support an injured companion on the surface.
- **Dolphins communicate** with high-pitched clicks called phonations. Some clicks are higher than any other animal noise and humans cannot hear them.
- **Dolphins use sound** to find things and can identify different objects even when blindfolded.

★ STAR FACT ★
Dolphins have rescued drowning humans by pushing them to the surface.

▲ *Dolphins are among the most intelligent of the animals, along with humans and chimpanzees.*

- **Dolphins can be trained** to jump through hoops, toss balls, or 'walk' backwards through the water on their tails.
- **Bottle-nosed dolphins** get their name from their short beaks (which also make them look like they are smiling). They are friendly and often swim near boats.

Pheasants and peafowl

- **A game bird** is a bird that is hunted for sport.
- **Game birds** spend most of the time strutting along the ground looking for seeds. They fly only in emergencies.
- **There are 250 species** of game bird, including pheasants, grouse, partridges, quails, wild turkeys and peafowl.
- **Most of the 48 species** of pheasant originated in China and central Asia.
- **Many hen (female) game birds** have dull brown plumage that helps them to hide in their woodland and moorland homes.
- **Many cock (male) game birds** have very colourful plumage to attract mates.
- **In the breeding season**, cocks strut and puff up their plumage to attract a mate. They also draw attention to themselves by cackling, whistling and screaming.
- **Pheasant cocks** often fight each other violently to win a particular mating area.
- **The jungle fowl** of Southeast Asia is the wild ancestor of the domestic chicken.
- **Peacocks** were carried as treasure from India throughout the ancient world.

◀ *The peacock (the male peafowl) of India and Sri Lanka is the most spectacular of all pheasants. When courting the drab peahen, the peacock throws up his tail feathers to create a gigantic turquoise fan.*

Kangaroos and koalas

- **Kangaroos** are big Australian mammals that hop around on their hind (back) legs.
- **A kangaroo's tail** can be over 1.5 m long. It is used for balance when hopping, and to hold the kangaroo up when walking.
- **Red kangaroos** can hop at 55 km/h for short distances.
- **Red kangaroos** can leap 9 m forwards in one huge bound, and jump over fences that are 2 to 3 m high.
- **There are two kinds of kangaroo** – red kangaroos and grey kangaroos. Red kangaroos live in the dry grasslands of central Australia. Grey kangaroos live in the southeast, in woods and grassland.
- **Kangaroos are marsupials** – animals whose babies are born before they are ready to survive in the outside word and so live for a while protected in a pouch on their mother's belly.

▲ *Koalas drink very little water, and their name comes from an Aboriginal word for 'no drink'.*

- **Koalas** are Australian mammals that look like teddy bears, but which are no relation to any kind of bear.
- **Like kangaroos**, koalas are marsupials. A koala baby spends 6 months in its mother's pouch and another 6 months riding on her back.
- **Koalas** spend 18 hours a day sleeping. The rest of the time they feed on the leaves of eucalyptus trees.
- **Other Australian marsupials** include the wombat, and several kinds of wallaby (which look like small kangaroos) and bandicoots (which look like rats).

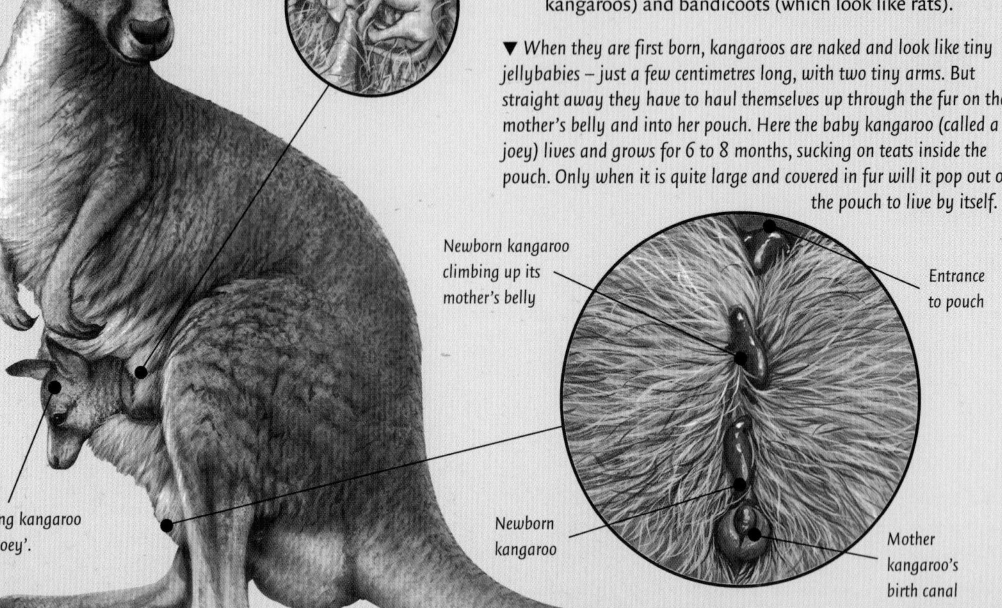

▼ *When they are first born, kangaroos are naked and look like tiny jellybabies – just a few centimetres long, with two tiny arms. But straight away they have to haul themselves up through the fur on their mother's belly and into her pouch. Here the baby kangaroo (called a joey) lives and grows for 6 to 8 months, sucking on teats inside the pouch. Only when it is quite large and covered in fur will it pop out of the pouch to live by itself.*

Migration

- **Migration** is when animals move from one place to another to avoid the cold or to find food and water.
- **Some migrations** are daily, some are seasonal, and some are permanent.
- **Starlings** migrate every day from the country to their roosts in the city.
- **Many birds, whales, seals and bats** migrate closer to the tropics in autumn to escape the winter cold.
- **One knot** (a kind of small bird) took just 8 days to fly 5,600 km, from Britain to West Africa.
- **Barheaded geese** migrate right over the top of the Himalayan mountains, flying as high as 8,000 m.
- **Migrating birds** are often brilliant navigators. Bristle-thighed curlews find their way from Alaska to tiny islands in the Pacific 9,000 km away.
- **Shearwaters**, sparrows and homing pigeons are able to fly home when released by scientists in strange places, thousands of kilometres away.

▶ *In summer, moose spend most of the time alone. But in winter they gather and trample areas of snow (called yards) to help each other get at the grass beneath.*

- **The Arctic tern** is the greatest migrator, flying 30,000 km from the Arctic to the Antarctic and back again each year.
- **Monarch butterflies** migrate 4,000 km every year, from North America to small clumps of trees in Mexico. Remarkably, the migrating butterflies have never made the journey before.

Eels

- **Eels** are long, slimy fish that look like snakes.

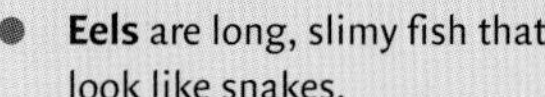

- **Baby eels** are called elvers.
- **Some eels** live in rivers, but most live in the sea, including moray eels and conger eels.
- **Moray eels** are huge and live in tropical waters, hunting fish, squid and cuttlefish.
- **Gulper eels** can live more than 7,500 m down in the Atlantic Ocean. Their mouths are huge to help them catch food in the dark, deep water – so big that they can swallow fish larger than themselves whole.
- **Every autumn**, some European common eels migrate over 7,000 km, from the Baltic Sea in Europe to the Sargasso Sea near the West Indies to lay their eggs.
- **Migrating eels** are thought to find their way partly by detecting weak electric currents created by the movement of the water.

◀ *Moray eels are fearsome predators that can grow to as long as 3 m. They hide in rock crevices during the day and come out at night to hunt.*

- **When European eels** hatch in the Sargasso Sea they are carried northeast by the ocean current, developing as they go into tiny transparent eels called glass eels.
- **The electric eels** of South America can produce an electric shock of over 500 volts – enough to knock over an adult human.
- **Garden eels** live in colonies on the seabed, poking out from holes in the sand to catch food drifting by. Their colonies look like gardens of weird plants.

What are mammals?

- **Mammals** are animals with furry bodies, warm blood, and a unique habit of suckling their young on milk from the mother's teats.
- **Humans and most other mammals** keep their body temperatures at around 37°C, although the three-toed sloth's temperature varies from 24°C to more than 40°C.
- **Fur and fat** protect mammals from the cold. When they do get cold, they curl up, seek shelter or shiver.
- **All mammals** except monotremes (see strange mammals) give birth to live young.
- **Most mammals** are placental – their young are nourished inside the mother's womb through an organ called the placenta until they are fully developed.
- **Marsupials** are not placental. Their young develop mainly in the mother's pouch.
- **The time from mating to birth** is called the pregnancy or gestation period. In mammals, it varies from 20 days for some mice to 22 months for elephants.

▲ *Pigs have 12 or so babies in a litter and 7 pairs of teats.*

- **Marsupials** have short pregnancies – the opossum's is just 12 days.
- **Mammals** vary in size from the finger-sized Etruscan shrew to the 30 m-long blue whale.
- **One of the earliest mammals** was a tiny, shrew-like creature called megazostrodon that lived alongside the dinosaurs about 120 million years ago.

Ocean fish

◀ *Flying fish beat their tails so fast they are able to 'fly' away from predators.*

- **Nearly 75%** of all fish live in the seas and oceans.
- **The biggest, fastest swimming fish**, such as swordfish and marlin, live near the surface of the open ocean, far from land. They often migrate vast distances to spawn (lay their eggs) or find food.
- **Many smaller fish** live deeper down, including seabed-dwellers like eels and flatfish (such as plaice, turbot and flounders).
- **All flatfish** start life as normal-shaped fish, but as they grow older, one eye slowly slides around the head to join the other. The pattern of scales changes so that one side is the top, the other is the bottom.
- **Plaice** lie on the seabed on their left side, while turbot lie on their right side. Some flounders lie on their left and some on their right.
- **The upper side** of a flatfish is usually camouflaged to help it blend in with the sea floor.
- **In the temperate waters** of the Atlantic there are rich fishing grounds for fish such as herring.
- **The swordfish** can swim at up to 80 km/h. It uses its long spike to slash or stab squid.
- **The bluefin tuna** can grow to as long as 3 m and weigh more than 500 kg. It is also a fast swimmer – one crossed the Atlantic in 199 days.

★ STAR FACT ★

Flying fish can glide over the sea for 400 m and soar up to 6 m above the waves.

Grasshoppers and crickets

- **Grasshoppers** are plant-eating insects related to crickets, locusts and katydids.
- **Grasshoppers** belong to two main families – short-horned, which includes locusts, and long-horned, which includes katydids and crickets.
- **Short-horned grasshoppers** have ears on the side of their body. Long-horned grasshoppers have ears in their knees.
- **Grasshoppers** have powerful back legs, which allow them to jump huge distances.
- **Some grasshoppers** can leap more than 3 m.
- **Grasshoppers** sing by rubbing their hind legs across their closed forewings.
- **A grasshopper's singing** is called stridulation.
- **Crickets** chirrup faster the warmer it is.
- **If you count** the number of chirrups a snowy tree cricket gives in 15 seconds, then add 40, you get the temperature in degrees Fahrenheit.

★ STAR FACT ★
A frightened lubber grasshopper oozes a horrible smelling froth from its mouth.

▼ *The spikes on the long-horned grasshopper's back legs are what make the chirruping sound as it rubs them against its forewings.*

Life in the mountains

- **Mountains** are cold, windy places where only certain animals can survive – including agile hunters such as pumas and snow leopards, and nimble grazers such as mountain goats, yaks, ibex and chamois.
- **The world's highest-living** mammal is the yak, a type of wild cattle. It can survive over 6,000 m up in the Himalayas of Tibet.
- **Mountain goats** have hooves with sharp edges that dig into cracks in the rock, and hollow soles that act like suction pads.

▲ *Sheep like these dall sheep are well equipped for life in the mountains, with their thick woolly coats and nimble feet.*

- **In winter**, the mountain goat's pelage (coat) turns white, making it hard to spot against the snow.
- **The Himalayan snowcock** nests higher than almost any other bird, often above 4,000 m in the Himalayas.
- **The Alpine chough** has been seen flying at 8,200 m up on Everest.
- **Lammergeiers** are the vultures of the African and southern European mountains. They break bones, when feeding, by dropping them from a great height on to stones and then eating the marrow.
- **The Andean condor** of the South American Andes is a gigantic scavenger which can carry off deer and sheep. It is said to dive from the skies like a fighter plane (see also vultures).
- **The puma**, or mountain lion, can jump well over 5 m up on to a rock ledge – that is like you jumping into an upstairs window.
- **The snow leopard** of the Himalayan mountains is now one of the rarest of all the big cats, because it has been hunted almost to extinction for its beautiful fur coat.

Life in the oceans

▲ *Many kinds of fish and other sea creatures live in the sunlit zone near the surface of the oceans.*

- **Oceans** cover 70% of the Earth and they are the largest single animal habitat.
- **Scientists divide the ocean** into two main environments – the pelagic (which is the water itself), and the benthic (which is the seabed).
- **Most benthic animals** live in shallow waters around the continents. They include worms, clams, crabs and lobsters, as well as bottom-feeding fish.
- **Scientists call the sunny surface waters** the euphotic zone. This extends down 150 m and it is where billions of plankton (microscopic animals and plants) live.
- **Green plant plankton** (algae) of the oceans produce 30% of the world's vegetable matter each year.
- **Animal plankton** include shrimps and jellyfish.
- **The surface waters** are also home to squid, fish and mammals such as whales.
- **Below the surface zone**, down to about 2,000 m, is the twilit bathyal zone. Here there is too little light for plants to grow, but many hunting fish and squid live.
- **Below 2,000 m** is the dark abyssal zone, where only weird fish like gulper eels and anglerfish live (see strange sea creatures).
- **The Sargasso**, a vast area in the west Atlantic where seaweed grows thick, is a rich home to many sea creatures.

Corals and anemones

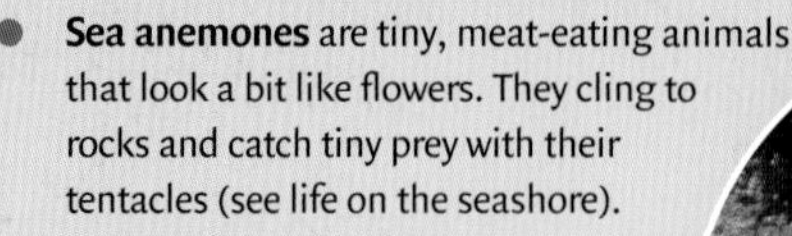

◀ *Sea anemones look like flowers with petals, but they are actually carnivorous animals with rings of tentacles.*

- **Sea anemones** are tiny, meat-eating animals that look a bit like flowers. They cling to rocks and catch tiny prey with their tentacles (see life on the seashore).
- **Coral reefs** are the undersea equivalent of rainforests, teeming with fish and other sea life. The reefs are built by tiny, sea-anemone-like animals called polyps.
- **Coral polyps** live all their lives in just one place, either fixed to a rock or to dead polyps.
- **When coral polyps die**, their cup-shaped skeletons become hard coral.
- **Coral reefs** are long ridges, and other shapes, made from billions of coral polyps and their skeletons.
- **Fringing reefs** are shallow coral reefs that stretch out from the seashore.
- **Barrier reefs** form a long, underwater wall a little way offshore.
- **The Great Barrier Reef** off eastern Australia is the longest reef in the world, stretching over 2,000 km. It can be seen from space (up to 200 km up) and is the only non-human, animal activity visible from space.
- **Coral atolls** are ring-shaped islands that formed from fringing reefs around an old volcano (which has long since sunk beneath the waves).
- **Coral reefs** take millions of years to form – the Great Barrier Reef is 18 million years old, for example. By drilling a core into ancient corals, and analysing the minerals and growth rate, scientists can read the history of the oceans back for millions of years.

Butterflies

- **Butterflies** are insects with four large wings that feed either on the nectar of flowers or on fruit.
- **Together with moths**, butterflies make up the scientific order Lepidoptera – the word means 'scaly wings'. There are more than 165,000 species of Lepidoptera – 20,000 butterflies and 145,000 moths.
- **Many butterflies** are brightly coloured and fly by day. They have slim, hairless bodies and club-shaped antennae (feelers).
- **The biggest butterfly** is the Queen Alexandra's birdwing of New Guinea, with 25-cm-wide wings. The smallest is the Western pygmy blue.
- **Butterflies can only fly** if their wing muscles are warm. To warm up, they bask in the sun so their wings soak up energy like solar panels.
- **The monarch butterfly** is such a strong flier it can cross the Atlantic Ocean (see migration).
- **The shimmering blue wings** of the South American morpho butterfly are very beautiful – in the 19th century millions of the butterflies were caught and made into brooches.
- **Most female butterflies** live only a few days, so they have to mate and lay eggs quickly. Most males court them with elaborate flying displays.
- **Butterflies** taste with their tarsi (feet). Females 'stamp' on leaves to see if they are ripe enough for egg laying.
- **Every butterfly's caterpillar** has its own chosen food plants – different from the flowers the adult feeds on.

▲ *Every species of butterfly has its own wing pattern, like a fingerprint – some drab like this, others brilliantly coloured.*

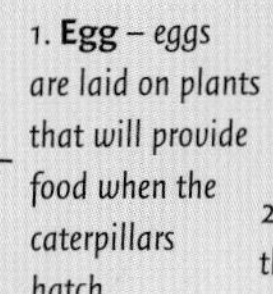

1. **Egg** – *eggs are laid on plants that will provide food when the caterpillars hatch*

2. **Larva** – *when the caterpillar hatches, it begins eating and growing straight away*

3. **Pupa** – *butterfly caterpillars develop hard cases and hang from a stem or leaf*

4. **Metamorphosis** – *it takes a few days to a year for the pupa to turn into an adult*

5. **Imago** – *the adult's new wings are damp and crumpled, but soon dry in the sun*

◀ *Few insects change as much as butterflies do during their lives. Butterflies start off as an egg, then hatch into a long, wiggly larva called a caterpillar, which eats leaves greedily and grows rapidly. When it is big enough, the caterpillar makes itself a case, which can be either a cocoon or a chrysalis. Inside, it metamorphoses (changes) into an adult, then breaks out, dries its new wings and flies away.*

★ **STAR FACT** ★

Butterflies fly like no other insects, flapping their wings like birds.

Octopuses and squid

- **Octopuses and squid** belong to a family of molluscs called cephalopods.
- **Octopuses** are sea creatures with a round, soft, boneless body, three hearts and eight long arms called tentacles.
- **An octopus's tentacles** are covered with suckers that allow it to grip rocks and prey.
- **Octopuses** have two large eyes, similar to humans, and a beak-like mouth.
- **When in danger** an octopus may send out a cloud of inky black fluid. Sometimes the ink cloud is the same shape as the octopus and may fool a predator into chasing the cloud.

★ STAR FACT ★
The 30-cm-long blue-ringed octopus's poison is so deadly that it kills more people than sharks.

- **Some octopuses can change colour** dramatically to startle a predator or blend in with its background.
- **The smallest octopus** is just 2.5 cm across. The biggest measures 6 m from tentacle tip to tentacle tip.
- **A squid** has eight arms and two tentacles and swims by forcing a jet of water out of its body.
- **Giant squid** in the Pacific can grow to 18 m or more long.

◀ *Most of the hundreds of species of octopus live on the beds of shallow seas around the world. Octopuses are quite intelligent creatures.*

Life on the grasslands

▲ *Until they were wiped out by European settlers, vast herds of bison (buffalo) roamed the North American prairies.*

- **Grasslands** form in temperate (moderate temperature) regions where there is too little rainfall for forests, but enough to allow grass to grow.
- **Temperate grasslands** include the prairies of North America, the pampas of South America, the veld of South Africa, and the vast steppes of Eurasia.
- **There is little cover** on grasslands, so many grassland animals have very good eyesight and large ears to detect predators from afar.
- **Some grassland animals escape** from predators by speed. These include jack rabbits, deer, pronghorn antelopes, wild asses and flightless birds like the emu.
- **Some animals**, such as mice and prairie dogs, escape by hiding underground in burrows.
- **Some birds hide** by building their nests in bushes. These include meadowlarks, quails and blackbirds.
- **The main predators** are dogs like the coyote and fox.
- **The North American prairies** have a small wild cat called the bobcat.
- **Prairie dogs** live in huge underground colonies called towns. One contained 400 million animals and covered over 60,000 square kilometres.
- **When they meet**, prairie dogs kiss each other to find out whether they are from the same group.

Seagulls and albatrosses

▲ *Seagulls catch small fish, steal eggs and young from other birds, scavenge on waste – and sometimes fly inland to find worms.*

★ STAR FACT ★

Herring gulls watch ducks diving for fish and then steal it when the ducks resurface.

- **Gulls are big sea birds** that live on coasts all around the world, nesting on cliffs, islands or beaches.
- **Gulls are related** to skuas and terns.
- **Skuas** have hooked claws and sharp bills, which they use to attack other birds and force them to disgorge (throw up) their food – which the skua then eats.
- **Skuas are such good acrobats** that they can catch the disgorged meal of another bird in mid-air.
- **The great skua** often pounces on seagulls, drowns them, and then steals their chicks.
- **Wandering albatrosses** are the biggest of all sea birds, with white bodies and dark wings.
- **The wandering albatross** has the biggest wingspan of any bird – 3.7 m across.
- **An albatross** will often follow a ship for days without stopping to rest.
- **Wild albatrosses** may live for more than 50 years.

Giraffes

- **Giraffes** are the tallest mammals, growing to more than 5 m. Their height allows them to reach and eat the leaves, twigs and fruit at the tops of trees.
- **A giraffe's legs** are almost 2 m long.
- **A giraffe's neck** may be over 2 m long, but it only has seven bones – the same number as humans.
- **Giraffes live** in Africa, south of the Sahara, in bush country.
- **The giraffe's long tongue** is so tough that it can wrap around the thorns of a thorn tree to grab twigs.
- **When drinking**, a giraffe has to spread its forelegs wide or kneel down to reach the water. This position makes it very vulnerable to attack by lions.

▲ *Giraffes are the world's tallest animals – but they are five times as light as elephants.*

- **When giraffes walk**, they move the two legs on one side of their body, then the two on the other side. Their long legs mean that when it comes to running they can gallop along faster than the speediest racehorse.
- **A giraffe's coat** is patched in brown on cream, and each giraffe has its own unique pattern. The reticulated giraffes of East Africa have triangular patches, but the South African Cape giraffes have blotchy markings.
- **During breeding time**, rival males rub their necks together and swing them from side to side. This is called necking.
- **When first born**, a baby giraffe is very wobbly on its legs and so cannot stand up for at least its first half an hour.

Whales

- **Whales**, dolphins and porpoises are large mammals called cetaceans that live mostly in the seas and oceans. Dolphins and porpoises are small whales.
- **Like all mammals**, whales have lungs – this means they have to come to the surface to breathe every 10 minutes or so, although they can stay down for up to 40 minutes. A sperm whale can hold its breath for 2 hours.
- **Whales breathe** through blowholes on top of their head. When a whale breathes out, it spouts out water vapour and mucus. When it breathes in, it sucks in about 2,000 litres of air within about 2 seconds.
- **Like land mammals**, whales nurse their babies with their own milk. Whale milk is so rich that babies grow incredibly fast. Blue whale babies are over 7 m long when they are born and gain an extra 100 kg or so a day for about 7 months.

▶ Killer whales or orcas are one of the biggest deep-sea predators, growing to as long as 9 m and weighing up to 10 tonnes. They feed on many types of fish, seals, penguins, squid, sea birds and sometimes even dolphins.

Dorsal fin

To swim, whales flap their fluke (tail) up and down

▲ Humpback whales live together in groups called pods and keep in touch with their own 'dialect' of noises.

- **Toothed whales**, such as the sperm whale and the orca or killer whale, have teeth and prey on large fish and seals. The six groups of toothed whale are sperm whales, beaked whales, belugas and narwhals, dolphins, porpoises, and river dolphins.
- **Baleen whales**, such as the humpback and blue, have a comb of thin plates called baleen in place of teeth. They feed by straining small, shrimp-like creatures called krill through their baleen. There are five baleen whale groups, including right whales, grey whales and rorquals. Rorquals have grooves on their throats and include humpback, minke and blue whales.

★ STAR FACT ★
Male humpbacks make elaborate 'songs' lasting 20 minutes or more – perhaps to woo females.

- **The blue whale** is the largest creature that ever lived. Blue whales grow to be over 30 m long and weigh more than 150 tonnes. In summer, they eat over 4 tonnes of krill every day – that is 4 million krill.
- **Whales keep in touch** with sounds called phonations. Large baleen whales make sounds which are too low for humans to hear, but they can be heard by other whales at least 80 km away.
- **Most baleen whales** live alone or in small groups, but toothed whales – especially dolphins – often swim together in groups called pods or schools.

What are birds?

- **Not all birds** can fly, but they all have feathers.
- **Feathers** are light, but they are linked by hooks called barbs to make them strong enough for flight.
- **Wrens** have 1,000 feathers, while swans have 20,000.
- **Birds have four kinds** of wing feather – large primaries, smaller secondaries, coverts and contours.
- **Every kind of bird** has its own formation, pattern and colour of feathers, called its plumage.
- **Instead of teeth**, birds have a hard beak or bill.
- **Unlike humans**, birds do not give birth to babies. Instead they lay eggs, usually sitting on them to keep them warm until they hatch (see birds' nests and eggs).
- **Birds fly in two ways** – by gliding with their wings held still, or by flapping their wings up and down.

★ STAR FACT ★
Birds are probably descended from dinosaurs and took to the air about 150 million years ago.

▲ *Most birds flap their wings to fly. Even birds that spend much of their time gliding have to flap their wings to take off and land.*

- **Gliding is less effort** than flapping, and birds that stay in the air a long time tend to be superb gliders – including birds of prey, swifts, gulls and gannets.
- **Albatrosses and petrels** have long narrow wings that help them sail upwards on rising air currents.

Life in rivers and lakes

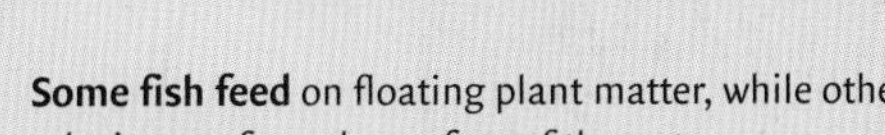

- **Rivers, lakes** and other freshwater habitats are home to all sorts of fish, including bream and trout.
- **Fast-flowing streams** are preferred by fish such as trout and grayling. Slow-flowing rivers and lakes are home to tench, rudd and carp.

▲ *Upland lakes like these are home to many fish, including char, powan and bullhead. Fish such as brown trout swim in the streams that tumble down into the lake.*

- **Some fish feed** on floating plant matter, while others take insects from the surface of the water.
- **Common bream and berbel** hunt on the riverbed, eating insect larvae, worms and molluscs.
- **Perch and pike** are predators of lakes and slow-flowing rivers.
- **Pike are the sharks** of the river – deadly hunters that lurk among weeds waiting for unwary fish, or even rats and birds. Pike can weigh as much as 30 kg.
- **Mammals of rivers and lakes** include voles, water rats and otters.
- **Birds of rivers and lakes** include birds that dive for fish (such as kingfishers), small wading birds (such as redshanks, avocets and curlews), large wading birds (such as herons, storks and flamingos), and waterfowl (such as ducks, swans and geese).
- **Insects** include dragonflies and water boatmen.
- **Amphibians** include frogs and newts.

Cobras and vipers

◀ *When defending itself, a cobra rears up and spreads the skin of its neck in a hood to make it look bigger. This often gives victims a chance to hit it away.*

- **Two kinds of poisonous snake** are dangerous to humans – vipers and elapids such as cobras and mambas.
- **Elapids** have their venom (poison) in short front fangs. A viper's fangs are so long that they usually have to be folded away.
- **The hamadryad cobra** of Southeast Asia is the world's largest poisonous snake, growing to over 5 m.

★ STAR FACT ★
Fer-de-lance snakes have 60 to 80 babies, each of which is deadly poisonous.

- **In India, cobras kill** more than 7,000 people every year. The bite of a king cobra can kill an elephant in 4 hours. The marine cobra lives in the sea and its venom is 100 times more deadly.
- **Snake charmers** use the spectacled cobra, playing to it so that it follows the pipe as if about to strike – but the snake's fangs have been removed to make it safe.
- **A spitting cobra** squirts venom into its attacker's eyes, and is accurate at 2 m or more. The venom is not deadly, but it blinds the victim and is very painful.
- **The black mamba** of Africa can race along at 25 km/h with its head raised and its tongue flickering.
- **A viper's venom** kills its victims by making their blood clot. Viper venom has been used to treat haemophiliacs (people whose blood does not clot well).
- **The pit vipers** of the Americas hunt their warm-blooded victims using heat-sensitive pits on the side of their heads (see animal senses).

Horses

     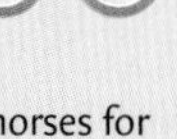

- **Horses** are big, four-legged, hooved animals, now bred mainly for human use.
- **Adult male horses** are stallions, females are mares, babies are foals, and young males are colts.
- **The only wild horses** are the Przewalski and the tarpan (possibly extinct) of central Asia.
- **The mustangs** (wild horses) of the USA are descended from tame horses.

▲ *All horses, wild and tame, may be descended from the prehistoric Merychippus (see evolution).*

- **Tame horses** are of three main kinds – light horses for riding (such as Morgans and Arabs), heavy horses for pulling ploughs and wagons (such as Pecherons and Suffolk punches), and ponies (such as Shetlands).
- **Most racehorses and hunting horses** are thoroughbred (pure) Arab horses descended from just three stallions that lived around 1700 – Darley Arabian, Godolphin Barb and Byerly Turk.
- **Lippizaners** are beautiful white horses, the best-known of which are trained to jump and dance at the Spanish Riding School in Vienna.
- **The shire horse** is probably the largest horse, bred after King Henry VIII had all horses under 1.5 m destroyed.
- **You can tell a horse's age** by counting its teeth – a 1-year-old has six pairs, a 5-year-old has twelve.
- **Quarter horses** are agile horses used by cowhands for cutting out (sorting cows from the herd). They got their name from running quarter-mile races.

Seals and sea lions

- **Seals, sea lions and walruses** are sea mammals that mainly live in water and are agile swimmers, but which waddle awkwardly when they come on land.
- **Most seals** eat fish, squid and shellfish. Crabeater seals eat mainly shrimps, not crabs.
- **Seals and sea lions** have ears, but only sea lions (which include fur seals) have ear flaps.

★ STAR FACT ★
The 4-m-long leopard seal of Antarctica feeds on penguins and even other seals.

- **Only sea lions** can move their back flippers under their body when travelling about on land.
- **When seals come ashore** to breed, they live for weeks in vast colonies called rookeries.
- **Walruses** are bigger and bulkier than seals, and they have massive tusks and face whiskers.
- **When hunters kill seal pups** for their fur, or to keep numbers down, it is called culling.
- **Elephant seals** spend up to 8 months far out in the ocean, continuously diving, with each dive lasting 20 minutes or so.
- **There are freshwater seals** in Lake Baikal in Russia.

◀ *All seals and sea lions have fur. Only the walrus lacks a furry coat.*

Moths

- **Moths belong**, to the insect group Lepidoptera.
- **Most moths** have fat, hairy bodies, and feathery or thread-like antennae.
- **Many moths** fly at dusk or at night. By day, they rest on tree trunks and in leaves, where their colour makes them hard for predators such as birds to spot. However, there are also many brightly coloured day-flying moths.
- **Tiger moths** give out high-pitched clicks to warn that they taste bad and so escape being eaten.
- **The biggest moths** are the Hercules moth and the bent wing ghost moth of Asia, with wingspans of over 25 cm.
- **Night-flying** moths shiver their wings to warm them up for flight.
- **Hawk moths** are powerful fliers and migrate long distances. The oleander hawk moth flies from tropical Africa to far northern Europe in summer.
- **The caterpillars of small moths** live in seeds, fruit, stems and leaves, eating them from the inside.

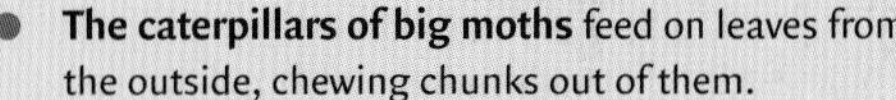

- **The caterpillars of big moths** feed on leaves from the outside, chewing chunks out of them.
- **When threatened**, the caterpillar of the puss moth rears up and thrusts its whip-like tail forward and squirts a jet of formic acid from its head end.
- **Every caterpillar spins silk**, but the cloth silk comes from the caterpillar of the white *Bombyx mori* moth, known as the silkworm.

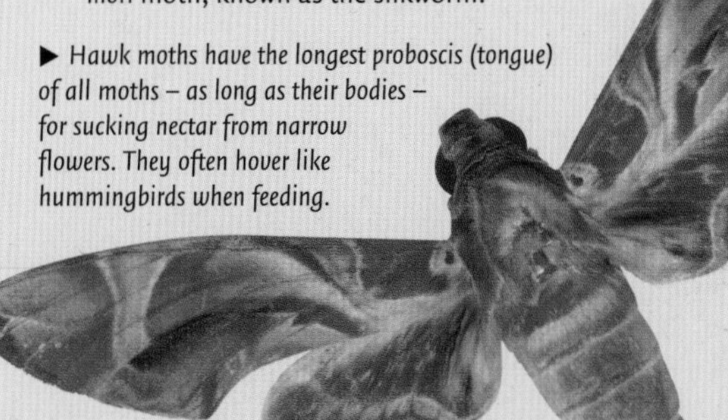

▶ *Hawk moths have the longest proboscis (tongue) of all moths – as long as their bodies – for sucking nectar from narrow flowers. They often hover like hummingbirds when feeding.*

Bird eggs and nests

★ STAR FACT ★
Great auks' eggs are pointed at one end to stop them rolling off their cliff-edge nests.

- **All birds** begin life as eggs. Each species' egg is a slightly different colour.
- **The plover's egg** is pear-shaped. The owl's is round.
- **Hornbills** lay just one egg a year. Partridges lay up to 20 eggs. Hens and some ducks can lay around 350 a year.
- **Most birds build nests** to lay their eggs in – usually bowl-shaped and made from twigs, grass and leaves.
- **The biggest nest** is that of the Australian mallee fowl, which builds a mound of soil 5 m across, with egg-chambers filled with rotting vegetation to keep it warm.
- **The weaverbirds** of Africa and Asia are very sociable. Some work together to weave huge, hanging nests out of straw, with scores of chambers. Each chamber is for a pair of birds and has its own entrance.
- **Ovenbirds** of Central and South America get their name because their nests look like the clay ovens made by local people. Some ovenbirds' nests can be 3 m high.
- **Flamingos** nest on lakes, building mud nests that look like upturned sandcastles poking out of the water. They lay one or two eggs on top.
- **The great treeswift** lays its single egg in a nest the size of an eggcup.

▶ *After they lay their eggs, most birds sit on them to keep their eggs warm until they are ready to hatch. This is called incubating the eggs.*

Defence

- **Animals** have different ways of escaping predators – most mammals run away, while birds take to the air.
- **Some animals** use camouflage to hide (see colours and markings). Many small animals hide in burrows.
- **Turtles and tortoises** hide inside their hard shells.

▼ *Meerkats stand on their hind legs and give a shrill call to alert other meerkats to danger.*

★ STAR FACT ★
The hognosed snake rolls over and plays dead to escape predators. It even smells dead.

- **Armadillos** curl up inside their bendy body armour.
- **The spiky-skinned** armadillo lizard of South Africa curls up and stuffs its tail in its mouth.
- **Hedgehogs**, porcupines and echidnas are protected by sharp quills (spines).
- **Skunks** and the stinkpot turtle give off foul smells.
- **Plovers** pretend to be injured to lure hunters away from their young.
- **Many animals defend themselves** by frightening their enemies. Some, such as peacock butterflies, flash big eye-markings. Others, such as porcupine fish and great horned owls, blow themselves up much bigger.
- **Other animals** send out warning signals. Kangaroo rats and rabbits thump their feet. Birds shriek.

Gorillas and other apes

- **Apes** are our closest relatives in the animal world. The great apes are gorillas, chimpanzees and the orang-utan. Gibbons are called lesser apes.
- **Like us**, apes have long arms, and fingers and toes for gripping. They are clever and can use sticks and stones as tools.
- **Gorillas** are the biggest of all the apes, weighing up to 225 kg and standing as tall as 2 m. But they are gentle vegetarians and eat leaves and shoots.
- **There are two gorilla species**, both from Africa – the western gorilla and eastern gorillas (including mountain gorillas).
- **Mountain gorillas** live in the mountains of Rwanda and Uganda. There are only about 650 of them.
- **When danger threatens a gorilla troop**, the leading adult male stands upright, pounds his hands against his chest, and bellows loudly.

◀ *Gorillas climb trees only to sleep at night or to pull down branches to make a one-night nest on the ground. They usually walk on all fours.*

- **Chimpanzees** are an ape species that live in the forests of central Africa.
- **Chimpanzees** are very clever and use tools more than any other animal apart from humans – they use leaves as sponges for soaking up water to drink, for example, and they crack nuts with stones.
- **Chimpanzees** communicate with each other through a huge range of grunts and screams. They also communicate by facial expressions and hand gestures, just as humans do. Experiments have shown that they can learn to respond to many words.
- **Only a few orang-utans** remain in the forests of Borneo and Sumatra. They get their name from a local word for 'old man of the woods'.

▶ *Gorillas live in troops (groups) of a dozen or so. They travel through the forests searching for food led by a mature male, called a silverback because of the silver hairs on his back. Gorillas like to groom each other and cuddle when they rest in the afternoon.*

Gorillas have no hair on their face or chest, and their palms and soles are also bare

Baby gorillas are carried their mother until they are years old

An adult male has a crest of hair on his head

Rhinos and hippos

- **Rhinoceroses** are big, tough-skinned animals of Africa and southern Asia.
- **African black and white** rhinos and the smaller Sumatran rhino have two horns in the middle of their heads. Indian and Javan rhinos have just one.
- **Powdered rhino horn** is believed by some to be a love potion, so thousands of rhinos have been slaughtered and most kinds are now endangered species.
- **Baluchitherium** lived 20 million years ago and was a type of rhino. At over 5 m tall, it was much bigger than any elephant.

★ **STAR FACT** ★
The African white rhinoceros's horn can grow to over 1.5 m long.

◀ *The African black rhino is almost extinct in the wild. Less than 3,000 are left on nature reserves. Some gamekeepers have tried cutting off their horns to make them less of a target for poachers.*

- **Hippopotamuses** are big, grey, pig-like creatures that live in Africa. They have the biggest mouth of any land animal.
- **When a hippo yawns** its mouth gapes wide enough to swallow a sheep whole, but it only eats grass.
- **Hippos spend their days** wallowing in rivers and swamps, and only come out at night to feed.
- **A hippo's eyes**, ears and nose are all on the top of its head, and so remain above the water when the rest of its body is completely submerged.
- **The word hippopotamus** comes from the Ancient Greek words for horse (hippo) and river (potamos).

Salmon

▲ *Salmon returning to their spawning ground make mighty leaps up raging torrents. The journey can take months.*

- **Salmon** are river and sea fish caught or farmed in huge quantities for food.
- **All salmon** are born in rivers and lakes far inland, then swim down river and out to sea.
- **Adult salmon** spend anything from 6 months to 7 years in the oceans, before returning to rivers and swimming upstream to spawn (lay their eggs).
- **Some salmon species**, including the chinook, spawn in North American rivers running into the North Pacific.
- **Cherry salmon** spawn in eastern Asian rivers, and amago salmon spawn in Japanese rivers.
- **Atlantic salmon** spawn in rivers in northern Europe and eastern Canada.
- **Amazingly, spawning salmon** return to the stream where they were born, up to 3,000 km inland. They may sense the chemical and mineral make-up of the water, helping them to recognise their own stream.
- **To reach their spawning grounds**, salmon have to swim upstream against strong currents, often leaping as high as 5 m to clear waterfalls.
- **When salmon** reach their spawning grounds, they mate. The female lays up to 20,000 eggs.
- **After spawning**, the weakened salmon head down river again, but few make it as far as the sea.

Turtles and tortoises

- **Turtles and tortoises** are reptiles that live inside hard, armoured shells. Together with terrapins, they make up a group called the chelonians.
- **Turtles** live in the sea, fresh water or on land, tortoises live on land, and terrapins live in streams and lakes.
- **The shield** on the back of a chelonian is called a carapace. Its flat belly armour is called a plastron.
- **Most turtles and tortoises** have no teeth, just jaws with very sharp edges, to eat plants and tiny animals.
- **Tortoises** live mostly in hot, dry regions and will hibernate in winter if brought to a cold country.
- **Turtles and tortoises** live to a great age. One giant tortoise found in 1766 in Mauritius lived 152 years.
- **The giant tortoise** grows to as long as 1.5 m.

★ STAR FACT ★
Giant tortoises were once kept on ships to provide fresh meat on long voyages.

- **The leatherback turtle** grows to as long as 2.5 m and weighs more than 800 kg.
- **Every three years**, green turtles gather together to swim thousands of kilometres to Ascension Island in the mid-Atlantic, where they lay their eggs ashore by moonlight at the highest tide. They bury the eggs in the sand, to be incubated by the heat of the sun.

▼ *Tortoises are very slow moving and placid.*

Antelopes and deer

- **Antelopes and deer** are four-legged, hooved animals. Along with cows, hippos and pigs, they belong to the huge group called artiodactyls – animals with an even number of toes on each foot.
- **Antelopes and deer** chew the cud like cows – they chew food again, after first partially digesting it in a special stomach.

◀ *Reindeer cope with harsh winters by finding lichen to eat under the snow – perhaps by smell.*

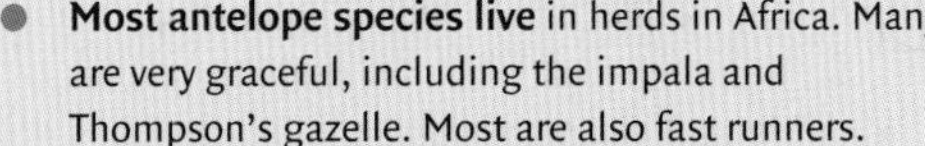

- **Most antelope species live** in herds in Africa. Many are very graceful, including the impala and Thompson's gazelle. Most are also fast runners.
- **The horns** on an antelope's head last its lifetime.
- **Deer have branching antlers** of bone (not horn) on their heads, which drop off and grow again each year.
- **Most deer species live** in woods and grasslands in mild regions such as northern Europe and North America.
- **The moose or elk** grows antlers more than 2 m wide.
- **Male deer** are called stags, young males are bucks, females are does and babies are fawns.
- **Usually only stags** have antlers. The only female deer to have them are caribou (or reindeer).

★ STAR FACT ★
Caribou can survive in the icy cold of Spitsbergen Island in the Arctic circle.

Evolution

▶ *All life on Earth may have evolved almost 4 billion years ago from organisms like this archaebacteria. Archaebacteria thrive in extreme conditions such as those on the early Earth. This one came from under the Antarctic ice. Others thrive in scorching undersea volcanic vents.*

★ STAR FACT ★
Many, many more species of animal have come and gone than are alive today.

- **Charles Darwin's** *Theory of Evolution*, first published in 1859, showed how all species of plant and animal adapt and develop over millions of years. Only the fittest survive.
- **Darwin's theory** depended on the fact that no two living things are alike.
- **Some animals** start life with characteristics that give them a better chance of surviving to pass the characteristics on to their offspring.
- **Other animals' characteristics** mean that they are less likely to survive.
- **Over many generations** and thousands of years, better-adapted animals and plants survive and flourish, while others die out or find a new home.
- **Fossil discoveries** since Darwin's time have supported his theory, and lines of evolution can be traced for thousands of species.
- **Fossils** also show that evolution is not always as slow and steady as Darwin thought. Some scientists believe change comes in rapid bursts, separated by long slow periods when little changes. Other scientists believe that bursts of rapid change interrupt periods of long steady change.
- **For the first 3 billion years** of Earth's history, the only life forms were microscopic, single-celled, marine (sea) organisms such as bacteria and amoeba. Sponges and jellyfish, the first multi-celled creatures, appeared by 700 million years ago (mya).
- **About 600 mya**, evolution speeded up dramatically in what is called the Precambrian explosion. Thousands of different organisms appeared within a very short space of time, including the first proper animals with bones and shells.
- **After the Precambrian**, life evolved rapidly. Fish developed, then insects and then, about 380 mya, amphibians – the first large creatures to crawl on land. About 340 mya, reptiles evolved – the first large creatures to live entirely on land.
- **Dinosaurs** developed from these early reptiles about 220 mya and dominated the Earth for 160 million years. Birds also evolved from the reptiles, and cynodonts (furry, mammal-like creatures).

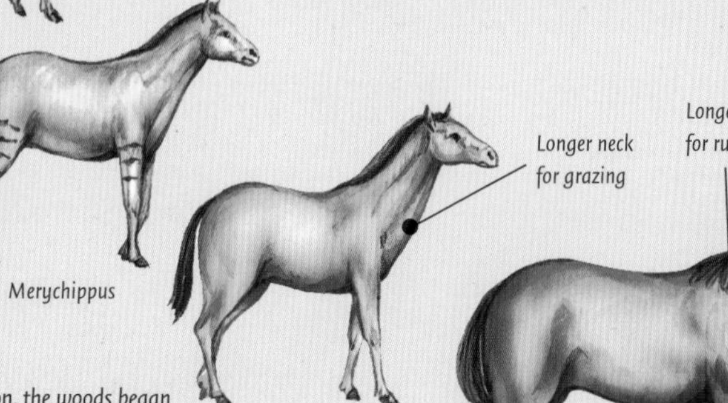

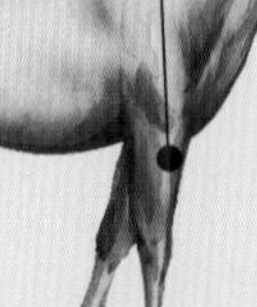

▶ *The gradual evolution of the horse shows how creatures adapt to changing conditions over million years. One of the horse's earliest ancestors, Hyracotherium, appeared about 50 mya. It was a small woodland creature which browsed on leaves and was suited to the widespread woodlands of the time. So was mesohippus. But from then on, the woods began to disappear and grasslands became more widespread – and it paid to be bigger to run fast to escape predators. The modern horse, Equus, is the latest result of evolutionary adaptation.*

What are insects?

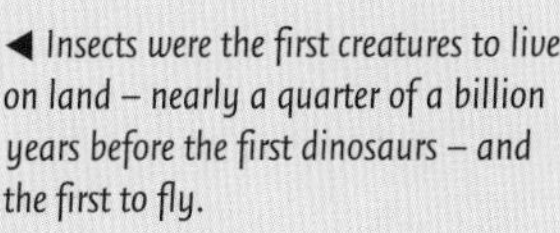

◀ *Insects were the first creatures to live on land – nearly a quarter of a billion years before the first dinosaurs – and the first to fly.*

- **Insects** may be tiny, but there are more of them than all the other animals put together – over 1 million known species.
- **They range** from tiny flies to huge beetles, and they are found everywhere there is land.
- **Insects** have six legs and a body divided into three sections – which is why they are called insects ('in sections'). The sections are the head, thorax (middle) and abdomen.
- **An insect's body** is encased in such a tough shell (its exoskeleton) that there is no need for bones.
- **Insect grow** by getting rid of their old exoskeleton and replacing it with a bigger one. This is called moulting.
- **Some insects change** dramatically as they grow. Butterflies, moths, and beetles undergo metamorphosis (see butterflies). Grasshoppers and mayflies begin as wingless nymphs, then gradually grow wings with each moult. Silverfish and springtails simply get bigger with each moult.
- **Insects' eyes** are called compound because they are made up of many lenses – from six (worker ants) to more than 30,000 (dragonflies).
- **Insects have** two antennae (feelers) on their heads.
- **Insects** do not have lungs. Instead, they breathe through holes in their sides called spiracles, linked to their body through tubes called tracheae.
- **The world's longest insect** is the giant stick insect of Indonesia, which can grow to 33 cm long.

Woodpeckers and toucans

- **Woodpeckers** are closely related to the colourful toucans and jacamars of tropical rainforests.
- **Woodpeckers**, toucans, barbets, jacamars and honeyguides all have two toes on each foot pointing forwards and two pointing backwards. Their toes help them cling to trees and branches.
- **Woodpeckers** use their powerful bills to bore into tree trunks to get at insects. They spear the insects with their incredibly long tongues.
- **Gila woodpeckers** escape the desert heat by nesting inside giant saguaro cacti (where it can be 30°C cooler).
- **Redhead woodpeckers** drill holes in trees and use them to store acorns for winter – wedging them in very tightly so that squirrels cannot steal them.

★ **STAR FACT** ★
At 23 cm, the toucan's bill is much longer than its body.

▲ *The toucan's giant beak is full of air holes, so it is not heavy enough to overbalance the bird. Toucans eat mainly small fruit.*

- **Woodpeckers** claim their territory not by singing, but by hammering their bills against trees.
- **Honeyguides** lead honey badgers to bees' nests. The badger gets the honey and the bird gets the beeswax.
- **When toucans sleep**, they turn their heads around and lay their bills down their backs.

Rabbits and rats

▶ *Rabbits and hares look like rodents. But they belong to another group of mammals called lagomorphs or "leaping shapes".*

- **Mice and rats** belong to a group of 1,800 species of small mammals called rodents. The group also includes voles, lemmings, squirrels, beavers, porcupines and guinea pigs.
- **All rodents** have two pairs of razor-sharp front teeth for gnawing nuts and berries, and a set of ridged teeth in their cheeks for chewing.
- **A rodent's front teeth**, called incisors, grow all the time. Only gnawing keeps them the same length.
- **Rats and mice** are by far the most common rodents – they have adapted well to living alongside humans.
- **Brown and black rats** carry germs for diseases such as food poisoning, plague and typhus.
- **Hares** live above ground and escape enemies through sheer speed. Rabbits live in burrows underground.
- **Baby hares** are born above ground, covered in fur and with their eyes open. Rabbits are born naked and blind in burrows.
- **Rabbits breed quickly** – a female can have 20 babies every month during the breeding season, and her babies will have their own families after 6 months.
- **One single rabbit** could have more than 33 million offspring in just 3 years, if they all survived to breed.
- **A single mouse** can produce up to 34 young in one litter.

▶ *Rats and mice have long thin tails, pointed noses, beady black eyes and four very sharp front teeth.*

Ducks and geese

- **Ducks, geese and swans** are known as waterfowl, and they all live on or near freshwater.
- **Waterfowl** can float for hours and have webbed feet for paddling along. On water they are graceful, but on land they waddle awkwardly, since their legs are set far back under their body for swimming.
- **Ducks** have shorter necks and wings, and flatter bills than swans. Male ducks are called drakes, and females, ducks. Babies are called ducklings.

◀ *Canada geese breed in the far north of Canada and Alaska, and migrate south to warmer regions in the autumn.*

- **Diving ducks** (such as the pochard, tufted duck and the scoter) dive for food such as roots, shellfish and insects on the river bed.
- **Dabbling ducks** (such as the mallard, widgeon, gadwall and the teal) dabble – they sift water through their beaks for food.
- **Some dabblers** lap water at the surface. Others up-end – sticking their heads into the water to sift out water weeds and snails from muddy water.
- **Swans** are the largest waterfowl. They have long elegant necks and pure white plumage – apart from the black-neck swan of South America and the Australian black swan.
- **Baby swans** are called cygnets and are mottled grey.
- **Geese** mostly graze on grass. Unlike ducks, which quack and swans which hiss, geese honk.
- **Baby geese** are called goslings.

Coral reef fish

- **Many colourful fish species** live in warm seas around coral reefs. They are often very bright, which makes them instantly recognizable to their own kind.
- **Butterfly fish and angelfish** have colourful, slender, oval bodies and are popular as aquarium fish.
- **Male triggerfish** boost their colour to attract females.
- **Cuckoo wrasse** are all born female, but big females change sex when they are between 7 and 13 years old.
- **Cleaner fish** are the health clinics of the oceans. Larger fish such as groupers queue up for cleaner fish to go over them, nibbling away pests and dead skin.
- **The banded coral shrimp** cleans up pests in the same way as cleaner fish do, from fish such as moray eels.
- **The sabre-toothed blenny** looks so like a cleaner fish that it can nip in close to fish before it takes a bite out of them.

★ STAR FACT ★
Cleaner fish will go to work inside a shark's mouth.

▲ *Coral reefs are home to many brilliantly coloured fish.*

- **Cheilinus** is a carnivorous fish of coral reefs which changes colour to mimic harmless plant-eating fish, such as parrotfish and goatfish. It swims alongside them, camouflaged, until it is close to its prey.

Ants and termites

- **Ants** are a vast group of insects related to bees and wasps. Most ants have a tiny waist and are wingless.
- **Ants** are the main insects in tropical forests, living in colonies of anything from 20 to millions.
- **Ant colonies** are all female. Most species have one or several queens which lay the eggs. Hundreds of soldier ants guard the queen, while smaller workers build the nest and care for the young.
- **Males** only enter the nest to mate with young queens, then die.
- **Wood ants** squirt acid from their abdomen to kill enemies.
- **Army ants** march in huge swarms, eating small creatures they meet.

▲ *African termites use mud and saliva to build amazing nests more than 12 m high, housing over 5 million termites.*

- **Groups of army ants** cut any large prey they catch into pieces which they carry back to the nest. Army ants can carry 50 times their own weight.
- **Ants known as slavemakers** raid the nests of other ants and steal their young to raise as slaves.
- **Termite colonies** are even more complex than ant ones. They have a large king and queen who mate, as well as soldiers to guard them and workers to do all the work.
- **Termite nests** are mounds built like cities with many chambers – including a garden used for growing fungus. Many are air-conditioned with special chimneys.

Swifts and hummingbirds

- **Swifts and hummingbirds** are on the wing so much that their feet have become weak – which is why they are called *Apodiformes*, meaning 'footless ones'.
- **Swifts** are among the fastest flying birds. Spine-tailed swifts of eastern Asia have been recorded at 240 km/h.
- **Swifts use** their short, gaping bills to catch insects on the wing.
- **Swifts may fly** through the night without landing. They may even sleep on the wing. European swifts fly all the way to Africa and back without stopping.
- **When swifts land**, they cling to vertical surfaces such as walls, cliffs and trees.
- **Great dusky swifts** nest and roost behind waterfalls, and have to fly through the water to get in and out.

★ STAR FACT ★
To hover, horned sungem hummingbirds beat their wings 90 times per second.

▲ *Hummingbirds have long bills to suck nectar from flowers.*

- **Hummingbirds** are about 325 species of tiny, bright, tropical birds which sip nectar from flowers.
- **Hummingbirds** are the most amazing aerial acrobats, hovering and twisting in front of flowers.
- **The bee hummingbird** is the world's smallest bird – including its long bill, it measures just 5 cm.

Lemurs and lorises

- **Lemurs** are small furry creatures with long tails and big eyes. They are primates, like monkeys and humans.
- **Lemurs** live only on the islands of Madagascar and Comoros, off the African east coast.
- **Most lemurs** are active at night and live in trees, but the ring-tailed lemur lives mostly on the ground and is active by day.

▲ *Ring-tailed lemurs get their name from their black-ringed tail which they raise to show where they are.*

- **Lemurs** eat fruit, leaves, insects and small birds.
- **The ring-tailed lemur** rubs its rear on trees to leave a scent trail for other lemurs to follow.
- **In the mating season**, ring-tailed lemurs have stink fights for females, rubbing their wrists and tails in stink glands under their arms and rear – then waving them at rivals to drive them off.
- **Lorises and pottos** are furry, big-eyed primates of the forests of Asia and Africa. All are brilliant climbers.
- **Bushbabies** are the acrobats of the loris family. They get their name because their cries sound like a human baby crying.
- **Bushbabies** are nocturnal animals and their big eyes help them see in the dark. Their hearing is so sensitive they have to block their ears to sleep during the day.
- **Tarsiers** of the Philippines are small, huge-eyed primates. They have very long fingers and can turn their heads halfway round to look backwards.

Pythons and boas

- **Constrictors** are snakes that squeeze their victims to death, rather than poisoning them. They include pythons, boas and anacondas.
- **A constrictor** does not crush its victim. Instead,it winds itself around, gradually tightening its coils until the victim suffocates.
- **Constrictors usually swallow** victims whole, then spend days digesting them. They have special jaws that allow their mouths to open very wide. A large meal can be seen as a lump moving down the body.
- **Pythons** are big snakes that live in Asia, Indonesia and Africa. In captivity, reticulated pythons grow to 9 m. Boas and anacondas are the big constrictors of South America.
- **Boas** capture their prey by lying in wait, hiding motionless under trees and waiting for victims to pass by. But like all snakes, they can go for many weeks without eating.
- **Like many snakes**, most constrictors begin life as eggs. Unusually for snakes, female pythons look after their eggs until they hatch by coiling around them. Even more unusually, Indian and green tree pythons actually keep their eggs warm by shivering.
- **Female boas** do not lay eggs, giving birth to live young.
- **Boas** have tiny remnants of back legs, called spurs, which males use to tickle females during mating.
- **Anacondas** spend much of their lives in swampy ground or shallow water, lying in wait for victims to come and drink. One anaconda was seen to swallow a 2-m-long caiman (a kind of crocodile).
- **When frightened**, the royal python of Africa coils itself into a tight ball, which is why it is sometimes called the ball python. Rubber boas do the same, but hide their heads and stick their tails out aggressively to fool attackers.

▲ Pythons are tropical snakes that live in moist forests in Asia and Africa. They are the world's biggest snakes, rivalled only by giant anacondas. Pythons are one long tube of muscle, well able to squeeze even big victims to death. They usually eat animals about the size of domestic cats, but occasionally they go for really big meals such as wild pigs and deer.

★ STAR FACT ★

A 4 to 5 m long African rock python was once seen to swallow an entire 60 kg impala (a kind of antelope) whole – horns and all.

Snails and slugs

- **Snails and slugs** are small, squidgy, slimy, soft-bodied crawling creatures. They belong to a huge group of animals called molluscs which have no skeleton. Squid and oysters are also molluscs.
- **Snails and slugs** are gastropods, a group that also includes whelks and winkles.
- **Gastropod** means 'stomach foot', because these animals seem to slide along on their stomachs.
- **Most gastropods** live in the sea. They include limpets which stick firmly to seashore rocks.

★ STAR FACT ★
Snails are a great delicacy in France, where they are called *escargot*.

◀ *Garden snails have a shell which they seal themselves into in dry weather, making a kind of trapdoor to save moisture. They have eyes on their horns.*

- **Most land snails and slugs** ooze a trail of sticky slime to help them move along the ground.
- **Garden snails** are often hermaphrodites, which means they have both male and female sex organs.
- **The great grey slugs** of western Europe court by circling each other for over an hour on a branch, then launching themselves into the air to hang from a long trail of mucus. They then mate for 7 to 24 hours.
- **Among the largest gastropods** are the tropical tritons, whose 45-cm shells are sometimes used as warhorns. Conches are another big kind of gastropod.
- **Some cone snails** in the Pacific and Indian oceans have teeth that can inject a poison which can actually kill people.

Life in tropical rainforests

- **Tropical rainforests** are the richest and most diverse of all animal habitats.
- **Most animals** in tropical rainforests live in the canopy (treetops), and are either agile climbers or can fly.
- **Canopy animals** include flying creatures such as bats, birds and insects, and climbers such as monkeys, sloths, lizards and snakes.

▲ *Year-round rainfall and warm temperatures make rainforests incredibly lush, with a rich variety of plant life.*

- **Many rainforest creatures** can glide through the treetops – these include gliding geckos and other lizards, flying squirrels and even flying frogs.
- **Some tree frogs** live in the cups of rainwater held by plants growing high up in trees.
- **Antelopes, deer, hogs, tapir** and many different kinds of rodent (see rabbits and rats) roam the forest floor, hunting for seeds, roots, leaves and fruit.
- **Beside rivers** in South East Asian rainforests, there may be rhinoceroses, crocodiles and even elephants.
- **Millions of insect species** live in rainforests, including butterflies, moths, bees, termites and ants. There are also many spiders.
- **Rainforest butterflies and moths** are often big or vividly coloured, including the shimmering blue morpho of Brazil and the birdwing butterflies.
- **Rainforest birds** can be vividly coloured too, and include parrots, toucans and birds of paradise.

Sharks

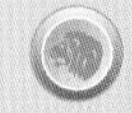

- **Sharks** are the most fearsome predatory fish of the seas. There are 375 species, living mostly in warm seas.
- **Sharks** have a skeleton made of rubbery cartilage – most other kinds of fish have bony skeletons.
- **The world's biggest fish** is the whale shark, which can grow to well over 12 m long. Unlike other sharks, the whale shark and the basking shark (at 9 m long) mostly eat plankton and are completely harmless.

★ STAR FACT ★
Great white sharks are the biggest meat-eating sharks, growing to over 7 m long.

- **A shark's main weapons** are its teeth – they are powerful enough to bite through plate steel.
- **Sharks** put so much strain on their teeth that they always have three or four spare rows of teeth in reserve.
- **Nurse sharks** grow a new set of teeth every 8 days.
- **Up to 20** people die from recorded shark attacks each year.
- **The killing machine** of the shark world is the great white shark, responsible for most attacks on humans.
- **Hammerhead sharks** can also be dangerous . They have T-shaped heads, with eyes and nostrils at the end of the T.

◀ *A shark's torpedo-shaped body makes it a very fast swimmer.*

Dinosaurs

- **Dinosaurs** were reptiles that dominated life on land from about 220 million to 65 million years ago, when all of them mysteriously became extinct.
- **Although modern reptiles** walk with bent legs splayed out, dinosaurs had straight legs under their bodies – this meant they could run fast or grow heavy.
- **Some dinosaurs** ran on two back legs, as birds do. Others had four sturdy legs like an elephant's.
- **Dinosaurs** are split into two groups according to their hipbones – saurischians had reptile-like hips and ornithischians had bird-like hips.
- **Saurischians** were either swift, two-legged predators called theropods, or hefty four-legged herbivores called sauropods.
- **Theropods** had acute eyesight, fearsome claws and sharp teeth. They included Tyrannosaurus rex, one of the biggest hunting animals to ever live on land – over 15 m long, 5 m tall and weighing more than 7 tonnes.
- **Sauropods** had massive bodies, long tails, and long, snake-like necks.
- **The sauropod Brachiosaurus** was over 23 m long, weighed 80 tonnes and towered 12 m into the air. It was one of the biggest creatures ever to live on land.
- **Most dinosaurs** are known from fossilized bones, but fossilized eggs, footprints and droppings have also been found. In 1913, mummified hadrosaur skin was found.
- **Some scientists** think the dinosaurs died out after a huge meteor struck the Earth off Mexico, throwing up a cloud that blocked the sun's light and heat.

▶ *Dinosaur means 'terrible lizard', and they came in all shapes and sizes. This is a plant-eating sauropod called Diplodocus.*

Pandas

▶ *Giant pandas are big, chubby animals, usually weighing well over 100 kg. When they stand on their hind legs they are as tall as a man. But pandas have inefficient digestive systems and to sustain their huge bulk they have to eat more continuously than most other animals.*

An extra thumb helps pandas hold the bamboo while they are chewing

Giant pandas eat only certain kinds of bamboo

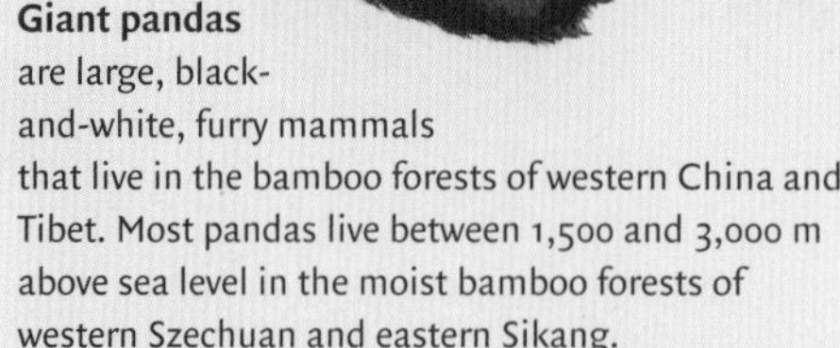

- **Giant pandas** are large, black-and-white, furry mammals that live in the bamboo forests of western China and Tibet. Most pandas live between 1,500 and 3,000 m above sea level in the moist bamboo forests of western Szechuan and eastern Sikang.
- **Giant pandas are among the rarest species** of animal in the world. There are probably fewer than 1,000 left. The giant panda's habitat has been cut back by the loss of forests for wood and farmland.
- **One reason** that giant pandas are rare is because they feed only on the shoots of bamboos. Some bamboos flower once every century and then die, and it is many years before the seeds grow into new plants.

! NEWS FLASH !
Chinese zoologists hope to clone giant pandas to save them for the future.

- **Giant pandas** spend most of their time sitting around on the ground eating, but they are surprisingly agile tree climbers.
- **Giant pandas spend 12 hours** a day feeding on bamboo shoots, because their digestive system is so ineffective that they have to eat more than 40 kg of bamboo a day.
- **To help it hold the bamboo**, the panda has an extra 'thumb' – it is not really a thumb, but a bone on the wrist which is covered by a fleshy pad.
- **The red panda** is a much smaller animal than the giant panda and it sleeps in trees, curled up like a cat.
- **Red pandas** look a little like raccoons and people once thought that pandas were related to raccoons, even though giant pandas look more like bears. DNA tests have shown that red pandas are close to raccoons, but that giant pandas are closer to bears.
- **In the wild**, giant pandas give birth to one or two cubs a year. The cubs are very tiny and the mother has to give up eating to look after them for the first 10 days or so. The cubs usually stay with their mother for nearly one year.
- **Attempts to breed** pandas in zoos have largely failed. Washington Zoo's giant panda Ling Ling, for instance, gave birth to several cubs in the 1970s and 1980s, but the cubs died very soon after birth.

▶ *Giant pandas look like clowns with their black eye patches and ears. No one knows quite what the purpose of these eye patches is. When giant pandas were first introduced to Europe in 1869 by French priest Père Armand David, many people believed they were hoaxes.*

Flies

▶ *Flies have only one pair of proper wings. The hind wings are small stumps called halteres which help a fly balance in flight.*

- **Flies** are one of the biggest groups of insects, common nearly everywhere – there are over 90,000 species.
- **Unlike other insects**, flies have only one pair of proper wings.
- **Flies** include bluebottles, black flies, gnats, horseflies, midges, mosquitoes and tsetse flies.
- **A house fly** flies at over 7 km/h – equal to flying 350,000 times its own length in an hour. If a jumbo jet flew at the same speed relative to its length for an hour, it would get almost right around the world.
- **Alaskan flies** can stand being frozen at temperatures of -60°C and still survive.
- **Flies suck up** their food – typically sap from rotting plants and fruit. Houseflies often suck liquids from manure. Blowflies drink juices from rotting meat.
- **The larvae (young) of flies** are called maggots, and they are tiny, white, wriggling tube-shapes.
- **Flies resemble or mimic** many other kinds of insects. There are wasp-flies, drone-flies, ant-flies, moth-flies and beetle-flies.
- **Many species** of fly are carriers of dangerous diseases. When a fly bites or makes contact, it can infect people with some of the germs it carries – especially the flies that suck blood. Mosquitoes spread malaria, and tsetse flies spread sleeping sickness.

★ **STAR FACT** ★
The buzzing of a fly is the sound of its wings beating. Midges beat their wings 1,000 times a second.

Sparrows and starlings

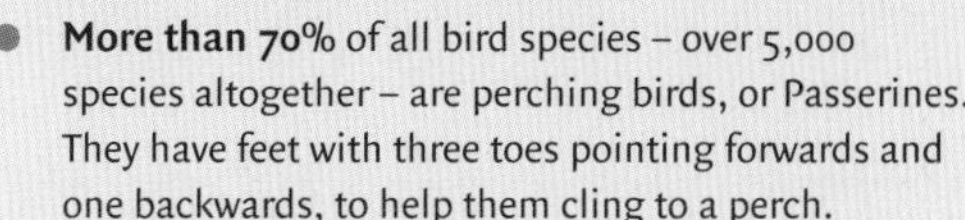

- **More than 70%** of all bird species – over 5,000 species altogether – are perching birds, or Passerines. They have feet with three toes pointing forwards and one backwards, to help them cling to a perch.
- **Perching birds** build neat, small, cup-shaped nests.
- **Perching birds sing** – this means that their call is not a single sound, but a sequence of musical notes.
- **Songbirds**, such as thrushes, warblers and nightingales, are perching birds with especially attractive songs.
- **Usually only male songbirds** sing – mainly in the mating season, to warn off rivals and attract females.
- **Sparrows** are small, plump birds, whose chirruping song is familiar almost everywhere.
- **Starlings** are very common perching birds which often gather in huge flocks, either to feed or to roost.
- **All the millions** of European starlings in North America are descended from 100 set free in New York's Central Park in the 1890s.

▲ *Starlings often gather on overhead cables ready to migrate.*

- **Many perching birds**, including mynahs, are talented mimics. The lyre bird of southeastern Australia can imitate car sirens and chainsaws, as well as other birds.
- **The red-billed quelea** of Africa is the world's most abundant bird. There are over 1.5 billion of them.

Spiders

- **Spiders** are small scurrying creatures which, unlike insects, have eight legs not six, and bodies with two parts not three.
- **Spiders** belong to a group of 70,000 creatures called arachnids, which also includes scorpions, mites and ticks.
- **Spiders** live in nooks and crannies almost everywhere in the world, especially where there is vegetation to feed tiny creatures.
- **Spiders are hunters** and most of them feed mainly on insects. Despite their name, bird-eating spiders rarely eat birds, preferring lizards and small rodents such as mice.
- **Spiders have eight eyes**, but most have poor eyesight and hunt by feeling vibrations with their legs.
- **Many spiders** catch their prey by weaving silken nets called webs. Some webs are simple tubes in holes. Others, called orb webs, are elaborate and round. Spiders' webs are sticky to trap insects.
- **The Australian trapdoor** spider ambushes its prey from a burrow with a camouflaged entrance flap.
- **Most spiders** have a poisonous bite which they use to stun or kill their prey. Tarantulas and sun spiders crush their victims with their powerful jaws.
- **The bite of black widow**, redback and funnel-web spiders is so poisonous that it can kill humans.

★ STAR FACT ★
Female black widow spiders eat their mates after mating.

▲ *Like all arachnids, spiders have eight legs, plus two 'arms' called pedipalps and a pair of fangs called chelicerae. They also have eight simple eyes.*

Cockles and mussels

- **Cockles and mussels** belong to a group of molluscs called bivalves, which includes oysters, clams, scallops and razorshells.
- **Bivalve** means 'having two valves', and all these creatures have two halves to their shells, joined by a hinge that opens rather like that of a locket.
- **Most bivalves feed** by filtering food out from the water through a tube called a siphon.
- **Cockles** burrow in sand and mud on the seashore. Mussels cling to rocks and breakwaters between the high and low tide marks.
- **Oysters** and some other molluscs line their shells with a hard, shiny, silvery white substance called nacre.
- **When a lump of grit** gets into an oyster shell, it is gradually covered in a ball of nacre, making a pearl.
- **The best pearls** come from the Pinctada pearl oysters that live in the Pacific Ocean. The world's biggest pearl was 12 cm across and weighed 6.4 kg. It came from a giant clam.
- **Scallops** can swim away from danger by opening and shutting their shells rapidly to pump out water. But most bivalves escape danger by shutting themselves up inside their shells.
- **A giant clam** found on the Great Barrier Reef was over 1 m across and weighed more than 0.25 tonnes.
- **There are colonies** of giant clams living many thousands of metres down under the oceans, near hot volcanic vents.

◀ *There are two main kinds of seashell – univalves like these (which are a single shell), and bivalves (which come in two, hinged halves).*

Reptiles and amphibians

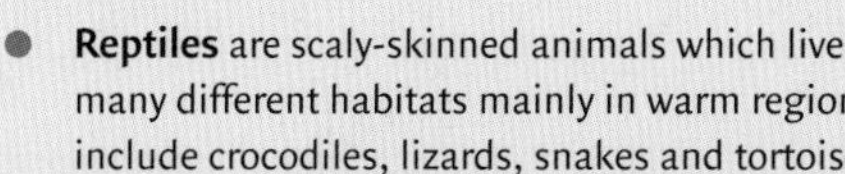

- **Reptiles** are scaly-skinned animals which live in many different habitats mainly in warm regions. They include crocodiles, lizards, snakes and tortoises.
- **Reptiles are cold-blooded**, but this does not mean that their blood is cold. A reptile's body cannot keep its blood warm, and it has to control its temperature by moving between hot and cool places.
- **Reptiles bask in the sun** to gain energy to hunt, and are often less active at cooler times of year.
- **A reptile's skin** looks slimy, but it is quite dry. It keeps in moisture so well that reptiles can survive in deserts. The skin often turns darker to absorb the sun's heat.
- **Although reptiles grow** most of their lives, their skin does not, so they slough (shed) it every now and then.

★ **STAR FACT** ★
Reptiles were the first large creatures to live entirely on land, over 350 million years ago.

▶ *Like all reptiles, crocodiles rely on basking in the sun to gain energy for hunting. At night, or when it is cold, they usually sleep.*

- **Amphibians** are animals that live both on land and in water. They include frogs, toads, newts and salamanders.
- **Most reptiles** lay their eggs on land, but amphibians hatch out in water as tadpoles, from huge clutches of eggs called spawn.
- **Like fish**, tadpoles have gills to breathe in water, but they soon metamorphose (change), growing legs and lungs.
- **Amphibians** never stray far from water.

Pets

- **There are over 500 breeds** of domestic dog. All are descended from the wolves first tamed 12,000 years ago to help humans hunt. Dogs have kept some wolf-like traits such as guarding territory and hiding bones.
- **Many pet dogs** were originally working dogs. Collies were sheepdogs. Terriers, setters, pointers and retrievers all get their names from their roles as hunting dogs.
- **The heaviest dog breed** is the St Bernard, which weighs over 90 kg. The lightest is the miniature Yorkshire terrier, under 500 g.
- **Cocker spaniels** were named because they were used by hunters to flush out woodcocks in the 14th century.
- **Chihuahuas** were named after a place in Mexico – the Aztecs thought them sacred.

▲ *Powerfully built, strong-jawed, pit bull terriers were first bred from bulldogs and terriers as fighting dogs, by miners in the 18th century.*

- **The first domestic cats** were wild African bushcats tamed by the Ancient Egyptians to catch mice 3,500 years ago.
- **Like their wild ancestors**, domestic cats are deadly hunters – agile, with sharp eyes and claws – and often catch mice and birds.
- **Cats spend** a great deal of time sleeping, in short naps, but can be awake and ready for action in an instant.
- **Tabby cats** get their name from Attab in Baghdad (now in Iraq), where striped silk was made in the Middle Ages.
- **A female cat** is called a queen. A group of cats is called a clowder. A female dog is a bitch. A group of dogs is a kennel.
- **All pet golden hamsters** are descended from a single litter which was discovered in Syria in 1930.

Fleas and lice

- **Fleas and lice** are small wingless insects that live on birds and mammals, including humans. Dogs, cats and rats are especially prone to fleas.
- **Fleas and sucking lice** suck their host's blood.
- **Chewing lice** chew on their host's skin and hair or feathers. Chewing lice do not live on humans.
- **Fleas and lice** are often too small to see easily. But adult fleas grow to over 2 mm long.
- **A flea** can jump 30 cm in the air – the equivalent of a human leaping 200 m in the air.
- **The fleas** in flea circuses perform tricks such as jumping through hoops and pulling wagons.
- **Fleas spread** by jumping from one animal to another, to suck their blood.

★ STAR FACT ★
Fleas jump with a force of 140 g – over 20 times that required to launch a space rocket.

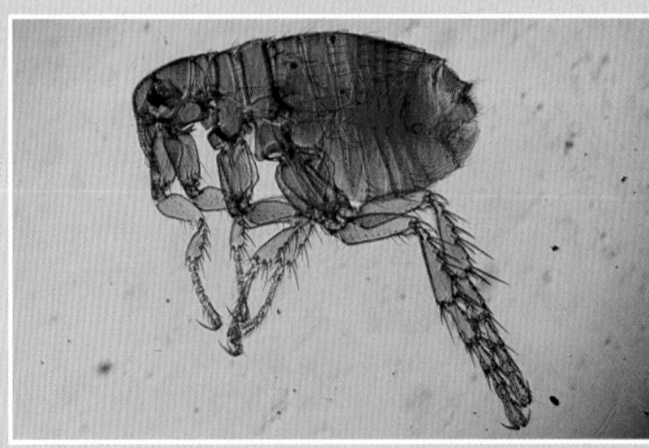

▲ *A much-magnified flea with its powerful back legs for jumping.*

- **When fleas lay their eggs**, they hatch as larvae and crawl off into the host's bedding, where they spin cocoons and emerge as adults 2 weeks later.
- **Head lice** gum their nits (eggs) to hair and spread from head to head through sharing of combs and hats.

Life in woodlands

- **Woodlands** in temperate zones between the tropics and the poles are home to many creatures.
- **Deciduous trees** lose their leaves in autumn. Evergreens keep theirs through cold winters.
- **In the leaf litter** under the trees live tiny creatures such as worms, millipedes, and ants and other insects.

▲ *On a walk through a deciduous wood, you may be lucky enough to catch a glimpse of a shy young red deer as it crosses a clearing.*

- **Spiders, shrews, salamanders and mice** feed on the small creatures in the leaf litter.
- **Some birds**, such as woodcocks, nest on the woodland floor and have mottled plumage to hide themselves.
- **Birds such as owls**, nuthatches, treecreepers, tits, woodpeckers and warblers live on and in trees, as well as insects such as beetles, moths and butterflies, and small mammals such as squirrels and raccoons.
- **Other small woodland mammals** include stoats, chipmunks, opossums, weasels, polecats, pinemartins and foxes.
- **Beavers, frogs, muskrats and otters** live near woodland streams.
- **The few large woodland mammals** include bears, deer, wolves and wild boar. Many of these have become rare because woods have been cleared away.
- **In winter**, many birds of deciduous woods migrate south, while small mammals like dormice hibernate.

Tigers

- **Tigers** are the largest of the big cats, with huge heads. The average male tiger's body grows to over 2 m long, plus a 1-m-long tail.
- **Tigers live** in the forests of Asia, Sumatra and Java, but as hunters kill them for their skin and farmers clear the forest for land, they are becoming very rare. They now live only on special reserves.
- **Tigers prey on large animals** such as deer, buffalo, antelopes and wild pigs. They hunt silently at night, stalking their prey, then making a sudden bound.
- **A tiger is fast and strong** but tires quickly, and it will give up if it fails to catch its prey the first time.
- **Adult tigers** usually live alone, and males try to keep other males out of their territory. But when two tigers meet, they may rub one another's head in greeting.
- **A male tiger's territory** often includes that of two or three females. But they only meet to mate.
- **Tigers mark** out their territory by scratching trees and urinating on them.
- **Usually, two to four cubs** are born at a time. The cubs are playful and boisterous, and are totally dependent on their mother for 2 to 3 years.

▲ *When a tiger roars, the sound can be heard for 4 or 5 kilometres through the forest.*

- **A tiger's stripes** make it instantly recognizable, but they make good camouflage in long grass and under trees. Each tiger has its own unique pattern of stripes.
- **White tigers** are rare. They have blue eyes, and their stripes are brown and white, not black and gold.

▼ *Tigers are forest dwellers and can climb trees, but most of the time they like to lie around. On hot days, they will often lie in rivers to cool off and, unusually for a cat, they can swim quite well.*

Most tigers have yellow eyes

In between the black stripes, the coat is amber or yellow

The fur on the throat, belly, and the insides of the legs is whitish

Male tigers usually have a ruff of hair around the face

Vultures

- **Vultures and condors** are the biggest birds of prey. They do not hunt, but feed on carrion (dead animals).
- **The palmnut vulture** is the only vegetarian bird of prey, and it feeds on oil nuts.
- **Many vultures are bald,** with no head feathers to mat with blood when digging into corpses.
- **The seven species** of New World vulture (those that live in the Americas) have a nostril hole right through their beak.
- **The Californian condor** is very rare. All the wild ones were captured in the mid 1980s, but some have since been bred in captivity and returned to the wild.
- **Vultures** are great fliers and spend hours soaring, scanning the ground for corpses with sharp eyes.

★ STAR FACT ★
The Andean condor is the world's biggest flying bird, with a wingspan of 3 m or more.

▲ *A vulture closes in to feed on a dead animal.*

- **Condors** have such a sharp sense of smell that they can pinpoint a corpse under a thick forest canopy.
- **Vultures** have such weak bills that flesh must be rotten before they can eat it.
- **The lammergeier** is known as the bearded vulture because it has a beard of black bristles on its chin.

Strange sea creatures

- **Deep-sea anglerfish** live deep in the ocean where it is pitch black. They lure prey into their mouths using a special, fishing-rod-like fin spine with a light at its tip.
- **Anglerfish** cannot find each other easily in the dark, so when a male meets a female he stays with her until mating time.

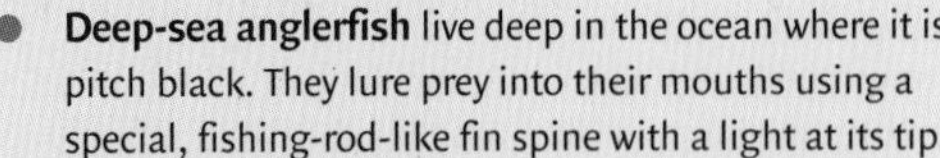

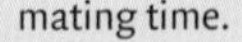

- **Hatchet fish** have giant eyeballs that point upwards so they see prey from below as silhouettes against the surface.
- **Viperfish** shine in the dark, thousands of metres down, and look like a jet airliner at night, with rows of lights along their bodies.

◀ *If threatened, the dragon fish will try to stab its attacker with its poisonous spines.*

- **Siphonophores** are colonies of tiny creatures that live in the deep oceans. They string themselves together in lines 20 m long and glow – so they look like fairy lights.
- **The cirrate octopod** looks like a jelly because its skin is 95% water – the water cannot be crushed by the intense pressure of the deep oceans where it lives.
- **The weedy seadragon** of Australia is a seahorse, but it looks just like a piece of flapping seaweed.
- **The sleeper shark** lives in the freezing depths of the North Atlantic and Arctic Oceans. It is 6.5 m long, but very slow and sluggish.
- **Flashlight fish** have light organs made by billions of bacteria which shine like headlights. The fish can suddenly block off these lights and change direction in the dark to confuse predators.
- **In the Arab-Israeli War** of 1967 a shoal of flashlight fish was mistaken for enemy frogmen and blown right out of the water.

Baby animals

- **All baby mammals** except monotremes (see strange mammals) are born from their mother's body, but most other creatures hatch from eggs.
- **Most creatures** hatch long after their parents have disappeared. Birds and mammals, though, usually look after their young.
- **Most birds** feed their hungry nestlings until they are big enough to find food themselves.
- **A pair of tits** may make 10,000 trips to the nest to feed their young.
- **Cuckoos** lay their egg in the nest of another, smaller bird. The foster parents hatch it and look after it as it grows. It then pushes its smaller, foster brothers and sisters out of the nest.

▶ *Lion cubs are looked after by several females until they are big enough to fend for themselves. Like many babies they have big paws, head and ears for their body.*

- **Mammals nurse** their young (they feed them on the mother's milk).The nursing period varies. It tends to be just a few weeks in small animals like mice, but several years in large animals like elephants.
- **Many animals** play when they are young. Playing helps them develop strength and co-ordination, and practise tasks they will have to do for real when adults.
- **When they are young**, baby opossums cling all over their mother as she moves around.
- **Some baby animals**, including baby shrews and elephants, go around in a long line behind the mother, clinging to the tail of the brother or sister in front.

Chameleons

- **Chameleons** are 85 species of lizard, most of which live on the island of Madagascar and in mainland Africa.
- **The smallest chameleon**, the dwarf Brookesia, could balance on your little finger. The biggest, Oustalet's chameleon, is the size of a small cat.
- **A chameleon** can look forwards and backwards at the same time, as each of its amazing eyes can swivel in all directions independently of the other.
- **Chameleons** feed on insects and spiders, hunting them in trees by day.
- **A chameleon's tongue** is almost as long as its body, but is normally squashed up inside its mouth.
- **A chameleon shoots** out its tongue in a fraction of a second to trap its victim on a sticky pad at the tip.
- **The chameleon's tongue** is fired out from a special launching bone on its lower jaw.
- **Most lizards** can change colour, but chameleons are experts, changing quickly to all sorts of colours.

▲ *Most of a chameleon's bulging eyes are protected by skin.*

- **Chameleons change colour** when they are angry or frightened, too cold or too hot, or sick – but they change colour less often to match their surroundings.
- **The colour of the skin** is controlled by pigment cells called melanophores, which change colour as they change size.

Life in cold regions

▲ *Other animals are the only substantial food in the Arctic wastes, so polar bears have to be carnivorous.*

- **The world's coldest places** are at the Poles in the Arctic and Antarctic, and high up mountains.
- **Only small animals** such as ice worms and insects can stand the extreme polar cold all year round.
- **Insects** such as springtails can live in temperatures as low as -38°C in Antarctica, because their body fluids contain substances that do not freeze easily.
- **Birds** such as penguins, snow petrels and skuas live in Antarctica. So do the leopard seals that eat penguins.
- **Polar seas** are home to whales, fish and shrimp-like krill.
- **Fish of cold seas** have body fluids that act like car anti-freeze to stop them freezing.
- **Mammals such as polar bears**, sea lions and walruses are so well insulated against the cold with their fur and fat that they can live on the Arctic ice much of the year.
- **Many animals** live on the icy tundra land in the far north of America and Asia. They include caribou, Arctic foxes and hares, and birds such as ptarmigans and snowy owls.
- **Arctic foxes and hares**, ermines and ptarmigans turn white in winter to camouflage them against the snow.

★ **STAR FACT** ★

Ptarmigans can survive through the bitter Arctic winter by eating twigs.

Starfish and sea urchins

    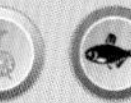    

- **Despite their name** starfish are not fish, but belong instead to a group of small sea creatures called echinoderms.
- **Sea urchins** and sea cucumbers are also echinoderms.
- **Starfish** have star-shaped bodies and are predators that prey mostly on shellfish such as scallops and oysters. They have five, strong arms which they use to prise open their victim. The starfish inserts its stomach into its victim and sucks out its flesh.
- **Each arm** of a starfish has on the underside hundreds of tiny, tube-like 'feet'. Bigger tubes inside the starfish's body pump water in and out of the 'feet', flexing the arms and driving the starfish along.
- **Starfish** often drop some of their arms off to escape an enemy, but the arms grow again.

◀ *Starfish that live in cooler water tend to be brown or yellow, whereas many tropical starfish can be bright red or even blue.*

- **Sea urchins** are ball-shaped creatures. Their shell is covered with bristling spines, which can be poisonous and can grow up to 40 cm long in some species.
- **A sea urchin's spines** are used for protection. Urchins also have sucker-like feet for moving.
- **A sea urchin's mouth** is a hole with five teeth, on the underside of its body.
- **Sea cucumbers** have no shell, but a leathery skin and a covering of chalky plates called spicules.
- **When threatened**, a sea cucumber chucks out pieces of its gut as a decoy and swims away. It grows a new one later.

Dragonflies

- **Dragonflies** are big hunting insects with four large transparent wings, and a long slender body that may be a shimmering red, green or blue.
- **Dragonflies have** 30,000 separate lenses in each of their compound eyes, giving them the sharpest vision of any insect.
- **A dragonfly** can see something that is stationary from almost 2 m away, and something moving two to three times farther away.
- **As it swoops** in on its prey, a dragonfly pulls its legs forwards like a basket to scoop up its victim.
- **Dragonflies** often mate in mid-air, and the male may then stay hanging on to the female until she lays her eggs.

★ STAR FACT ★
Dragonflies can reach speeds of almost 100 km/h to escape from birds.

- **Dragonfly eggs** are laid in water or in the stem of a water plant, and hatch in 2 to 3 weeks.
- **Newly hatched dragonflies** are called nymphs and look like fatter, wingless adults.
- **Dragonfly nymphs** are ferocious hunters, often feeding on young fish and tadpoles.
- **Dragonfly nymphs** grow and moult over a many years, before they climb on to a reed or rock to emerge as an adult.

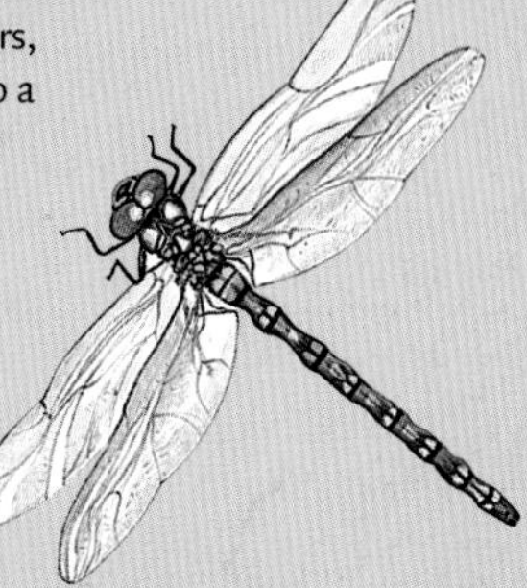

▶ *Dragonflies are big insects even today, but hundreds of millions of years ago, there were dragonflies with wings that were well over 70 cm across.*

Owls

- **Owls** are nocturnal and hunt by night, unlike most other hunting birds.
- **There are two big families of owl** – barn owls and typical owls.
- **There are 135 species** of typical owl, including the great horned owl.
- **There are 12 species** of barn owl. The common barn owl is the most widespread – it is found on every continent but Antarctica.

◀ *An owl's big eyes face straight ahead to focus. However, owls cannot move their eyes so have to swivel their whole head to look to the side or the rear.*

- **Small owls** eat mostly insects. Bigger owls eat mice and shrews. Eagle owls can catch young deer.
- **In the country**, the tawny owl's diet is 90% small mammals, but many now live in towns where their diet is mainly small birds such as sparrows and starlings.
- **Owls have huge eyes** that allow them to see in almost pitch darkness.
- **An owl's hearing** is four times as sharp as a cat's.
- **An owl can pinpoint** sounds with astonishing accuracy from the slight difference in the sound levels it receives in each of its ears.
- **Most bird's eyes** look out to the sides, but an owl's look straight forward like a human's. This is probably why the owl has been a symbol of wisdom since ancient times.
- **The flight feathers** on an owl's wing muffle the sound of the bird's wingbeat so that it can swoop almost silently down on to its prey.

Turkeys and hens

- **Turkeys**, chickens, geese and ducks are all kinds of poultry – farm birds bred to provide meat, eggs and feathers.
- **Chickens** were first tamed 5,000 years ago, and there are now over 200 breeds, including bantams and Rhode Island reds.
- **Female chickens** and turkeys are called hens. Male chickens are called roosters or cockerels. Male turkeys are toms. Baby turkeys are poults.
- **To keep hens laying**, their eggs must be collected daily. If not, the hens will wait until they have a small clutch of eggs, then try to sit on them to hatch them.

> ★ **STAR FACT** ★
> All domestic chickens are descended from the wild red jungle fowl of India.

◀ *Roosters are renowned for their noisy cries every morning as the sun comes up. This harsh cry is called a crow.*

- **Battery hens** spend their lives in rows of boxes or cages called batteries inside buildings.
- **Free-range hens** are allowed to scratch outdoors for insects and seeds.
- **Chickens** raised only for eating are called broilers.
- **Turkeys** are a kind of pheasant. There are several species, but all are descended from the native wild turkey of North America, first tamed by Native Americans 1,000 years ago.
- **Male turkeys** have a loose fold of bare, floppy skin called a wattle hanging down from their head and neck.

Strange mammals

- **The duck-billed platypus** and the echidnas live in Australia and are the only monotremes – mammals that lay eggs.
- **Duck-billed platypuses** are strange in other ways, too. They have a snout shaped like a duck's bill and webbed feet, which is why they are so happy in water.

▼ *The Tasmanian devil may be small, but it can be very fierce.*

- **Platypuses hatch** from eggs in a river-bank burrow.
- **Platypus babies** lick the milk that oozes out over the fur of their mother's belly.
- **Echidnas** are also known as spiny anteaters because they are covered in spines and eat ants.
- **After a female echidna** lays her single egg, she keeps it in a pouch on her body until it hatches.
- **The Tasmanian devil** is a small, fierce, Australian marsupial (see kangaroos and koalas). It hunts at night and eats almost any meat, dead or alive.
- **Tasmanian devils** stuff their victims into their mouth with their front feet.
- **The sugar glider** is a tiny, mouse-like jungle marsupial which can glide for 45 m between trees.
- **The aardvark** is a strange South African mammal with a long snout and huge claws. It can shovel as fast as a mechanical digger to make a home or find ants.

What is a fish?

- **Fish** are mostly slim, streamlined animals that live in water. Many are covered in tiny shiny plates called scales. Most have bony skeletons and a backbone.
- **There are well over 21,000 species** of fish, from the 8-mm-long pygmy goby to the 12-m-long whale shark.

▼ *Angling (catching fish) is a popular pastime all around the world. The fish is hooked as it bites the lure or bait.*

★ STAR FACT ★
The drum fish makes a drumming sound with its swim bladder.

- **Fish** are cold-blooded.
- **Fish breathe** through gills – rows of feathery brushes inside each side of the fish's head.
- **To get oxygen**, fish gulp water in through their mouths and draw it over their gills.
- **Fish** have fins for swimming, not limbs.
- **Most fish** have a pectoral fin behind each gill and two pelvic fins below to the rear, a dorsal fin on top of their body, an anal fin beneath, and a caudal (tail) fin.
- **Fish let gas in** and out of their swim bladders to float at particular depths.
- **Some fish** communicate by making sounds with their swim bladder. Catfish use them like bagpipes.

Worms

- **Worms** are long, wriggling, tube-like animals. Annelids are worms such as the earthworm whose bodies are divided into segments.
- **There are 15,000 species** of annelid. Most live underground in tunnels, or in the sea.
- **The world's largest earthworm** is the giant earthworm of South Africa, which can grow to as long as 6.5 m.
- **Earthworms** spend their lives burrowing through soil. Soil goes in the mouth end, passes through the gut and comes out at the tail end.
- **An earthworm** is both male and female (called a hermaphrodite), and after two earthworms mate, both develop eggs.
- **Over half the annelid species** are marine (sea) bristleworms, such as ragworms and lugworms. They are named because they are covered in bristles, whch they use to paddle over the seabed or dig into the mud.
- **The sea mouse** is a bristleworm with furry hairs.
- **Flatworms** look like ribbons or as though an annelid worm has been ironed flat. Of the thousands of flatworm species, many live in the sea or in pond algae.

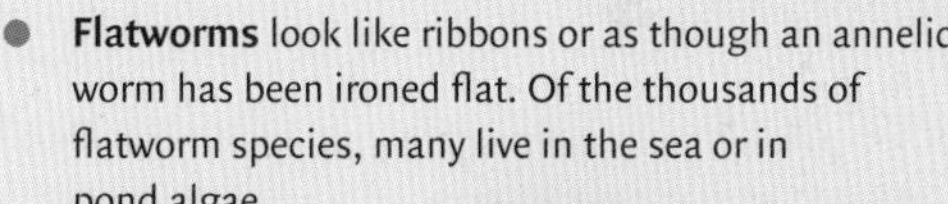

- **Flukes** are flatworms that live as parasites inside other animals. Diseases like bilharzia are caused by flukes.
- **Tapeworms** are parisitic flatworms that live inside their host's gut and eat their food.

▶ *Plants would not grow half as well without earthworms to aerate the soil as they burrow in it, mix up the layers and make it more fertile with their droppings.*

HUMAN BODY

KEY

 Breathing and blood

 Skeleton and muscle

 Body control

 Food and water

 Growing and changing

 Health and disease

Airways

- **The upper airways** include the nose and the sinuses, the mouth and the pharynx (throat).
- **The lower airways** include the larynx (see vocal cords), the trachea (windpipe) and the airways of the lungs.
- **The sinuses** are air chambers within the bones of the skull that form the forehead and face. If mucus blocks them when you get a cold, your speech is affected.
- **The soft palate** is a flap of tissue at the back of the mouth, which is pressed upwards when you swallow to stop food getting into your nose.
- **Your throat** is the tube that runs down through your neck from the back of your nose and mouth.
- **Your throat branches** in two at the bottom. One branch, the oesophagus, takes food to the stomach.The other, the larynx, takes air to the lungs.
- **The epiglottis** is the flap that tilts down to block off the larynx to stop food entering it when you swallow.
- **The tonsils and the adenoids** are bunches of lymph nodes (see lymphatic system) that swell to help fight ear, nose and throat infections, especially in young children.
- **The adenoids** are at the back of the nose, and the tonsils are at the back of the upper throat.

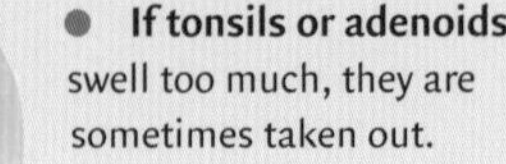

- **If tonsils or adenoids** swell too much, they are sometimes taken out.

> ★ STAR FACT ★
> Your throat is linked to your ears by tubes which open when you swallow to balance air pressure.

Lungs

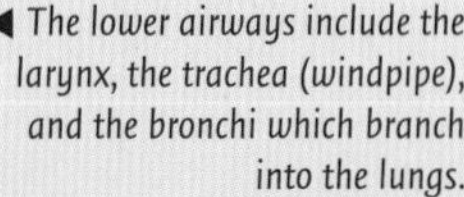

◀ *The lower airways include the larynx, the trachea (windpipe), and the bronchi which branch into the lungs.*

Smell

▲ *Scents are closely linked to emotions in the brain, and perfume can be a powerful way of triggering feelings.*

- **Smells are scent molecules** which are carried in the air and breathed in through your nose. A particular smell may be noticeable even when just a single scent molecule is mixed in with millions of air molecules.
- **The human nose** can tell the difference between more than 10,000 different chemicals.
- **Dogs can pick up** smells that are 10,000 times fainter than the ones humans can detect.
- **Inside the nose**, scent molecules are picked up by a patch of cells called the olfactory epithelium.
- **Olfactory** means 'to do with the sense of smell'.
- **The olfactory epithelium** contains over 25 million receptor cells.
- **Each of the receptor cells** in the olfactory epithelium has up to 20 scent-detecting hairs called cilia.
- **When they are triggered** by scent molecules, the cilia send signals to a cluster of nerves called the olfactory bulb, which then sends messages to the part of the brain that recognizes smell.
- **The part of the brain** that deals with smell is closely linked to the parts that deal with memories and emotions. This may be why smells can evoke memories.
- **By the age of 20**, you will have lost 20% of your sense of smell. By 60, you will have lost 60% of it.

Central nervous system

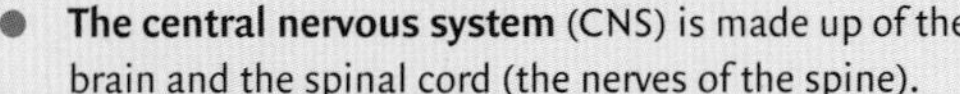

- **The central nervous system** (CNS) is made up of the brain and the spinal cord (the nerves of the spine).
- **The CNS** contains billions of densely packed interneurons – nerve cells with very short connecting axons (see nerve cells).

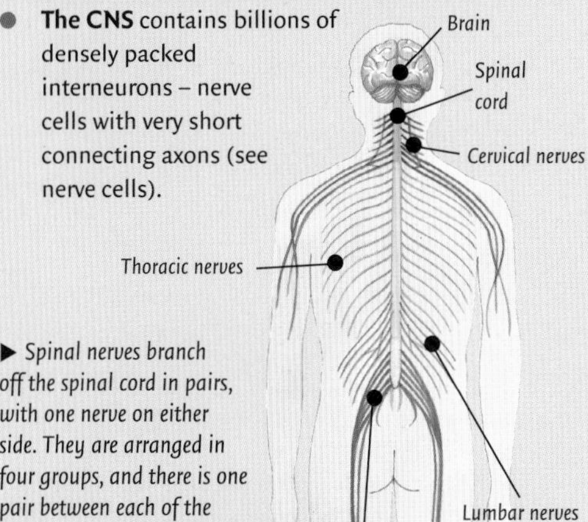

▶ *Spinal nerves branch off the spinal cord in pairs, with one nerve on either side. They are arranged in four groups, and there is one pair between each of the neighbouring 32 vertebrae.*

- **The CNS is cushioned** from damage by a surrounding bath of cerebrospinal fluid.
- **There are 43 pairs** of nerves branching off the CNS.
- **The job of the nerves** is to send sense and movement signals to the brain.
- **Cranial nerves** are the 12 pairs of nerves that branch off the CNS in the head, branching out of the brain.
- **Spinal nerves** are the 31 pairs of nerves that branch off the spinal cord.
- **The spinal nerves** are made up of 8 cervical nerve pairs, 12 thoracic pairs, 5 lumbar, 5 sacral and 1 coccyx pair.
- **Many spinal nerves** join up just outside the spine in five spaghetti junctions called plexuses.

> ★ **STAR FACT** ★
> The CNS sends out messages to more than 640 muscles around the body.

Carbohydrates

- **Carbohydrates** in food are your body's main source of energy. They are plentiful in sweet things and in starchy food such as bread, cakes and potatoes (see diet).
- **Carbohydrates** are burned by the body to keep it warm and to provide energy for growth and muscle movement, as well as to maintain basic body processes.
- **Carbohydrates** are among the most common of all organic (life) substances. Plants, for instance, make carbohydrates when they take energy from sunlight.
- **Carbohydrates** include huge molecules made of long strings of sugars. Sucrose (the sugar in sugar lumps and caster sugar) is just one of these sugars.
- **Simple carbohydrates** such as glucose, fructose (the sweetness in fruit) and sucrose are sweet and soluble (they will dissolve in water).
- **Complex carbohydrates** (or polysaccharides) such as starch are made when the molecules of simple carbohydrates join together.
- **A third type of carbohydrate** is cellulose (see diet).
- **The carbohydrates** you eat are turned into glucose for your body to use at once, or stored in the liver as the complex sugar glycogen (body starch).
- **The average adult** needs 2,000 to 4,000 Calories a day.
- **A Calorie** is the heat needed to warm 1 litre of water by 1 °C.

▼ *Bread is especially rich in complex carbohydrates such as starch, as well as simpler ones such as glucose and sucrose. Both were made by the original cereal plant whose seeds were ground into flour.*

Veins

- **Veins** are pipes in the body for carrying blood.
- **Unlike arteries**, most veins carry 'used' blood back to the heart – the body cells have taken the oxygen they need from the blood, so it is low in oxygen.
- **When blood** is low in oxygen, it is a dark, purplish blue colour – unlike the bright red of the oxygenated blood carried by the arteries.
- **The only veins** that carry oxygenated blood are the four pulmonary veins, which carry blood from the lungs the short distance to the heart.
- **The two largest veins** in the body are the vena cavae that flow into the heart from above and below.
- **Inside most large veins** are flaps that act as valves to make sure that the blood only flows one way.

★ **STAR FACT** ★
At any moment 75% of the body's blood is in veins.

- **The blood in veins** is not pumped as hard by the heart, so the blood pressure is lower than in arteries and vein walls do not need to be as strong.
- **Unlike arteries**, veins collapse when empty.
- **Blood is helped through** the veins by pressure placed on the vein walls by the surrounding muscles.

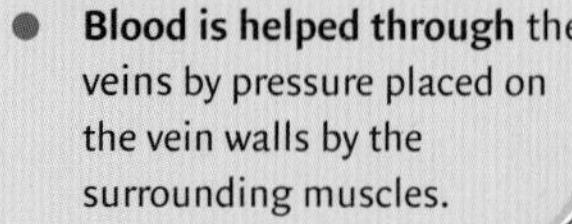

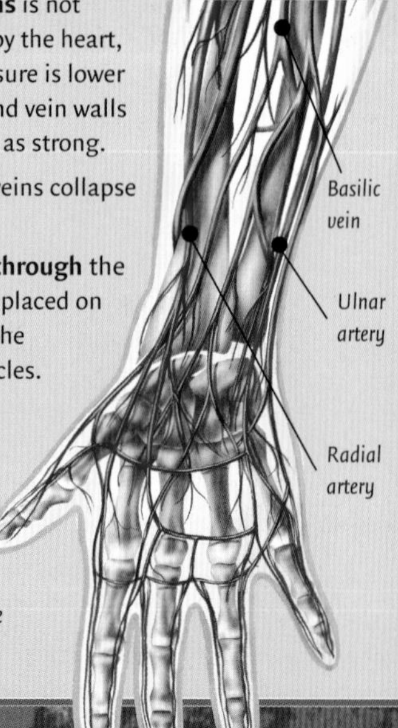

▶ *This illustration of the lower arm shows the main veins (in blue) and the main arteries (in red).*

Teeth

▼ *Teeth have long roots that slot into sockets in the jawbones, but they sit in a fleshy ridge called the gums. In the centre of each tooth is a living pulp of blood and nerves. Around this is a layer of dentine, then on top of that a tough shield of enamel.*

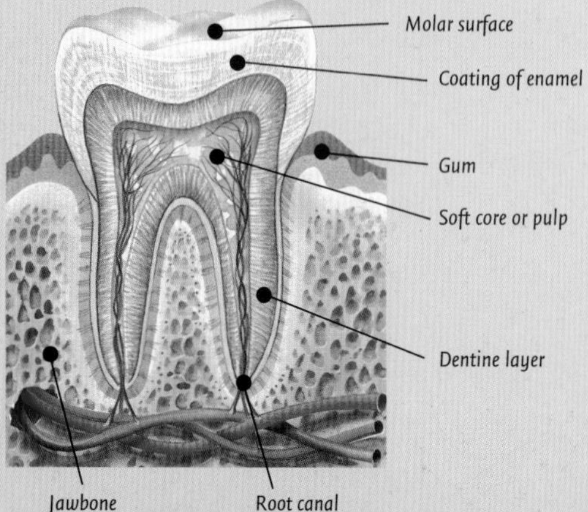

- **Milk teeth** are the 20 teeth that start to appear when a baby is about six months old.
- **When you are six**, you start to grow your 32 adult teeth – 16 top in the top row and 16 in the bottom.
- **Molars** are the (usually) six pairs of big, strong teeth at the back of your mouth. They have flattish tops and are a good shape for grinding food.
- **The molars** in the four corners of your jaw are wisdom teeth. These grow last and sometimes never appear.
- **Premolars** are four pairs of teeth in front of the molars.
- **Incisors** are the four pairs of teeth at the front of your mouth. They have sharp edges for cutting food.
- **Canines** are the two pairs of big, pointed teeth behind the incisors. Their shape is good for tearing food.
- **The enamel** on teeth is the body's hardest substance.
- **Dentine** inside teeth is softer but still hard as bone.
- **Teeth** sit in sockets in the jawbones.

The thyroid gland

- **The thyroid** is a small gland about the size of two joined cherries. It is at the front of your neck, just below the larynx (see airways and vocal cords).
- **The thyroid** secretes (releases) three important hormones – tri-odothyronine (T3), thyroxine (T4) and calcitonin.
- **The thyroid hormones** affect how energetic you are by controlling your metabolic rate.
- **Your metabolic rate** is the rate at which your cells use glucose and other energy substances.

▶ *The thyroid is part of your energy control system, telling your body cells to work faster or slower in order to keep you warm or to make your muscles work harder.*

> ★ **STAR FACT** ★
> Everyone has a different metabolic rate. It goes up when you work hard or are afraid.

- **T3 and T4** control metabolic rate by circulating into the blood and stimulating cells to convert more glucose.
- **If the thyroid** sends out too little T3 and T4, you get cold and tired, your skin gets dry and you put on weight.
- **If the thyroid** sends out too much T3 and T4, you get nervous, sweaty and overactive, and you lose weight.
- **The amount of T3 and T4** sent out by the thyroid depends on how much thyroid-stimulating hormone is sent to it from the pituitary gland (see the brain).
- **If the levels of T3 and T4** in the blood drop, the pituitary gland sends out extra thyroid-stimulating hormone to tell the thyroid to produce more.

Water

  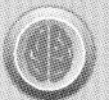  

- **Your body** is mainly made of water – over 60%.
- **You can survive weeks** without food, but no more than a few days without water.
- **You gain water** by drinking and eating, and as a by-product of cell activity.
- **You lose water** by sweating and breathing, and in your urine and faeces (see excretion).
- **The average person** takes in 2.2 litres of water a day – 1.4 litres in drink and 0.8 litres in food. Body cells add 0.3 litres, bringing the total water intake to 2.5 litres.
- **The average person** loses 1.5 litres of water every day in urine, 0.5 litres in sweat, 0.3 litres as vapour in the breath, and 0.2 litres in faeces.
- **The water balance** in the body is controlled mainly by the kidneys and adrenal glands.
- **The amount of water** the kidneys let out as urine depends on the amount of salt there is in the blood (see body salts).

▶ *If you sweat a lot during heavy exercise, you need to make up for all the water you have lost by drinking. Your kidneys make sure that if you drink too much, you lose water as urine.*

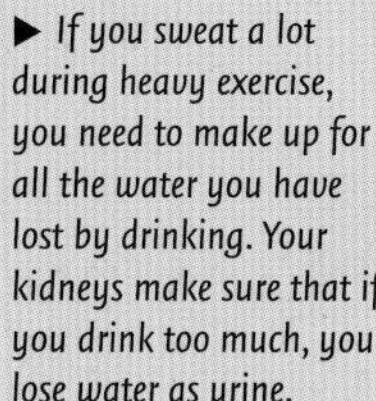

- **If you drink a lot**, the saltiness of the blood is diluted (watered down). To restore the balance, the kidneys let out a lot of water in the form of urine.
- **If you drink little** or sweat a lot, the blood becomes more salty, so the kidneys restore the balance by holding on to more water.

Diet

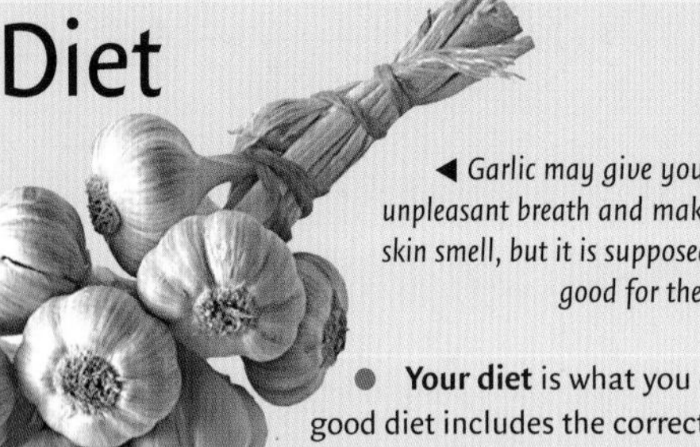

◀ *Garlic may give you fairly unpleasant breath and make your skin smell, but it is supposed to be good for the heart.*

- **Your diet** is what you eat. A good diet includes the correct amount of proteins, carbohydrates, fats, vitamins, minerals, fibre and water.
- **Most of the food** you eat is fuel for the body, provided mostly by carbohydrates and fats.
- **Carbohydrates** are foods made from kinds of sugar, such as glucose and starch. They are found in foods such as bread, rice, potatoes and sweet things.
- **Fats** are greasy foods that will not dissolve in water. Some, such as the fats in meat and cheese, are solid. Some, such as cooking oil, are liquid.
- **Fats are not** usually burned up straight away, but stored around your body until they are needed.
- **Proteins** are needed to build and repair cells, and they are made from chemicals called amino acids.
- **There are 20** different amino acids. Your body can make 11 of them. The other nine are called essential acids and they come from food.
- **Meat and fish** are very high in protein.
- **A correctly balanced vegetarian diet** can provide all the essential amino acids.
- **Fibre** or roughage is supplied by cellulose from plant cell walls. Your body cannot digest fibre, but needs it to keep the bowel muscles properly exercised.

▶ *Citrus fruits are a good source of vitamin C, which is vital for healthy teeth, gums and bones.*

Babies

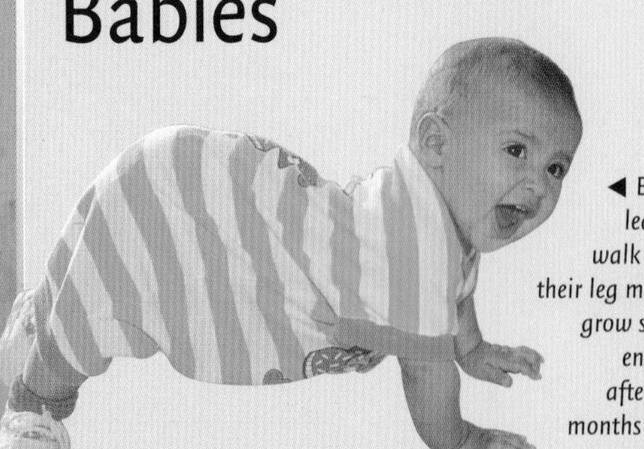

◀ *Babies learn to walk when their leg muscles grow strong enough, after nine months or so.*

- **A baby's head** is three-quarters of the size it will be as an adult – and a quarter of its total body height.
- **The bones** of a baby's skeleton are fairly soft, to allow for growth. They harden over time.
- **Baby boys grow faster** than baby girls during the first seven months.
- **A baby** has a very developed sense of taste, with taste buds all over the inside of its mouth.
- **Babies have** a much stronger sense of smell than adults – perhaps to help them find their mother.
- **There are two gaps** called fontanelles between the bones of a baby's skull, where there is only membrane (a 'skin' of thin tissue), not bone. The gaps close and the bones join together by about 18 months.
- **A baby is born** with primitive reflexes (things it does automatically) such as grasping or sucking a finger.
- **A baby's body weight** will usually triple in its first year.
- **A baby seems to learn** to control its body in stages, starting first with its head, then moving on to its arms and legs.

★ STAR FACT ★
A baby's brain is one of the fastest growing parts of its body.

The brain

 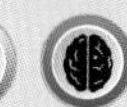   

- **The human brain** is made up of more than 100 billion nerve cells called neurons.
- **Each neuron** is connected to as many as 25,000 other neurons – so the brain has trillions and trillions of different pathways for nerve signals.
- **Girls' brains** weigh 2.5% of their body weight, on average, while boys' brains weigh 2%.
- **About 0.85 litres** of blood shoots through your brain every minute. The brain may be as little as 2% of your body weight, but it demands 15% of your blood supply.
- **An elephant's brain** weighs four times as much as the human brain. However, our brains are far bigger in relation to our bodies than those of most other animals.
- **The cerebral cortex** is the outside of the upper part of the brain, and if laid out flat, it would cover a bed.
- **The brain** is divided into two halves (hemisheres). Each controls the oposite side of the body.
- **Conscious thoughts and actions** happen in the cerebral cortex.
- **A human brain** has a cerebral cortex four times as big as a chimpanzee, about 20 times as big as a monkey's, and about 300 times as big as a rat's.
- **Unconscious, automatic activities** such as breathing, hunger, sleep and so on are controlled by structures such as the hypothalamus and the hippocampus in the middle of the brain.
- **The cerebellum** mainly controls body co-ordination and balance.

Hypothalamus controls body heat, water and hunger, and also wakes you up

Cerebrum – where you think and decide what to say and other clever things

Thalamus affects sensory levels, awareness and alertness

Limbic system affects body functions, emotions and smell

Pituitary gland controls hormones

Hippocampus, linked to moods, willpower, learning and memory

Amygdala, linked with moods and memories

Cerebellum controls co-ordination

Brain stem controls heartbeat and breathing

▲ *In this illustration, the right hemisphere (half) of the cerebrum is shown in pink, surrounding the regions that control basic drives such as hunger, thirst and anger.*

! NEWS FLASH !
Scientists can now grow human brain cells in a laboratory dish.

▼ *Taking the top off the skull shows the brain to be a soggy, pinky-grey mass which looks rather like a giant walnut.*

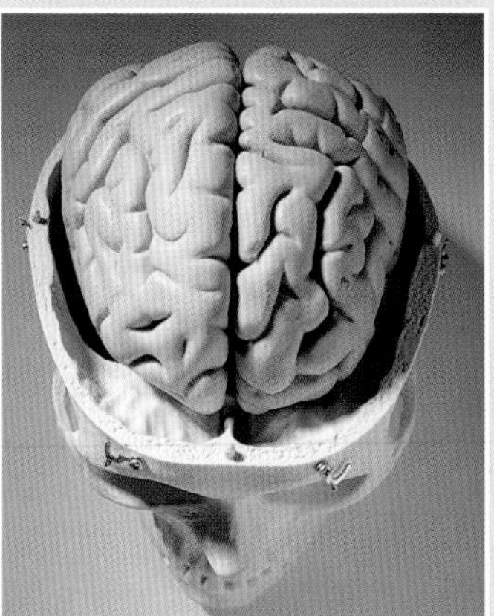

Tendons and ligaments

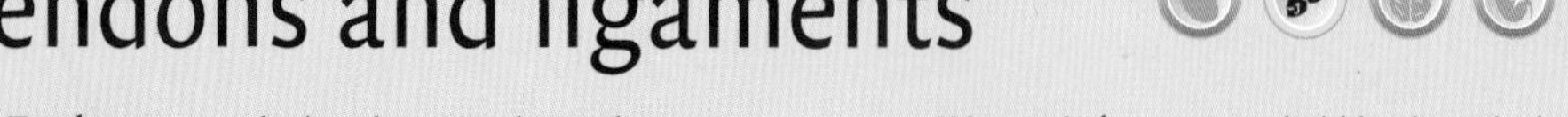

- **Tendons** are cords that tie a muscle to a bone or a muscle to another muscle.
- **Most tendons** are round, rope-like bundles of fibre. A few, such as the ones in the abdomen wall, are flat sheets called aponeuroses.
- **Tendon fibres are made** from a rubbery substance called collagen.
- **Your fingers are moved** mainly by muscles in the forearm, connected to the fingers by long tendons.
- **The Achilles tendon** pulls up your heel at the back.
- **Ligaments** are cords attached to bones on either side of a joint. They strengthen the joint.
- **Ligaments** also support various organs, including the liver, bladder and uterus (womb).

★ STAR FACT ★
The Achilles tendon is named after the Greek hero Achilles whose only weakness was his heel.

- **Women's breasts** are held in shape by bundles of ligaments.
- **Ligaments are made up** of bundles of tough collagen and a stretchy substance called elastin.

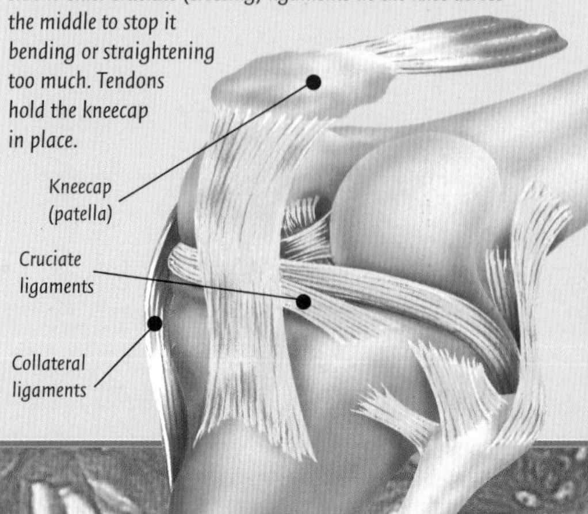

▶ *Collateral (side) ligaments stop the knee wobbling from side to side. Cruciate (crossing) ligaments tie the knee across the middle to stop it bending or straightening too much. Tendons hold the kneecap in place.*

Vaccination

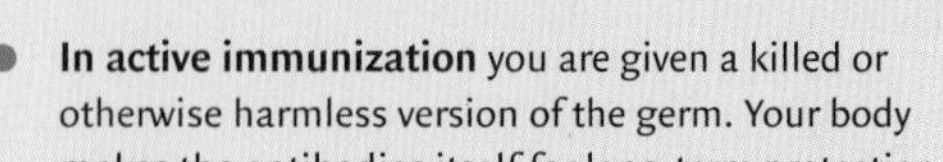

- **Vaccination** helps to protect you against an infectious disease by exposing you to a mild or dead version of the germ in order to make your body build up protection, in the form of antibodies.
- **Vaccination** is also called immunization, because it builds up your resistance or immunity to a disease.
- **In passive immunization** you are injected with substances such as antibodies which have been exposed to the germ. This gives instant but short-term protection.

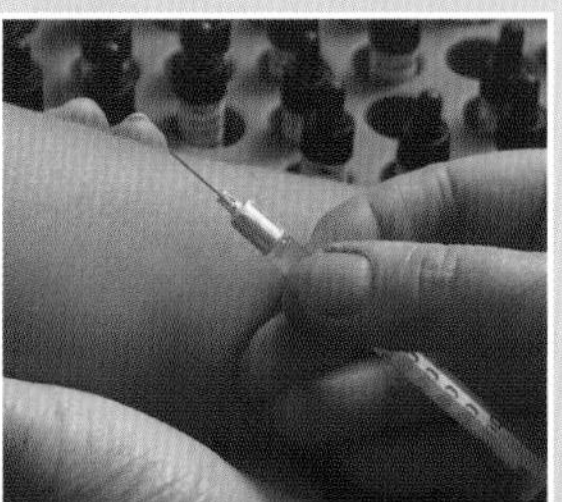

◀ *Diseases such as diphtheria, rubella and whooping cough are now rare in many countries thanks to vaccination. The dangerous disease smallpox – once very common – has been wiped out.*

- **In active immunization** you are given a killed or otherwise harmless version of the germ. Your body makes the antibodies itself for long-term protection.
- **Children in many countries** are given a series of vaccinations as they grow up, to protect them against diseases such as diphtheria, tetanus and polio.
- **There is a small risk** of a serious reaction against a vaccine. The measles vaccine carries a 1 in 87,000 chance of causing encephalitis (brain inflammation).
- **In cholera, typhoid, rabies and flu vaccines**, the germ in the vaccine is killed to make it harmless.
- **In measles, mumps, polio and rubella vaccines**, the germ is live attenuated – this means that its genes or other parts have been altered to make it harmless.
- **In diphtheria and tetanus vaccines**, the germ's toxins (poisons) are removed to make them harmless.
- **The hepatitis B vaccine** can be prepared by genetic engineering.

Thinking

- **Some scientists** claim that we humans are the only living things that are conscious – we alone are actually aware that we are thinking.
- **No one knows** how consciousness works – it is one of science's last great mysteries.
- **Most thoughts** seem to take place in the cerebrum (at the top of your brain), and different kinds of thought are linked to different areas, called association areas.

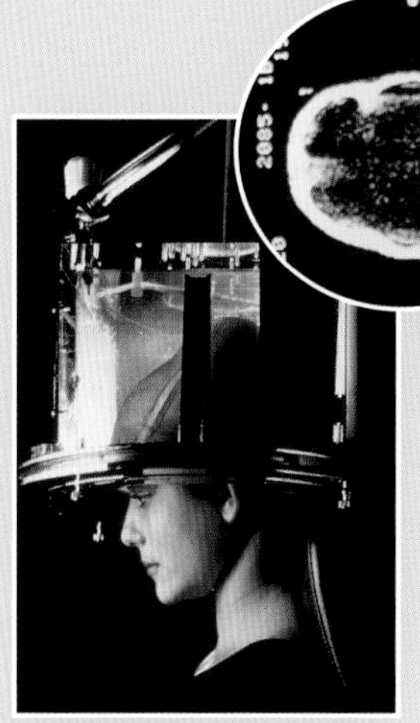

▲ Modern scanning techniques have taught us a great deal about the human brain and brain processes by allowing us to see brains in action.

- **Each half of the cerebrum** has four rounded ends called lobes: two at the front (frontal and temporal lobes) and two at the back (occipital and parietal lobes).
- **The frontal lobe** is linked to your personality and it is where you have your bright ideas.
- **The temporal lobe** is where you hear and understand what people say to you.
- **The occipital lobe** is where you work out what your eyes see.
- **The parietal lobe** is where you register touch, heat and cold, and pain.
- **The left half of the brain** (left hemisphere) controls the right side of the body. The right half (right hemisphere) controls the left side.
- **One half of the brain** is always dominant (in charge). Usually, the left brain is dominant, which is why 90% of people are right-handed.

Chromosomes

- **Chromosomes** are the microscopically tiny, twisted threads inside every cell that carry your body's life instructions in chemical form.
- **There are 46 chromosomes** in each of your body cells, divided into 23 pairs.
- **One of each chromosome pair** came from your mother and the other from your father
- **In a girl's 23 chromosome pairs**, each half exactly matches the other (the set from the mother is equivalent to the set from the father).
- **Boys** have 22 matching chromosome pairs, but the 23rd pair is made up of two odd chromosomes.
- **The 23rd chromosome pair** decides what sex you are, and the sex chromosomes are called X and Y.
- **Girls** have two X chromosomes, but boys have an X and a Y chromosome.
- **In every matching pair**, both chromosomes give your body life instructions for the same thing.
- **The chemical instructions** on each chromosome come in thousands of different units called genes.
- **Genes for the same feature** appear in the same locus (place) on each matching pair of chromosomes in every human body cell. Scientists one day hope to find out how the entire pattern, called the genome, works.

▼ Girls turn out to be girls because they get an X – not a Y – chromosome from their father.

Circulation

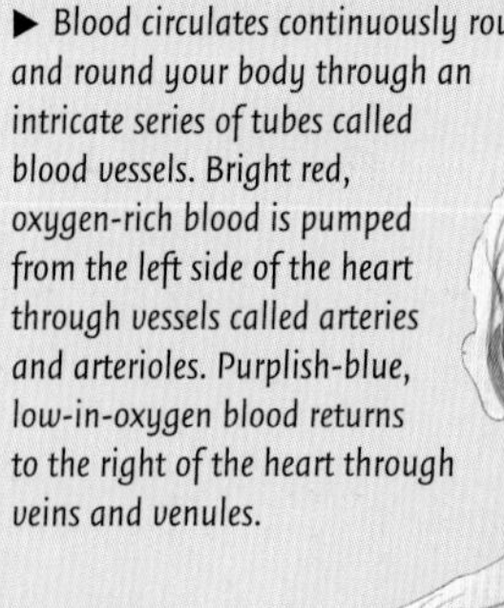

▶ *Blood circulates continuously round and round your body through an intricate series of tubes called blood vessels. Bright red, oxygen-rich blood is pumped from the left side of the heart through vessels called arteries and arterioles. Purplish-blue, low-in-oxygen blood returns to the right of the heart through veins and venules.*

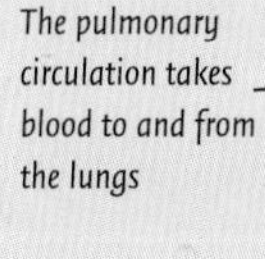

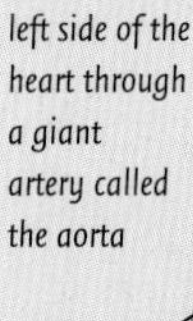

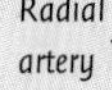

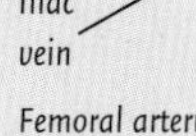

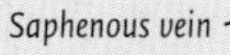

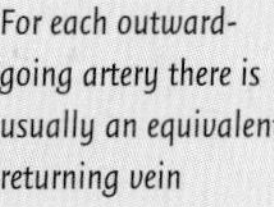

- **Your circulation** is the system of tubes called blood vessels which carries blood out from your heart to all your body cells and back again.
- **Blood circulation** was discovered in 1628 by the English physician William Harvey (1578-1657), who built on the ideas of Matteo Colombo.
- **Each of the body's** 600 billion cells gets fresh blood once every few minutes or less.
- **On the way out** from the heart, blood is pumped through vessels called arteries and arterioles.

★ STAR FACT ★

It takes less than 90 seconds on average for the blood to circulate through all of the body's 100,000 km of blood vessels!

- **On the way back** to the heart, blood flows through venules and veins.
- **Blood flows** from the arterioles to the venules through the tiniest tubes called capillaries.
- **The blood circulation** has two parts – the pulmonary and the systemic.
- **The pulmonary circulation** is the short section that carries blood which is low in oxygen from the right side of the heart to the lungs for 'refuelling'. It then returns oxygen-rich blood to the left side of the heart.
- **The systemic circulation** carries oxygen-rich blood from the left side of the heart all around the body, and returns blood which is low in oxygen to the right side of the heart.
- **Inside the blood**, oxygen is carried by the haemoglobin in red blood cells (see blood cells).

◀ *Red blood cells can actually be brown in colour, but they turn bright scarlet when their haemoglobin is carrying oxygen. After the haemoglobin passes its oxygen to a cell, it fades to dull purple. So oxygen-rich blood from the heart is red, while oxygen-poor blood that is returning to the heart is a purplish-blue colour.*

Birth

- **Babies are usually born** 38-42 weeks after the mother becomes pregnant.
- **Usually a few days** or weeks before a baby is born, it turns in the uterus (womb) so its head is pointing down towards the mother's birth canal (her cervix and vagina).
- **Birth begins** as the mother goes into labour – when the womb muscles begin a rhythm of contracting (tightening) and relaxing in order to push the baby out through the birth canal.
- **There are three stages** of labour. In the first, the womb muscles begin to squeeze, bursting the bag of fluid around the baby. This is called breaking the waters.
- **In the second stage** of labour, the baby is pushed out through the birth canal. Then the umbilical cord – its lifeline to its mother – is cut and the baby starts to breathe on its own.
- **In the third stage** of labour, the placenta is shed and comes out through the birth canal.
- **A premature baby** is one born before it is fully developed.
- **A miscarriage** is when the developing baby is 'born' before the 28th week of pregnancy and cannot survive.
- **A Caesarian section** is an operation that happens when a baby can't be born through the birth canal and emerges from the womb through a cut made in the mother's belly.

▼ *A mother makes a special bond with her baby.*

Diagnosis

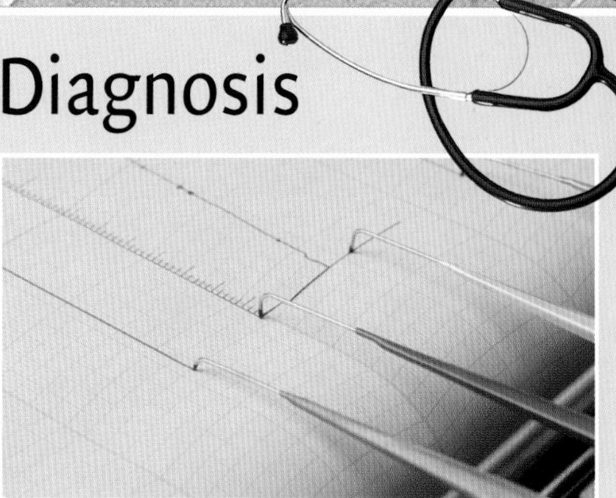

▲ *To diagnose certain illnesses correctly, a doctor may need to carry out a number different tests.*

- **Diagnosis** is when a doctor works out what a patient is suffering from – the illness and perhaps its cause.
- **The history** is the patient's own account of their illness. This provides the doctor with a lot of clues.
- **The prognosis** is the doctor's assessment of how the illness will develop in future.
- **Symptoms** are the effects or signs of the illness.
- **After taking a history** the doctor may carry out a physical examination, looking at the patient's body for symptoms such as swelling and tenderness.
- **A stethoscope** is a set of ear tubes which allows the doctor to listen to body sounds such as breathing and the heart beating.
- **With certain symptoms,** a doctor may order special tests, such as laboratory tests of blood and urine samples. Devices such as ultrasounds and X-rays may also be used to take special pictures.
- **Doctors** nowadays may use computers to help them make a diagnosis.
- **Diagnosis** can take a few seconds or many months.

! NEWS FLASH !
In future, some illnesses may be diagnosed entirely by computer.

The cortex

- **A cortex** is the outer layer of any organ, such as the brain or the kidney.
- **The brain's cortex** is also known as the cerebral cortex. It is a layer of interconnected nerve cells around the outside of the brain, called 'grey matter'.
- **The cerebral cortex** is where many signals from the senses are registered in the brain.

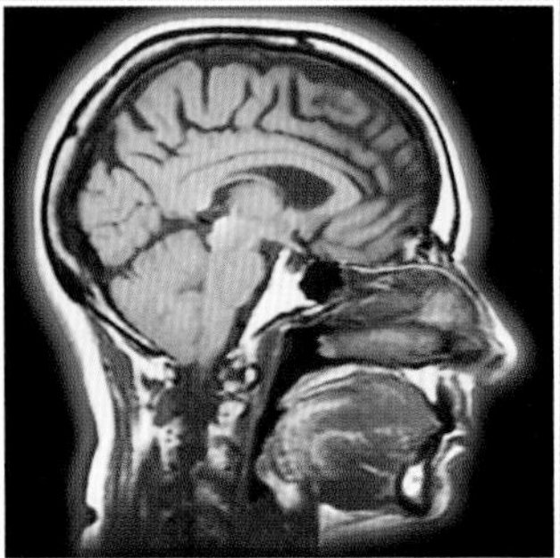

◀ The surface of the cortex is wrinkled into folds which are called gyri, with valleys in between them called sulci. The pattern of wrinkles can be seen clearly in this scan, which creates a slice through the brain.

- **The visual cortex** is around the lower back of the brain. It is the place where all the things you see are registered in the brain.
- **The somatosensory cortex** is a band running over the top of the brain like a headband. This where a touch on any part of the body is registered.
- **The motor cortex** is a band just in front of the sensory cortex. It sends out signals to body muscles to move.
- **The more nerve endings** there are in a particular part of the body, the more of the sensory cortex it occupies.
- **The lips and face** take up a huge proportion of the sensory cortex.
- **The hands** take up almost as much of the sensory cortex as the face.

★ STAR FACT ★
Everyone has their own unique pattern of wrinkles on their cerebral cortex.

Bone

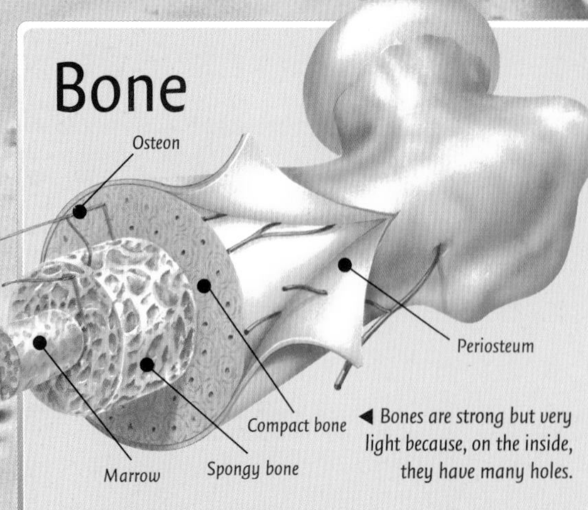

◀ Bones are strong but very light because, on the inside, they have many holes.

- **Bones are so strong** that they can cope with twice the squeezing pressure that granite can, or four times the stretching tension that concrete can, before breaking.
- **Weight for weight,** bone is at least five times as strong as steel.
- **Bones are so light** they only make up 14% of your body's total weight.
- **Bones get their rigidity** from hard deposits of minerals such as calcium and phosphate.
- **Bones get their flexibility** from tough, elastic, rope-like fibres of collagen.
- **The hard outside of bones** (called compact bone) is reinforced by strong rods called osteons.
- **The inside of bones** (called spongy bone) is a light honeycomb, made of thin struts or trabeculae, perfectly angled to take stress. The core of some bones is soft, jelly-like bone marrow.
- **Bones are living tissue** packed with cells called osteocytes. Each osteocyte, though, is housed in its own hole or lacuna.
- **In some parts of each bone,** there are special cells called osteoblasts which make new bone. In other parts, cells called osteoclasts break up old bone.
- **Bones grow** by getting longer near the end – at a region called the epiphyseal plate.

The spinal cord

- **The spinal cord** is the bundle of nerves running down the middle of the backbone.
- **The spinal cord** is the route for all nerve signals travelling between the brain and the body.
- **The spinal cord** can actually work independently of the brain, sending out responses to the muscles directly.
- **The outside** of the spinal cord is made of the long tails or axons of nerve cells and is called white matter; the inside is made of the main nerve bodies and is called grey matter.
- **Your spinal cord** is about 43 cm long and 1 cm thick; it stops growing when you are about five years old.
- **Damage to the spinal cord** can cause paralysis.
- **Injuries below the neck** can cause paraplegia – paralysis below the waist.
- **Injuries to the neck** can cause quadraplegia – paralysis below the neck.
- **Descending pathways** are groups of nerves that carry nerve signals down the spinal cord – typically signals from the brain for muscles to move.
- **Ascending pathways** are groups of nerves that carry nerve signals up the spinal cord – typically signals from the skin and internal body sensors going to the brain.

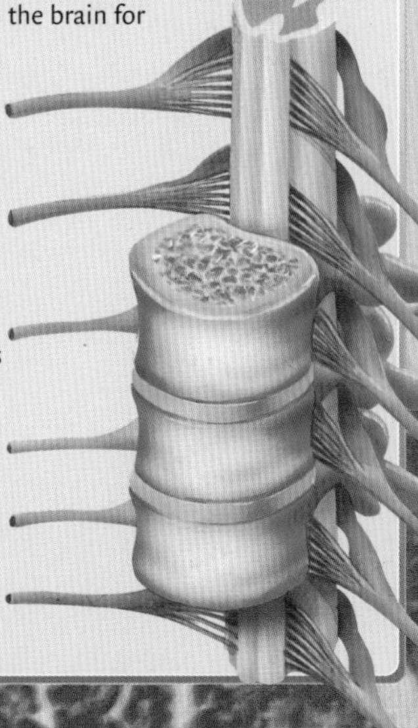

▶ *The spinal cord is encased in a tunnel in the backbone at the back of each vertebra. Nerves branch off to the body in pairs either side.*

Vitamins

- **Vitamins** are special substances the body needs to help maintain chemical processes inside cells.
- **Plants can make** their own vitamins, but humans must take most of their own from food.
- **A lack of any vitamin** in the diet can cause illness.
- **Before the 18th century,** sailors on long voyages used to suffer the disease scurvy, caused by a lack of vitamin C from fresh fruit in their diet.
- **There are at least 15 vitamins** known.
- **The first vitamins** discovered were given letter names like B. Later discoveries were given chemical names.
- **Some vitamins** such as A, D, E and K dissolve in fat and are found in animal fats and vegetable oils. They may be stored in the body for months.
- **Some vitamins** such as C and the Bs, dissolve in water and are found in green leaves, fruits and cereal grains. They are used daily.

> ★ **STAR FACT** ★
> Lack of vitamin A ruins night vision, because it is needed for the working of the retina.

- **Vitamins D and K** are the only ones made in the body. Vitamin D is essential for bone growth in children. It is made by the skin when exposed to the sun – 15 minutes three times a week may be enough.

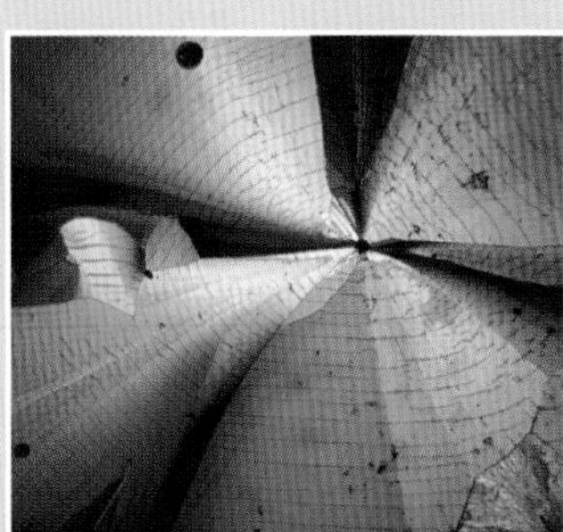

▶ *This is a microscope photograph of a crystal of vitamin C, also known as ascorbic acid. This vitamin helps the body fight infections such as colds.*

Disease

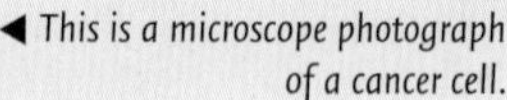

◀ *This is a microscope photograph of a cancer cell.*

- **A disease** is something that upsets the normal working of any living thing. It can be acute (sudden, but short-lived), chronic (long-lasting), malignant (spreading) or benign (not spreading).
- **Some diseases** are classified by the body part they affect (such as heart disease), or by the body activity they affect (such as respiratory, or breathing, disease).
- **Heart disease** is the most common cause of death in the USA, Europe and Australia.
- **Some diseases** are classified by their cause. These include the diseases caused by the staphylococcus bacteria, such as pneumonia.
- **Diseases can be** either contagious (able to be passed on) or non-contagious.
- **Infectious diseases** are caused by germs such as bacteria and viruses (see germs). They include the common cold, polio, flu and measles. Their spread can be controlled by good sanitation and hygiene, and by vaccination programmes.
- **Non-infectious diseases** may be inherited or they may be caused by such things as eating harmful substances, poor nutrition or hygiene, getting old or being injured.
- **Endemic diseases** are diseases that occur in a particular area of the world, such as sleeping sickness in Africa.
- **Cancer** is a disease in which malignant cells multiply abnormally, creating growths called tumours.
- **Cancer kills** 6 million people a year around the world. The risk increases as you get older.

Blood groups

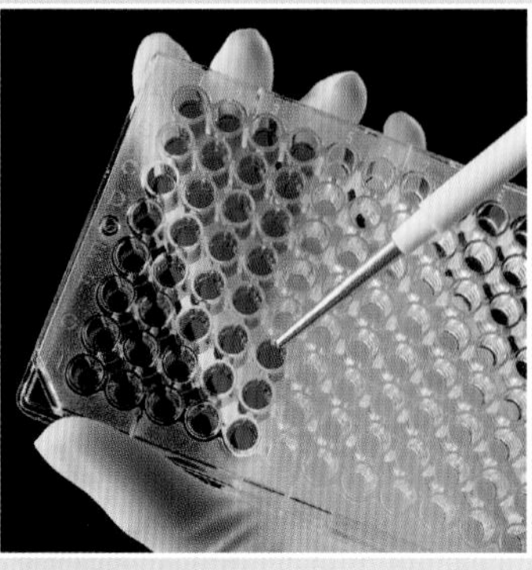

◀ *Lives often depend on a patient receiving blood donated by someone else. But unless the blood belongs to a suitable group, the patient's body will react against it.*

- **Most people's blood** belongs to one of four groups or types – A, O, B and AB.
- **Blood type O** is the most common.
- **Blood is also** either Rhesus positive (Rh+) or Rhesus negative (Rh-).
- **Around 85% of people** are Rh+. The remaining 15% are Rh-.
- **If your blood is Rh+** and your group is A, your blood group is said to be A positive. If your blood is Rh- and your group is O, you are O negative, and so on.
- **The Rhesus factors** got their name because they were first identified in Rhesus monkeys.
- **A transfusion** is when you are given blood from another person's body. Your body will only accept blood from certain groups which match with yours.
- **Blood transfusions** are given when someone has lost too much blood because of an injury or operation. It is also given to replace diseased blood.

> ★ **STAR FACT** ★
> A pregnant mother who is Rh- may develop damaging antibodies against the baby in her own womb if it is Rh+.

Digestion

- **Digestion** is the process by which your body breaks down the food you eat into substances that it can absorb (take in) and use.
- **Your digestive tract** is basically a long, winding tube called the alimentary canal (gut). It starts at your mouth and ends at your anus.
- **If you could lay** your gut out straight, it would be nearly six times as long as you are tall.
- **The food you eat** is softened in your mouth by chewing and by chemicals in your saliva (spit).
- **When you swallow**, food travels down your oesophagus (gullet) into your stomach. Your stomach is a muscular-walled bag which mashes the food into a pulp, helped by chemicals called gastric juices.
- **When empty**, your stomach holds barely 0.5 litres, but after a big meal it can stretch to more than 4 litres.
- **The half-digested food** that leaves your stomach is called chyme. It passes into your small intestine.
- **Your small intestine** is a 6 m long tube where chyme is broken down further, into molecules small enough to be absorbed through the intestine wall into the blood.

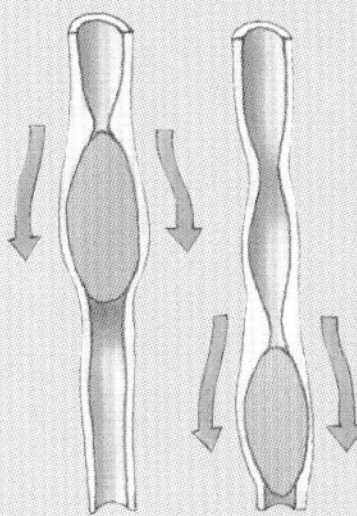

◀ *Food is moved through your digestive system by the muscles of the gut wall contracting (tightening) and relaxing. This rippling movement is called peristalsis. Whenever food enters the gut, rings of muscle contract behind it, while muscles in front relax, easing the food slowly forward.*

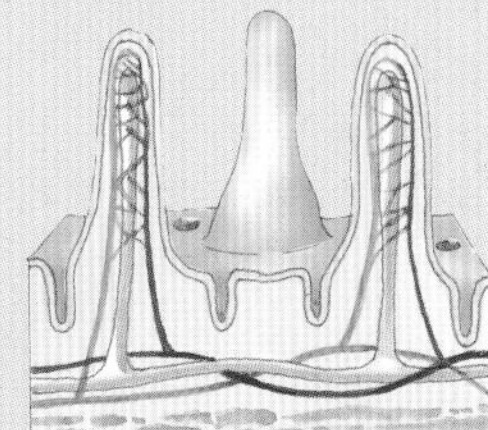

▶ *The small intestine is lined with tiny, finger-like folds called villi. On the surface of each villi are even tinier, finger-like folds called microvilli. These folds give a huge area for absorbing food.*

★ **STAR FACT** ★

On average, food takes 24 hours to pass right the way through your alimentary canal and out the other end.

- **Food that cannot be** digested in your small intestine passes on into your large intestine. It is then pushed out through your anus as faeces when you go to the toilet (see excretion).
- **Digestive enzymes** play a vital part in breaking food down so it can be absorbed by the body.

▼ *The food you eat is broken down into the nutrients your body needs as it passes down through your oesophagus into your stomach and your small intestine. Undigested food travels through your large intestine and leaves your body via your anus.*

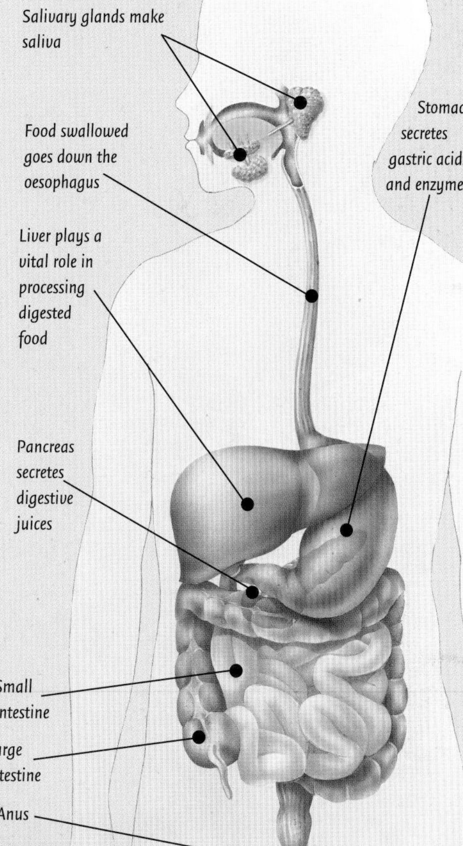

Joints

- **Body joints** are places where bones meet.
- **The skull** is not one bone, but 22 separate bones bound tightly together with fibres so that they can't move.
- **Most body joints** (apart from fixed joints like the skull's fibrous joints) let bones move, but different kinds of joint let them move in different ways.
- **Hinge joints**, such as the elbow, let the bones swing to and fro in two directions like door hinges do.
- **In ball-and-socket joints**, such as the hip, the rounded end of one bone sits in the cup-shaped socket of the other and can move in almost any direction.
- **Swivel joints** turn like a wheel on an axle. Your head can swivel to the left or to the right on your spine.

★ STAR FACT ★
The knee joint can bend, straighten and (when slightly bent) rotate.

- **Saddle joints** such as those in the thumb have the bones interlocking like two saddles. These joints allow great mobility with considerable strength.
- **The relatively inflexible** joints between the spine's bones (vertebrae) are cushioned by pads of cartilage.
- **Flexible synovial joints** such as the hip-joint are lubricated with 'synovial fluid' and cushioned by cartilage

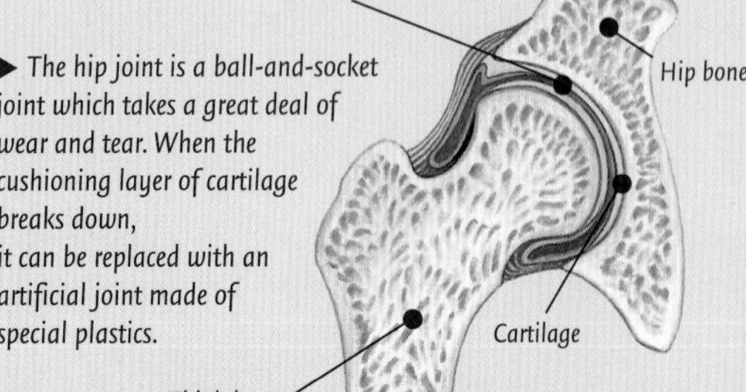

▶ *The hip joint is a ball-and-socket joint which takes a great deal of wear and tear. When the cushioning layer of cartilage breaks down, it can be replaced with an artificial joint made of special plastics.*

Nerve cells

- **Nerves** are made of cells called neurons.
- **Neurons** are spider-shaped cells with a nucleus at the centre, lots of branching threads called dendrites, and a winding tail called an axon which can be up to 1 m long.
- **Axon terminals** on the axons of one neuron link to the dendrites or cell body of another neuron.
- **Neurons link up** like beads on a string to make your nervous system.

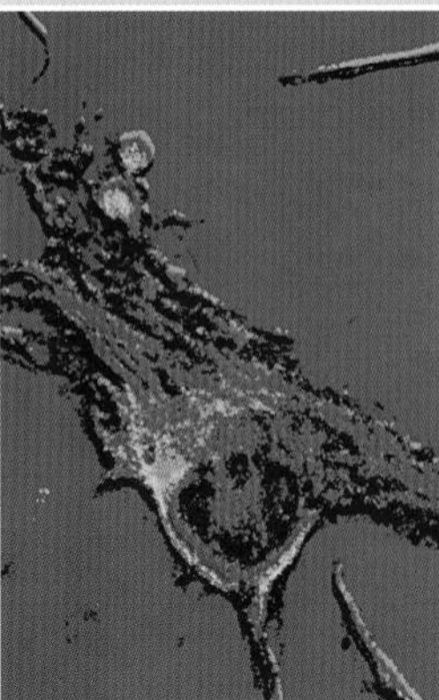

▲ *Microscopically tiny nerve cells like this were first seen by being stained with silver nitrate by the Italian scientist Camillo Golgi in the late 19th century.*

- **Most cells are** short-lived and are constantly being replaced by new ones. Some neurons, however, are never replaced after you are born.
- **Nerve signals** travel as electrical pulses, each pulse lasting about 0.001 seconds.
- **When nerves are resting** there are extra sodium ions with a positive electrical charge on the outside of the nerve cell, and extra negative ions inside.
- **When a nerve fires**, little gates open in the cell wall all along the nerve, and positive ions rush in to join the negative ions. This makes an electrical pulse.
- **Long-distance nerves** are insulated by a sheath of a fatty substance, myelin to keep the signal strong.
- **Myelinated (myelin-sheathed) nerves** shoot signals through at about 100 metres per second.
- **Ordinary nerves** send signals at about 1-2 metres per second.

The lungs

- **Your lungs** are a pair of soft, spongy bags inside your chest.
- **When you breathe** in, air rushes in through your nose or mouth, down your trachea (windpipe) and into the hundreds of branching airways in your lungs.
- **The two biggest airways** are called bronchi, and they both branch into smaller airways called bronchioles.

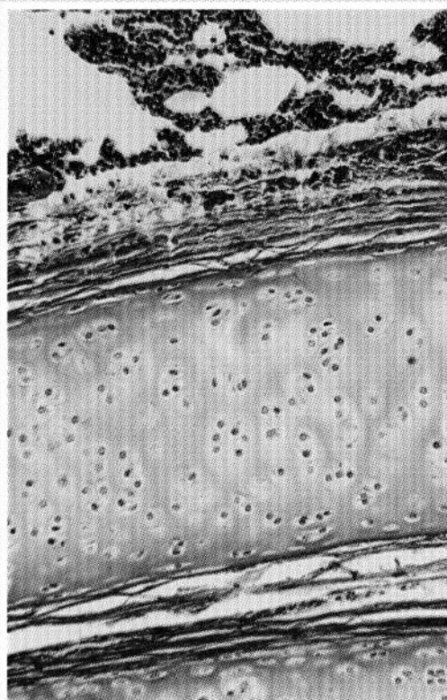

▲ *Taken through a powerful microscope, this photo of a slice of lung tissue shows a blood vessel and the very thin walls of an alveolus next to it.*

- **The surface of your airways** is protected by a slimy film of mucus, which gets thicker to protect the lungs when you have a cold.
- **At the end of each bronchiole** are bunches of minute air sacs called alveoli (singular alveolus).
- **Alveoli** are wrapped around with tiny blood vessels, and alveoli walls are just one cell thick – thin enough to let oxygen and carbon dioxide seep through them.
- **There are 300 million alveoli** in your lungs.
- **The huge surface area** of all these alveoli makes it possible for huge quantities of oxygen to seep through into the blood. Equally huge quantities of carbon dioxide can seep back into the airways for removal when you breathe out.

★ STAR FACT ★

Opened out and laid flat, the alveoli would cover half a football field.

The liver

   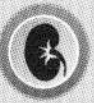  

- **The liver** is your chemical processing centre.
- **The liver is your** body's biggest internal organ, and the word hepatic means 'to do with the liver'.
- **The liver's prime task** is handling all the nutrients and substances digested from the food you eat and sending them out to your body cells when needed.
- **The liver turns** carbohydrates into glucose, the main energy-giving chemical for body cells.
- **The liver keeps** the levels of glucose in the blood steady. It releases more when levels drop, and by storing it as glycogen, a type of starch, when levels rise.
- **The liver packs off** any excess food energy to be stored as fat around the body.
- **The liver breaks down** proteins and stores vitamins and minerals.
- **The liver produces bile**, the yellowish or greenish bitter liquid that helps dissolve fat as food is digested.
- **The liver clears the blood** of old red cells and harmful substances such as alcohol, and makes new plasma (see blood).
- **The liver's chemical processing units** are thousands of hexagonal-shaped units called lobules. These take in unprocessed blood on the outside and dispatch it through a collecting vein in the centre of each.

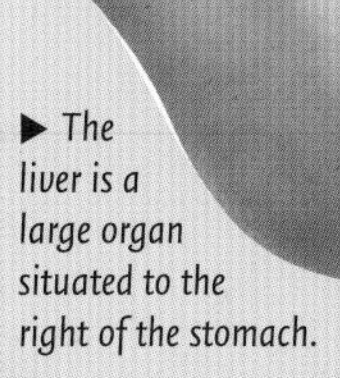

▶ *The liver is a large organ situated to the right of the stomach.*

Genes

- **Genes** are the body's chemical instructions for your entire life – for growing up, surviving, having children and, perhaps, even for dying.
- **Individual genes** are instructions to make particular proteins, the body's building-block molecules.
- **Small sets of genes** control features such as the colour of your hair or your eyes, or create a particular body process such as digesting fat from food.
- **Each of your body cells** (except egg and sperm cells) carries identical sets of genes. This is because all your cells were made by other cells splitting in two, starting with the original egg cell in your mother.
- **Your genes are a mixture** – half come from your mother and half from your father (see chromosomes). But none of your brothers or sisters will get the same mix, unless you are identical twins.
- **Genes make us unique** – making us tall or short, fair or dark, brilliant dancers or speakers, healthy or likely to get particular illnesses, and so on.
- **Genes are sections** of DNA – a microscopically tiny molecule inside each cell.
- **DNA** is shaped in a double helix with linking bars, like a twisted rope ladder.

★ STAR FACT ★
There are more than 30,000 individual genes inside every single cell of your body.

- **The bars of DNA** are four special chemicals called bases – guanine, adenine, cytosine and thymine.
- **The bases in DNA** are set in groups of three called codons, and the order of the bases in each codon varies to provide a chemical code for the cell to make a particular amino acid. The cell puts together different amino acids to make different proteins.

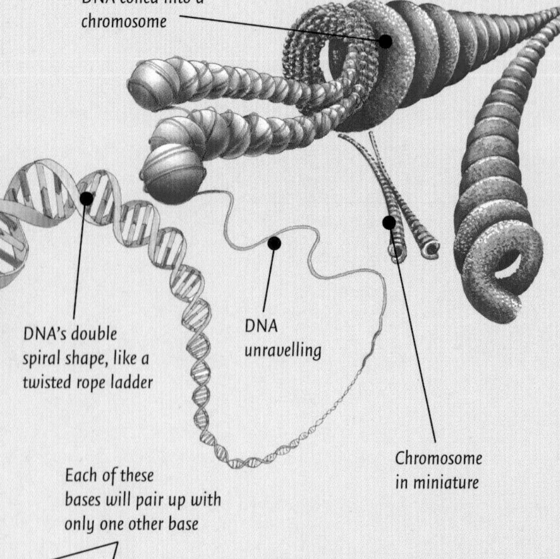

◀ DNA (Deoxyribonucleic Acid) is the amazing tiny molecule inside every cell that carries all your genes in a chemical code – the genetic code. Most of the time it is coiled up inside the chromosomes, but when needed it unravels to reveal its double helix shape. Each of the four bases that make the rungs pairs with only one other: guanine with cytosine, and adenine with thymine. So the sequence of bases along one strand of the DNA is a perfect mirror image of the sequence on the other side. When the strand temporarily divides down the middle, each strand can be used like a template to make a copy. This is how instructions are issued.

Breathing

- **You breathe** because every single cell in your body needs a continuous supply of oxygen to burn glucose, the high-energy substance from digested food that cells get from blood.
- **Scientists** call breathing 'respiration'. Cellular respiration is the way that cells use oxygen to burn glucose.
- **The oxygen in air** is taken into your lungs, and then carried in your blood to your body cells.
- **Waste carbon dioxide** from your cells is returned by your blood to your lungs, to be breathed out.
- **On average** you breathe in about 15 times a minute. If you run hard, the rate soars to around 80 times a minute.
- **Newborn babies** breathe about 40 times a minute.
- **If you live to the age of 80**, you will have taken well over 600 million breaths.
- **A normal breath** takes in about 0.4 litres of air. A deep breath can take in ten times as much.
- **Your diaphragm** is a dome-shaped sheet of muscle between your chest and stomach, which works with your chest muscles to make you breathe in and out.
- **Scientists** call breathing in 'inhalation', and breathing out 'exhalation'.

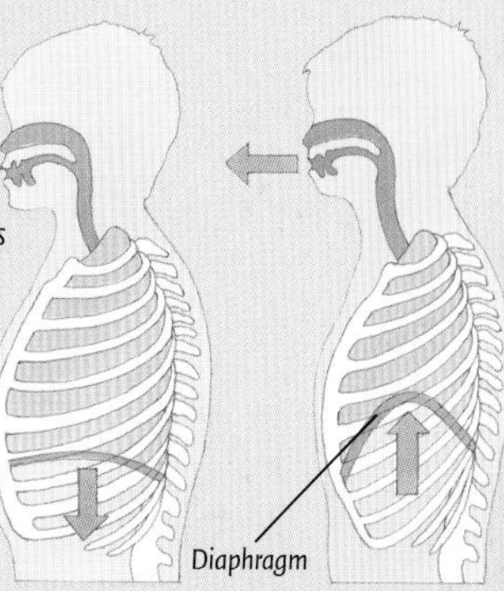

▶ Air is sucked in through your nose and mouth as your diaphragm pulls your lungs down and your chest muscles pull your ribs up and out. Air is forced out again when the diaphragm arches up and the rib muscles relax to allow the ribs to tilt down.

Co-ordination

- **Co-ordination** means balanced or skilful movement.
- **To make you move**, your brain has to send signals out along nerves telling all the muscles involved exactly what to do.

◀ Ball skills demand incredible muscle co-ordination. The eyes follow the ball to tell the brain exactly where it is. At the same time, the brain also relies on a high-speed stream of sensory signals from the proprioceptor cells in order to tell it exactly where the leg is, and to keep the body perfectly balanced.

- **Co-ordination of the muscles** is handled by the cerebellum at the back of your brain (see the brain).
- **The cerebellum** is told what to do by the brain's motor cortex (see the cortex).
- **The cerebellum sends** its commands via the basal ganglia in the middle of the brain.
- **Proprioceptor** means 'one's own sensors', and proprioceptors are nerve cells that are sensitive to movement, pressure or stretching.
- **Proprioceptors are all over your body** – in muscles, tendons and joints – and they all send signals to your brain telling it the position or posture of every body part.
- **The hair cells** in the balance organs of your ear are also proprioceptors (see balance).

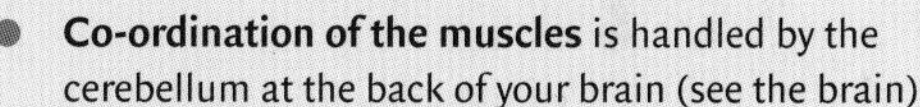

★ STAR FACT ★
Proprioceptors are what allow you to touch forefingers behind your back.

Mood

- **Mood is** your state of mind – whether you are happy or sad, angry or afraid, overjoyed or depressed.
- **Moods and emotions** seem to be strongly linked to the structures in the centre of the brain, where unconscious activities are controlled (see the brain).
- **Moods** have three elements – how you feel, what happens to your body, and what they make you do.
- **Some scientists** think the way you feel causes changes in the body – you are happy so you smile, for example.
- **Other scientists** think changes in the body alter the way you feel – smiling makes you happy.
- **Yet other scientists** think moods start automatically – before you even know it – when something triggers off a reaction in the thalamus in the centre of the brain.

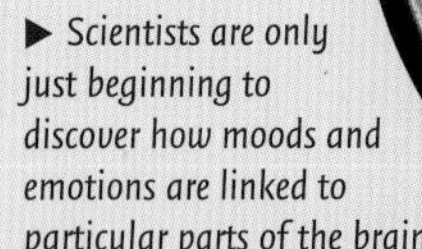

★ **STAR FACT** ★
In one experiment, people injected with adrenaline found rotten jokes much funnier!

- **The thalamus** then sends mood signals to the brain's cortex and you become aware of the mood.
- **The thalamus** also sets off automatic changes in the body through nerves and hormones.
- **Certain memories or experiences** are so strongly linked in your mind that they can trigger a certain mood.

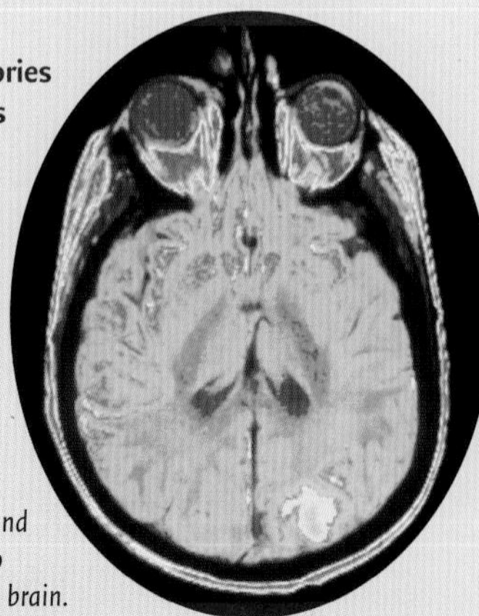

▶ *Scientists are only just beginning to discover how moods and emotions are linked to particular parts of the brain.*

Fats

- **Fats** are an important source of energy. Together with proteins and carbohydrates, they make up your body's three main components of foods.
- **While carbohydrates** are generally used for energy immediately, your body often stores fat to use for energy in times of shortage.
- **Weight for weight**, fats contain twice as much energy as carbohydrates.
- **Fats (or lipids)** are important organic (life) substances, found in almost every living thing. They are made from substances called fatty acids and glycerol.
- **Food fats** are greasy, vegetable or animal fats that will not dissolve in water.
- **Most vegetable fats** such as corn oil and olive oil are liquid, although some nut fats are solid.

◀ *Fats are either saturated or unsaturated. Cheese is a saturated fat, which means its fatty acids are saturated with as much hydrogen as they can hold. Saturated fats are linked to high levels of the substance cholesterol in the blood and may increase certain health risks such as heart attack.*

- **Most animal fats** as in meats, milk and cheese are solid. Milk is mainly water with some solid animal fats. Most solid fats melt when warmed.
- **Fats called triglycerides** are stored around the body as adipose tissue (body fat). These act as energy stores and also insulate the body against the cold.
- **Fats called phospholipids** are used to build body cells.
- **In your stomach**, bile from your liver and enzymes from your pancreas break fats down into fatty acids and glycerol. These are absorbed into your body's lymphatic system or enter the blood.

Capillaries

- **Capillaries** are the smallest of all your blood vessels, only visible under a microscope. They link the arterioles to the venules (see circulation).
- **Capillaries** were discovered by Marcello Malphigi in 1661.
- **There are 10 billion capillaries** in your body.
- **The largest capillary** is just 0.2 mm wide – thinner than a hair.

▲ *The work done by an athlete's muscles generates a lot of heat – which the body tries to lose by opening up capillaries in the skin, turning the skin bright red.*

- **Each capillary** is about 0.5 mm to 1 mm long.
- **Capillary walls** are just one cell thick, so it is easy for chemicals to pass through them.
- **It is through the capillary walls** that your blood passes oxygen, food and waste to and from each one of your body cells.
- **There are many more capillaries** in active tissues such as muscles, liver and kidneys than there are in tendons and ligaments.
- **Capillaries** carry more or less blood according to need. They let more blood reach the surface when you are warm. They let less blood reach the surface to save heat when you are cold.

★ STAR FACT ★

The average capillary is 0.001 mm in diameter – just wide enough for red blood cells to pass through one at a time.

Germs

- **Germs** are microscopic organisms that enter your body and harm it in some way.
- **The scientific word** for 'germ' is 'pathogen'.
- **When germs** begin to multiply inside your body, you are suffering from an infectious disease.
- **An infection** that spreads throughout your body (flu or measles, for example) is called a systemic infection.
- **An infection** that affects only a small area (such as dirt in a cut) is called a localized infection.
- **It is often the reaction** of your body's immune system to the germ that makes you feel ill.
- **Bacteria** are single-celled organisms. They are found almost everywhere in huge numbers, and they multiply rapidly.
- **Most bacteria are harmless**, but there are three harmful groups – cocci are round cells, spirilla are coil-shaped, and bacilli are rod-shaped. These harmful bacteria cause diseases such as tetanus and typhoid.
- **Viruses** can only live and multiply by taking over other cells – they cannot survive on their own. They cause diseases such as colds, flu, mumps and AIDS.
- **Parasites** are animals such as tapeworms that may live in or on your body, feeding on it and making you ill.
- **Fungal spores** and tiny organisms called protozoa can also cause illness.

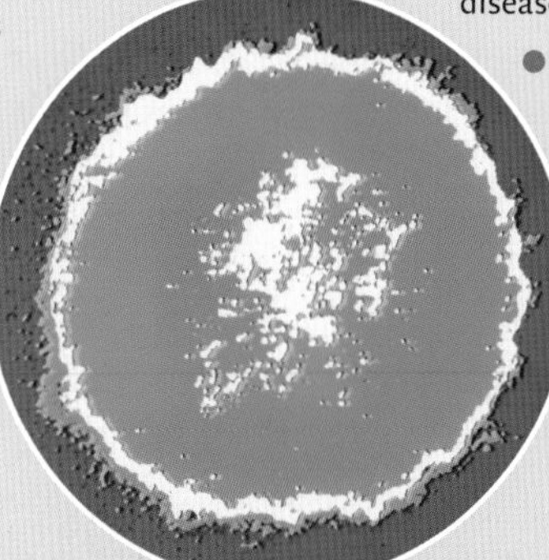

◀ *The disease AIDS (Acquired Immune Deficiency Syndrome) is caused by a virus called HIV. This virus gets inside vital cells of the body's immune system and weakens its ability to fight against other infections.*

Motor nerves

▲ *Motor nerves fire to make muscles move to hit the ball.*

- **Motor nerves** tell your muscles to move.
- **Each major muscle** has many motor nerve-endings that instruct it to contract (tighten).
- **Motor nerves cross over** from one side of your body to the other at the top of your spinal cord. This means that signals from the right side of your brain go to the left side of your body, and vice versa.
- **Each motor nerve** is paired to a proprioceptor on the muscle and its tendons (see co-ordination). This sends signals to the brain to say whether the muscle is tensed or relaxed.
- **If the strain** on a tendon increases, the proprioceptor sends a signal to the brain. The brain adjusts the motor signals to the muscle so it contracts more or less.
- **Motor nerve signals** originate in a part of the brain called the motor cortex (see the cortex).
- **All the motor nerves** (apart from those in the head) branch out from the spinal cord.
- **The gut** has no motor nerve-endings but plenty of sense endings, so you can feel it but cannot move it consciously.
- **The throat** has motor nerve-endings but few sense endings, so you can move it but not feel it.
- **Motor neuron disease** is a disease that attacks motor nerves within the central nervous system.

Glucose

- **Glucose** is the body's energy chemical, used as the fuel in all cell activity.
- **Glucose is a kind of sugar** made by plants as they take energy from sunlight. It is common in many fruits and fruit juices, along with fructose (see carbohydrates).
- **The body gets its glucose** from carbohydrates in food, broken down in stages in the intestine.
- **From the intestine**, glucose travels in the blood to the liver, where excess is stored in the form of glycogen.
- **For the body to work effectively**, levels of glucose in the blood (called blood sugar) must always be correct.
- **Blood sugar levels** are controlled by two hormones, glucagon and insulin, sent out by the pancreas.
- **When blood sugar is low**, the pancreas sends glucagon to the liver to tell it to change more glycogen to glucose.
- **When blood sugar is high**, the pancreas sends insulin to the liver to tell it to store more glucose as glycogen.

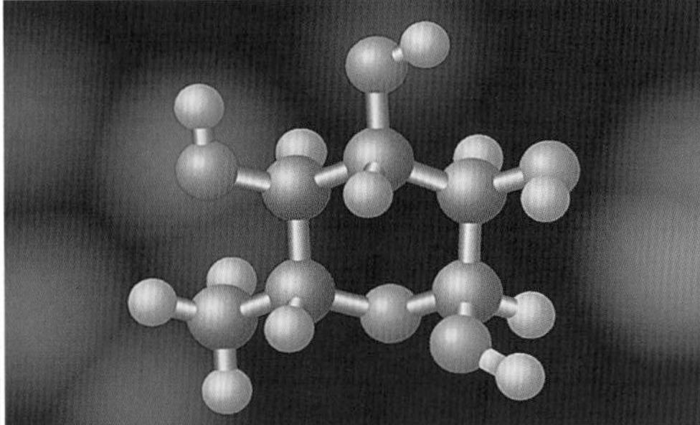

▲ *Glucose is built from 6 carbon, 12 hydrogen and 6 oxygen atoms.*

- **Inside cells**, glucose may be burned for energy, stored as glycogen, or used to make triglyceride fats (see fats).

★ **STAR FACT** ★

Adrenaline and other hormones from the adrenals boost blood sugar levels.

The immune system

- **The immune system** is the complicated system of defences that your body uses to prevent or fight off attack from germs and other invaders.
- **Your body** has a variety of barriers, toxic chemicals and booby traps to stop germs entering it. The skin is a barrier that stops many germs getting in, as long as it is not broken.
- **Mucus is a thick, slimy fluid** that coats vulnerable internal parts of your body such as your stomach. It also acts as a lubricant (oil), making swallowing easier.
- **Mucus lines your airways** and lungs to protect them from smoke particles as well as from germs. Your airways may fill up with mucus when you have a cold, as your body tries to minimize the invasion of airborne germs.

★ **STAR FACT** ★

Your vulnerable eyes are protected by tears which wash away germs. Tears also contain an enzyme called lysozome which kills bacteria.

- **Itching, sneezing, coughing and vomiting** are your body's ways of getting rid of unwelcome invaders. Small particles that get trapped in the mucus lining of your airways are wafted out by tiny hairs called cilia.
- **The body** has many specialized cells and chemicals which fight germs that get inside you.
- **Complement** is a mixture of liquid proteins in the blood which attacks bacteria.
- **Interferon** are proteins which help the body's cells to attack viruses and also stimulate killer cells (see lymphocytes).
- **Certain white blood cells** are cytotoxic, which means they are poisonous to invaders.
- **Phagocytes** are big white blood cells that swallow up invaders and then use an enzyme to dissolve them (see antibodies). They are drawn to the site of an infection whenever there is inflammation.

▶ *HIV, the AIDS virus, attacks the body's immune cells and prevents them dealing with infections.*

▼ *The body's range of interior defences against infection is amazingly complex. The various kinds of white blood cells and the antibodies they make are particularly important.*

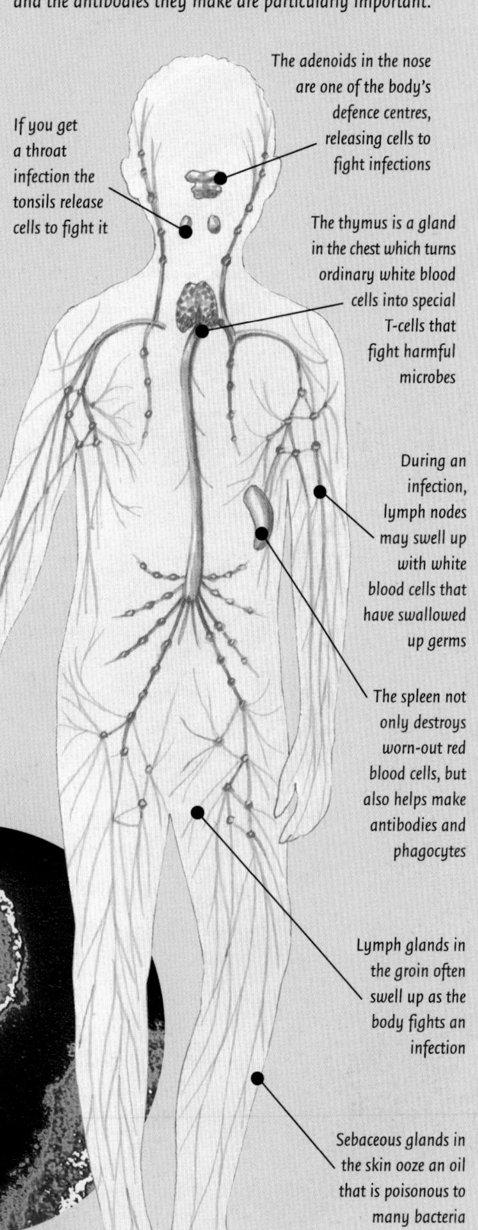

Heredity

- **Your heredity** is all the body characteristics you inherit from your parents, whether it is your mother's black hair or your father's knobbly knees.
- **Characteristics** are passed on by the genes carried on your chromosomes (see genes, chromosomes).
- **The basic laws** of heredity were discovered by the Austrian monk Gregor Mendel 150 years ago.
- **Your body characteristics** are a mix of two sets of instructions – one from your mother's chromosomes and the other from your father's.
- **Each characteristic** is the work of only one gene – either your mother's or your father's. This gene is said to be 'expressed'.
- **The gene that is not expressed** does not vanish. Instead, it stays dormant (asleep) in your chromosomes, possibly to pass on to your children.
- **A gene** that is always expressed is called the dominant gene.
- **A recessive gene** is one that loses out to a dominant gene and stays dormant.
- **A recessive gene** may be expressed when there is no competition – that is, when the genes from both of your parents are recessive.

▲ *The gene for blue eyes is recessive, but if a girl gets a blue-eye gene from both of her parents, she may have blue eyes.*

Fitness

◀ *Skiing is one of the most demanding of all sports, and top skiers need to be extremely fit to cope with the extra strain on their bodies.*

- **Fitness** is about how much and what kind of physical activity you can do without getting tired or strained.
- **Fitness depends** on your strength, flexibility (bendiness) and endurance (staying power).
- **One key to fitness** is cardiovascular fitness – that is, how well your heart and lungs respond to the extra demands of exercise.
- **One measure of cardiovascular fitness** is how quickly your pulse rate returns to normal after exercise – the fitter you are, the quicker it returns.
- **Another measure of cardiovascular fitness** is how slowly your heart beats during exercise – the fitter you are, the slower it beats.
- **Being fit** improves your physical performance.
- **Being fit often** protects against illness.
- **Being fit can** slow down the effects of ageing.
- **Cardiovascular fitness** reduces the chances of getting heart disease.
- **Fitness tests** involve comparing such things as height, weight and body fat, and measuring blood pressure and pulse rate before and after exercise. Other tests may measure how you manage a standard exercise, such as running over a fixed distance.

Heartbeat

- **The heartbeat** is the regular squeezing of the heart muscle to pump blood around the body.
- **Four heart valves** make sure blood only moves one way.
- **The heartbeat** is a sequence called the cardiac cycle and it has two phases – systole and diastole.
- **Systole** is when the heart muscle contracts (tightens). Diastole is the resting phase between contractions.
- **Systole begins** when a wave of muscle contraction sweeps across the heart and squeezes blood from each of the atria into the two ventricles.
- **When the contraction** reaches the ventricles, they squeeze blood into the arteries.
- **In diastole**, the heart muscle relaxes and the atria fill with blood again.
- **Heart muscle** on its own would contract automatically.
- **Nerve signals** make the heart beat faster or slower.

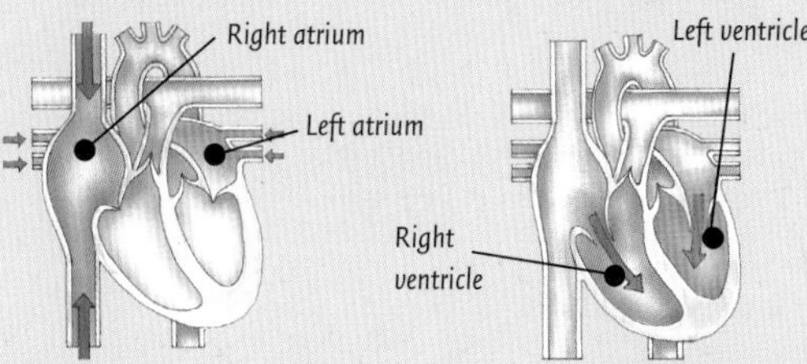

▲ *Blood floods into the relaxed atria.*

▲ *The wave of contraction squeezes blood into ventricles.*

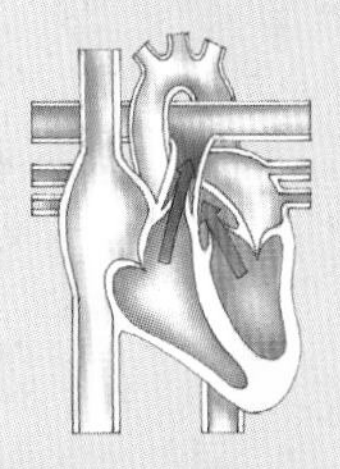

▲ *Blood is squeezed out the ventricles into the arteries.*

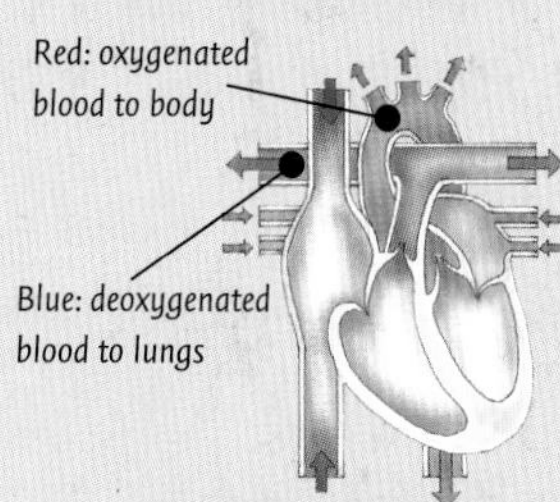

▲ *Blood starts to fill up the now relaxed atria again.*

Blood

◀ *Blood contains red cells and white cells, but is mainly a watery liquid called plasma.*

- **Blood** is the liquid that circulates around your body. It carries oxygen and food to body cells, and takes carbon dioxide and other waste away. It fights infection, keeps you warm, and distributes chemicals that control body processes.
- **Blood is made up of** red cells, white cells and platelets, all carried in a liquid called plasma.
- **Plasma** is 90% water, plus hundreds of other substances, including nutrients, hormones and special proteins for fighting infection.
- **Blood plasma** turns milky immediately after a meal high in fats.
- **Platelets** are tiny pieces of cell that make blood clots start to form to stop bleeding.
- **Blood clots also** involve a lacy, fibrous network made from a protein called fibrin. Fibrin is set in action by a sequence of chemicals called factors (factors I through to 8).
- **The amount of blood** in your body depends on your size. An adult who weighs 80 kg has about 5 litres of blood. A child who is half as heavy has half as much blood.
- **People who live high up mountains** have at least 20% more blood to carry more oxygen – this is because the higher you are, the less oxygen there is in the air.
- **If a blood donor** gives 0.5 litres of blood, the body replaces the plasma in a few hours, but it takes a few weeks to replace the red cells.

★ STAR FACT ★

Oxygen turns blood bright red when you bleed. In your veins it can be almost brown.

The heart

- **Your heart** is the size of your fist. It is inside the middle of your chest, slightly to the left.
- **The heart is a powerful pump** made almost entirely of muscle.
- **The heart contracts** (tightens) and relaxes automatically about 70 times a minute to pump blood out through your arteries.
- **The heart has two sides** separated by a muscle wall called the septum.
- **The right side** is smaller and weaker, and it pumps blood only to the lungs.
- **The stronger left side** pumps blood around the body.
- **Each side of the heart** has two chambers. There is an atrium (plural atria) at the top where blood accumulates (builds up) from the veins, and a ventricle below which contracts to pump blood out into the arteries.
- **Each of the heart's four chambers** ejects about 70 ml of blood with each beat.
- **There are two valves** in each side of the heart to make sure that blood flows only one way – a large one between the atrium and the ventricle, and a small one at the exit from the ventricle into the artery.
- **The coronary arteries** supply the heart. If they become clogged, the heart muscle may be short of blood and stop working. This is what happens in a heart attack.

★ STAR FACT ★

During an average lifetime, the heart pumps 200 million litres of blood – enough to fill New York's Central Park to a depth of 15 m.

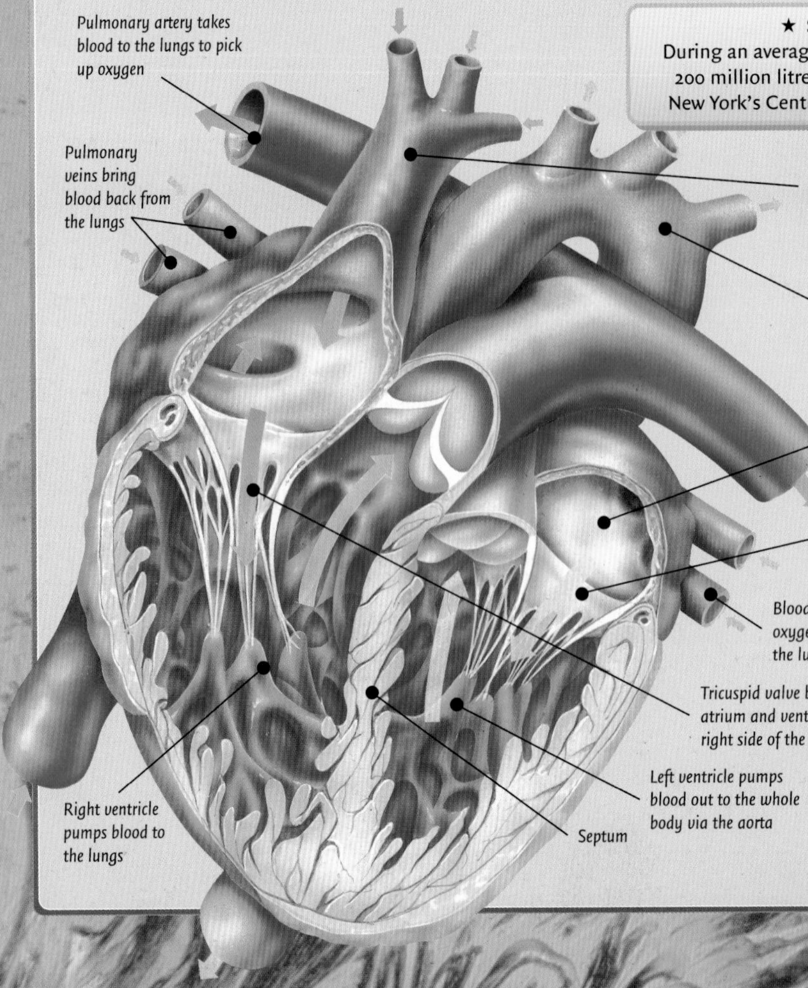

Pulmonary artery takes blood to the lungs to pick up oxygen

Pulmonary veins bring blood back from the lungs

Two big veins called the venae cavae bring blood low in oxygen back from the body to the right side of the heart

A large artery called the aorta sends blood rich in oxygen out to the whole body

Blood loaded with oxygen from the lungs enters the left atrium

Mitral valve between the atrium and ventricle of the left side of the heart

Blood rich in oxygen returns from the lungs

Tricuspid valve between the atrium and ventricle of the right side of the heart

Left ventricle pumps blood out to the whole body via the aorta

Septum

Right ventricle pumps blood to the lungs

◀ *The heart is a remarkable double pump, with two pumping chambers, the left and the right ventricles. It contracts automatically to squeeze jets of blood out of the ventricles and through the arteries.*

Pregnancy

- **Pregnancy** begins when a woman's ovum (egg cell) is fertilized by a man's sperm cell. Usually this happens after sexual intercourse, but it can begin in a laboratory.
- **When a woman becomes pregnant** her monthly menstrual periods stop. Tests on her urine show whether she is pregnant.
- **During pregnancy**, the fertilized egg divides again and again to grow rapidly – first to an embryo (the first eight weeks), and then to a foetus (from eight weeks until birth).
- **Unlike an embryo**, a foetus has grown legs and arms, as well as internal organs such as a heart.
- **Pregnancy lasts nine months**, and the time is divided into three trimesters (periods of about 12 weeks).
- **The foetus** lies cushioned in its mother's uterus (womb) in a bag of fluid called the amniotic sac.
- **The mother's blood** passes food and oxygen to the foetus via the placenta, or afterbirth.
- **The umbilical cord** runs between the foetus and the placenta, carrying blood between them.
- **During pregnancy** a woman gains 30% more blood, and her heart rate goes up.
- **During pregnancy** a woman's breasts grow and develop milk glands.

▼ After about 16 weeks, a pregnant woman may go for an ultrasound scan to check that the foetus is healthy.

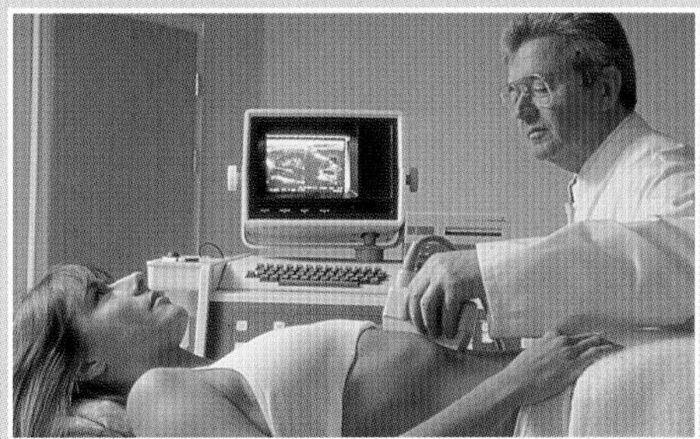

Muscle movement

◀ A very high-powered electron microscope reveals purple myofibrils of myosin – each little more than 0.00001 mm wide. The orange is actin.

- **Most muscles are long and thin** and they work by pulling themselves shorter, sometimes contracting by up to half their length.
- **Skeletal muscles,** which make you move, are made of cells which have not just one nucleus like other cells do, but many nuclei in a long fibre, called a myofibre.
- **Muscles are made** from hundreds or thousands of these fibres bound together like fibres in string.
- **Muscle fibres** are made from tiny strands called myofibrils, each marked with dark bands, giving the muscle its name of stripey or 'striated' muscle.

> ★ **STAR FACT** ★
> If all the muscles in your body pulled together, they could lift a bus.

- **The stripes** in muscle are alternate bands of filaments of two substances: actin and myosin.
- **The actin and myosin** interlock, like teeth on a zip.
- **When a nerve signal** comes from the brain, chemical 'hooks' on the myosin twist and yank the actin filaments along, shortening the muscle.
- **The chemical hooks** on myosin are made from a stem called a cross-bridge and a head made of a chemical called adenosine triphosphate or ATP.
- **ATP is sensitive to calcium**, and the nerve signal from the brain that tells the muscle to contract does its work by releasing a flood of calcium to trigger the ATP.

Reflexes

- **Reflexes** are muscle movements that are automatic (they happen without you thinking about them).
- **Inborn reflexes** are reflexes you were born with, such as urinating or shivering when you are cold.
- **The knee-jerk** is an inborn reflex that makes your leg jerk up when the tendon below your knee is tapped.
- **Primitive reflexes** are reflexes that babies have for a few months after they are born.
- **One primitive reflex** is when you put something in a baby's hand and it automatically grips it.
- **Conditioned reflexes** are those you learn through habit, as certain pathways in the nervous system are used again and again.
- **Conditioned reflexes** help you do anything from holding a cup to playing football without thinking.
- **Reflex reactions** are what pull your hand from hot things before you have had time to think about it.

▲ *Many sportsmen rely on lightning reflexes – actions too fast for the brain to even think about.*

- **Reflex reactions** work by short-circuiting the brain. The alarm signal from your hand sets off motor signals in the spinal cord to move the hand.
- **A reflex arc** is the nerve circuit from sense to muscle via the spinal cord.

The kidneys

        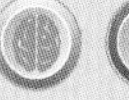  

- **The kidneys** are a pair of bean-shaped organs inside the small of the back.
- **The kidneys** are the body's water control and blood-cleaning plants.
- **The kidneys** are high-speed filters that draw off water and important substances from the blood. They let unwanted water and waste substances go (see urine).
- **The kidneys filter** about 1.3 litres of blood a minute.

Nephrons

Ureter

◀ *This cross-section diagram of a kidney shows blood entering through arteries (red) and leaving through veins (blue). Waste fluid drains away through the ureter (shown in yellow).*

- **All the blood** flows through the kidneys every ten minutes, so blood is filtered 150 times a day.
- **The kidneys manage** to recycle every re-useable substance from the blood. It takes 85 litres of water and other blood substances from every 1,000 litres of blood, but only lets out 0.6 litres as urine.
- **The kidneys** save nearly all the amino acids and glucose from the blood and 70% of the salt.
- **Blood entering each kidney** is filtered through a million or more filtration units called nephrons.
- **Each nephron** is an incredibly intricate network of little pipes called convoluted tubules, wrapped around countless tiny capilliaries. Useful blood substances are filtered into the tubules, then re-absorbed back into the blood in the capilliaries.
- **Blood enters each nephron** through a cup called the Bowman's capsule via a bundle of capilliaries.

Puberty

- **Puberty** is the time of life when girls and boys mature sexually.
- **The age of puberty varies**, but on average it is between 11 and 13 years.
- **Puberty is started** by two hormones sent out by the pituitary gland (see the brain) – the follicle-stimulating hormone and the luteinizing hormone.
- **During puberty, a girl** will develop breasts and grow hair under her arms and around her genitals.
- **Inside her body**, a girl's ovaries grow ten times as big and release sex hormones (see reproduction – girls).
- **The sex hormones** oestrogen and progesterone spur the development of a girl's sexual organs and control her monthly menstrual cycle.

★ STAR FACT ★
By the time a boy is 15, his testicles can make 200 million new sperm a day.

▲ *In their early teens, girls go through puberty and begin to develop the sexual characteristics that will make them women.*

- **A year or so after puberty begins**, a girl has her menarche (the first menstrual period). When her periods come regularly, she is able to have a baby.
- **For a boy during puberty**, his testes grow and hair sprouts on his face, under his arms and around his genitals.
- **Inside his body**, a boy's testes begin to make sperm.

The lymphatic system

- **The lymphatic system** is your body's sewer, the network of pipes that drains waste from the cells.
- **The 'pipes' of the lymphatic system** are called lymphatics or lymph vessels.
- **The lymphatics** are filled by a watery liquid called lymph fluid which, along with bacteria and waste chemicals, drains from body tissues such as muscles.
- **The lymphatic system** has no pump to make it circulate. Instead, lymphatic fluid is circulated as a side effect of the heartbeat and muscle movement.
- **At places** in the lymphatic system there are tiny lumps called nodes. These are filters which trap germs that have got into the lymph fluid.
- **In the nodes**, armies of white blood cells called lymphocytes neutralize or destroy germs.
- **When you have** a cold or any other infection, the lymph nodes in your neck or groin, or under your arm, may swell, as lymphocytes fight germs.

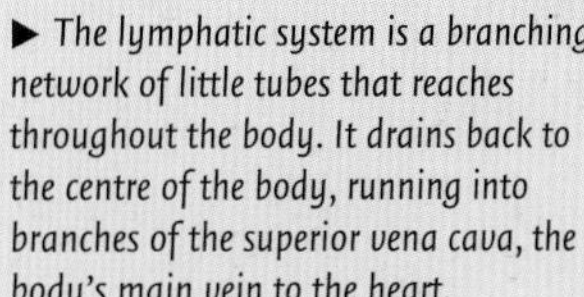

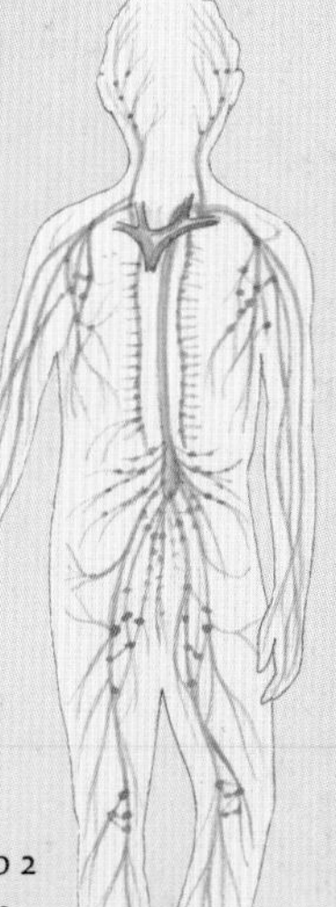

▶ *The lymphatic system is a branching network of little tubes that reaches throughout the body. It drains back to the centre of the body, running into branches of the superior vena cava, the body's main vein to the heart.*

- **Lymph fluid** drains back into the blood via the body's main vein, the superior vena cava.
- **The lymphatic system** is not only the lymphatics and lymph nodes, but includes the spleen, the thymus, the tonsils and the adenoids (see the immune system).
- **On average**, at any time about 1 to 2 litres of lymph fluid circulate in the lymphatics and body tissues.

Reproduction – girls

- **A girl or woman's reproductive system** is where her body stores, releases and nurtures the egg cells (ova – singular, ovum) that create a new human life when joined with a male sperm cell.
- **All the egg cells** are stored from birth in the ovaries – two egg-shaped glands inside the pelvic region. Each egg is stored in a tiny sac called a follicle.
- **One egg cell** is released every monthly menstrual cycle by one of the ovaries.
- **A monthly menstrual cycle starts** when follicle-stimulating hormone (FSH) is sent by the pituitary gland in the brain to spur follicles to grow.
- **As follicles grow**, they release the sex hormone oestrogen. Oestrogen makes the lining of the uterus (womb) thicken.
- **When an egg is ripe**, it slides down a duct called a Fallopian tube.
- **If a woman** has sexual intercourse at this time, sperm from the man's penis may swim up her vagina, enter her womb and fertilize the egg in the Fallopian tube.
- **If the egg is fertilized**, the womb lining goes on thickening ready for pregnancy, and the egg begins to develop into an embryo.
- **If the egg is not fertilized**, it is shed with the womb lining in a flow of blood from the vagina. This shedding is called a menstrual period.

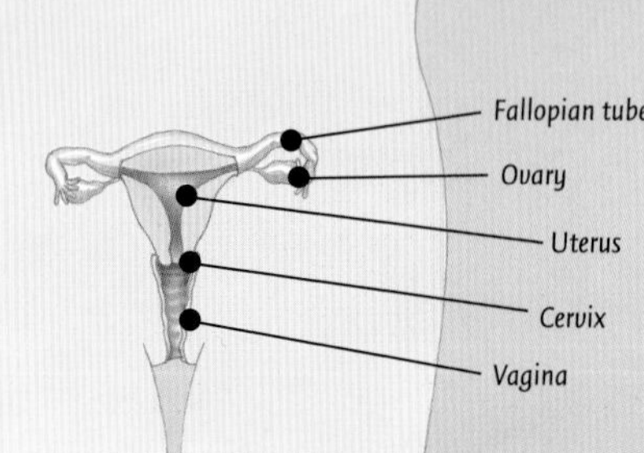

◀ *This is a frontal view of the inside of a female reproductive system, showing the two ovaries and Fallopian tubes, which join to the uterus.*

Lymphocytes

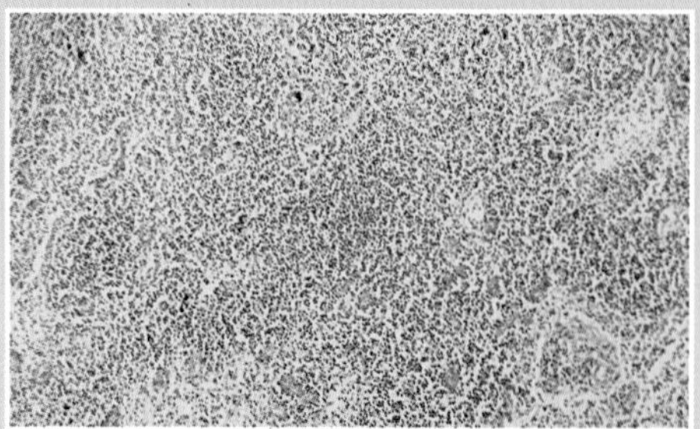

▲ *A lymph node packed with lymphocytes fighting infection.*

- **Lymphocytes** are white blood cells that play a role in the body's immune system, which targets invading germs.
- **There are two kinds of lymphocyte** – B lymphocytes (B-cells) and T lymphocytes (T-cells).
- **B-cells** develop into plasma cells that make antibodies to attack bacteria such as those which cause cholera, as well as some viruses (see antibodies).
- **T-cells** work against viruses and other micro-organisms that hide inside body cells. T-cells help identify and destroy these invaded cells or their products. They also attack certain bacteria.
- **There are two kinds of T-cell** – killers and helpers.
- **Helper T-cells** identify invaded cells and send out chemicals called lymphokines as an alarm, telling killer T-cells to multiply.
- **Invaded cells** give themselves away by abnormal proteins on their surface.
- **Killer T-cells** lock on to the cells identified by the helpers, then move in and destroy them.
- **Some B-cells,** called memory B-cells, stay for a long time, ready for a further attack by the same organism.

★ **STAR FACT** ★

If you get flu, it is your T lymphocytes that come to the rescue and fight off the virus.

The ear

- **Pinnae** (singular, pinna) are the ear flaps you can see on the side of your head, and they are simply collecting funnels for sounds.
- **A little way inside your head**, sounds hit a thin, tight wall of skin, called the eardrum, making it vibrate.
- **When the eardrum vibrates**, it shakes three little bones called ossicles. These are the smallest bones in the body.
- **The three ossicle bones** are the malleus (hammer), the incus (anvil) and the stapes (stirrup).

> ★ **STAR FACT** ★
> If your hearing is normal, you can hear sounds as deep as 20 Hertz (Hz) – vibrations per second – and as high as 20,000 Hz.

- **When the ossicles vibrate**, they rattle a tiny membrane called the oval window, intensifying the vibration.
- **The oval window** is 30 times smaller than the eardrum.
- **Beyond the oval window is the cochlea** – a winding collection of three, liquid-filled tubes, which looks a bit like a snail shell.
- **In the middle tube** of the cochlea there is a flap which covers row upon row of tiny hairs. This is called the organ of Corti.
- **When sounds make** the eardrum vibrate, the ossicles tap on the oval window, making pressure waves shoot through the liquid in the cochlea and wash over the flap of the organ of Corti, waving it up and down.
- **When the organ of Corti waves**, it tugs on the tiny hairs under the flap. These send signals to the brain via the auditory nerve – and you hear a sound.

▼ Most of your ear is hidden inside your head. It is an amazingly complex and delicate structure for picking up the tiny variations in air pressure created by a sound.

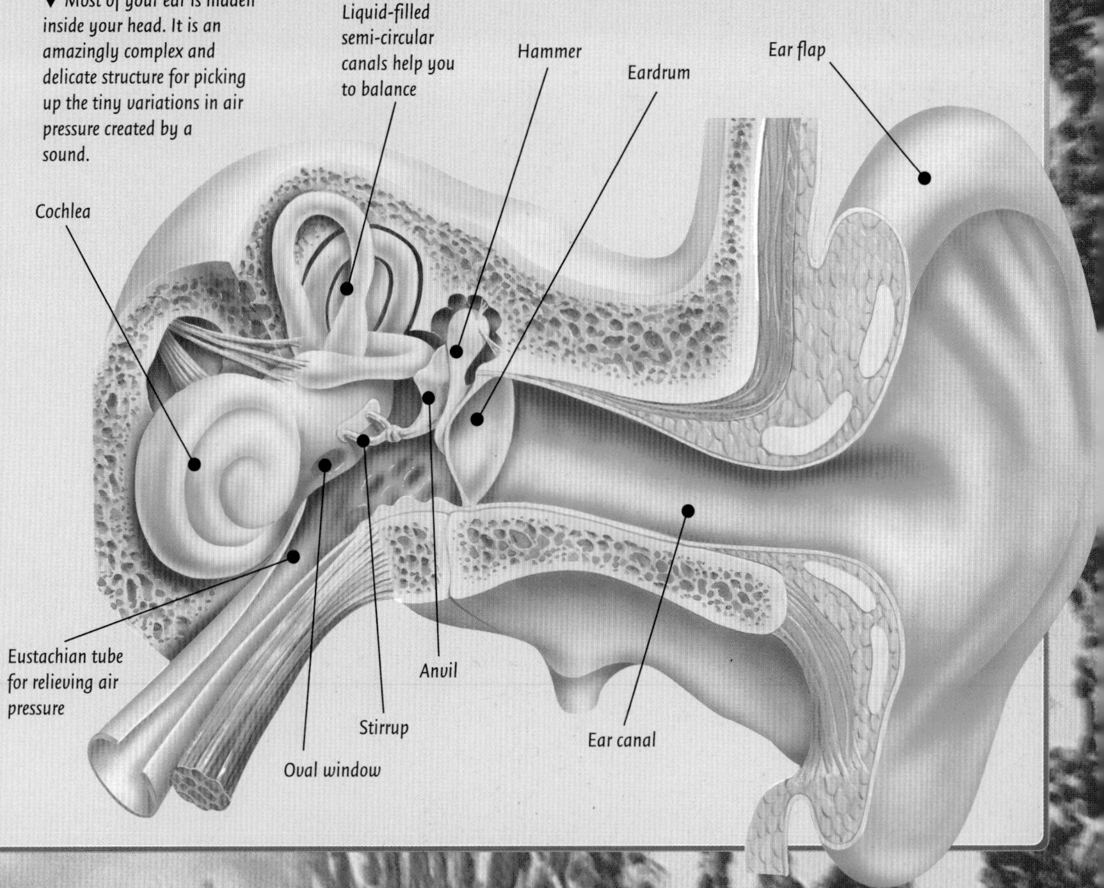

Liquid-filled semi-circular canals help you to balance
Hammer
Eardrum
Ear flap
Cochlea
Eustachian tube for relieving air pressure
Anvil
Stirrup
Oval window
Ear canal

Excretion

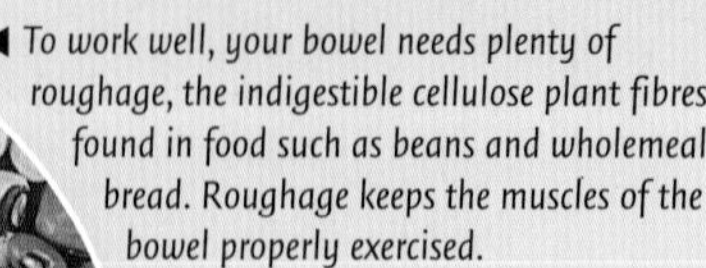

◀ *To work well, your bowel needs plenty of roughage, the indigestible cellulose plant fibres found in food such as beans and wholemeal bread. Roughage keeps the muscles of the bowel properly exercised.*

- **Digestive excretion** is the way your body gets rid of food that it cannot digest.
- **Undigested food** is prepared for excretion in your large intestine or bowel.
- **The main part** of the large intestine is the colon, which is almost as long as you are tall.
- **The colon** converts the semi-liquid 'chyme' (see digestion) of undigested food into solid waste, by absorbing water.
- **The colon** soaks up 1.5 litres of water every day.
- **The colon walls** also absorb sodium and chlorine and get rid of bicarbonate and potassium.
- **Billions of bacteria** live inside the colon and help turn the chyme into faeces. These bacteria are harmless as long as they do not spread to the rest of the body.
- **Bacteria in the colon** make vitamins K and B – as well as smelly gases such as methane and hydrogen sulphide.
- **The muscles of the colon** break the waste food down into segments ready for excretion.

★ **STAR FACT** ★
About a third of all faeces is not old food but 'friendly' gut bacteria and intestinal lining.

Cartilage

- **Cartilage is a rubbery** substance used in various places around the body. You can feel cartilage in your ear flap if you move it back and forward.
- **Cartilage is made** from cells called chondrocytes embedded in a jelly-like ground substance with fibres of collagen, all wrapped in an envelope of tough fibres.
- **There are three types**: hyaline, fibrous and elastic.
- **Hyaline cartilage** is the most widespread in your body. It is almost clear, pearly white and quite stiff.
- **Hyaline cartilage** is used in many of the joints between bones to cushion them against impacts.
- **Fibrous cartilage** is really tough cartilage used in between the bones of the spine and in the knee.
- **Cartilage in the knee** makes two dish shapes called menisci between the thigh and shin bones. Footballers often damage these cartilages.
- **Elastic cartilage** is very flexible and used in your airways, nose and ears.
- **Cartilage grows** quicker than bone, and the skeletons of babies in the womb are mostly cartilage, which gradually ossifies (hardens to bone).
- **Osteoarthritis** is when joint cartilage breaks down, making movements painful.

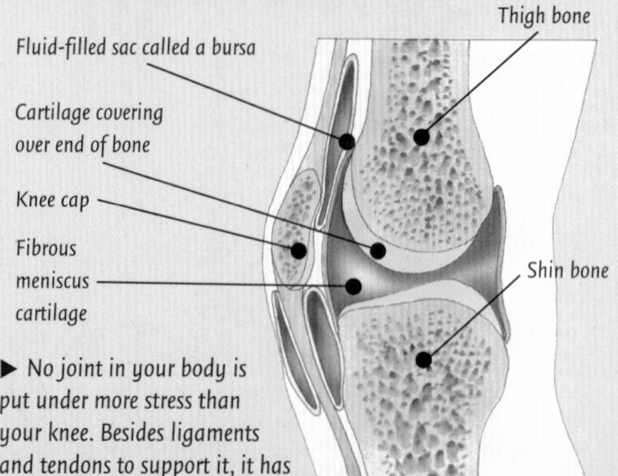

▶ *No joint in your body is put under more stress than your knee. Besides ligaments and tendons to support it, it has a thick cushion of cartilage.*

Hormones

- **Hormones are** the body's chemical messengers, released from stores at times to trigger certain reactions in different parts of the body.
- **Most hormones** are endocrine hormones which are spread around your body in your bloodstream.
- **Each hormone** is a molecule with a certain shape that creates a certain effect on target cells.
- **Hormones are controlled** by feedback systems. This means they are only released when their store gets the right trigger – which may be a chemical in the blood or another hormone.
- **Major hormone sources** include: the thyroid gland; the pituitary glands; the adrenal glands; the pancreas; a woman's ovaries; a man's testes.
- **The pituitary** is the source of many important hormones, including growth hormones which spur growing.
- **Adrenalin** is released by the adrenals to ready your body for action.

▲ *In hairy moments, adrenalin boosts your breathing and heartbeat, makes your eyes widen and your skin sweat.*

- **Endorphins and enkephalins** block or relieve pain.
- **Oestrogen and progesterone** are female sex hormones that control a woman's monthly cycle.
- **Testosterone** is a male sex hormone which controls the workings of a man's sex organs.

Exercise

- **If you exercise hard,** your muscles burn energy 20 times as fast as normal, so they need much more oxygen and glucose (a kind of sugar) from the blood.
- **To boost oxygen,** your heart beats twice as fast and pumps twice as much blood, and your lungs take in ten times more air with each breath.
- **To boost glucose,** adrenalin triggers your liver to release its store of glucose.

▲ *A sportsman such as a football player builds up his body's ability to supply oxygen to his muscles by regular aerobic training.*

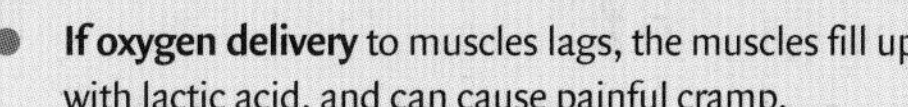

- **If oxygen delivery** to muscles lags, the muscles fill up with lactic acid, and can cause painful cramp.
- **The fitter you are,** the quicker your body returns to normal after exercise.
- **Aerobic exercise** is exercise that is long and hard enough for the oxygen supply to the muscles to rise enough to match the rapid burning of glucose.
- **Regular aerobic exercise** strengthens your heart and builds up your body's ability to supply extra oxygen through your lungs to your muscles.
- **Regular exercise** thickens and multiplies muscle fibres and strengthens tendons.
- **Regular exercise** can help reduce weight when it is combined with a controlled diet.

★ **STAR FACT** ★

When you exercise hard, your body burns up energy 20 times as fast as normal.

The eye

- **Your eyes** are tough balls filled with a jelly-like substance called vitreous humour.
- **The cornea** is a thin, glassy dish across the front of your eye. It allows light rays through the eye's window, the pupil, and into the lens.
- **The iris** is the coloured muscular ring around the pupil. The iris narrows in bright light and widens when light is dim.
- **The lens** is just behind the pupil. It focuses the picture of the world on to the back of the eye.
- **The back of the eye** is lined with millions of light-sensitive cells. This lining is called the retina, and it registers the picture and sends signals to the brain via the optic nerve.

★ STAR FACT ★
The picture registered on your retina looks large and real – yet it is upside down and just a few millimetres across.

- **There are two kinds** of light-sensitive cell in the retina – rods and cones. Rods are very sensitive and work in even dim light, but they cannot detect colours. Cones respond to colour.
- **Some kinds of cone** are very sensitive to red light, some to green and some to blue. One theory says that the colours we see depend on how strongly they affect each of these three kinds of cone (see colour vision).
- **Each of your two eyes** gives you a slightly different view of the world. The brain combines these views to give an impression of depth and 3-D solidity.
- **Although each eye** gives a slightly different view of the world, we see things largely as just one eye sees it. This dominant eye is usually the right eye.

▼ This illustration shows your two eyeballs, with one cut away to reveal the cornea and lens (which projects the picture of the world) and the light-sensitive retina (which registers it).

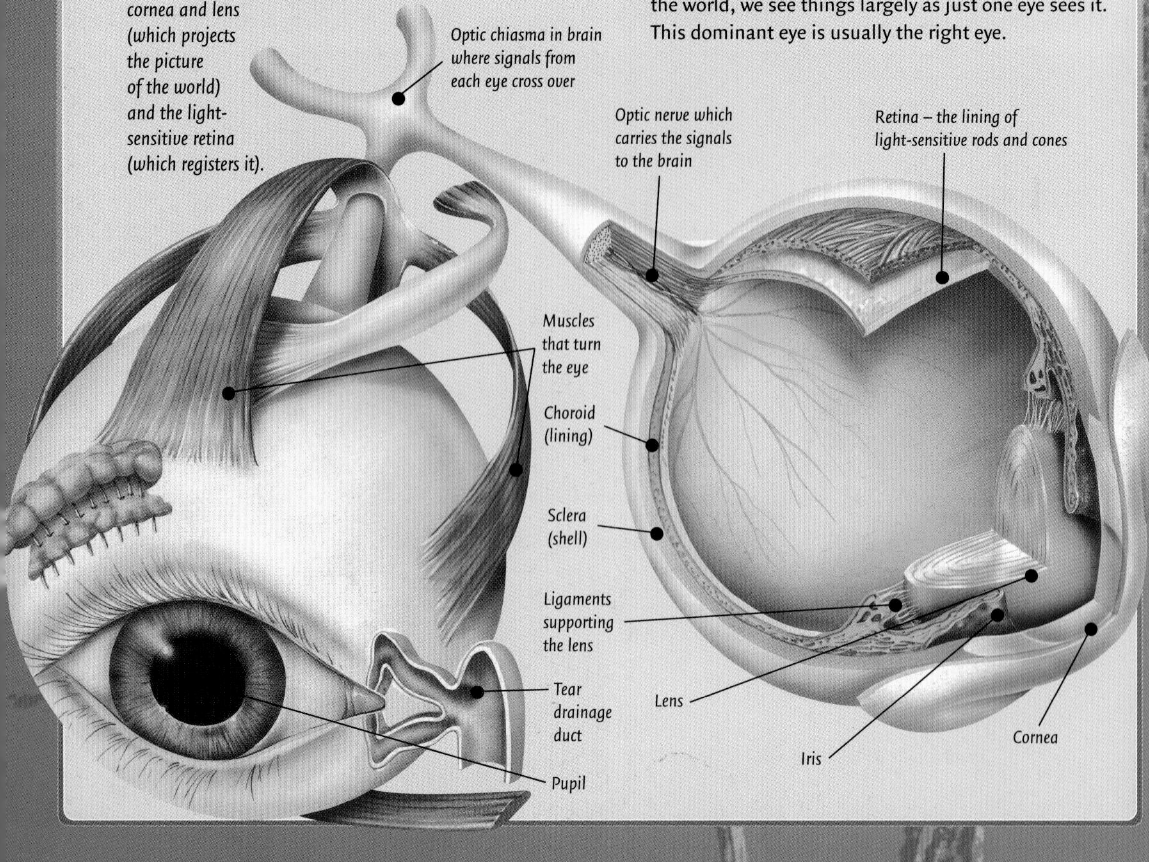

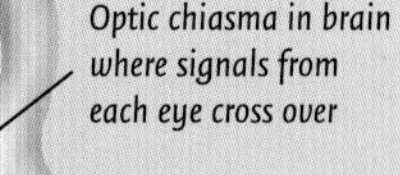

Osmosis and diffusion

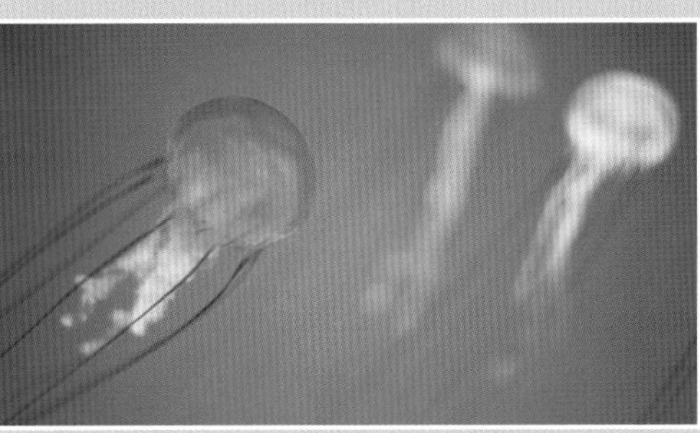

▲ *Like these jellyfish, every living cell must maintain the correct balance of chemicals inside and outside of them.*

- **To survive**, every living cell must take in the chemicals it needs and let out the ones it does not through its thin membrane (casing). Cells do this in several ways, including osmosis, diffusion and active transport.
- **Osmosis** is when water moves to even the balance between a weak solution and a stronger one.
- **Diffusion** is when the substances that are dissolved in water or mixed in air move to even the balance.
- **Osmosis** happens when the molecules of a dissolved substance are too big to slip through the cell membrane – only the water can move.
- **Osmosis** is vital to many body processes, including the workings of the kidney and the nerves.
- **Urine** gets its water from the kidneys by osmosis.
- **In diffusion**, a substance such as oxygen moves in and out of cells, while the air or water it is mixed in stays put.
- **Diffusion** is vital to body processes such as cellular respiration (see breathing), when cells take in oxygen and push out waste carbon dioxide.
- **Active transport** is the way a cell uses protein-based 'pumps' or 'gates' in its membrane to draw in and hold substances that might otherwise diffuse out.
- **Active transport** uses energy and is how cells draw in most of their food such as glucose.

Reproduction – boys

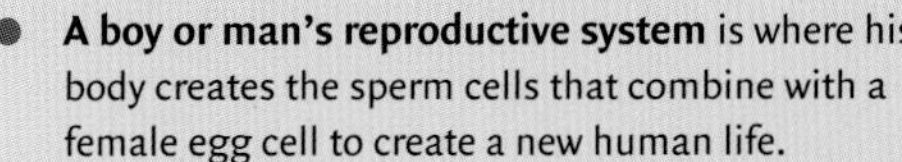

- **A boy or man's reproductive system** is where his body creates the sperm cells that combine with a female egg cell to create a new human life.
- **Sperm cells** look like microscopically tiny tadpoles. They are made in the testes, inside the scrotum.
- **The testes and scrotum** hang outside the body where it is cooler, because this improves sperm production.
- **At 15**, a boy's testes can make 200 million sperm a day.
- **Sperm leave** the testes via the epididymis – a thin, coiled tube, about 6 m long.
- **When the penis** is stimulated during sexual intercourse, sperm are driven into a tube called the vas deferens and mix with a liquid called seminal fluid to make semen.
- **Semen** shoots through the urethra (the tube inside the penis through which males urinate) and is ejaculated into the female's vagina.
- **The male sex hormone** testosterone is also made in the testes.
- **Testosterone** stimulates bone and muscle growth.
- **Testosterone** also stimulates the development of male characteristics such as facial hair and a deeper voice.

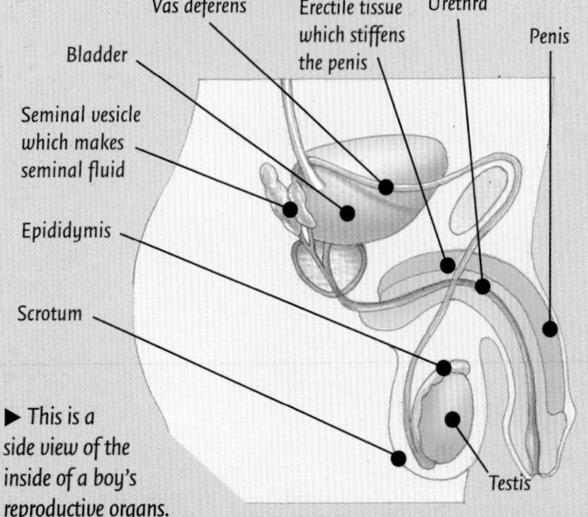

▶ *This is a side view of the inside of a boy's reproductive organs.*

Ageing

▲ *Changes in health standards mean that more and more people than ever before are remaining fit in old age.*

- **Most people live** for between 60 and 100 years, although a few live even longer than this.
- **The longest officially confirmed age** is that of Frenchwoman Jeanne Calment, who died in 1997, aged 122 years and 164 days.
- **Life expectancy** is how long statistics suggest you are likely to live.
- **On average in Europe**, men can expect to live about 75 years and women about 80. However, because health is improving generally, people are living longer.
- **As adults grow older**, their bodies begin to deteriorate (fail). Senses such as hearing, sight and taste weaken.
- **Hair goes grey** as pigment (colour) cells stop working.
- **Muscles weaken** as fibres die.
- **Bones become more brittle** as they lose calcium. Cartilage shrinks between joints, causing stiffness.
- **Skin wrinkles** as the rubbery collagen fibres that support it sag. Exposure to sunlight speeds this up, which is why the face and hands get wrinkles first.
- **Circulation and breathing weaken.** Blood vessels may become stiff and clogged, forcing the heart to work harder and raising blood pressure.

Microscopes

- **Optical microscopes** use lenses and light to magnify things (make them look bigger). By combining two or more lenses, they can magnify specimens up to 2,000 times and reveal individual blood cells.
- **To magnify things more**, scientists use electron microscopes – microscopes that fire beams of tiny charged particles called electrons.
- **Electrons** have wavelengths 100,000 times smaller than light and so can give huge magnifications.
- **Scanning electron microscopes** (SEMs) are able to magnify things up to 100,000 times.
- **SEMs** show such things as the structures inside body cells.
- **Transmission electron microscopes** (TEMs) magnify even more than SEMs – up to 5 million times.
- **TEMs** can reveal the individual molecules in a cell.
- **SEM specimens** (things studied) must be coated in gold.
- **Optical microscope specimens** are thinly sliced and placed between two glass slides.
- **Microscopes help** to identify germs.

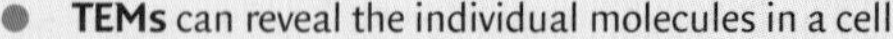

▼ *Microscopes reveal a lot about the body.*

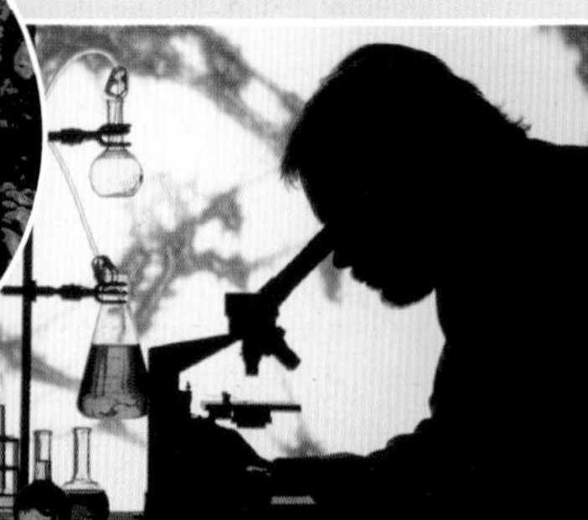

Ribs

- **The ribs** are the thin, flattish bones that curve around your chest.
- **Together,** the rib bones, the backbone and the breastbone make up the rib cage.
- **The rib cage** protects vital organs such as heart, lungs, liver, kidneys and stomach.

▶ *The ribs provide a framework for the chest and form a protective cage around the heart, lungs and other organs.*

True ribs

Sternum

False ribs

★ STAR FACT ★
The bones of the ribs contain red marrow and are one of the body's major blood-cell factories.

- **You have 12 pairs** of ribs altogether.
- **Seven pairs** are true ribs. Each rib is attached to the breastbone and curves around to join one of the vertebrae that make up the backbone via a strip of costal cartilage.
- **There are three pairs** of false ribs. These are attached to vertebrae but are not linked to the breastbone. Instead, each rib is attached to the rib above it by cartilage.
- **There are two pairs** of floating ribs. These are attached only to the vertebrae of the backbone.
- **The gaps between** the ribs are called intercostal spaces, and they contain thin sheets of muscle which expand and relax the chest during breathing.
- **Flail chest** is when many ribs are broken (often in a car accident) and the lungs heave the chest in and out.

The pancreas

- **The pancreas** is a large, carrot-shaped gland which lies just below and behind your stomach.
- **The larger end** of the pancreas is on the right, tucking into the gut (see digestion). The tail end is on the left, just touching your spleen.
- **The pancreas** is made from a substance called exocrine tissue, embedded with hundreds of nests of hormone glands called the islets of Langerhans.
- **The exocrine tissue** secretes (releases) pancreatic enzymes such as amylase into the intestine to help digest food (see enzymes).
- **Amylase** breaks down carbohydrates into simple sugars such as maltose, lactose and sucrose.
- **The pancreatic enzymes** run into the intestine via a pipe called the pancreatic duct, which joins to the bile duct. This duct also carries bile (see the liver).
- **The pancreatic enzymes** only start working when they meet other kinds of enzyme in the intestine.
- **The pancreas** also secretes the body's own antacid, sodium bicarbonate, to settle an upset stomach.
- **The islets of Langerhans** secrete two important hormones – insulin and glucagon.
- **Insulin and glucagon** regulate blood sugar levels (see glucose).

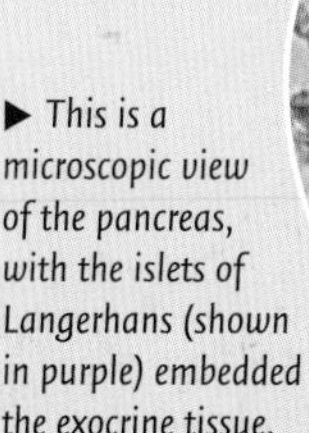
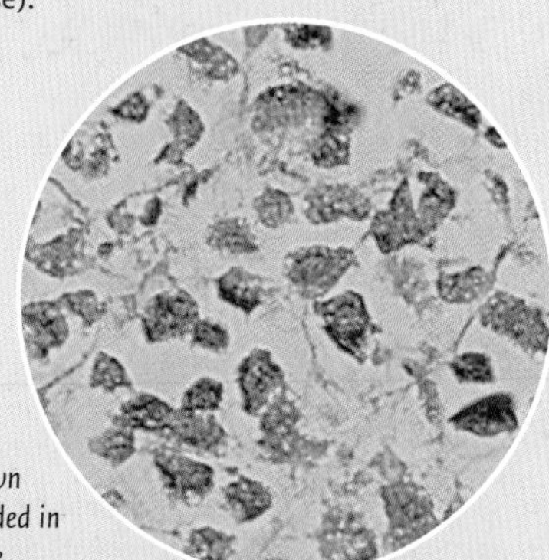

▶ *This is a microscopic view of the pancreas, with the islets of Langerhans (shown in purple) embedded in the exocrine tissue.*

Sensory nerves

- **Sensory nerves** are the nerves that carry information to your brain from sense receptors all over your body.
- **Each sense receptor** in the body is linked to the brain by a sensory nerve.
- **Most sensory nerves** feed their signals to the somatosensory cortex – the strip around the top of the brain where sensations are registered (see the cortex).
- **Massive bundles** of sensory nerve cells form the nerves that link major senses such as the eyes, ears and nose to the brain.
- **The eyes are linked to the brain** by the optic nerves.
- **The ears are linked to the brain** by the auditory nerves.
- **The nose is linked to the brain** by the olfactory tracts.
- **In the skin**, many sense receptors are simply 'free', exposed sensory nerve-endings.
- **The sciatic nerve** to each leg is the longest nerve in the body. Its name is from the Latin for 'pain in the thigh'.

▲ *Some of our most pleasant feelings, such as being hugged or stroked, are sent to the brain by sensory nerves.*

- **We can tell** how strong a sensation is by how fast the sensory nerve fires signals to the brain. But no matter how strong the sensation is, the nerve does not go on firing at the same rate and soon slows down.

Sex hormones

▲ *A girl's sexual development depends on female sex hormones.*

- **The sexual development** of girls and boys depends on the sex hormones (see reproduction).
- **Sex hormones** control the development of primary and secondary sexual characteristics, and regulate all sex-related processes such as sperm and egg production.
- **Primary sexual characteristics** are the development of the major sexual organs, such as the genitals.
- **Secondary sexual characteristics** are other differences between the sexes, such as men's beards.
- **There are three main types of sex hormones** – androgens, oestrogens and progesterones.
- **Androgens** are male hormones such as testosterone. They make a boy's body develop features such as a beard, deepen his voice and make his penis grow.
- **Oestrogen** is the female hormone made mainly in the ovaries. It not only makes a girl develop her sexual organs, but controls her monthly menstrual cycle.
- **Progesterone** is the female hormone that prepares a girl's uterus (womb) for pregnancy every month.
- **Some contraceptive pills** have oestrogen in them to prevent the ovaries releasing their egg cells.

★ STAR FACT ★

Boys have female sex hormones and girls male sex hormones, but they usually have no effect.

Muscles

- **Muscles are special fibres** that contract (tighten) and relax to move parts of the body.
- **Voluntary muscles** are all the muscles you can control by will or thinking, such as your arm muscles.
- **Involuntary muscles** are the muscles you cannot control at will and that work automatically, such as the muscles that move food through your intestine.
- **Most voluntary muscles** cover the skeleton and are therefore called skeletal muscles. They are also called striated (striped) muscle because there are dark bands on the bundles of fibre that form them.
- **Most involuntary muscles** form sacs or tubes such as the intestine. They are called smooth muscle because they lack the bands or stripes of voluntary muscles.
- **Heart muscle** is a unique combination of skeletal and smooth muscle. It has its own built-in contraction rhythm of 70 beats a minute, and special muscle cells that work like nerve cells for transmitting the signals for waves of muscle contraction to sweep through the heart.

> ★ **STAR FACT** ★
> Your body's smallest muscle is the stapedius, inside the ear – about as big as this I.

- **Most muscles are arranged in pairs**, because although muscles can shorten themselves, they cannot forcibly make themselves longer. So the flexor muscle that bends a joint is paired with an extensor muscle to straighten it out again.
- **With practice, most muscles** can be controlled individually, but they normally operate in combinations that are used to working together.
- **Your body's longest muscle** is the sartorius on the inner thigh.
- **Your body's widest muscle** is the external oblique which runs around the side of the upper body.
- **Your body's biggest muscle** is the gluteus maximus in your buttock (bottom).

▶ *Under a microscope, you can see that muscles are made from bundles and bundles of tiny fibres.*

▶ *You have more than 640 skeletal muscles and they make up over 40% of your body's entire weight, covering your skeleton like a bulky blanket. The illustration here shows only the main surface muscles of the back, but your body has at least two layers, and sometimes three layers of muscle beneath its surface muscles. Most muscle is firmly anchored at both ends and attached to the bones either side of a joint, either directly or via tough fibres called tendons.*

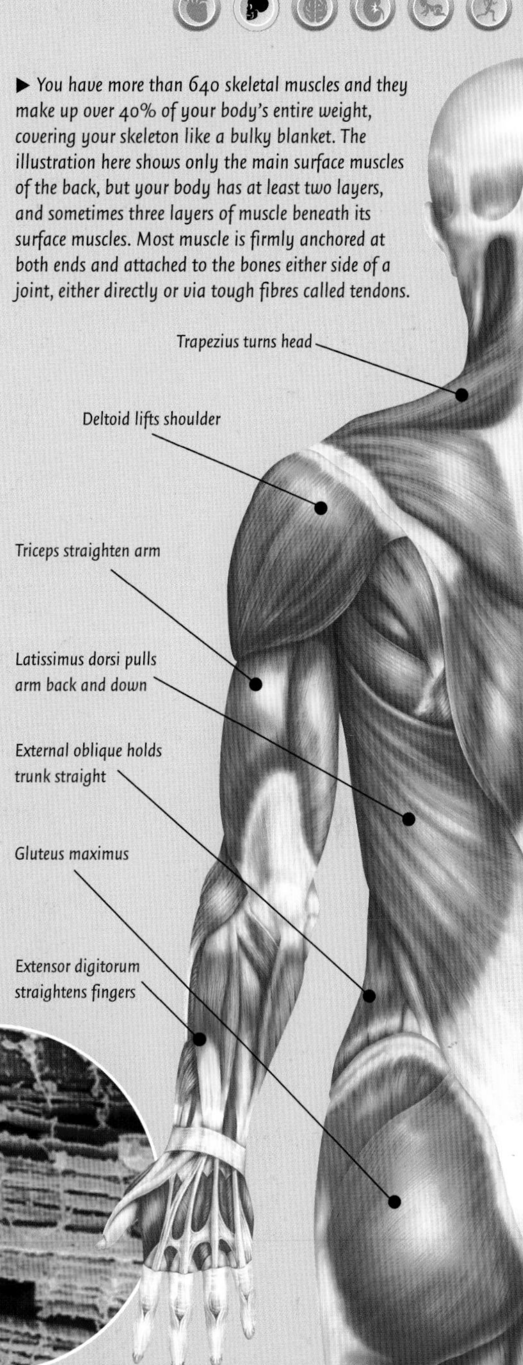

Anatomy

▶ *Much of our basic knowledge of human anatomy comes from the anatomists of the 16th and 17th centuries, who meticulously cut up corpses and then accurately drew what they saw.*

- **Anatomy** is the study of the structure of the human body.
- **Comparative anatomy** compares the structure of our bodies to those of animals' bodies.
- **The first great anatomist** was the Ancient Roman physician, Galen (AD 129-199).
- **The first great book** of anatomy was written in 1543 by the Flemish scientist Andreas Vesalius (1514-1564). It is called *De Humani Corporis Fabrica* ('On the Fabric of the Human Body').
- **To describe the location** of body parts, anatomists divide the body into quarters.
- **The anatomical position** is the way the body is positioned to describe anatomical terms – upright, with the arms hanging down by the sides, and the eyes, palms and toes facing forwards.
- **The central coronal plane** divides the body into front and back halves. Coronal planes are any slice across the body from side to side, parallel to the central coronal plane.
- **The ventral or anterior** is the front half of the body.
- **The dorsal or posterior** is the back half of the body.
- **Every part of the body** has a Latin name, but anatomists use a simple English name if there is one.

Sleeping

- **When you are asleep,** your body functions go on as normal – even your brain goes on receiving sense signals. But your body may save energy and do routine repairs.
- **Lack of sleep** can be dangerous. A newborn baby needs 18 to 20 hours sleep a day. An adult needs 7 to 8.
- **Sleep is controlled** in the brain stem (see the brain). Dreaming is stimulated by signals fired from a part of the brain stem called the pons.
- **When you are awake,** there is little pattern to the electricity created by the firing of the brain's nerve cells. But as you sleep, more regular waves appear.
- **While you are asleep,** alpha waves sweep across the brain every 0.1 seconds. Theta waves are slower.
- **For the first 90 minutes** of sleep, your sleep gets deeper and the brain waves become stronger.
- **After about 90 minutes** of sleep, your brain suddenly starts to buzz with activity, yet you are hard to wake up.
- **After 90 minutes** of sleep, your eyes begin to flicker from side to side under their lids. This is called Rapid Eye Movement (REM) sleep.

▲ *We all shut our eyes to sleep. Other marked changes to the body include the brain's activity pattern and slower heartbeat.*

- **REM sleep** is thought to show that you are dreaming.
- **While you sleep,** ordinary deeper sleep alternates with spells of REM lasting up to half an hour.

Body salts

- **Body salts** are not simply the salt (sodium chloride) some people sprinkle on food – they are an important group of chemicals which play a vital role in your body.
- **Examples of components** in body salts include potassium, sodium, chloride and manganese.
- **Body salts are important** in maintaining the balance of water in the body, and on the inside and the outside of body cells.
- **The body's thirst centre** is the hypothalamus (see the brain). It monitors salt levels in the blood and sends signals telling the kidneys to keep water or to let it go.
- **You gain salt** in the food you eat.
- **You can lose salt** if you sweat heavily. This can make muscles cramp, which is why people take salt tablets in the desert or drink a weak salt solution.

★ STAR FACT ★
A saline drip is salt solution dripped via a tube into the arm of a patient who has lost blood.

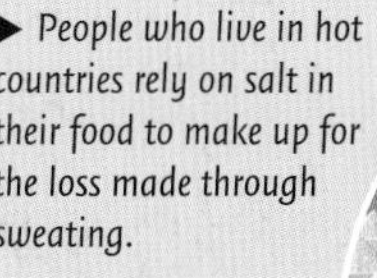

▶ *People who live in hot countries rely on salt in their food to make up for the loss made through sweating.*

- **Too much salt** in food may result in high blood pressure.
- **When dissolved in water**, the chemical elements that salt is made from split into ions – atoms with either a positive or a negative electrical charge.
- **The balance** of water and salt inside and outside of body cells often depends on a balance of potassium ions entering the cell and sodium ions leaving it.

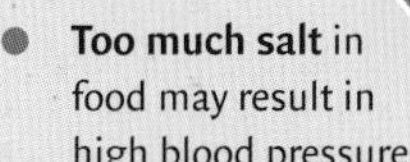
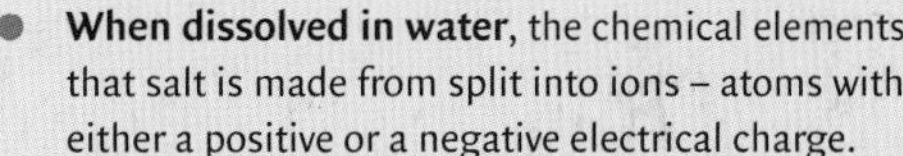

Marrow

- **Marrow** is the soft tissue in the middle of some bones.
- **Bone marrow can be red** or yellow, depending on whether it has more blood tissue or fat tissue.
- **Red bone marrow** is the body's factory, where all blood cells apart from some white cells are made.
- **All bone marrow** is red when you are a baby, but as you grow older, more and more turns yellow.
- **In adults**, red marrow is only found in the ends of the limbs' long bones: the breastbone, backbone, ribs, shoulder blades, pelvis and the skull.
- **Yellow bone marrow** is a store for fat, but it may turn to red marrow when you are ill.

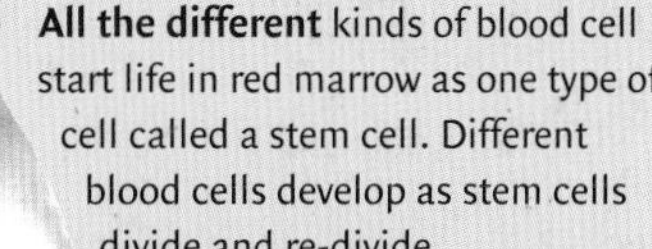

▶ *Inside the tough casing of most bones is a soft, jelly-like core called the marrow, which can be either red or yellow. The red marrow of particular bones is the body's blood cell factory, making 5 million new cells a day.*

- **All the different** kinds of blood cell start life in red marrow as one type of cell called a stem cell. Different blood cells develop as stem cells divide and re-divide.
- **Some stem cells** divide to form red blood cells and platelets.
- **Some stem cells** divide to form lymphoblasts. These divide in turn to form various different kinds of white cells – monocytes, granulocytes and lymphocytes.
- **The white cells** made in bone marrow play a key part in the body's immune system. This is why bone marrow transplants can help people with illnesses that affect their immune system.

The skeleton

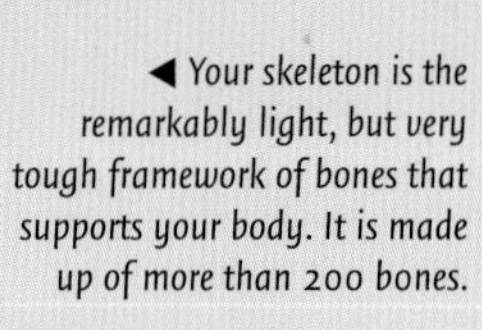
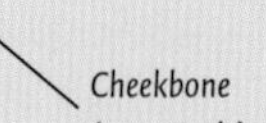
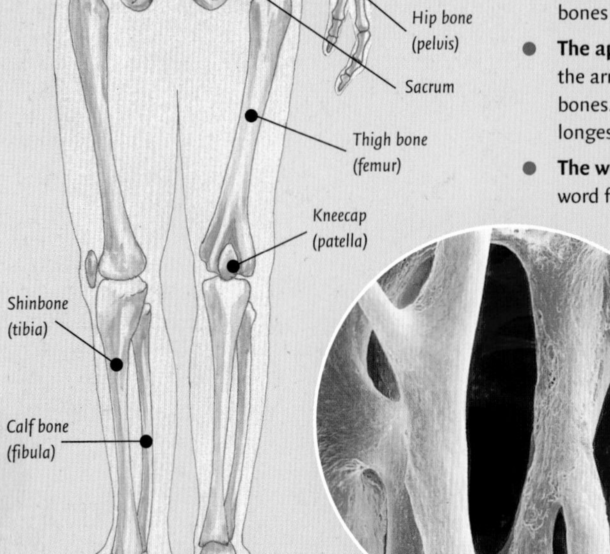

◀ Your skeleton is the remarkably light, but very tough framework of bones that supports your body. It is made up of more than 200 bones.

- **Your skeleton** is a rigid framework of bones, which provides an anchor for your muscles, supports your skin and other organs, and protects vital organs.
- **An adult's skeleton has 206 bones** joined together by rubbery cartilage. Some people have extra vertebrae (the bones of the backbone, or spine).
- **A baby's skeleton has 300** or more bones, but some of these fuse (join) together as the baby grows older.

> ★ **STAR FACT** ★
> There are 26 bones in each of your feet – exactly the same number as in your hands.

- **The parts of an adult skeleton** that have fused into one bone include the skull and the pelvis (see the skull). The pelvis came from fusing the ilium bones, the ischium bones and the pubis. The ischium is the bone that you sit down on.
- **The skeleton** has two main parts – the axial skeleton and the appendicular skeleton.
- **The axial skeleton** is the 80 bones of the upper body. It includes the skull, the vertebrae of the backbone, the ribs and the breastbone. The arm and shoulder bones are suspended from it.
- **The appendicular skeleton** is the other 126 bones – the arm and shoulder bones, and the leg and hip bones. It includes the femur (thigh bone), the body's longest bone.
- **The word skeleton** comes from the Ancient Greek word for 'dry'.
- **Most women and girls** have smaller and lighter skeletons than men and boys. But in women and girls, the pelvis is much wider than in men and boys. This is because the opening has to be wide enough for a baby to get through when it is born.

◀ A microscopic view of the inside of a bone shows just why the skeleton is so light and strong. Bone is actually full of holes, like a honeycomb. Its structure is provided by criss-crossing struts called trabeculae, each angled perfectly to cope with stresses and strains.

Operations

- **A surgical operation** is when a doctor cuts into or opens up a patient's body to repair or remove a diseased or injured body part.
- **An anaesthetic** is a drug or gas that either sends a patient completely to sleep (a general anaesthetic), or numbs part of the body (a local anaesthetic).
- **Minor operations** are usually done with just a local anaesthetic.
- **Major operations** such as transplants are done under a general anaesthetic.
- **Major surgery** is performed by a team of people in a specially–equipped room called an operating theatre.
- **The surgical team** is headed by the surgeon. There is also an anaesthetist to make sure the patient stays asleep, as well as surgical assistants and nurses.
- **The operating theatre** must be kept very clean to prevent any infection getting into the patient's body during the operation.

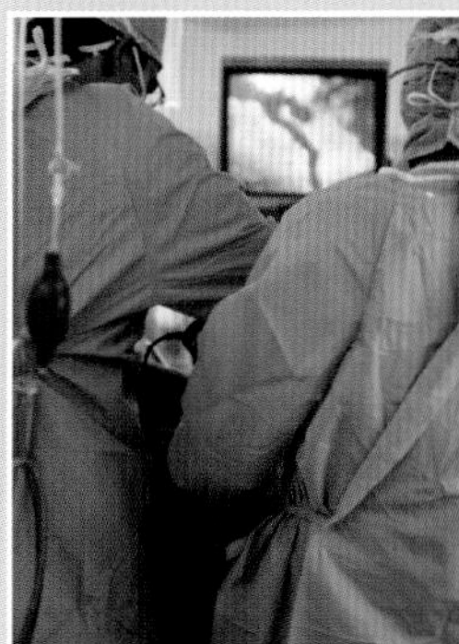

▶ *Many tricky operations are now performed using miniature cameras which help the surgeon see tiny details inside the body.*

- **In microsurgery**, a microscope is used to help the surgeon work on very small body parts such as nerves or blood vessels.
- **In laser surgery**, the surgeon cuts with a laser beam instead of a scalpel. The laser seals blood vessels as it cuts, and it is used for delicate operations such as eye surgery.
- **An endoscope is** a tube-like instrument with a TV camera at one end. It can be inserted into the patient's body during an operation to look at body parts.

The arm

     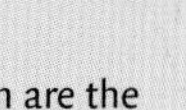

- **The arm is made** from three long bones, linked by a hinge joint at the elbow.
- **The two bones** of the lower arm are the radius and the ulnar.
- **The radius** supports the thumb side of the wrist.
- **The ulnar** supports the outside of the wrist.
- **The wrist** is one of the best places to test the pulse, since major arteries come nearer the surface here than at almost any other place in the body.

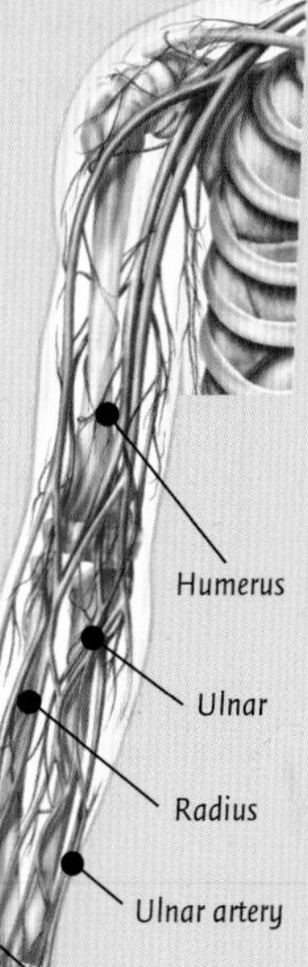

▶ *Look at the inside of your wrist on a warm day and you may be able to see the radial artery beneath the skin.*

- **The two major muscles** of the upper arm are the biceps (which bends the elbow) and the triceps (which straightens it).
- **The hand is made** from 26 bones, including the carpals (wrist bones), the metacarpals (hand bones) and the phalanges (finger bones).
- **There are no strong muscles** in the hand. When you grip firmly, most of the power comes from muscles in the lower arm, linked to the bones of the hand by long tendons.
- **The shoulder** is one of the weak points of the skeleton, since it is set in a very shallow socket. But it is supported by six major muscle groups, including the powerful deltoid (shoulder) muscle.

★ STAR FACT ★

The upper arm bone is called the humerus or, jokingly, the funny bone.

Antibodies

◀ *Bacteria, viruses and many other micro-organisms have antigens which spur B-cells into action to produce antibodies as this artists impression shows.*

- **Antibodies** are tiny proteins that make germs vulnerable to attack by white blood cells called phagocytes (see the immune system).
- **Antibodies are produced** by white blood cells derived from B lymphocyctes (see lymphocytes).
- **There are thousands** of different kinds of B-cell in the blood, each of which produces antibodies against a particular germ.
- **Normally, only a few B-cells** carry a particular antibody. But when an invading germ is detected, the correct B-cell multiplies rapidly to cause the release floods of antibodies.
- **Invaders** are identified when your body's immune system recognizes proteins on their surface as foreign. Any foreign protein is called an antigen.
- **Your body was armed** from birth with antibodies for germs it had never met. This is called innate immunity.
- **If your body comes across** a germ it has no antibodies for, it quickly makes some. It then leaves memory cells ready to be activated if the germ invades again. This is called acquired immunity.
- **Acquired immunity** means you only suffer once from some infections, such as chickenpox. This is also how vaccination works.
- **Allergies** are sensitive reactions that happen in your body when too many antibodies are produced, or when they are produced to attack harmless antigens.
- **Autoimmune diseases** are ones in which the body forms antibodies against its own tissue cells.

Blood cells

! NEWS FLASH !
In the future, doctors may be able to make artificial red blood cells.

- **Your blood has two main kinds of cell** – red cells and white cells – plus pieces of cell called platelets (see blood).
- **Red cells** are button-shaped and they contain mainly red protein called haemoglobin.
- **Haemoglobin** is what allows red blood cells to ferry oxygen around your body.
- **Red cells** also contain enzymes which the body uses to make certain chemical processes happen (see enzymes).
- **White blood cells** are big cells called leucocytes and most types are involved in fighting infections.
- **Most white cells** contain tiny little grains and are called granulocytes.
- **Most granulocytes** are giant white cells called neutrophils. They are the blood's cleaners, and their task is to eat up invaders.
- **Eosinophils and basophils** are granulocytes that are involved in allergy or fighting disease. Some release antibodies that help fight infection (see antibodies).

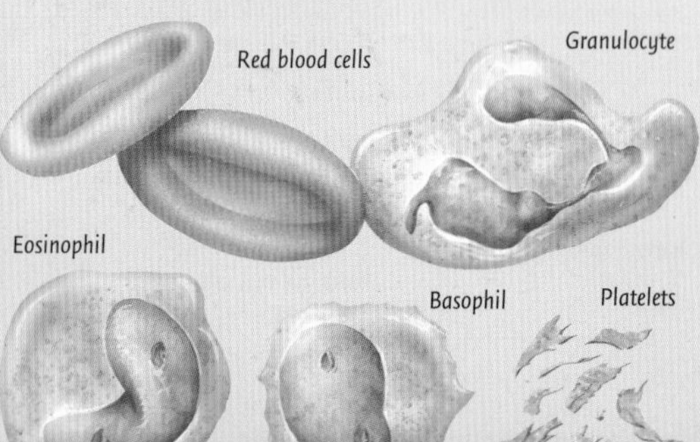

◀ *These are some of the most important kinds of cell in the blood – red cells, three kinds of white cells, and platelets.*

Body systems

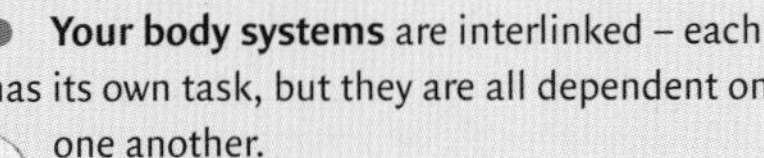

- **Your body systems** are interlinked – each has its own task, but they are all dependent on one another.
- **The skeleton** supports the body, protects the major organs, and provides an anchor for the muscles.
- **The skeletal muscles** are the ones that let you move. (Muscles are also involved in other systems.)
- **The nervous system** is the brain and the nerves – the body's control and communications network.
- **The digestive system** breaks down food into chemicals that the body can use.

◀ The cardiovascular system is the heart and the blood circulation. It keeps the body cells supplied with food and oxygen, and defends them against germs.

★ STAR FACT ★
The reproductive system is the only system that can be removed without threatening life.

- **The immune system** is the body's defence against germs. It includes white blood cells, antibodies and the lymphatic system (which circulates lymph fluid and drains away cell waste).
- **The urinary system** controls the body's water balance, removing extra water as urine and getting rid of impurities in the blood. The excretory system gets rid of undigested food.
- **The respiratory system** takes air into the lungs to supply oxygen, and lets out waste carbon dioxide.
- **The reproductive system** is the smallest of all the systems. It is basically the sexual organs that enable people to have children. It is the only system that is different between men and women.

Transplants

- **More and more body parts** can now be replaced, either by transplants (parts taken from other people or animals) or by implants (artificial parts).
- **Common transplants** include – the kidney, the cornea of the eye, the heart, the lung, the liver and the pancreas.
- **Some transplant organs** (such as the heart, lungs and liver) are taken from someone who has died.
- **Other transplants** (such as kidneys) may be taken from living donors.

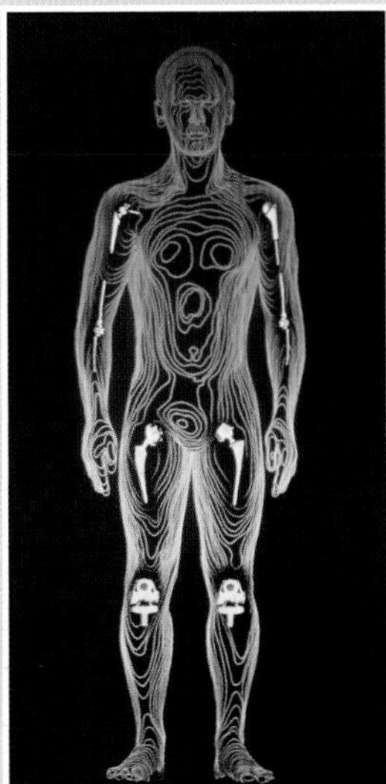

▶ These are just some of the artificial implants now put in place – hip, knee, shoulder and elbow. Old people often need implants to replace joints that have deteriorated.

- **After the transplant organ** is taken from the donor, it is washed in an oxygenated liquid and cooled to preserve it.
- **One problem** with transplants is that the body's immune system identifies the transplant as foreign and attacks it. This is called rejection.
- **To cut down** the chance of rejection, patients may be given cyclosporin or other drugs to suppress their immune system.
- **Heart transplant** operations last 4 hours.
- **During a heart transplant**, the patient is connected to a heart-lung machine which takes over the heart's normal functions.

! NEWS FLASH !
Surgeons think that in future they may be able to do head transplants.

Pulse

- **Your pulse** is the powerful high-pressure surge or wave that runs through your blood and vessels as the heart contracts strongly with each beat (see the heart).
- **You can feel your pulse** by pressing two fingertips on the inside of your wrist where the radial artery nears the surface (see the arm).
- **Other pulse points** include the carotid artery in the neck and the brachial artery inside the elbow.
- **Checking the pulse** is a good way of finding out how healthy someone is, which is why doctors do it.
- **Normal pulse rates** vary between 50 and 100 beats a minute. The average for a man is about 71, for a woman it is 80, and for children it is about 85.
- **Tachycardia** is the medical word for an abnormally fast heartbeat rate.
- **Someone who has tachycardia** when sitting down may have drunk too much coffee or tea, or taken drugs, or be suffering from anxiety or a fever, or have heart disease.

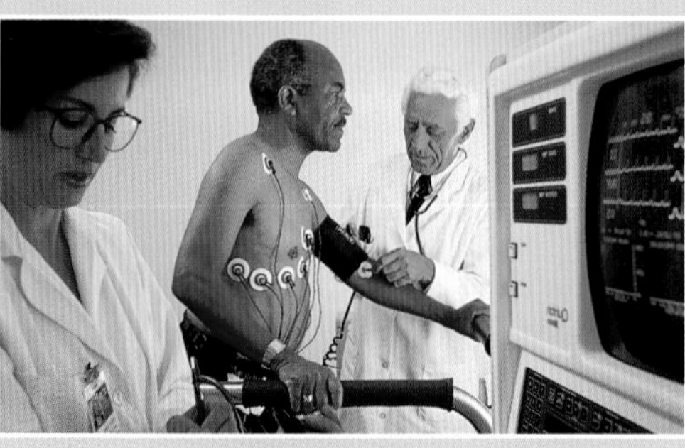

▲ *By monitoring how much heart rate goes up and down during exercise, an ECG can show how healthy someone's heart is.*

- **Bradycardia** is an abnormally slow heartbeat rate.
- **Arrhythmia** is any abnormality in a person's heart rate.
- **Anyone with a heart problem** may be connected to a machine called an electrocardiogram (ECG) to monitor (watch) their heartbeat.

Urine

- **Urine** is one of your body's ways of getting rid of waste (see water).
- **Your kidneys** produce urine, filtering it from your blood.
- **Urine runs from** each kidney down a long tube called the ureter, to a bag called the bladder.
- **Your bladder fills** up with urine over several hours. When it is full, you feel the need to urinate.

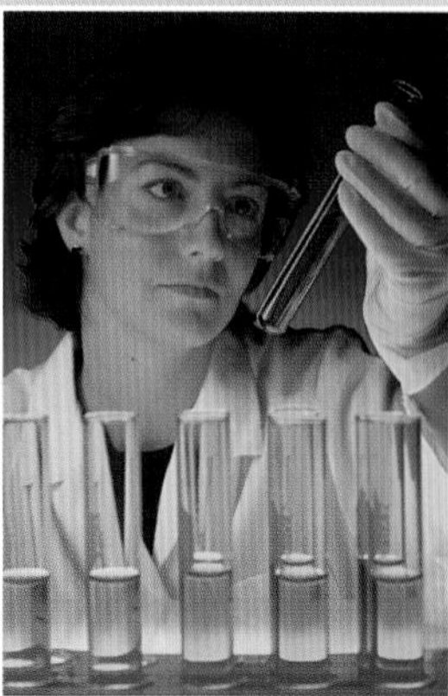

▲ *Doctors can get clues to illnesses by testing what substances there are in urine. Diabetes, for instance, is shown up by the presence of glucose in the urine.*

- **Urine is mostly water**, but there are substances dissolved in it. These include urea, various salts, creatinine, ammonia and blood wastes.
- **Urea** is a substance that is left after the breakdown of amino acids (see diet).
- **Urine gets its smell** from substances such as ammonia.
- **Urine gets its colour** from a yellowish blood waste called urochrome. Urochrome is left after proteins are broken down.
- **If you sweat a lot** – perhaps during a fever – your kidneys will let less water go and your urine will be stronger in colour.

★ STAR FACT ★

During your life, you will urinate 45,000 litres – enough to fill a small swimming pool!

Cells

- **Cells** are the basic building blocks of your body. Most are so tiny you would need 10,000 to cover a pinhead.
- **There are over 200 different kinds** of cell in your body, including nerve cells, skin cells, blood cells, bone cells, fat cells, muscle cells and many more.
- **A cell is basically** a little parcel of organic (life) chemicals with a thin membrane (casing) of protein and fat. The membrane holds the cell together, but lets nutrients in and waste out.
- **Inside the cell** is a liquid called cytoplasm, and floating in this are various minute structures called organelles.
- **At the centre** of the cell is the nucleus – this is the cell's control centre and it contains the amazing molecule DNA (see genes). DNA not only has all the instructions the cell needs to function, but also has the pattern for new human life.

★ STAR FACT ★
There are 75 trillion cells in your body!

- **Each cell** is a dynamic chemical factory, and the cell's team of organelles is continually busy – ferrying chemicals to and fro, breaking up unwanted chemicals, and putting together new ones.
- **The biggest cells** in the body can be nerve cells. Although the main nucleus of nerve cells is microscopic, the tails of some cells can extend for a metre or more through the body, and be seen even without a microscope.
- **Among the smallest cells** in the body are red blood cells. These are just 0.0075 mm across and have no nucleus, since nearly their only task is ferrying oxygen.
- **Most body cells** live a very short time and are continually being replaced by new ones. The main exceptions are nerve cells – these are long-lived, but rarely replaced.

Mitochondria are the cell's power stations, turning chemical fuel supplied by the blood as glucose into energy packs of the chemical ATP (see muscle movement)

The endoplasmic reticulum is the cell's main chemical factory, where proteins are built under instruction from the nucleus

The ribosomes are the individual chemical assembly lines, where proteins are put together from basic chemicals called amino acids (see diet)

The nucleus is the cell's control centre, sending out instructions via a chemical called messenger RNA whenever a new chemical is needed

The lysosomes are the cell's dustbins, breaking up any unwanted material

The Golgi bodies are the cell's despatch centre, where chemicals are bagged up inside tiny membranes to send where they are needed

◀ This illustration shows a typical cell, cutaway to show some of the different organelles (special parts of a cell) that keep it working properly. The instructions come from the nucleus in the cell's 'control centre', but every kind of organelle has its own task.

Skin

- **Skin is your protective coat**, shielding your body from the weather and from infection, and helping to keep it at just the right temperature.
- **Skin is your largest sense receptor**, responding to touch, pressure, heat and cold (see touch).
- **Skin makes** vitamin D for your body from sunlight.
- **The epidermis** (the thin outer layer) is just dead cells.
- **The epidermis is made mainly** of a tough protein called keratin – the remains of skin cells that die off.
- **Below the epidermis** is a thick layer of living cells called the dermis, which contains the sweat glands.
- **Hair roots** have tiny muscles that pull the hair upright when you are cold, giving you goose bumps.

★ **STAR FACT** ★
Even though its thickness averages just 2 mm, your skin gets an eighth of all your blood.

- **Skin is 6 mm thick** on the soles of your feet, and just 0.5 mm thick on your eyelids.
- **The epidermis** contains cells that make the dark pigment melanin – this gives dark-skinned people their colour and fair-skinned people a tan.

▶ *This is a cross-section of skin, hugely magnified, showing its key components.*

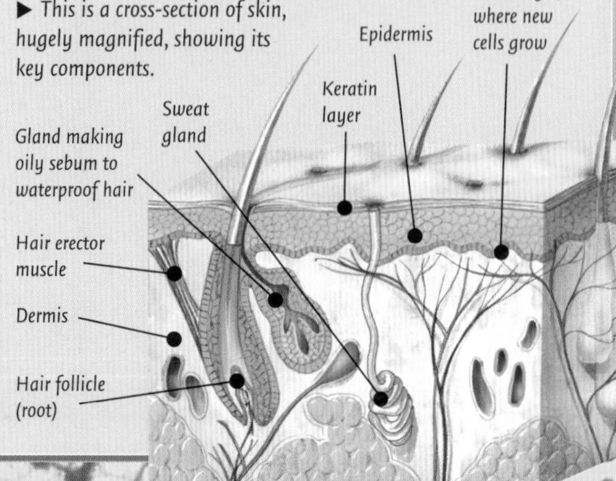

Temperature

▶ *Sweating from the sweat glands (see right) in the skin keeps you cool – not only by letting warm water out of your body, but also because as the moisture evaporates it cools your skin.*

- **The inside of your body** stays at a constant temperature of 37°C (98°F), rising a few degrees only when you are ill.
- **Your body creates heat** by burning food in its cells, especially the 'energy sugar' glucose.
- **Even when you are resting**, your body generates so much heat that you are comfortable only when the air is slightly cooler than you are.
- **When you are working hard**, your muscles can generate as much heat as a 2 kW heater.
- **Your body loses heat** as you breathe in cool air and breathe out warm air. Your body also loses heat by giving it off from your skin.

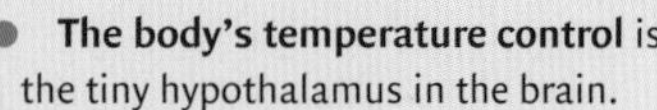

- **The body's temperature control** is the tiny hypothalamus in the brain.
- **Temperature sensors** in the skin, in the body's core, and in the blood by the hypothalamus tell the hypothalamus how hot or cold your body is.
- **If it is too hot**, the hypothalamus sends signals to your skin telling it to sweat more. Signals also tell blood vessels in the skin to widen – this increases the blood flow, increasing the heat loss from your blood.
- **If it is too cold**, the hypothalamus sends signals to the skin to cut back skin blood flow, as well as signals to tell the muscles to generate heat by shivering.
- **If it is too cold**, the hypothalamus may also stimulate the thyroid gland to send out hormones to make your cells burn energy faster and so make more heat.

Drugs

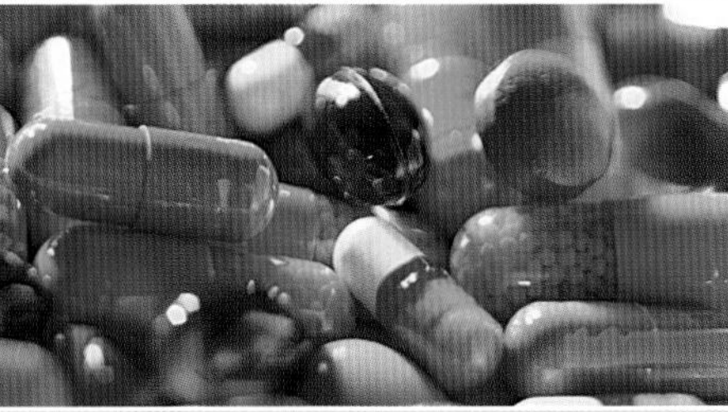

▲ *Thousands of different drugs are today used to treat illness.*

- **Antibiotic drugs** are used to treat bacterial infections such as tuberculosis (TB) or tetanus. They were once grown as moulds (fungi) but are now made artificially.
- **Penicillin** was the first antibiotic drug, discovered in a mould in 1928 by Alexander Fleming (1881-1955).
- **Analgesic drugs** such as aspirin relieve pain, mainly by stopping the body making prostaglandin, the chemical that sends pain signals to the brain.
- **Tranquillizers** are drugs that calm. Minor tranquillizers are drugs such as prozac, used to relieve anxiety.
- **Major tranquillizers** are used to treat mental illnesses such as schizophrenia.
- **Psychoactive drugs** are drugs that change your mood. Many, including heroin, are dangerous and illegal.
- **Stimulants** are drugs that boost the release of the nerve transmitter noradrenaline, making you more lively and awake. They include the caffeine in coffee.
- **Narcotics** are powerful painkillers such as morphine that mimic the body's own natural painkiller endorphin.
- **Depressants** are drugs such as alcohol which do not depress you, but instead slow down the nervous system.

! NEWS FLASH !
In future, more drugs may be made by animals with altered genes. Insulin is already made in the pancreas of pigs and oxen.

Synapses

- **Synapses** are the very tiny gaps between nerve cells.
- **When a nerve signal** goes from one nerve cell to another, it must be transmitted (sent) across the synapse by special chemicals called neurotransmitters.
- **Droplets of neurotransmitter** are released into the synapse whenever a nerve signal arrives.
- **As the droplets of neurotransmitter** lock on to the receiving nerve's receptors, they fire the signal onwards.
- **Each receptor site** on a nerve-ending only reacts to certain neurotransmitters. Others have no effect.
- **Sometimes** several signals must arrive before enough neurotransmitter is released to fire the receiving nerve.
- **More than 40 neurotransmitter chemicals** have been identified.
- **Dopamine** is a neurotransmitter that works in the parts of the brain that control movement and learning. Parkinson's disease may develop when the nerves that produce dopamine break down.
- **Serotonin** is a neurotransmitter that is linked to sleeping and waking up, and also to your mood.
- **Acetylcholine** is a neurotransmitter that may be involved in memory, and also in the nerves that control muscle movement.

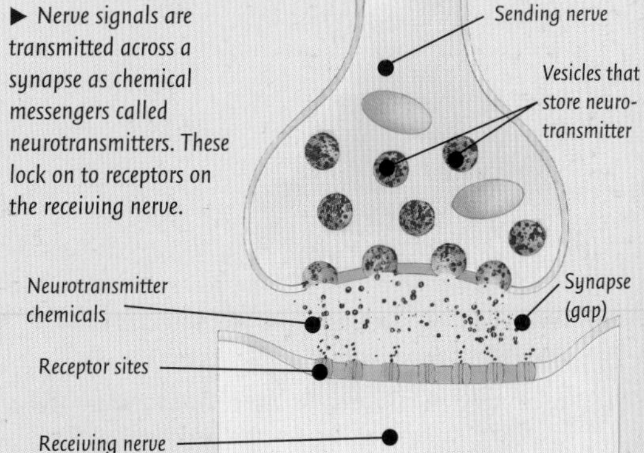

▶ *Nerve signals are transmitted across a synapse as chemical messengers called neurotransmitters. These lock on to receptors on the receiving nerve.*

The nervous system

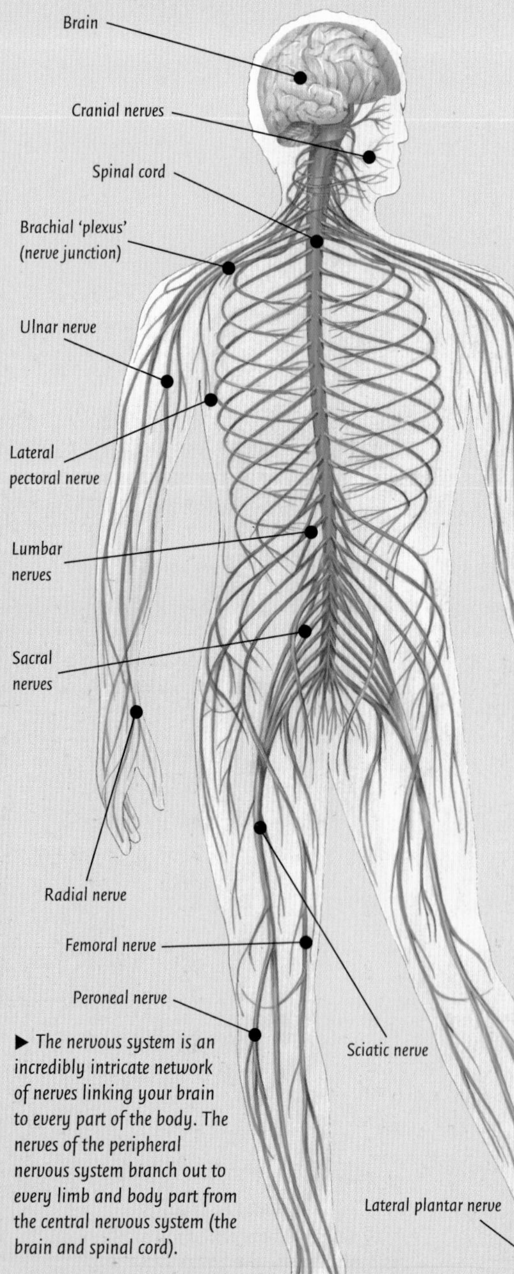

▶ *The nervous system is an incredibly intricate network of nerves linking your brain to every part of the body. The nerves of the peripheral nervous system branch out to every limb and body part from the central nervous system (the brain and spinal cord).*

▶ *A human being has a nervous system with about 60 billion nerve cells. A spider has about 100,000.*

- **The nervous system** is your body's control and communication system, made up of nerves and the brain. Nerves are your body's hot-lines, carrying instant messages from the brain to every organ and muscle – and sending back an endless stream of data to the brain about what is going on both inside and outside your body.
- **The central nervous system** (CNS) is the brain and spinal cord (see central nervous system).
- **The peripheral nervous system** (PNS) is made up of the nerves that branch out from the CNS to the rest of the body.
- **The main branches of the PNS** are the 12 cranial nerves in the head, and the 31 pairs of spinal nerves that branch off the spinal cord.
- **The nerves of the PNS** are made up of long bundles of nerve fibres, which in turn are made from the long axons (tails) of nerve cells, bound together like the wires in a telephone cable.
- **In many places**, sensory nerves (which carry sense signals from the body to the brain) run alongside motor nerves (which carry the brain's commands telling muscles to move).
- **Some PNS nerves** are as wide as your thumb. The longest is the sciatic, which runs from the base of the spine to the knee.
- **The autonomic nervous system** (ANS) is the body's third nervous system. It controls all internal body processes such as breathing automatically, without you even being aware of it.
- **The ANS** is split into two complementary (balancing) parts – the sympathetic and the parasympathetic. The sympathetic system speeds up body processes when they need to be more active such as when the body is exercising or under stress. The parasympathetic slows them down.

★ **STAR FACT** ★

Millions of nerve signals enter your brain every single second of your life.

Valves

- **Valves play** a crucial part in the circulation of your blood and lymph fluid (see the lymphatic system), ensuring that liquids flow only one way.
- **The heart has four valves** to make sure blood flows only one way through it.
- **On each side of the heart** there is a large valve between the atrium and the ventricle, and a smaller one where the arteries leave the ventricle.
- **The mitral valve** is the large valve on the left. The tricuspid is the large valve on the right.
- **The aortic valve** is the smaller valve on the left. The pulmonary is the smaller valve on the right.
- **Heart valves** can sometimes get blocked, making the heart work harder or leak. Both cause what a doctor using a stethoscope hears as a heart murmur.
- **The mitral** is the valve most likely to give problems, causing an illness called mitral stenosis.
- **A faulty heart valve** may be replaced with a valve from a human or pig heart, or a mechanical valve.

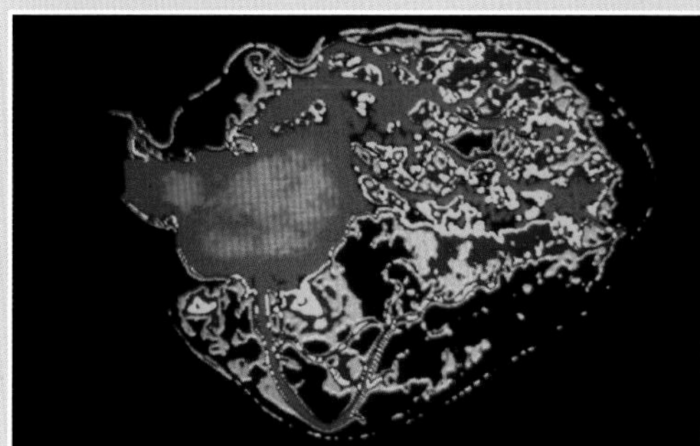

▲ *Heart valve problems may arise if the blood supply to the heart is impaired – something that may show up on an angiogram like this.*

- **Valves in the arteries and veins** are simply flaps that open only when the blood is flowing one way.
- **The lymphatic system** also has its own small valves to ensure lymph is squeezed only one way.

The skull

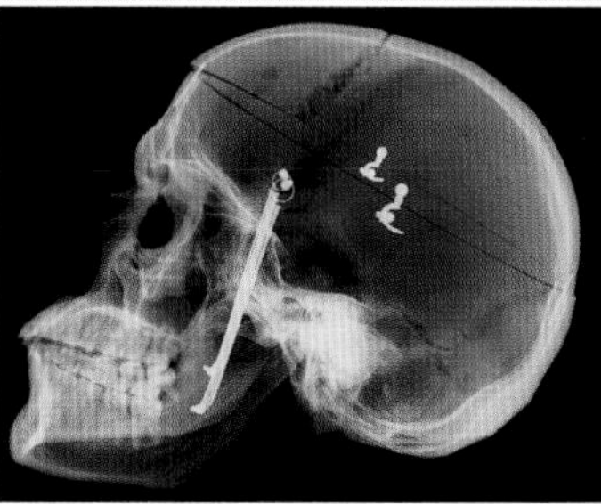

▶ *An X-ray of the skull shows the cranial cavity which holds the brain. This is an old skull: the bright white bits are wires and clamps holding it together.*

- **The skull** or cranium is the hard, bone case that protects your brain.
- **The skull looks** as though it is a single bone. In fact, it is made up of 22 separate bones, cemented together along rigid joints called sutures.
- **The dome on top** is called the cranial vault and it is made from eight curved pieces of bone fused (joined) together.
- **As well as the sinuses** of the nose (see airways), the skull has four large cavities – the cranial cavity for the brain, the nasal cavity (the nose) and two orbits for the eyes.
- **There are holes in the skull** to allow blood vessels and nerves through, including the optic nerves to the eyes and the olfactory tracts to the nose.
- **The biggest hole** is in the base. It is called the foramen magnum, and the brain stem goes through it to meet the spinal cord.
- **In the 19th century**, people called phrenologists thought they could work out people's characters from little bumps on their skulls.
- **Archaeologists** can reconstruct faces from the past using computer analysis of ancient skulls.

★ **STAR FACT** ★

A baby has soft spots called fontanelles in its skull because the bones join slowly over about 18 months.

Hair

◀ *The colour of your hair depends upon melanin made in melanocytes at the root.*

- **Humans are one of** very few land mammals to have almost bare skin. But even humans have soft, downy hair all over, with thicker hair in places.
- **Lanugo** is the very fine hair babies are covered in when they are inside the womb, from the fourth month of pregnancy onwards.
- **Vellus hair** is fine, downy hair that grows all over your body until you reach puberty.
- **Terminal hair** is the coarser hair on your head, as well as the hair that grows on men's chins and around an adult's genitals.
- **The colour of your hair** depends on how much there are of pigments called melanin and carotene in the hairs.
- **Hair is red or auburn** if it contains carotene.
- **Black, brown and blonde hair** get their colour from black melanin.
- **Each hair** is rooted in a pit called the hair follicle. The hair is held in place by its club-shaped tip, the bulb.
- **Hair grows** as cells fill with a material called keratin and die, and pile up inside the follicle.
- **The average person** has 120,000 head hairs and each grows about 3 mm per week.

★ **STAR FACT** ★
Hair in poor condition is said to be lifeless. In fact, all hair is lifeless since it is made of keratin, the material left by dead cells.

Balance

▲ *This gymnast's body is feeding her brain a continual stream of data about its position to help her stay perfectly balanced.*

- **To stay upright**, your body must send a continual stream of data about its position to your brain – and your brain must continually tell your body how to move to keep its balance.
- **Balance** is controlled in many parts of the brain including the cerebellum.
- **Your brain** finds out about your body position from many sources, including your eyes and the semicircular canals and other chambers in the inner ear.
- **Proprioceptors** are sense receptors in your skin, muscles and joints (see co-ordination).
- **The semicircular canals** are three, tiny, fluid-filled loops in your inner ear (see the ear).
- **Two chambers** called the utricle and saccule are linked to the semicircular canals.
- **When you move your head**, the fluid in the canals and cavities lags a little, pulling on hair detectors which tell your brain what is happening.
- **The canals** tell you whether you are nodding or shaking your head, and which way you are moving.
- **The utricle and saccule** tell you if you tilt your head or if its movement speeds up or slows down.

Colour vision

- **Seeing in colour** depends on eye cells called cones.
- **Cones do not** work well in low light, which is why things seem grey at dusk.
- **Some cones** are more sensitive to red light, some are more sensitive to green and some to blue.
- **The old trichromatic theory** said that you see colours by comparing the strength of the signals from each of the three kinds of cone – red, green and blue.

★ STAR FACT ★
You have over 5 million colour-detecting cones in the retina of each eye.

- **Trichromatic theory** does not explain colours such as gold, silver and brown.
- **The opponent-process theory** said that you see colours in opposing pairs – blue and yellow, red and green.
- **In opponent-process theory,** lots of blue light is thought to cut your awareness of yellow, and vice versa. Lots of green cuts your awareness of red, and vice versa.
- **Now scientists** combine these theories and think that colour signals from the three kinds of cone are further processed in the brain in terms of the opposing pairs.
- **Ultraviolet light** is light waves too short for you to see, although some birds and insects can see it.

◀ *Seeing all the colours of the world around you depends on the colour-sensitive cone cells inside your eyes.*

Enzymes

- **Enzymes are** molecules – mostly protein – which alter the speed of chemical reactions in living things.
- **There are thousands of enzymes** in your body – it could not function without them.
- **Some enzymes** need an extra substance, called a coenzyme, to work. Many coenzymes are vitamins.
- **Most enzymes** have names ending in 'ase', such as lygase, protease and lipase.
- **Pacemaker enzymes** play a vital role in controlling your metabolism – the rate your body uses energy.
- **One of the most important enzyme groups** is that of the messenger RNAs, which are used as communicators by the nuclei of body cells (see cells).
- **Many enzymes** are essential for the digestion of food, including lipase, protease, amylase, and the peptidases. Many of these are made in the pancreas.
- **Lipase** is released mainly from the pancreas into the alimentary canal (gut) to help break down fat.
- **Amylase** breaks down starches such as those in bread and fruit into simple sugars (see carbohydrates). There is amylase in saliva and in the stomach.
- **In the gut**, the sugars maltose, sucrose and lactose are broken down by maltase, sucrase and lactase.

▼ *After you eat a meal, a complex series of enzymes gets to work, breaking the food down into the simple molecules that can be absorbed into your blood.*

Tissue and organs

- **Each of the many different kinds of cell** in your body combines to make substances called tissues.
- **As well as cells**, some tissues include other materials.
- **Connective tissues** are made from particular cells (such as fibroblasts), plus two other materials – long fibres of protein (such as collagen) and a matrix. Matrix is a material in which the cells and fibres are set like the currants in a bun.
- **Connective tissue** holds all the other kinds of tissue together in various ways. The adipose tissue that makes fat, tendons and cartilage is connective tissue.
- **Bone and blood** are both connective tissues.
- **Epithelial tissue** is good lining or covering material, making skin and other parts of the body.

★ STAR FACT ★
All your body is made from tissue and tissue fluid (liquid that fills the space between cells).

▶ *Lungs are largely made from special lung tissues (see right), but the mucous membrane that lines the airways is epithelial tissue.*

- **Epithelial tissue** may combine three kinds of cell to make a thin waterproof layer – squamous (flat), cuboid (box-like) and columnar (pillar-like) cells.
- **Nerve tissue** is made mostly from neurons (nerve cells), plus the Schwann cells that coat them.
- **Organs** are made from combinations of tissues. The heart is made mostly of muscle tissue, but also includes epithelial and connective tissue.

Touch

▲ *As we grow up, we gradually learn to identify more and more things instantly through touch.*

- **Touch, or physical contact,** is just one of the sensations that are spread all over your body in your skin. The others include pressure, pain, hot and cold.
- **There are sense receptors** everywhere in your skin, but places like your face have more than your back.
- **There are 200,000** hot and cold receptors in your skin, plus 500,000 touch and pressure receptors, and nearly 3 million pain receptors.
- **Free nerve-endings** are rather like the bare end of a wire. They respond to all five kinds of skin sensation and are almost everywhere in your skin.
- **There are specialized receptors** in certain places, each named after their discoverer.
- **Pacini's corpuscles** and Meissner's endings react instantly to sudden pressure.
- **Krause's bulbs**, Merkel's discs and Ruffini's endings respond to steady pressure.
- **Krause's bulbs** are also sensitive to cold.
- **Ruffini's endings** also react to changes in temperature.

★ STAR FACT ★
Your brain knows just how hard you are touched from how fast nerve signals arrive.

The vocal cords

- **Speaking and singing** depend on the larynx (voice-box) in your neck (see airways).
- **The larynx** has bands of fibrous tissue called the vocal cords, which vibrate as you breathe air out over them.
- **When you are silent**, the vocal cords are relaxed and apart, and air passes between freely.
- **When you speak or sing**, the vocal cords tighten across the airway and vibrate to make sounds.
- **The tighter** the vocal cords are stretched, the higher-pitched sounds you make.
- **The basic sound** produced by the vocal cords is a simple 'aah'. But by changing the shape of your mouth, lips, and especially your tongue, you can change this simple sound into letters and words.
- **Babies' vocal cords** are just 6 mm long.
- **Women's vocal cords** are about 20 mm long.
- **Men's vocal cords** are about 30 mm long. Because men's cords are longer than women's, they vibrate more slowly and give men deeper voices.
- **Boys' vocal cords** are the same length as girls' until they are teenagers – when they grow longer, making a boy's voice 'break' and get deeper.

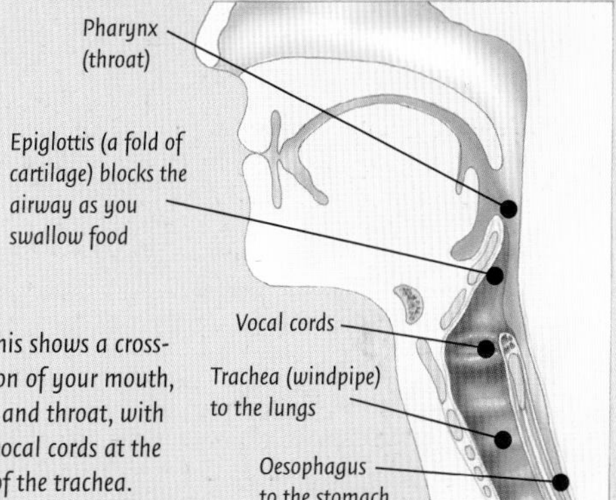

▶ *This shows a cross-section of your mouth, nose and throat, with the vocal cords at the top of the trachea.*

X-rays

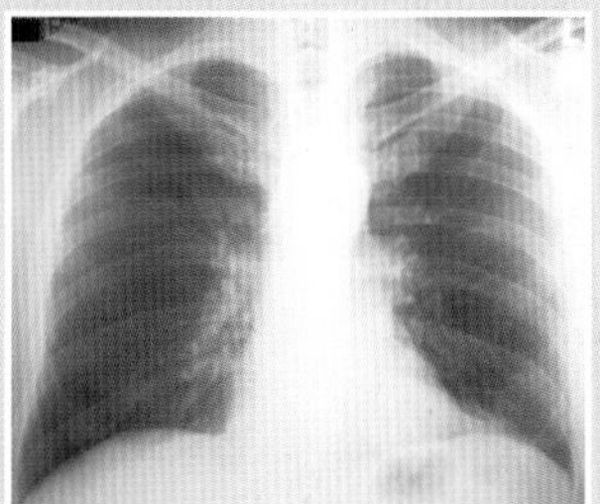

◀ *An X-ray gives a clear picture of the inside of the chest, showing the ribs, the spine and the branching airways in the lung. Any lung problems and blockages show up as white shadows.*

- **X-rays** are a form of electromagnetic radiation, as are radio waves, microwaves, visible light and ultraviolet. They all travel as waves, but have different wavelengths.
- **X-ray waves** are much shorter and more energetic than visible light waves. X-rays are invisible because their waves are too short for our eyes to see.
- **X-rays are made** when negatively charged particles called electrons are fired at a heavy plate made of the metal tungsten. The plate bounces back X-rays.
- **Even though they are invisible** to our eyes, X-rays register on photographic film.
- **X-rays are so energetic** that they pass through some body tissues like a light through a net curtain.
- **To make an X-ray photograph**, X-rays are shone through the body. The X-rays pass through some tissues and turn the film black, but are blocked by others, leaving white shadows on the film.
- **Each kind of tissue** lets X-rays through differently. Bones are dense and contain calcium, so they block X-rays and show up white on film. Skin, fat, muscle and blood let X-rays through and show up black on film.
- **X-ray radiation** is dangerous in high doses, so the beam is encased in lead, and the radiographer who takes the X-ray picture stands behind a screen.
- **X-rays are** very good at showing up bone defects. So if you break a bone, it will be probably be X-rayed.
- **X-rays also** reveal chest and heart problems.

Scans

- **Diagnostic imaging** means using all kinds of complex machinery to make pictures or images of the body to help diagnose and understand a problem.
- **Many imaging techniques** are called scans, because they involve scanning a beam around the patient.
- **CT scans** rotate an X-ray beam around the patient while moving him or her slowly forward. This gives a set of pictures showing different slices of the patient.
- **CT** stands for computerized tomography.
- **MRI scans** surround the patient with such a strong magnet that all the body's protons (tiny atomic particles) turn the same way. A radio pulse is then used to knock the protons in and out of line, sending out radio signals that the scanner picks up to give the picture.

> ★ STAR FACT ★
> PET scans allow scientists to track blood through a live brain and see which areas are in action.

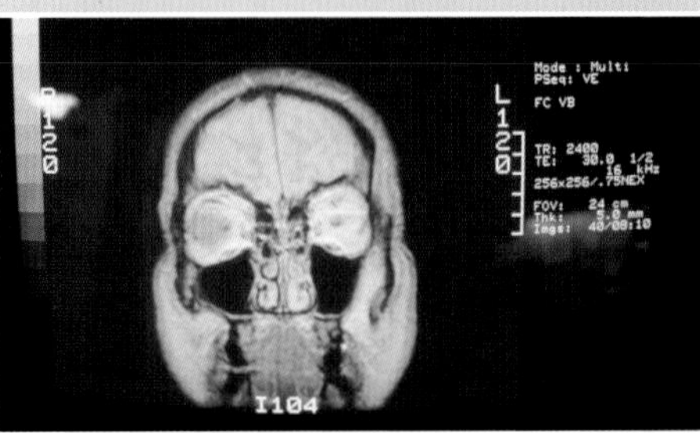

▲ *One of a series of CT scans of the head and brain.*

- **MRI** stands for magnetic resonance imaging.
- **PET scans** involve injecting the patient with a mildly radioactive substance, which flows around with the blood and can be detected because it emits (gives out) particles called positrons.
- **PET** stands for positron emission tomography.
- **PET scans** are good for spotting heart stroke problems.

Backbone

- **The backbone** (or spine) extends from the base of the skull down to the hips.
- **The backbone is not a single bone**, but a column of drum-shaped bones called vertebrae (singular, vertebra).
- **There are 33 vertebrae** altogether, although some of these fuse or join as the body grows.
- **Each vertebra** is linked to the next by facet joints, which are like tiny ball-and-socket joints.
- **The vertebrae are separated** by discs of rubbery material called cartilage. These cushion the bones when you run and jump.
- **The bones of the spine** are divided into five groups from top to bottom. These are the cervical (7 bones), the thoracic (12 bones), the lumbar (5 bones), the sacrum (5 bones fused together), and the coccyx (4 bones fused together).
- **The cervical spine** is the vertebrae of the neck. The thoracic spine is the back of the chest, and each bone has a pair of ribs attached to it. The lumbar spine is the small of the back.
- **A normal spine** curves in an S-shape, with the cervical spine curving forwards, the thoracic section curving backwards, the lumbar forwards, and the sacrum backwards.
- **On the back** of each vertebra is a bridge called the spinal process. The bridges on each bone link together to form a tube which holds the spinal cord, the body's central bundle of nerves.

◀ *The backbone is not straight – instead, its 33 vertebrae curve into an S-shape.*

> ★ STAR FACT ★
> The story character the Hunchback of Notre Dame suffered from kyphosis – excessive curving of the spine.

Arteries

- **An artery** is a tube-like blood vessel that carries blood away from the heart.
- **Systemic arteries** deliver oxygenated blood around the body.
- **An arteriole** is a smaller branch off an artery.
- **Arterioles branch** into microscopic capillaries.
- **Blood flows through** arteries at up to 30 cm per second.
- **Arteries run alongside** most of the veins that return blood to the heart.
- **The walls of arteries** are muscular and can expand or relax to control the blood flow.
- **Arteries have** thicker, stronger walls than veins, and the pressure of the blood in them is a lot higher.
- **Over-thickening of the artery walls** may be one cause of hypertension (high blood pressure).
- **In old age** the artery walls can become very stiff. This hardening of the arteries, called arteriosclerosis, can cut blood flow to the brain.

★ **STAR FACT** ★
Blood in arteries moves quickly in a pulsing way, while blood in a vein oozes slowly.

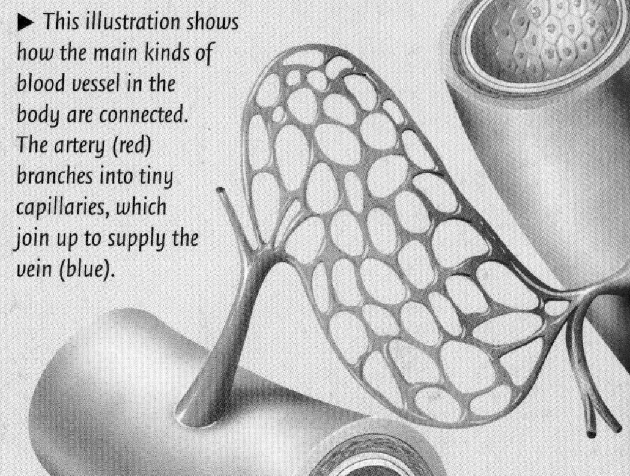

▶ This illustration shows how the main kinds of blood vessel in the body are connected. The artery (red) branches into tiny capillaries, which join up to supply the vein (blue).

Memory

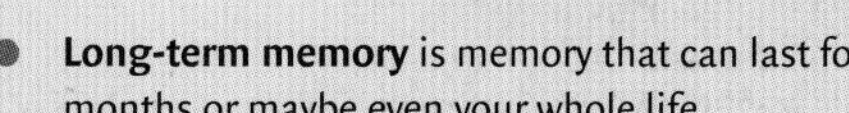

- **When you remember** something, your brain probably stores it by creating new nerve connections.
- **You have** three types of memory – sensory, short-term and long-term.
- **Sensory memory** is when you go on feeling a sensation for a moment after it stops.
- **Short-term memory** is when the brain stores things for a few seconds, like a phone number you remember long enough to dial.

▲ Learning to play the violin involves non-declarative memory – in which nerve pathways become reinforced by repeated use. This is why practising is so important.

- **Long-term memory** is memory that can last for months or maybe even your whole life.
- **Your brain** seems to have two ways of remembering things for the long term. Scientists call these declarative and non-declarative memories.
- **Non-declarative memories** are skills you teach yourself by practising, such as playing badminton or the flute. Repetition establishes nerve pathways.
- **Declarative memories** are either episodic or semantic. Each may be sent by the hippocampus region of the brain to the correct place in the cortex, the brain's wrinkly outer layer where you do most of your thinking.
- **Episodic memories** are memories of striking events in your life, such as breaking your leg or your first day at a new school. You not only recall facts, but sensations.
- **Semantic memories** are facts such as dates. The brain seems to store these in the left temporal lobe, at the front left–hand side of your brain.

INDEX

A

B

C

D

E

F

G

H

M

N

T

U

Acknowledgements

Artists: Jim Chanel, Kuo Kang Chen, Gary Hincks, Rob Jakeway, Janos Marffy, Mike Saunders, Guy Smith, Mike White,

The publishers would like to thank the following sources for the photographs used in this book:

Page 19 (T/R) Genesis photo library; Page 36 (B/L) Genesis photo library; Page 59 (T/R) Genesis photo library; Page 62 (T/R) Genesis photo library; Page 68 (B/R) Corbis; Page 75 (T/C) Corbis; Page 77 (T/R) Corbis; Page 83 (T/R) Corbis; Page 95 (C/L) Corbis; Page 111 (T/C) Corbis; Page 126 (B/L) Corbis. Page 130 (B/R) Corbis; Page 143 (B/R) Corbis; Page 151 (B/R) Corbis; Page 166 (T/C) Science photo library.Page 228 (B) Science Photo Library; Page 232 (T/R) The Stock Market; Page 237 (T/R) The Stock Market.

All other photographs are from MKP Archives